I Saw the Lord

I Saw the Lord

A Biblical Theology of Vision

ABNER CHOU

WIPF & STOCK · Eugene, Oregon

I SAW THE LORD
A Biblical Theology of Vision

Copyright © 2013 Abner Chou. All rights reserved. Except for brief quotations in critical publications or reviews, no part of this book may be reproduced in any manner without prior written permission from the publisher. Write: Permissions, Wipf and Stock Publishers, 199 W. 8th Ave., Suite 3, Eugene, OR 97401.

Wipf & Stock
An Imprint of Wipf and Stock Publishers
199 W. 8th Ave., Suite 3
Eugene, OR 97401

www.wipfandstock.com

ISBN 13: 978-1-62032-301-4

Manufactured in the U.S.A.

Scripture quotations taken from the New American Standard Bible®, Copyright © 1960, 1962, 1963, 1968, 1971, 1972, 1973,1975, 1977, 1995 by the Lockman Foundation. Used by permission. (www.Lockman.org)

To my wife and children (Nehemiah, Naomi, and Meital):
May you always look to and love Jesus, who alone is worthy

Contents

Preface | ix
Abbreviations | xi

1 Introduction | 1
2 Precedents for a Biblical Theology of Vision | 5
3 Unity of Vision as Foundation for a Biblical Theology of Vision | 21
4 Isaiah's Vision: Vision of Salvation | 48
5 Ezekiel's Vision: Vision of Presence | 83
6 Daniel's Vision: Vision of King and Kingdom | 114
7 Paul's Vision: Vision of Inauguration and Anticipation | 147
8 John's Vision: Vision of the Culmination of History and Theology | 188
9 Conclusion | 232

Bibliography | 239
Scripture Index | 249

Preface

THIS BOOK BEGAN IN my devotional readings of the visions of Isaiah, Ezekiel, Daniel, Paul, and John. As I meditated on these passages, I was struck how these texts exalted Christ in quite similar ways. Such realizations resulted in a paper presented at the national conference of the Evangelical Theological Society. Those present encouraged me to explore this idea further and from that, a book was born.

However, no book "is born" so easily. My journey to this point was facilitated by a labor of love from the community around me. My family has been amazingly supportive. How many five-year-old sons ask God to "help *abba* in writing the book today"? My other children have also demonstrated immense patience and love for me. I am thankful to the Lord for my wife's patience in putting up with a more absent-minded husband. She bears with my discussions on writing and has been a listening ear to my thoughts. She also has found creative ways to encourage me throughout this entire process, which the Lord has used to get me through.

In like fashion, the faculty and staff at The Master's College and Seminary have supported my efforts to investigate these matters. They have given me constructive feedback and encouragement which has helped shape this book and seen it through to completion. I would like to especially acknowledge my (former) administrative assistant, Amy Kidder, who painstakingly read all my drafts to look for typographical errors as well as for clarity of thought. I would have never thought that social media would be an aid in these endeavors. However, a group called "Nerdy Language Majors" on Facebook has been a great place of discussion on related ideas. Their feedback and input has also been quite useful. Finally, I thank my students who have interacted with me and showed tremendous enthusiasm for their professor's work. Much of what I am writing here is for their sake; to help them grasp God's Word better as a whole as well as to exhibit a pursuit of biblical research for God's glory.

Nonetheless, despite all of their efforts, my work will fall short due to my own weakness and limitations. I know there will always be better ways to express ideas or to frame the argument. There will always be more to be said or more concise and direct ways to say them. There will always be a need to demonstrate more exhaustively a thesis or address certain issues more adeptly or to better qualify ideas. The work of those above helped me make inroads into these areas better than I could have done on my own. Any errors or weaknesses of this work are my own.

In spite of this, my prayer is that God would use this book to help his people better understand the books of Isaiah, Ezekiel, Daniel, and Revelation as well as the writings of Paul. Most of all, I hope that this book would drive the reader to have a higher view of God and Christ. All of the theology of this book ultimately is fulfilled by the Son and that is what makes him so unique and central. I desire that the reader eagerly anticipate that moment when the Son is highly exalted for his unparalleled work in redemptive history and when he returns to fulfill all theology. If one leaves with such a conviction, I have done my job. The work on this book has given me greater clarity about the theologies of the writers aforementioned as well as their unity in the glory of Christ. I hope it does the same for those who take and read this book as well. May all glory go to the Lord, who alone is worthy as the vision proclaims.

Abbreviations

ABD	*The Anchor Bible Dictionary*. Edited by David Noel Freedman. 6 vols. New York: Doubleday, 1992.
ANE	Ancient Near East
AOTC	Apollos Old Testament Commentary
BASOR	*Bulletin of the American Schools of Oriental Research*
BBR	*Bulletin for Biblical Research*
BDAG	Walter Bauer, Frederick W. Danker, W. F. Arndt, and F. W. Gingrich. *Greek-English Lexicon of the New Testament and Other Early Christian Literature*. 3rd ed. Chicago: University of Chicago Press, 2000.
BibSac	*Bibliotheca Sacra*
CBQ	*Catholic Biblical Quarterly*
EBC	*Expositor's Bible Commentary*. Edited by Frank Gaebelein. 12 vols. Grand Rapids: Zondervan, 1992.
HALOT	Ludwig Köhler, Walter Baumgartner, M. E. J. Richardson, Johann Jakob Stamm. *The Hebrew Aramaic Lexicon of the Old Testament*. 2 vols. Leiden: Brill, 2000.
HUCA	*Hebrew Union College Annual*
IBHS	Bruce K. Waltke and M. O'Connor. *An Introduction to Biblical Hebrew Syntax*. Winona Lake, IN: Eisenbrauns, 1990.
ICC	International Critical Commentary
Int	*Interpretation*
ITC	International Theological Commentary
JBL	*Journal of Biblical Literature*
JETS	*Journal of the Evangelical Theological Society*
JSNTSup	Journal for the Study of the New Testament Supplement
JSOT	*Journal for the Study of the Old Testament*

Abbreviations

LXX	Septuagint
MSJ	*Master's Seminary Journal*
MT	Masoretic Text
NAC	New American Commentary
NICNT	New International Commentary on the New Testament
NICOT	New International Commentary on the Old Testament
NIDOTTE	*New International Dictionary of Old Testament Theology and Exegesis.* Edited by Willem VanGemeren. 5 vols. Grand Rapids: Zondervan, 1997.
NIGTC	New International Greek Testament Commentary
NovT	*Novum Testamentum*
NT	New Testament
OT	Old Testament
RevExp	*Review and Expositor*
SBJT	*Southern Baptist Journal of Theology*
TLOT	*Theological Lexicon of the Old Testament.* Edited by Ernst Jenni and Claus Westermann. 3 vols. Translated by Mark Biddle. Peabody, MA: Hendrickson, 1997.
TOTC	Tyndale Old Testament Commentary
TynBul	*Tyndale Bulletin*
VT	*Vetus Testamentum*
WBC	Word Biblical Commentary
WTJ	*Westminster Theological Journal*

1

Introduction

WHILE ALL SCRIPTURE IS profitable, certain texts have captivated the attention of God's people. The visions of Isaiah (Isa 6), Ezekiel (Ezek 1), Daniel (Dan 7), Paul (Damascus road), and John (Rev 4–5) are among those passages. The words of these texts have become part of our worship, both in Scripture reading and song. We talk about conversion in terms of a "Damascus road" experience. Scholars have pondered the depths of these passages. Such focus has not been limited to recent years. Rather, fascination with these texts has existed essentially from the time they were written.[1] The visions have gripped the people of God in a unique way.

There is good reason for this. Few texts can portray the heights of heaven and the glory of God as these do. The descriptions stretch human language and imagination as they encapsulate the eternal and sublime into finite expression. In that sense, there is a level of mystery in these accounts. What are the functions and nature of the living creatures in Ezekiel or the seraphim of Isaiah? How do we meditate and process the resplendent glory of God reflected in the visions of Ezekiel or John? What is the significance of the various elements seen in God's heavenly throne room? The questions go on and draw us further in to be enthralled with the visions of heaven.

Moreover, the visions have a dynamic and epic quality. They communicate some of the most dramatic scenes in all of Scripture. A prophet falls upon his face to be called into ministry. A murderer is transfixed by the glory of God and gives his life for the cause he once persecuted. The Lamb, who is alone worthy, receives the sealed book to complete all history as the entire cosmos breaks out in praise. Such moments, in the context of or within the actual vision itself, testify to the power of these passages. They reinforce the loftiness of God and fuel thereby our worship as a community.

However, what is interesting is that we are not captured by *it* but by *them*. I mean to say that one vision does not grab our attention alone, but rather a set of heavenly

---

1. As we will later discuss, *1 En.* reflects such fascination and was composed near the time of Ezekiel and Daniel.

visions. Why is this? What binds them all together, even in our minds? Such questions form the basis for a biblical theology of vision.

A BIBLICAL THEOLOGY OF VISION

What is a biblical theology of vision? I propose that a biblical theology of vision is comprised of two elements which need some definition. The first of these is the concept of *innertextuality*.[2] Innertextuality deals with how an author uses his own material to develop theological themes within a book. In this discussion, a biblical theology of vision concerns how the author connects his vision with the rest of his writing(s). As we will see, the biblical writer uses words and phrases from his vision throughout his writing(s) to further explain his vision. Based upon this, I would suggest that the vision is representative of key ideas within the author's theology and message. In a sense, the vision depicts the fulfillment of his theology. This accounts for why these visions are so dense. Each vision is thoroughly theological, explained by the author throughout the rest of his work.

The second component concerns the idea of *intertextuality*. This concept describes how an author incorporates another text outside of his writings into his message.[3] In a biblical theology of vision, this refers to how the biblical writer incorporates another prophet's or apostle's vision and theology into his own book. The prophets and apostles thereby weave their visions together. As we will discuss, scholars have noted similarities between these visions. They visualize the throne room of God and describe his glory as he sits on his throne. However, I would suggest that such intertextual overlap goes beyond similarity. Instead of seeing the visions as related by a common motif or tradition, it appears that they are different facets of the same event (just like the Gospels at times portray the same event from different angles). Put differently, the prophets and apostles all saw the same thing, but from varying vantage points or "zooming in or out" of different parts of this occasion. Thus, I am suggesting that while the biblical writers may not have exhaustively viewed or described the entire scene, they nonetheless were witnessing (the components of) the inauguration of the Son of Man. This shows why we are attracted not just to one vision, but to this grouping. Implicitly, we sense an underlying unity between these visions.

How do these two factors come together in a biblical theology of vision? If each vision relates to the author's theology and the visions are one, then the theologies of these visions also come together. In essence, our job is to trace the uniqueness of each vision and theology and how they join together to portray and anticipate the climactic moment and ramifications of when Christ officially receives dominion over all the cosmos. That is a biblical theology of vision.

---

2. Sailhamer, *Pentateuch as Narrative*, 207–13.
3. Hays, *Echoes of Scripture*, 14–21; Tull, "Intertextuality and the Hebrew Scriptures," 88–92.

APPROACH

How can we go about both proving this thesis as well as exploring it? To be sure, I will need some evidence to prove that the visions depict the same eschatological event. My approach begins by showing the possibility/reality of a biblical theology of vision. The next chapter will survey early reflections upon the vision texts as well as the observations of modern scholarship (some may not be interested or familiar with this and may want to skip to my exegetical discussion in chapter 3). From this, we may note that even in the intertestamental period, Jewish readers of Isaiah, Ezekiel, and Daniel began to merge the visions together into a single eschatological event. This mentality may be in the background of the NT's use of the visions, especially since John also fuses these visions into a single moment. In addition, modern scholarship has affirmed the similarities between the visions. Some have even pointed out the connection between Paul's Damascus road with the visions of his predecessors. Kim is the foremost of those individuals, and my work is in a sense an expansion of his. Moreover, others believe that John's experience repeats the same experience of those who saw the visions beforehand. All of this points to the fact that biblical writers are not seeing distinct visions but rather recapitulations of the same thing. What I suggest is nothing new or novel.

Past readers of Scripture have grounds for such conclusions. The third chapter discusses how exegetical examination bears out the unity of visions. When we apply the principles of harmonization (that are used in the Gospels) to the visions, we can see that the similarities do point out the significant overlap between the visions that draw them together. Furthermore, the dissimilarities can be reasonably harmonized no differently than we would do with the Gospel accounts. Thus, the evidence demonstrates that a biblical theology of vision is possible. The visions do seem to merge, and this fuses together the theologies connected with each individual vision.

Based upon this, we can explore how a biblical theology of vision works out in the various texts. Our approach will be to examine Isaiah, Ezekiel, Daniel, Paul, and John to see how each of their visions relate to their theologies. My goal here is to as thoroughly possible (so pardon the length of those chapters) explore the writer's message around the organizing principle of the vision. Within this, vision and theology share a symbiotic relationship. Analyzing the vision helps us tie the writer's theology together, and understanding his theology helps us better understand the significance of the vision and the event it ultimately portrays. Along that line, as revelation progresses, we can also trace how different authors pick up on the visions and theologies of their predecessors. These intertextual interactions reveal how their visions are actually reflections of the same event, how their unique theologies work together, and how all of this moves toward the full unveiling and fulfillment of the vision in all its theological significance. Isaiah provides us the fundamental framework that later writers develop. This climaxes in the Apocalypse, which provides the consummation of vision and theology in Jesus Christ. This moment in redemptive history is truly epic as it sums together the theologies of Isaiah, Ezekiel, Daniel, Paul, and John.

I should make two last comments before we proceed. First, I use the term "visionary event" to communicate the moment or occasion in redemptive history that the various visions are essentially describing. As mentioned above, the prophet or apostle sees components in his own vision that can be synthesized with other visions into a "whole." That "whole" is what I am labeling the "visionary event." As I will argue, that primarily pertains to the coronation of the Son of Man.

Second, there is much that falls beyond the scope of what I can discuss or accomplish here. Some of these matters include authorship and literary unity, which I must assume and defer to other works to defend.[4] While I am unable to interact with the entire discussion surrounding intertextuality, I use this term to refer to the interaction of a biblical author with prior revelation per his intent and will employ Hays' methodology for detecting echoes or allusions.[5] In addition, a whole host of scholarly issues surround this study, ranging from *merkabah* mysticism to the new perspective on Paul. Although some of those matters will be pertinent and helpful in this discussion, the goal is not to interact with them as much as it is to trace the innertextuality and intertextuality of vision. My intent is to argue for the unity of these visions and then lay out the theological beauty of each individual vision and how Isaiah, Ezekiel, Daniel, Paul, and John all saw and wrote about an inexplicable moment: the summing up of all things in Christ.

---

4. See Oswalt, *Isaiah 1–39*, 23–29; Motyer, *Isaiah*, 25–30; Block, *Ezekiel*, 1:9–12; Cooper, *Ezekiel*, 27–29; Miller, *Daniel*, 22–42; Archer, *A Survey of Old Testament Introduction*, 421–36; Guthrie, *New Testament Introduction*, 496–528; Osborne, *Revelation*, 2–5.

5. My own use of intertextuality avoids the deconstructive notion often associated with literary studies. Instead, I focus upon intertextuality as a function of the author. See Vanhoozer, *Is There a Meaning*; Stein, "Author-Oriented Approach"; Broyles, "Traditions, Intertextuality, and Canon," 158–59. Hays' criteria for an intertextual link will serve as the criteria I will use in this study. See Hays, *Echoes*, 26–27, 29–30. Hays lists a possibility that intertextuality occurs as a hermeneutical event in Paul's mind. That is the view that this work would subscribe; otherwise, how could we speak of Isaiah's use of Ezekiel or an author relating his vision to his work? I will also use echoes and allusions interchangeably to denote an author's intertextual activity.

2

Precedents for a Biblical Theology of Vision

IN THE LIGHT OF several thousand years of interpretative history, claiming a completely new idea smacks of hubris. Lack of precedent tends to falsify an idea rather than prove its worth. Accordingly, this chapter aims to show that while not articulated in the official terms of a "biblical theology of vision," the ideas of *inter*textuality and *inner*textuality have been present in the interpretative history of the visions. My thesis is not a brand new idea, but rather one that was thought through in intertestamental literature and has been discussed in the modern era.

Along that line, my goal is not to provide an exhaustive history of the way past generations have perceived the vision or to rehearse the arguments or various issues surrounding such interactions. Many others have waded through those waters over the years.[1] I also do not intend to explore (much less advocate) the theological messages of the texts that will be discussed in this chapter. Rather, my major criteria of discussion revolve around the notion of precedent: showing that people before me have concluded that various visions are highly related, if not different angles of the same occasion. Within this discussion, I have also winnowed down my focus to two major areas: early Jewish literature and the modern era. The former provide us with evidence that early traditions already began stitching the OT visions together. A unity of vision did not result from recent trends or ideologies but instead was possibly recognized by ancient sensitivities regarding these texts. The latter shows that these ideas are still a part of modern scholarship, which has extended the discussion to the NT, particularly to John and Paul. Understanding both of these factors makes my thesis not only plausible, but the logical synthesis of a rich interpretative tradition.

---

1. Halperin, *Faces of the Chariot*; Kim, *Paul*; Kim, *The Origin of Paul's Gospel*; Rowland, *Christian Origins*; Collins and Collins, *King and Messiah*; Segal, *Paul the Convert*; Rowland, *The Open Heaven*. These are just a few that have critical treatments of the tradition.

A BRIEF NOTE ON INNERTEXTUALITY

This chapter will primarily address the issue of intertextuality since the notion of innertextuality is more widely researched, documented, and accepted by scholars. For example, note Oswalt's comment on Isa 6:

> The vision which 6:1–8 report was clearly fundamental to the entire course of Isaiah's ministry and to the shape of his book. The glory, the majesty, the holiness, and the righteousness of God became the ruling concept of his ministry. Furthermore, it is this experience that explains Isaiah's contempt for, and horror of, any kind of national or individual life, which did not pay adequate attention to the one God.[2]

Kim makes a similar observation concerning Paul's theology and vision:

> Paul's designation of Christ as the Son of God based on the Damascus Christophany corresponds to Jesus' intention in his self-designation as the Son of Man, and that the Damascus Christophany contributed to Paul's conception of the church as the body of Christ and the true Israel.[3]

We can find similar logic surrounding the visions of the other prophets. Ezekiel's vision of God's presence in his first chapter draws the entire book together. Dan 7 provides a cross-section of all the visions in Daniel. Rev 4–5 also seems to occupy a unique place in the book.[4] Because the connection between a biblical writer's vision and his theology is not widely disputed among scholars, I have chosen not to belabor this point in the chapter.

DISCUSSION OF EARLY LITERATURE

A Proclivity of Harmonization

Moving to our discussion of the intertextuality of visions, extra-canonical literature (e.g., *1 Enoch*), as well as the discoveries of the Judean desert, testify that people harmonized the visions early on.[5] Before discussing those attempts, we can observe that such efforts were part of a wider movement that desired to correlate various OT texts.

---

2. Oswalt, *Isaiah 1–39*, 176.

3. Kim, *Origin of Paul's Gospel*, 165. See also Schreiner, *Pauline Theology*, 44–47; Bruce, *Paul*, 74.

4. See Hartenstein, "Cherubim and Seraphim," 177; Walvoord, *Daniel*, 145; Beale, *Revelation*, 172–73.

5. I recognize the discussion of the various compositional layers in *1 Enoch* and other extra-biblical books. Since most scholars date the range of composition up through the first century a.d., my point that various traditions merge texts together early on still stands. Of more concern is whether or not the texts I employ (particularly the Similitudes) are of Christian origin or influence. If that is the case, then perhaps the notion of harmonization stems from only a Christian reading of the OT rather than a wider recognized phenomenon. However, Knibb and Collins both conclude that this section of Enoch is distinctively Jewish rather than Christian. See Collins and Collins, *King and Messiah*, 87; Knibb, "The Date of the Parables of Enoch," 350.

Scholars observe that such individuals employed the rabbinical method of *gezerah sheva*, which refers to the collation of texts based upon lexical associations.[6] The very presence of this *modus operandi* supports the synthesis I suggest. In any case, this discussion helps us to see that the harmonization of visions was not coincidental, but based instead upon a mentality that desired to systematize texts and concepts together.

General trends in early Jewish eschatology evidence such synthesis. For example, Nickelsburg observes that *1 Enoch* and *Jubilees* contain new creation and resurrection motifs reminiscent of Dan 12:3.[7] These books describe how the righteous will be raised to live in a blessed new world (*1 En.* 91:14–16; Jub. 23:27–29; cf. Dan 12:2a) and how the wicked will be judged in everlasting shame (*1 En.* 90:30; cf. Dan 12:2b).[8] God will reign forever, displaying his total sovereignty. Allusions to Jeremiah are also thrown in as the writer of *1 Enoch* refers to the "seventy generations" of the consummation of judgment (*1 En.* 10:12; cf. Jer 25:11).[9] The writer of Enoch combines all of this information with Isaiah. The latter part of Isaiah is echoed in *1 En.* 91:14–16, where God will invade the earth to establish a new heaven and earth (cf. Isa 65:17). In this way, *1 Enoch* weaves together an eschatological portrait built upon Daniel, Isaiah, and Jeremiah.

Other books contain similar juxtapositions. Perrin points out how this works in *4 Ezra*.[10] The text describes that the Messiah takes his stand upon a great mountain to judge and reign, which alludes to Isa 2:2–4, 11:1–10, as well as Dan 2:35. The *Assumption of Moses* correlates Dan 12:3 and the "shining of the stars" with Israel's future celestial dwellings (10:9). Within this, the writer intertwines the notion of divine retribution and judgment akin to both Daniel and Isaiah (cf. Isa 66:23–24; Dan 12:3). In fact, *Jub.* 23:12–31, *T. Mos.* 5–10 and *1 En.* 91–93 all have the substructure of the "weeks" probably linked with Daniel's own seventy-weeks prophecy (cf. Dan 9:23–27).[11] Overall, these books have a similar pattern. They pieced together various OT texts into a singular picture of eschatology.[12]

In addition, scholarly discussions on the conceptualization of the Son of Man/Messiah during this time period support the notion that people were looking at texts intertextually. For example, *1 Enoch* draws heavily from Dan 7:13. Both passages describe the "Son of Man" receiving glory from a divine figure (*1 En.* 48:2; Dan 7:13).

---

6. Longenecker, *Biblical Exegesis*, 34: "Where the same words are applied to two separate cases it follows that the same considerations apply to both."

7. Nickelsburg, "Apocalyptic and Myth," 394.

8. Ibid.

9. Nickelsburg, "Eschatology," 579.

10. Perrin, "Son of Man in Ancient Judaism and Primitive Christianity," 22.

11. Nickelsburg, "Apocalyptic and Myth," 393.

12. Rowland, *Christian Origins*, 87–88. Rowland notes that within the diversity of Jewish apocalyptic traditions, Jewish eschatology at this time maintains certain key elements, including a new age of prosperity that follows a time of great distress. The Jews did have certain conceptions of eschatology early on.

However, that is not the only way *1 Enoch* depicts the Son of Man. He is also an individual akin to the Servant in Isaiah. The terms "elect one" and "righteous one" found in *1 Enoch* (cf. 38:2; 40:4; 61:5) match similar ideas presented in Isa 53:11. This individual judges from his throne in heaven (46:7; 61:8) similarly to Dan 7:13 and Isa 42:4. The throne of glory mentioned in *1 Enoch* may refer to Ezekiel's vision (*1 En.* 45:3; cf. Ezek 1:26).[13]

First Enoch is not alone in amalgamating various messianic texts. Both 4QpGen^a (4Q252 5:1–7) and 4QpIsa^a (4Q161 3:11–25) interpret Gen 49:10 messianically and link that passage with Jer 23:5, Zech 3:8, and Isa 11 through the term "branch."[14] Similarly, 11QMelchizedek makes reference to the Son of Man by linking Lev 25, Isa 52:7, 61:2–3, Dan 9:25, with Ps 82 and 110. There, the messianic messenger found in Daniel merges with the Isaianic Servant and the ultimate Davidic figure in Psalm 110.[15] A reference to the Son of Man is also found in *4 Ezra* in a vision scene like that in Dan 7. However, it also references him in the context of Zion, the holy mountain (*4 Ezra* 13:6–7; Ps 2:6), where he has lips that breathe forth judgment (*4 Ezra* 13:9; cf. Isa 11:4) and is referenced as the son (*4 Ezra* 7:28; cf. 2 Sam 7:14; Ps 2:7).[16]

All of these examples show that the Jews read various passages of the OT together quite early on. They merged different works together based upon similarity of topic and motif as well as linguistic connections. The diversity of the use of OT texts testifies that such efforts did not come from a single strand of tradition. The Similitudes of Enoch and *4 Ezra* are not dependent upon each other, as various scholars have concluded. Instead, as Perrin suggests, "These uses are independent of one another; the common dependence is upon Dan 7:13 on the one hand and upon the general world apocalyptic concepts on the other."[17] This points out a more general approach that the Jewish writers took with certain biblical texts. They appear to believe that the writings had an underlying unity and could, in their diversity, speak to a set of subjects.[18] This accords with the grander recognition that Jewish apocalypticism was present in the

---

13. Muilenburg, "Son of Man in Daniel," 204.

14. Knibb, "Messianism in the Pseudepigrapha," 166.

15. Collins and Collins, *King and Messiah*, 79–86. I will not belabor the point of whether Melchizedek is messianic, angelic, or divine. That misses the point of the collation of various texts. Nonetheless, Collins' conclusion that the text brings out how there was a "growing interest in imagining a savior figure who was divine in some sense" is sound and is helpful to this discussion.

16. The Greek could read παῖς instead of υἱός. If this is the case, then one could translate it as "servant" and make an allusion to Isaiah's Servant again.

17. Perrin, *Teaching of Jesus*, 198; Walker, "Origin of the Son of Man Concept," 485. In *1 Enoch*, the Son of Man, the plotline is far more linear and follows Daniel more closely. The Son of Man is inaugurated to judge the earth. However, in *4 Ezra*, the language is far more veiled and symbolic, pointing how a messianic figure (not named the Son of Man however) from the mountain will conquer another prominent figure.

18. Lindars, *New Testament Apologetic*. Both Walker and Perrin support Lindars in the idea that the Jewish communities of the time viewed the OT as a cohesive whole such that one text was a pointer to a conglomeration of texts.

intertestamental period and dealt with the topics of the heavenly world, astronomy, Jewish history, and human destiny.[19] The Jewish authors attempted to harmonize texts together to describe their viewpoint of the world, history, and eschatology.

The above examples of eschatology and Messiah are particularly pertinent for this discussion, since the vision texts directly relate to both of those subjects. As we turn to a specific discussion of the visions, we have an initial paradigm in which we can anchor our findings. The juxtaposition of visions in early Jewish writings does not merely reflect their aptitude for biblical terminology or literary artistry, but rather a belief that the visions participate in a unified eschatological scheme. This harmonization of visions took place as they endeavored to synthesize OT information about the Messiah and the culmination of history.[20]

Textual Examination

The goal of this textual examination is two-fold. First, I will attempt to show that various early Jewish texts combine the visions of Isaiah, Ezekiel, and Daniel. Second, I will also point out that oftentimes such harmonization is geared toward the eschatological inauguration of the Son of Man per Dan 7. The Enochian corpus, *4 Ezra*, and selected documents from Qumran provide evidence that affirms these two points.

First Enoch provides a multifaceted look at an early harmonization of vision, as the heavenly courtroom scene occurs several times throughout the book (*1 En.* 14; 24–25; 46–48; 71). While the book is not a unified literary work, such compositional issues do not weigh as heavily in this discussion other than the following observations. First, scholars agree that the latest "layer" of composition occurs no later than the first century A.D. and is therefore still a quite early example of early interpretation of the visions.[21] Second, the compositional elements testify that various writers might have viewed the visions similarly. Finally, I would argue that *1 Enoch* is dependent on Daniel rather than the other way around. Arguments for this scheme include the common base of Dan 7 in a variety of literary works including *4 Ezra* and *1 Enoch* in its various compositional fragments (e.g., Book of Watchers, Book of Giants, Similitudes). If *1 Enoch* were truly the base of these texts, then we would expect Daniel, *4 Ezra*, and the Book of Giants to correspond to the imagery of *1 Enoch*. However, the differences

---

19. Rowland, *Christian Origins*, 57–60.

20. Collins and Collins, *King and Messiah*, 98–100; Rowland, *Christian Origins*, 57–60; Nickelsburg, "Eschatology," 579. This does *not* mean that there was a unified opinion about the nature of eschatology or Messiah. Instead, I argue that the Jews attempted to collate (in a variety of ways) OT data about these topics and in the process, harmonized the visions. While diversity in the tradition exists, Collins acknowledges that the Jews of the intertestamental period did recognize a type of messianic figure. Similarly, Rowland states that Jewish eschatology at this time maintains certain key elements, including a new age of prosperity that follows a time of distress. So, although plurality exists in the theological viewpoints of the second-temple period, a marked goal for unity and systematization also is present.

21. Boyarin, *Jewish Gospels*, 74; Nickelsburg, *1 Enoch*, 7.

between these works are substantial, particularly between *4 Ezra* and *1 Enoch*.[22] This has led scholars to recognize that Dan 7 is the common denominator between them.[23] Furthermore, the presence of chronological markers in Daniel distinguishes it from the rest of apocryphal literature, which lacks this feature. This gives the appearance that the Jewish apocalypses are adapting Daniel to a new context[24] Along this line, the fact that *1 Enoch* describes God as the "Great Glory" as opposed to Ancient of Days indicates that *Enoch* altered Daniel's account in light of later Jewish sensitivities. Stokes suggests that the Jews desired to portray God not as an elderly gentleman but rather as the glory upon whom no one can gaze.[25] This explanation makes more sense than the Jews desiring to re-portray God's glory as an elderly individual. The dependence of *1 Enoch* on Daniel indicates that *1 Enoch* (even in its compositional variety) utilizes OT visions rather than the other way around.

First Enoch 14 provides an initial example of such interaction. Contextually, this text comes toward the end of the second major section of the book, known as the "Book of Watchers" (*1 Enoch* 6–16). Based upon Gen 6, disobedient angelic beings (the Watchers) have cohabited with mankind, producing evil giants. The heavenly court convenes to have Enoch announce judgment against these angels.[26]

This vision account draws from Daniel, Isaiah, and Ezekiel. The opening lines begin to indicate such convergence. The protagonist "looks and sees" (ἐθεώρουν δὲ καὶ εἶδον; *1 En.* 14:18). The former term occurs in Dan 7:13, whereas the latter is found in both the LXX of Isa 6:1 and Ezek 1:4. The juxtapositions continue in the description of the heavenly scene. Enoch beholds a "lofty throne" (θρόνον ὑψηλόν; *1 En.* 14:18), which is identical wording to the LXX of Isa 6:1. The throne is likened to crystal, a description found in Ezek 1:22. In addition, the writer mentions the famous wheels of Ezekiel's chariot-throne (τροχὸς; *1En.* 14:18) with the description of brilliant light and the cherubim (v. 14), terms also found in Ezekiel's visions (cf. 10:1–3). Underneath this throne flows a river of fire (*1 En.* 14:19), as mentioned in Dan 7:10. God, described as the "Great Glory," takes his seat (*1 En.* 14:20), as seen in the visions of Isaiah, Ezekiel, and Daniel (cf. Isa 6:1; Ezek 1:26; Dan 7:9). He is as brilliant as the sun (*1En.* 14:20), a phrase that is reminiscent of Ezekiel (1:27). His garments are also white (*1 En.* 14:20) mirroring the words of Daniel (7:9). Because of such glory, the angels are unable to see his face (*1 En.* 14:21), a description that echoes the language of Isaiah (6:2). Repeatedly, the visions of Isaiah, Ezekiel, and Daniel are joined together in discussions of this throne room scene.

We might contend that the author has drawn from previous visions for the sake of depicting the heavenly locale and not necessarily the same event. Even if this was

---

22. Collins and Collins, *King and Messiah*, 94–98.
23. Stokes, "The Throne Visions," 351–56.
24. Korner, "'And I Saw ..,'" 170.
25. Stokes, "The Throne Visions," 348.
26. Nickelsburg, *1 Enoch*, 7. See also Bauckham, "Apocalypses," 139.

the case, people were at least inclined to synthesize the visions together. However, there appears to be more to *1 Enoch* 14 than merely a heavenly scene. As mentioned above, this occasion precedes Enoch's commission to judge the Watchers. Arguably, this lays the groundwork for the book's concern for eschatology. Scholars observe that this subject is of primary concern for the book.[27] The argument is one of *Urzeit* to *Endzeit* typology; the first judgment mirrors the ultimate.[28] We find such logic in the NT, where biblical writers compare the end of time with the days of Noah (Matt 24:37–38; 1 Pet 3:20). Accordingly, Enoch's experience would set up for the heavenly courtroom to provide eschatological judgment. This explanation accounts for why later eschatological courtroom scenes in *1 Enoch* draw upon the imagery of *1 Enoch* 14 (cf. *1 En.* 24–25; 46; 71).[29] These earlier scenes anticipate the final judgment mentioned later in the book. Thus, *1 Enoch* ultimately combines the visions into a singular eschatological event. That event, describing God's final judgment against the world, is quite similar to Dan 7.

Hence, *1 Enoch* 14 connects with passages in the Similitudes (*1 En.* 46; 62; 71). Like *1 Enoch* 14, these texts also describe a scene similar to Dan 7, where the Head of Days takes his seat on the heavenly throne.[30] Like *1 Enoch* 14, the Similitudes texts refer to the visions of Isaiah, Ezekiel, and Daniel. Some of those texts include God sitting on a throne (47:3), his fiery, white appearance (46:1), and the description of the throne and its surroundings (71:2) which were found in *1 En.* 14. Also, as discussed earlier, the titles of the "messianic" figure in these accounts draw from Isaiah (Righteous One; cf. 38:2; Isa 53:11) and Daniel (Son of Man, cf. 62:7; Dan 7:13).

Additional details in the Similitudes indicate a harmonization of visions, particularly the description of the heavenly hosts. *First Enoch* 61:10–12 and 71:7 use the terms seraphim, kerubim, and ofanim to describe the angels in God's presence. The first term refers to the angelic creatures in Isaiah's vision (6:2), the second term to the angelic beings in one of Ezekiel's visions (10:1–3), and the latter term actually means "wheel" and links again with Ezekiel's vision (1:15). In addition, *Enoch* also describes a myriad of angels that cannot be counted, which mirrors Daniel's vision (7:10). Enoch synthesizes the angelic descriptions together.

---

27. Nickelsburg, *1 Enoch*, 55.

28. Nickelsburg, "Apocalyptic and Myth," 383.

29. See ibid., 390–91. This suggestion seems to have traction in the development of *1 Enoch*. The "Animal Apocalypse" as well as the "Apocalypse of Weeks" draws on language from the Book of Watchers, but links it with an eschatological scene of judgment. *First Enoch* 24–25, which presents another scene of God's heavenly rule from a mountain, is explicitly eschatological in nature (25:3–4). This utilizes terminology and motifs found in *1 En.* 14:18–21 with a throne, a holy one sitting upon it, and judgment and blessing ensuing. It also draws upon language not only found in the visions of Daniel, Isaiah, and Ezekiel (cf. mountain and throne in Dan 2:35; Ezek 40:2; Isa 2:2; 11:9 and *1 En.* 25:3). In the compositional layers of *1 Enoch*, we can then notice a pattern of connecting the judgment that was as a paradigm for the judgment that will be.

30. Nickelsburg, *1 Enoch 37–82*, 155.

Understanding this convergence of visions helps in resolving certain tensions observed in the Similitudes section. Nickelsburg notes that while *1 Enoch* 46 draws from Dan 7, it dramatically differs from that text in that it portrays the Son of Man as judge over the nations.[31] Dan 7 does not describe the Son of Man in detail acting in such a manner. However, in the innertextuality of Daniel, the Son of Man, appears to parallel the "stone" that crushes all the nations (2:34).[32] Hence, it is already implied that the Son of Man will judge the nations. Similarly, in the visions of Isaiah and Ezekiel, God acts to judge as well. Scholars note that such visions precede proclamations of divine judgments (cf. Isa 6:11–13; Ezek 3:7–11).[33] Thus, Nickelsburg is correct in saying that *1 Enoch* does deviate slightly from Dan 7. However, such variations actually demonstrate that *1 Enoch* involves other material from Daniel and the visions of Isaiah and Ezekiel. This provides some support to the suggestion that the visions are both innertextual and intertextual in nature.

The Similitudes texts are eschatological. In these passages, the purpose of this court is not to judge the Watchers, as it was earlier on in the book. Instead, the messianic individual will judge all the kings and nations of the earth (*1 En.* 46:5). He will crush those who have been proud, reverse the injustices of the earth, and condemn those who have not obeyed God (46:6). He will in fact destroy the wicked with the breath of his mouth (62:2) and they will receive the eternal judgment of the underworld (46:6b).[34] The Son of Man will also exact justice against the "stars of heaven," or the supernatural beings who rebelled against God long ago (46:7–8).[35] At the same time, he will vindicate the righteous, whose prayers for salvation will now be fulfilled (47:1–4). The Son of Man will then reign forever over the earth, which now will have the peace, fullness, and righteousness of original creation (*1En.* 62:2–16; 71:15–17). Such descriptions of ultimate judgment, the condemnation of angels, and final victory all carry eschatological overtones. In the flow of the book, it appears that the earlier description of Enoch's vision in *1 Enoch* 14 prepares readers for the eschatological description in the Similitudes. This helps us see the validity of *Urzeit* to *Endzeit* scheme as mentioned earlier. Even more, the Similitude texts suggest that the writers of Enoch combined the visions to portray a single eschatological episode. They fit Isaiah and Ezekiel into the framework depicted by Dan 7.

Accordingly, *1 Enoch* is an essential example of how early Jewish writers synthesized the visions of Isaiah, Ezekiel, and Daniel and linked them in various ways with a climactic eschatological event. The book arguably provides the most detailed treatment of this synthesis. For this reason, scholars repeatedly identify *1 Enoch* with

---

31. Ibid.

32. Miller, *Daniel*, 91; Lucas, *Daniel*, 74; Ford, *Daniel*, 86–87.

33. Oswalt, *Isaiah 1–39*, 173–75; Block, *Ezekiel*, 1:77–79. See also Nickelsburg, *1 Enoch 37–82*, 155. Nickelsburg himself acknowledges the connection.

34. Nickelsburg, *1 Enoch 37–82*, 159.

35. Ibid., 159–60.

a "throne tradition," because they recognize its tie with these texts in light of similar language and type of scene.[36] The book raises our attention to such harmonization, which allows us to detect other works that follow suit. Although these other texts may use passages slightly differently or have far less depth than *1 Enoch*, they show that *1 Enoch* was not alone in seeing the intertextuality of visions.

Second and *Third Enoch* follow in this tradition. In *2 Enoch*, Enoch travels to the seventh heaven and witnesses the heavenly courtroom (20:1—25:5). He sees both cherubim and seraphim (21:1), the angels mentioned in the visions of Ezekiel and Isaiah, respectively. They surround God's throne and sing the anthem found in Isa 6:3 (*2 En.* 21:2). In fact, Enoch's response to this entire scene mirrors Isaiah's, as both proclaim their own woe (*2 En.* 21:3; cf. Isa 6:5). As Enoch ascends to the very throne room itself in the tenth heaven, he beholds the face of God (*2 En.* 22:1). Instead of being consumed, Enoch is transformed to stand before God's presence forever (vv. 2–7).[37] Such inauguration may slightly mirror the scene in Dan 7 where the Son of Man is exalted. In this way, *2 Enoch* mixes the visions of Isaiah, Ezekiel, and Daniel together.

Third Enoch also merges Isaiah, Ezekiel, and Daniel.[38] The book discusses the journey of the writer, Rabbi Ishmael, into heaven, where he meets an angelic being, Metatron. The character of Metatron may relate to the Son of Man figure in Dan 7 (cf. *3 En.* 3:4; 4:1). The text explicitly mentions the *merkabah* (the chariot-throne described in Ezekiel), alluding to Ezekiel's vision (*3 En.* 1:1). The mention of seraphim, cherubim, and ofanim also alludes to both Isaiah and Ezekiel, as discussed above (1:8). In this vision, the author discovers that Enoch has been made the ruler over all the kingdoms of the earth and that he mediates God's presence to the world (*3 En.* 10:1–6). *Third Enoch* maintains the idea found in *1 Enoch*, that the visions converge to present the eschatological ruler of the world. In fact, Alexander comments:

> The *Hêkālôt* texts draw motifs from Ezekiel 1 and from other OT theophanies but they are not straightforward expositions of the biblical text. They present themselves as fresh visions, as attempts to see again what Ezekiel saw. In elaborate descriptions of the heavenly world, of God's throne, of the angelic hierarchies, and of the celestial liturgy, they depict God as a heavenly emperor, the angels as a celestial civil service (*pāmalyâ šel ma'ălâ*; cf. the Roman term *familia Caesaris*).[39]

Outside of the Enochian corpus, *4 Ezra* also attests to the convergence of visions. Ezra witnesses God's revelation concerning the downfall of the Roman Empire and

---

36. See Allen, *Ezekiel 1–19*, 26–27.

37. Andersen, "Enoch, Second Book of," 517, 519.

38. Alexander, "Enoch, Third Book of," 522. The date of *3 Enoch* is around the sixth or seventh century A.D. This does not qualify it as "early Jewish literature," but it does illustrate a consistency with early thinking about the visions in Jewish traditions moving towards the medieval period.

39. Ibid. 523.

the rest of the evil nations.[40] After this, the Messiah will come forth to judge and rule (13:1–4). *Fourth Ezra* itself proclaims that the events it describes are the full interpretation of Daniel (*4 Ezra* 12:12).[41] Various scholars identify that the background of the passage comes from Dan 7.[42] However, as we have discussed, the Messianic figure in *4 Ezra* is reminiscent of the Isaiah portrayal of the Messianic ruler who destroys with the breath of his mouth (*4 Ezra* 13:4; cf. Isa 11:4). He also wages war from a great mountain (13:12), an image shared by the visions of Isaiah (2:2), Ezekiel (40:2), and Daniel (2:35). *Four Ezra* has employed biblical imagery far differently than *1 Enoch*. This does not discredit what we have observed. Rather, this testifies that those associated with Enochian traditions were not the only ones engaged in such activity. It appears that in explaining the eschatology of Dan 7, the writer(s) of *4 Ezra* also incorporated other scriptural allusions, including the visions, in their own way. Thus, *4 Ezra* is indicative of a broader pattern of thought in Judaism that uses Dan 7 as a framework of eschatology. Collins confirms this:

> There is no allusion to the Similitudes in *4 Ezra* and no reason to posit any influence between them. Precisely for that reason, they are independent witnesses to common assumptions about the meaning of Daniel 7 in first-century Judaism. Very similar assumptions underlie the use of Son of Man imagery derived from Daniel in the Gospels.[43]

In addition, the writings from Qumran attest to this kind of activity. Some parallels are shared between 11QMelchizedek and the scene found in *Enoch*.[44] The document expounds upon the nature of the Jubilee (cf. Lev 25:10–55) explaining that this period is actually the latter days. This time not only marks atonement, but also the ultimate judgment through Melchizedek, who will take his stand among the "gods" or angelic beings (11QMelchizedek 10; cf. Ps 82:1).[45] He will judge in order that good news may be proclaimed (note the language of Isa 52:7 in 11QMelchizedek 23) and that God may reign over Israel and all the earth (11QMelchizedek 16, 23). Collins observes that in this scene of inauguration and judgment, "Melchizedek" parallels Daniel's vision of the Son of Man.[46] In this case, the information of Psalms and Isaiah merged into the eschatological framework of Dan 7 somewhat similarly to *1 Enoch* above.

---

40. Ibid.

41. Collins and Collins, *King and Messiah*, 94–98.

42. Perrin, "Son of Man in Ancient Judaism and Primitive Christianity," 23–24; Knibb, "Messianism in the Pseudepigrapha," 170; Rowland, *Christian Origins*, 57–58.

43. Collins and Collins, *King and Messiah*, 96.

44. Ibid., 82–86.

45. Knibb, "Messianism in the Pseudepigrapha," 173; Collins and Collins, *King and Messiah*, 84–86.

46. Collins and Collins, *King and Messiah*, 86.

It seems that 4QMess Ar (4Q534) also relates to the Enochic tradition.[47] This should not be too surprising, since a form of 1 *Enoch* was at Qumran.[48] In any case, if such reconstructions of the fragment are accurate, the document reveals an individual who ascends into the celestial temple and heavens to receive the mystery of the world. Upon doing so, the plots of men fail (1.9) such that he will reign over all the provinces as he slays the wicked by his breath.[49] The individual who accomplishes this is called the "chosen one" in language similar to the Similitudes of Enoch (cf. *1 En.* 39:6).[50] The mention of mystery and the entire motif of a heavenly area from which one claims rule echoes Daniel (cf. Dan 4:17). The mention of a chosen one reminds us of the messianic language in Isaiah (cf. Isa 42:1). Furthermore, the description of how this individual slays the wicked by his breath comes from Isaiah (Isa 11:4). Finally, Davila suggests that this entire scene may be a proto-typical description of the individual who descends into the chariot as seen by Ezekiel.[51] Consequently, this Qumran manuscript seems to have combined motifs from Isaiah, Ezekiel, and Daniel into a single "end judgment" event.[52]

These various texts illustrate that ancient readers merged the visions of the OT (or passages highly related to them) together. This finding argues that they viewed such texts as having substantial overlap in describing the heavenly courtroom. Moreover, various traditions synthesized the visions with an eschatological event. This attests that such harmonization is not strictly about describing heaven, but rather a particular occasion in heaven; the time when a Messianic figure is inaugurated to judge and rule over the cosmos. Such efforts early on testify that the notion of the intertextuality between the visions of Isaiah, Ezekiel, and Daniel is not a novel idea, but instead has been an endeavor from nearly the very beginning.

DISCUSSION OF RECENT LITERATURE

Modern scholarship testifies that the observations of early Jewish thinkers were not foregone ideas. Even more, recent literature also builds a bridge between the OT visions and the NT visions, which supports a biblical theology of vision.

Scholars recognize that YHWH's throne is a major idea within Israel's culture and ideology. Halperin's work is crucial in this regard. For example, Halperin argues that at the end of Ezekiel's vision, a scribal error has occurred such that instead of

---

47. Davila, "4QMess," 379. Note the similarity of language, as well as the use of the term "Watchers."
48. Bauckham, "Apocalypses," 137.
49. Davila, "4QMess," 374.
50. Ibid.
51. Ibid., 374–76.
52. As with parts of *1 Enoch*, this seems to relate to the victory during Noah's time over the Watchers (2.16–18). However, remembering the connection in Enochic literature between *Urzeit* and *Endzeit*, the situation in this text is an intentional foreshadowing of an eschatological situation.

seeing God's exalted glory (ברום), the MT states that Ezekiel saw the blessing (ברוך) from God's glory (Ezek 3:12–13).[53] Halperin explains the choice for the supposed textual variant in this way:

> What caused the error? Any hand-copied text, sacred or profane, is bound to have its share of random blunders made by overworked or distracted scribes. But I do not think this is one of them. I believe that the copyist had found a context for the *merkabah* vision in another dramatic vision, this time described by Isaiah ... Once *barukh* has replaced *berum*, the resemblance of Ezekiel 3:12–13 to this passage in Isaiah [6] is almost eerie.[54]

However, if the MT reading is original, then Halperin's observation becomes even more important. Ezekiel bears striking resemblance to Isaiah's vision. Interestingly enough, Halperin goes on to cite the book of Daniel as his primary example of the first Jewish reactions to the *merkabah* ideology in Ezekiel.[55] This statement inherently ties Daniel and Ezekiel together. In the flow of his argumentation, Halperin makes a case for unity between the visions of Isaiah, Ezekiel, and Daniel.

Halperin also cites an interesting observation about the angelic creatures to support this idea. One of the greatest difficulties in harmonizing the visions concerns the similarities and differences between living creatures, the cherubim, and the seraphim.[56] Halperin recognizes the complexity of this matter.[57] Moreover, he shows how Ezekiel himself resolves this issue. After seeing the four-faced living creatures, Ezekiel later calls them cherubim (Ezek 10:19). Even more, Halperin notes that these creatures are never mentioned side by side in Isaiah, Ezekiel, or Revelation.[58] He interprets that to mean these various titles refer to the same creatures. This too removes an obstacle, allowing the visions to cohere together.

Halperin is not alone in his sentiments. Rowland concurs, as the following observation illustrates:

> In light of the sophistication of the exegetical methods applied to the Scriptures to enable the will of God in specific situations to be discerned, we may well imagine that the hints found in passages like Genesis 1 and Ezekiel 1 would lead the expositor to untold extravagances, as he sought to understand the process of creation and the immediate environs of the Creator. These passages (to which we might add others like Isa 6.1ff) offered the exegete a glimpse into another world,

---

53. I suggest that the MT reading may actually be correct in a later chapter. Halperin admits that while the evidence points to the MT reading (he acknowledges the change must have occurred quite early), the proposed alteration makes more sense. Nonetheless, we can account for the reading of ברך by arguing for its consistency with Isaiah's vision as well as Ezekiel's later statements in chapter 43.

54. Halperin, *Faces of the Chariot*, 44–45.

55. Ibid., 75. "There is little question that the author(s) of Daniel made heavy use of Ezekiel's *merkabah* vision." The next chapter will discuss the many observations Halperin makes concerning the overlap between the two.

56. I will discuss this in the next chapter.

57. Halperin, *Faces of the Chariot*, 41.

58. Ibid., 73.

a disclosure of the way things were before the universe existed and the nature of God who sat enthroned in glory on the cherubim chariot above the firmament.[59]

I could add a plethora of scholars who have recognized the similarities between the visions via a "throne-theophany tradition."[60] Allen sums up the discussion well:

> The throne vision had already featured in the account of Isaiah's prophetic call in Isa 6. Isaiah saw YHWH present in judgment, sitting in council, with the verdict of judgment passed and awaiting execution. At an earlier period Micaiah ben Imlah had seen a vision of the enthroned YHWH in session with his council of judgment, discussing how the death sentence might be carried out (1 Kgs 22:19–22). In line with this tradition, the throne vision that Ezekiel gradually describes functions as a theophany of judgment. Indeed, this passage became part of a continuing tradition. In second-century B.C. Judah, two more visions were described that spoke in terms of a throne with wheels, in echo of Ezek 1:15–21. In the Book of the Watchers, the intent of the vision is to reprove the supernatural Watchers for their sins (*1 Enoch* 14:3; 15:1—16:3; for the wheels of the throne, see 14:18). Likewise, in Dan 7:9 the wheeled throne has a setting of a divine court of judgment. There seems to be a conscious reminiscence of Ezek 1 in its description of a theophany of judgment upon the kingdoms of the earth.[61]

This affirms much of what I have argued. The Jewish people, in a variety of ways, recognized the resemblances of the vision texts and based their own writings (e.g., *1 Enoch*) upon merging those texts together. However, scholars do not merely leave the discussion here, but also extend the implications of this tradition to John and Paul.

Arguably, this is where the discussion must go. The similarities in the wording and imagery in the NT evidence a significant influence of OT visions on NT theology. The concept of Jesus as God-man who sits on a glorious throne (cf. Matt 25:31; 22:1) seems to continue the motif found in Isaiah, Ezekiel, Daniel, and *1 Enoch*.[62] Jesus' own identification as the Son of Man who rides upon the clouds (Luke 21:27), as well as later descriptions of him going to the clouds (Acts 1:9, 11), seem to draw upon such OT terminology.[63] Similarly, Halperin points out that even Pentecost, the inauguration of the latter days, draws upon the imagery of Ezek 1, including the overwhelming fiery sights and rumbling sounds accompanying the presence of the Spirit (Acts 2:1–4; cf. Ezek 1:20, 24).[64]

---

59. Rowland, *Christian Origins*, 61. While we may disagree on the "untold extravagances," the notion that Isa 6 and Ezek 1 provide the foundation for an entire ideology about heaven and God's throne is significant.

60. See Kim, *Paul*, 175. Kim has an impressive list of individuals who affirm the throne-theophany tradition. See also Kanagaraj, "Merkabah Mysticism and the Gospel of John," 349; Allen, *Ezekiel 1–19*, 26–27; Goldingay, *Daniel*, 164; Bruce, *Acts*, 466–67. Halperin mentions that early Christian scholars such as Jerome address this very reality. See Halperin, *Faces of the Chariot*, 58.

61. Allen, *Ezekiel 1–19*, 26–27.

62. Collins and Collins, *King and Messiah*, 87.

63. Boyarin, *Jewish Gospels*, 46–47.

64. Halperin, *Faces of the Chariot*, 17.

Beyond this, both John and Paul pick up on the language of the visions. John mentions angelic creatures, God sitting on a throne, and the appearance of a messianic figure. Revelation truly appears to be a synthesis of all prior visions.[65] Even the phrase "and I saw" (Καὶ εἶδον; cf. Rev 5:1) seems to draw from an apocalyptic phrase found in books like Isaiah, Ezekiel, and Daniel.[66] The overlap and influence of these texts upon John led Kanagaraj to conclude:

> Such a presentation of Jesus' kingship indicates that John is addressing to some extent the Jews of his time who had great interest in Merkabah mysticism—the experience of seeing God on the throne in human-like form, after the pattern of Ezekiel 1, Isaiah 6, and Daniel 7.[67]

In addition, Paul recalls OT visions in his experience on the Damascus road. Kim's work has been seminal in this regard.[68] Kim traces both lexical as well as theological connections between Paul's theology and his vision experience. Kim links this with a broader tradition-history surrounding Ezek 1 and the *merkabah*.[69] Interestingly enough, the apostle uses the language of OT visions (e.g., εἰκών) in the context of "seeing" the Lord (cf. 2 Cor 3:18; 4:4–6; 1 Cor 9:1; 15:8).[70] Other Pauline scholars maintain these connections.[71]

Our discussion thus far shows how scholars have recognized connections between the OT visions, early Jewish literature, and the NT. What are we to make of these observations? Initially, we may see that scholars acknowledge the continuity between the visions of the NT with the OT. By this, we find further precedent towards a biblical theology of vision. However, we can go beyond this. For one, we can identify what the associations between OT, NT, and extra-biblical literature do not imply. They do not mean that the apostles wholly accepted the theology of early Jewish writings. They also do not indicate that the NT writers were controlled or completely influenced by their contemporaries. The apostles do not synthesize their visions in order to follow *1 Enoch* or other Jewish literature.

Rather, understanding the backdrop of early Jewish works helps us more clearly to see what Paul and John intended in their own writings. The NT does not exist in a vacuum. The apostles' wording and use of OT imagery would have lead their readers to a certain conclusion; namely, that like their contemporaries, they claimed the

---

65. Ibid., 91. See Osborne, *Revelation*, 226.

66. Korner, "'And I Saw . . . ,'" 170–71. Beale states, "To sum up, in purely literary terms Ezekiel and Daniel are the dominant influences. Since the structure of Ezekiel 1–2 and allusions to it fade in 5:2ff. and the structure of Daniel 7 continues in 5:2ff., it is probable that the whole vision reflects the dominant framework of Daniel 7. This is based on the observation that chs. 4–5 form one vision and should be studied as a unit" (Beale, *Revelation*, 316).

67. Kanagaraj, "Merkabah Mysticism and the Gospel of John," 349.

68 Kim, *Origin of Paul's Gospel*, 260–68.

69. Ibid.

70. Kim, *Paul*, 178–79.

71. See Schreiner, *Pauline Theology*, 44–47; Bruce, *Paul*, 47.

visions were one, reflections of the same eschatological event. However, Paul and John announce theological conclusions about this unity of vision that are radically different than their counterparts. They proclaim that Jesus is the one central in the visionary event. As such, all the glory and theology associated with the visions of Isaiah, Ezekiel, and Daniel entirely hinge upon the crucified and resurrected Savior. The hope of the OT is in Christ. While this observation does not substitute for an exegetical defense of the unity of visions (see the next chapter), such background sharpens our reading of the NT's assertions. This also points us in the direction of a biblical theology of vision.

Halperin provides one more piece of evidence for this idea. He suggests the "I" statements in such visions indicate recapitulation. There is a reason for why certain individuals experience the same type of events (e.g., both Ezekiel and John consume a scroll). The commonality stems from the fact that one individual is actually stepping in the shoes of the original prophet:

> Who, then, is the "I" who ate the sweet and bitter scroll, and who speaks in Revelation? It is, of course, the putative author, John of Patmos. But it is also Ezekiel. Better: it is Ezekiel as he would have spoken had he fully understood the implications of what had been revealed to him.[72]

And in clearer terms:

> When an apocalyptic visionary "sees" something that looks like Ezekiel's *merkabah*, we may assume that he is seeing the *merkabah* vision as he persuaded himself it really was, as Ezekiel would have seen it had he been inspired wholly and not in part.[73]

The significance of this idea cannot be overstated. Halperin suggests therefore (as Kim and others have allowed) that the visions of the NT writers are recapitulations of their OT counterparts. As such, this idea points towards the thesis of visionary intertextuality: the prophets and apostles all saw different facets of the same vision.

SYNTHESIS

I have not intended to provide a comprehensive review of argumentation and issues that pervade the discussion of the visions and their history of interpretation. Rather, by examining certain ancient texts as well as by observing the conclusions of modern scholarship, we can see that my view is certainly not novel. On the contrary, the notion that the prophets and apostles were all viewing the same visionary event from

---

72. Halperin, *Faces of the Chariot*, 71.

73. Ibid.; Kowalski, "Transformation of Ezekiel," 301. Moyise supports this: "The most obvious explanation is that John has taken on the 'persona' of Ezekiel. Through meditation and study (of which there are ample precedents), John has absorbed something of the character and mind of the prophet" ("Old Testament," 78). While Moyise relates John's use of Ezekiel to the apostle's study of the prophet (which could be the case), he recognizes closeness between these two individuals that most likely extends to their visions as well.

different angles is actually reflected in the interpretation of some of the first readers of the vision texts as well as in contemplations of the modern time. This attests that these passages have thoroughly occupied their readers for centuries, illustrating the importance of formulating a biblical theology of vision. This is not an investigation into some tertiary issue in theology, but something quite central. Likewise, considering the lengthy period of ongoing discussion and analysis, evidence for such a theology is not sparse. Various readers have identified similarities between the visions, and some have even tied the visions together into an eschatological event based upon the paradigm of Dan 7. Some even argue that the visions may be recapitulations of each other. All of this analysis does not necessarily prove that my thesis is right, but merely indicates that we should not disregard the idea of the visions' unity as some new-fangled idea. Instead, the fact that others have made similar observations invites a serious exegetical discussion on the visions themselves to determine whether something in those texts points to their unity, as others seem to have recognized in the past. This is the investigation to which we will now turn.

3

Unity of Vision as Foundation for Biblical Theology of Vision

THE BIG QUESTION

ARE THE VISIONS ACTUALLY different perspectives of the same event? That is the "big question" of this book. After all, by definition, a theology of vision (note the singular), with all its implications, requires unity of vision. Granted, we could formulate a theology of visions (note the plural) even if the visions were all distinct. There are enough similarities that the visions share some sort of intertextual connection. Exploring these relationships would produce a discussion of the biblical perception of God's glory, sovereignty, judgment, and salvation and how they topically relate (and what those who do not fully accept my argument can still gain from this work if it is read along those lines). However, the unity of vision can demonstrate such realities with greater precision and cohesion. This chapter seeks to address whether such a demonstration is possible.

That task seems easier said than done. This "big question" involves a lot of smaller inquiries. What is a fair methodology for evaluating this proposition? How can we discern similar events from identical ones? Were the biblical writers aware that they saw the same thing? How does progressive revelation factor into the discussion? Of course, we may also ask about particular dissimilarities (e.g., the different angelic appearance in Isa 6:2; Ezek 1:4; Rev 4:8) or wonder whether it is even reasonable to read the intertextuality between visions in this manner.[1]

---

1. Block, *Ezekiel*, 1:97. Block argues that Isaiah's vision differs from Ezekiel's vision: "The observation that they used one pair of wings to cover their bodies recalls Isaiah's inaugural vision (Isa. 6:2). However, those creatures are called *sĕrāpîm*, "burning ones," and they have six wings, two of which are used for flying."

While such complexities are many, the solution may not be as elusive as it appears. I would contend that when we start asking the right questions, a harmony of visions is much more obvious than we might have thought.

FUNDAMENTAL ISSUE: HARMONIZATION

When thinking about the unity of the visions, we are actually contemplating the matter of harmonization. The question of whether the visions refer to the same event parallels the issue of whether certain Gospel accounts describe the same part of the life of Christ. Although the Gospel harmonization may deal with "historical material" and the other with more prophetic texts, the difficulty remains the same. Fundamentally, harmonization wrestles with how to prove that multiple accounts refer to the same event. Recognizing this challenge helps us establish a fair and effective methodology to answer the question.

Before addressing the methodology proper, a brief discussion of the background and nature of harmonization can contribute to our understanding of this discussion. Harmonization of scriptural texts (e.g., the Gospels or historical books of the OT) results from a series of factors. It assumes that the Bible is accurate, which forces synthesis rather than contradiction.[2] It also recognizes that the reader of Scripture can identify similar material between two texts.[3] Based upon Scripture's accuracy, comparable material ought to fit together and describe the same occasion. With such presuppositions, people are actually inclined to identify correspondences and harmonize texts.[4] As Dillard states, "The question is not 'should we harmonize or not,' for harmonization is a virtually universal and inevitable feature of daily life."[5] Parents piece together different accounts of their children's behavior. The news media sifts through various testimonies to report what actually occurred. We may read through varying news accounts to form a circumspect view of those events. Harmonization happens intuitively and has been an essential feature of biblical interpretation. History attests to this reality. Harmonies have existed from the time of the OT and continue to the present day. They include scribal efforts at resolving tensions between Chronicles and Kings, Tatian's *Diatessaron*, Ammonius' parallel texts of the Gospels, as well as other works compiled by Calvin and Eusebius of Caesarea.[6] Far from being abnormal, harmonization is quite conventional.

---

2. Thomas and Gundry, *Harmony on the Gospels*, 265–68; Dillard, "Harmonization," 156.

3. Dillard, "Harmonization," 153.

4. Ibid.

5. Ibid.

6. For a summary of harmonies, see Thomas and Gundry, *Harmony on the Gospels*, 269–73. The tradition of a harmony of the Gospels arguably began in the second century with Tatian's *Diatessaron* and continued through church history. See also Perrin, *Thomas, the Other Gospel*; Dillard, "Harmonization," 153–54. Dillard points out that intrabiblical exegesis in the OT relates various accounts together. See also Fishbane, *Biblical Interpretation*, 221–28 for more information on the subject.

That being said, we can now address the concern that a harmonization of vision may be unnatural. If harmonization is a part of humanity's experience, as Dillard argues, and how we habitually read texts, then it makes sense that we might gravitate to such questions. Moreover, if we have applied such approaches to various passages in the history of biblical interpretation, why not do the same to these texts? The tradition of harmonization demonstrates that such activity should be the default rather than an afterthought. In fact, scholars have already acknowledged the striking similarities between the vision accounts. That is precisely why a throne-theophany tradition exists. Likewise, as discussed in chapter 2, ancient writers also recognized such connections in their literature. We have begun to ask the right questions; we just have yet to fully answer them. This conclusion by no means guarantees that the visions all reflect a single entity, but it does illustrate that there is no need to be reticent about the issue.

METHOD OF HARMONIZATION

As we have noted, people seem to pick up on harmonization quite naturally. What causes the reader of OT historical books or the Gospels to understand that multiple accounts may refer to the same event? Similarly, what causes a reader to comprehend that individual accounts do not harmonize together? By identifying these "trigger factors," we can formulate a methodology of harmonization. In essence, this discussion aims to bring to light what the reader does subconsciously and instinctively.[7]

We may describe an event by comparing the familiar criteria of "who, what, when, where, and why." Events often contain certain people/characters (who) that interact in particular ways (what). This takes place at a specific time (when) and place (where) for a certain reason (why). Accordingly, harmonization investigates whether the similarity between the who, what, when, where, and why of multiple accounts actually indicates sameness rather than just likenesses.[8] For example, if the Gospels record the same action (what) that takes place at the same place (where) and time (when) with all the same characters (who), then it stands to reason that they all describe the same event. Thus, no one argues that Jesus rose from the dead four times (Matt 28:5–8; Mark 16:2–8; Luke 24:1–8; John 20:1) or that he fed the five thousand more than once (Matt 14:15–21; Mark 6:35–44; Luke 9:12–17; John 6:4–13). The specification of these events in their timing, characters, and location indicates the shared identity of these occasions.

Within these criteria, certain happenings may contain a distinctive or unrepeatable feature. If multiple texts contain such characteristics, then those accounts likely refer to the same event. No one believes David killed Goliath more than once (1 Sam 17:4; 2 Sam 21:19; 1 Chr 20:5) or that Jesus' transfiguration occurred three different times (Matt 17:1–13; Mark 9:2–8; Luke 9:28–36). We view each of the characters and

---

7. Dillard, "Harmonization," 153.
8. Ibid.; Blomberg, "Limits of Harmonization," 161.

their activities as too exceptional for repetition to take place. Such unique qualities compel us to harmonize these texts regardless of the differences.[9]

A method of harmonization also includes a process for dealing with dissimilarities. Traditionally, scholars resolved inconsistencies by an "additive" harmonization by which they juxtaposed one fact against another.[10] For instance, the differing resurrection texts may refer to distinct events within the complex circumstances of the resurrection.[11] We may also address the doubling of characters in one account over the other by the same means (cf. Mark 16:5; Luke 24:4). Mark emphasizes one angel and omits the other, whereas Luke discusses both of them.[12] Thus, certain accounts can supply details omitted by another.

Additive harmonization is not the only tool for reconciling differences. We can also account for these supposed incongruities by appealing to textual criticism, recognizing that one author may word events differently than another, and approaching works with the understanding that an author may be selective due to the purpose of his writing.[13] For example, scholars reconcile alternative portrayals of Goliath's death through textual criticism.[14] Distinct theological purposes may account for the difference of timing surrounding when Jesus cursed the fig tree (Matt 21:18-22; Mark 11:12—14:25).[15] In the end, those who argue for harmonization bear the burden of proof. The explanations mentioned above are accepted as legitimate solutions. One has to demonstrate that these factors are a part of the author's intent to make a successful case for harmonizing disparities.

If we cannot resolve overt contradictions through the factors discussed above, then the descriptions must not refer to the same event. For this reason, some believe that Jesus cleansed the temple twice (John 2:13-22; Matt 21:12-13; Mark 11:15-18; Luke 19:45-48). The Synoptics differ with John over the timing (when) of the event. The Synoptics place the event late in Jesus' ministry, while John sets it early. Mark's, Luke's, and John's accounts are highly chronological.[16] Hence, it is less likely that

---

9. Bergen, *Samuel*, 449–50. This assumption compels commentators to harmonize Goliath's death in the three texts through textual criticism. Elhanan may be another name for David. Another possibility is that both 2 Sam 21:19 and 1 Chr 20:5 texts suffered corruption. In this case, the reading would be that Elhanan, son of Jaare the Bethelehemite, killed the brother of Goliath (see NET Bible note on 2 Sam 21:19). No matter what the conclusion, the presupposition that Goliath could not die twice or be killed by two different people drives the entire discussion.

10. Ibid., 161.

11. Blomberg, "Limits of Harmonization," 160; Carson, *John*, 633–36.

12. Blomberg, "Limits of Harmonization," 161.

13. Ibid., 141–44. Blomberg provides textual critical, linguistic, historical contextual, form critical, audience critical, source critical, and redactionary factors to resolve supposed discrepancies between the texts.

14. See Bergen, *Samuel*, 449–50.

15. Blomberg, "Limits of Harmonization," 158.

16. Carson, *John*, 177–78. Carson has an excellent discussion concerning the two views of a single temple cleansing versus two. He concludes that strict chronology in the Johannine account argues

one author moved the account earlier or later for theological reasons. Their agenda would seem to dictate a more chronological approach.[17] Furthermore, textual critical evidence indicates that the specific descriptions are in their original positions or contexts. Thus, the claims represent a legitimate discrepancy, and so Jesus most likely cleansed the temple two times. Based upon similar logic, Jesus could have called his disciples more than once (John 1:35–51; Matt 4:18–22; Mark 1:16–20; Luke 5:1–11). The difference of timing (when) as well as the interactions within each (what) may indicate that they are distinct.[18] Furthermore, Peter could have denied Jesus more than three times (Matt 26:69–75; Mark 14:66–72; Luke 22:54–62; John 18:15–18, 25–27).[19] Some have argued that the difference between Peter's interlocutors (who) and the timing of these denials (when) suggest up to six distinct denials.[20] Though I do not support that notion, it does illustrate the parameters of discussing harmonization.[21]

Overall, the methodology for harmonization examines whether overlap of similarities is both extensive and exclusive. It asks "who, what, when, where, and why" questions to determine whether the descriptions of various passages match. It also seeks to determine whether certain details establish an event as unrepeatable such that the various passages must harmonize. It deals with differences between the accounts to see whether they can be resolved using a variety of means.

FURTHER FACTORS OF CONSIDERATION

Three points remain for discussion before we may apply this method to the visions. First, a harmonization of the intertextuality of visions must also involve the

---

against an interpolation of the event, even for theological reasons. Scholars tend to harmonize, but that is not always justified. Rather, in this case, the timing in the Johannine account as well as in the Synoptics argues for two distinctive events.

17. Ibid.

18. See Thomas and Gundry, *Harmony of the Gospels*, 52 n. j.

19. Carson, "Matthew," 8:557–58. Carson notes the various possibilities in harmonizing Peter's denials. Here, in contrast with his discussion on the temple cleansing, he seems to indicate that the accounts can be harmonized more closely into at least a maximum of four denials if not three.

20. Lindsell, *The Battle for the Battle*, 174–76.

21. Carson, "Matthew," 8:557–58. One could harmonize certain characters together. For example, the group of bystanders in John 19:25 could include (or even be a generic plural for) the second servant girl who approaches Peter (cf. Matt 26:71–72, Mark 14:69; Luke 22:58). The relative of Malchus could also be the specific individual in mind in Luke 22:59 and the bystanders of Matt 26:73 and Mark 14:70–71. The timing of the first denial in John's narrative (18:18) remains the predominant factor in this matter. Hence, it is much more likely that either all the events can be successfully harmonized to three denials, or that there are at most four denials (one prior to the trial before Annas and three afterwards).

Another example of disharmonization concerns Jesus' teaching. The Lord could have repeated his message in a certain locale more than once. The happening is not unique or distinctive. Hence, we cannot merely harmonize based upon the similarities in teaching. Rather, time, place, and people present also play a role in the discussion.

innertextuality of the visions. A theology of vision includes the relationship between a biblical writer's vision and his message. I have suggested that the writer expounds upon the nature of his vision, as it provides the "key elements" of his theology. The previous chapter provides initial support for this aspect of a biblical theology of vision.[22] Thus, the biblical writer's message sheds light on what he saw. These additional details provided by the writer help in the discussion of harmonization.

Second, although we will employ such innertextual information, I ought to balance that out by detailing the discourse boundaries of the visions before proceeding. Where does the vision begin and end? What textual material are we going to compare for the purpose of harmonization? This is particularly important when we deal with visions that occur at a prophet or apostle's calling. We may be tempted to blend what the prophet sees and his interaction with that vision together. Admittedly, this makes it impossible for harmonization to occur (since Jesus talking with Paul is hard to harmonize with Isaiah's or Ezekiel's account and vice versa). However, such a reading is actually not entirely accurate. Scholars recognize that within the entire experience of a prophet or apostle's calling there are two components: the "vision proper" which is what the recipient sees, and then his interaction with the vision proper as well.[23] Thus, within Isaiah's calling (6:1–13), Isaiah sees the Lord (vv. 1–3) and then responds to what he has witnessed (vv. 4–13).[24] Similarly, Paul sees Jesus (Acts 9:3) and then interacts with the implications of that vision when Jesus speaks to him (v. 4).[25] For this study, my goal is to compare the "vision proper" of these individuals because I am trying to show the unity of what they actually saw (as opposed to how they responded). While their response to the vision proper may be helpful in interpreting what is taking

---

22. Oswalt, *Isaiah 1–39*, 176; Kim, *Origin of Paul's Gospel*, 165; Bruce, *Paul*, 74; Schreiner, *Pauline Theology*, 44–47. Kim's notions about Paul have played significantly into the formation of this thesis. Both Bruce and Schreiner see that the Damascus Christophany participated in Paul's conversion. They acknowledged that it shifted his thinking and thereby formulated his theology.

23. See Block, *Ezekiel*, 1:77–78; House, "Isaiah's Call," 218–19; Motyer, *Isaiah*, 75; Smith, *Isaiah*, 186; Watts, *Isaiah 1–33*, 104. Scholars agree that the prophet's vision proper is a subunit within his calling followed by his response to seeing the heavenly scene. Watts particularly argues that the vision is a distinctive unit within the prophet's calling and cites parallel scenes in the vision proper of other visions (not involved with an individual's calling).

24. Motyer, *Isaiah*, 77; Oswalt, *Isaiah 1–39*, 182. Note what Oswalt states, "At this point, the prophet becomes aware of himself. He has been aware of the desperate need implicit in the political situation. He has been made aware of the awesome holiness of God with all that that means, of his transcendence and yet his immanence, and now he is suddenly and brutally aware of himself." This marks the transition from what he sees to how he responds.

25. Polhill, *Acts*, 233. Polhill notes that Paul's experience on the Damascus road mirrors those of his predecessors. That includes the experience of seeing Christ's glory and then Paul's reaction to that glory when he speaks. Paul seems to make the same distinction in his experience of the glory of the resurrected Christ and then falling to the ground, which allows for the interaction to take place. This parallels other call experiences, where the prophet (like Ezekiel) sees the vision and then falls to receive instruction (cf. Ezek 2:1). By mirroring these prior call experiences, Paul also makes a distinction between what he saw and how he responded.

place (see above on innertextuality), we should not confuse the vision proper with its consequent reaction.

So what are the textual units that communicate the vision proper? Scholars accept that the vision proper in Isaiah and Ezekiel are Isa 6:1–3 and Ezek 1:1–28.[26] Daniel's vision in chapter 7 breaks down into three parts: his observation of the beasts (7:1–8), his vision of the throne room (7:9–14), and then the interpretation of the vision (7:15–28).[27] Both topic and grammar indicate that Dan 7:9–14 is its own unit.[28] As for John's vision, commentators see Revelation 4–5 as one unit. Similarly to Isaiah and Ezekiel, John's limited participation (cf. Rev 5:4–5) is actually viewed as outside the vision proper.[29] These passages outline the core textual units that provide the "vision proper," the scene that the various prophets and apostles witnessed at their calling (or on other occasions) and responded to. We will use these texts for comparison and harmonization.

Finally, I will discuss the where, what, when, who, and why of Isaiah, Ezekiel, Daniel, and John.[30] An analysis of Paul's Damascus road vision will follow. I include the apostle Paul's vision separately, since it contains less textual data than the others. Seyoon Kim's works have already argued for its association with these visions.[31] Thus, my approach to that discussion will be slightly different. I will highlight Kim's key findings and show how they relate to my thesis.

---

26. Motyer, *Isaiah*, 77; Oswalt, *Isaiah 1–39*, 182. See also Block, *Ezekiel*, 1:78. In Isaiah, the *wayyiqtol* in verse 4 actually signals a structural break in his calling, dividing vision proper from his encounter with what he just saw. Some disagree with this demarcation, arguing that verse 4 is part of the vision proper (see Oswalt, *Isaiah 1–39*, 182; House, "Isaiah's Call," 218–19, Smith, *Isaiah*, 186). They argue that verse 4 transitions from the vision proper to Isaiah's consequent reaction. The transitional nature of verse 4 makes it hard to classify strictly as belonging to one section or the other. Nonetheless, that very transitional nature also argues that a transition is taking place. This indicates that the demarcation between "vision proper" and consequent reaction is highly legitimate.

27. Miller, *Daniel*, 203.

28. This text particularly stands out through its topical distinction from series of beasts in verses 1–8 as well as Daniel's personal involvement in the subsequent verses (7:15–28). Grammatically, Daniel 7:9–14 also does not continue with the prepositional connector "after this" (בָּאתַר דְּנָה) or "behold" (וַאֲרוּ), which bind the previous section (cf. Dan 7:4–8). The lack of an initial *waw* conjunction in Dan 7:15 indicates that verse 15 begins a new section as well. In contrast to these grammatical distinctions, it appears that Daniel 7:9–14 is a cohesive unit. It divides neatly into two subsections that discuss the glory of the Ancient of Days (7:9–12) and the Son of Man's interaction with the Ancient of Days (7:13–14). The conjunctions confirm this (בֵּאדַיִן in v. 11 and *waw* in vv. 12 and 14).

29. Aune, *Revelation 1–5*, 329; Osborne, *Revelation*, 254. Aune rightly notes that the discourse marker "and I saw" separates verses 2–5 from the rest of the narrative within the vision. Osborne agrees, seeing the "and I saw" in verse 6 as leading into the centerpiece of the vision.

30. I have deviated from the normal order of "who, what, when, where, and why" to facilitate a clearer presentation.

31. Kim, *Origin of Paul's Gospel*, 93.

THE QUESTION OF "WHERE"

We may now apply the method and factors discussed above to the visions. We begin by discussing the issue of the locale described in the visions. All the visions revolve in some fashion around the heavenly courtroom of God and his throne (cf. Isa 6:1; Ezek 1:1; Dan 7:9; Rev 4:3). They also share significant overlap in the details of this scene. The mention of wheels on the throne in Dan 7:9 corresponds to the same type of chariot-throne found in Ezek 1:26. In fact, Collins states, "The fiery wheels on the stationary throne, however, undoubtedly derive from Ezekiel's *Merkavah* vision (Ezek 1:15–21; 10:2)."[32] Thus, Daniel incorporates Ezekiel's vision into his scene. In addition, Daniel and John record multiple thrones around God's chariot-throne (Dan 7:9; Rev 4:4). Overall, Isaiah, Ezekiel, Daniel, and John significantly overlap in how they describe the heavenly courtroom.

One may object to the issue of "where" by noting that Ezekiel's chariot-throne seems to appear on earth as opposed to heaven (see Ezek 1:4; 8–11; 43). Initially, I can point out that Daniel has already tied the chariot-throne of Ezekiel with the heavenly court. This signals that Ezekiel's vision will be somehow involved in that heavenly courtroom scene (even if later revelation will reveal it). However, I do not even need to appeal to Daniel necessarily. Ezekiel already states that he saw visions (note the plural, which seems to include all of Ezekiel's visions) of heaven (1:1). As Cooper comments on this verse, "The picture created by Ezekiel's description is of the door being opened into the heavenly throne room of God."[33] In fact, Block translates the phrase "visions of heaven" as "visions of heavenly realities."[34] Thus, while his visions elaborate upon the significance of the chariot-throne, fundamentally, in the context of Ezek 1:1, all of that innertextuality amplifies what was revealed to Ezekiel about heaven. Ezekiel's visions explain the agenda of the chariot-throne found in the heavenly court. This coincides with a later and larger discussion concerning the agenda of the visionary event, which pertains to how the Lord from his throne in heaven will resolve all the history of the world in the Son. Ezekiel's subsequent visions about how the heavenly chariot-throne interacts with the earth fits quite well within that paradigm. Nonetheless, it appears that Daniel and Ezekiel are both consistent insofar as they describe the chariot-throne as part of something heavenly, even if it will pertain to earth, as both of them explain.

Along that vein, the scene in heaven does seem to anticipate the very specific occasion of heaven coming to earth. The temple imagery in these visions may promote that association. Isaiah specifically places his vision in the context of the temple (6:4). God's heavenly glory fills this structure. John also witnesses heavenly temple imagery

---

32. Collins, *Daniel*, 302. Collins counters Halperin and Zimmerli, who argue that this is just incidental. Cf. Miller, *Daniel*, 205.

33. Cooper, *Ezekiel*, 60.

34. Block, "Text and Emotion," 428–29.

with an altar (Rev 6:9; 8:3), which is reminiscent of Isaiah (6:6) and Ezekiel (10:2).[35] In John's vision, God's eschatological workings move from the heavenly temple to earth (cf. Rev 15:1–8). Such temple imagery in these visions seems to bridge heaven to earth. Consistently, Ezekiel's vision initially focuses upon the throne of God in heaven (Ezek 1:1) but later also places the vision in an earthly temple context. The same glory that Ezekiel saw at Chebar both leaves and fills the temple (cf. 8:3–5; 10:15–18; 43:1–7).

This suggests that we are not merely seeing a scene in heaven but the heavenly courtroom prepared for a certain occasion. The "stage" is ready for the "event," so to speak. The prophets and apostles envision the throne room of God while it brings together heaven and earth through the temple.[36] Our investigation of the other factors will evidence this claim further.

THE QUESTION OF "WHAT"

What actually happens in (and even around) the visionary event itself? I have already hinted that the visions seem to all converge around the Son of Man's inauguration. Daniel and John support this observation. Their visions provide the clearest description of what is taking place. Daniel describes the inauguration of the Son of Man and how all kingdoms are placed under his control (Dan 7:9–13). Similarly, John describes Jesus as the one who receives the scroll, which indicates that Jesus inherits the entire cosmos as his own to rule.[37] Scholars recognize that both visions portray the event of the Son of Man's investiture or enthronement.[38] They both show how the Son of Man comes before the throne of God, the Ancient of Days (Dan 7:9; Rev 4:2; 5:7) to receive dominion. Thus, Dan 7 and Rev 4–5 seem to record the same "happening" (what).

Isaiah's vision proper is brief and appears to only record the Lord sitting on his throne surrounded by the angels (Isa 6:1–3).[39] However, the innertextuality of the

---

35. Beale, *Revelation*, 391; Aune, *Revelation 1–5*, 404–6. See also, Beale, *Temple and the Church's Mission*, 37, 336–40. The imagery of the chariot presents a microcosm of creation and temple. See also Allen, *Ezekiel 1–19*, 28:34. Furthermore, the temple imagery becomes even more apparent in Ezekiel when we consider the fuller vision in Ezek 10:1–22 and 43:3–7. See later discussion.

36. Motyer, *Isaiah*, 76: "The temple is no mere symbol of his indwelling presence; it is the reality of it. But there is also the specific truth that in the temple the Lord meets with his people on the basis of sacrifice. This in particular is the point where heaven touches earth. The vision thus prepares for its climax in verse 7."

37. Beale, *Revelation*, 340.

38. Aune, *Revelation 1–5*, 336. Aune notes that both Daniel and Revelation technically refer to the Son's investiture rather than enthronement. While the former emphasizes the conferral of authority, whereas the latter denotes his official rule, scholars assume the latter flows from the former. In this book, I will use the terms essentially interchangeably.

39. Block, *Ezekiel*, 1:78. Amongst other subdivisions, commentators distinguish the vision proper and the prophet's calling. The vision occurs as the prophet watches, and then its specific nuances for the prophet occur when he begins to interact with the vision. Accordingly, Isaiah's vision pertains to the first four verses of the chapter describing the holy God sitting on the throne. As Isaiah begins to speak in verse 5, the text transitions into describing his calling.

vision with the rest of the book provides a fuller picture of what occurs. Isaiah's vision seems to relate to Isa 52:13—53:12. In Isa 6, YHWH is "high and lifted up" (יָרוּם וְנִשָּׂא). The phrase next appears when the prophet applies the same description to the suffering Servant's exaltation (52:13).[40] This provides an initial indication that the passages are interconnected. These texts share further parallels. Isaiah's vision opens with YHWH sitting on his throne (6:1) as his glory fills the earth (6:3). The Servant song begins by stating that the Servant has been successful (52:13) in fulfilling his contextual calling to bring justice to the nations (cf. 42:1, 4) and to display God's glory to the ends of the earth (cf. 49:2-3).[41] Isaiah's calling continues with a description of how God purifies Isaiah, who dwells amongst a sinful people (6:5-7). In like manner, the Servant song describes how the Servant cleanses the people of Israel and the nations (53:5, 11-12). These similarities suggest that Isa 52:13—53:12 more fully explains the nature of the prophet's original vision. God seems to bestow his own dominion (being "high and lifted up") upon his Servant because of his atoning work. In the context of the Servant song, this results in the Servant's reign over all the world and the spread of YHWH's glory throughout creation (42:1, 4; 49:2; 52:13; 53:12). In the flow of the book, Isa 6 appears to depict the opening part of this inauguration, which is completed by the Servant song.

Isaiah's innertextual association of Isa 6 with the Servant's exaltation sounds similar to both Daniel and John. In fact, John confirms the parallel in two ways. First, he quotes from Isa 6:10 and claims that Isaiah spoke of Christ (John 12:38-41). Some believe that John claims Jesus was on the throne in Isa 6.[42] Others note that technically the apostle states he saw the *glory* of Jesus and spoke of him.[43] In that case, the apostle means that the Servant shares the same glory of God presented in Isaiah's visions.[44] The connection between Isaiah's vision and the Servant song accounts for either interpretation. It appears that John understands the textual links within Isaiah. Second, John's apocalyptic vision confirms this innertextuality as well. The visions in Isaiah and Revelation contain various parallels. Both record how Isaiah and John saw God seated on the throne (Isa 6:1; Rev 4:1-2). Both depict the angelic beings singing the same chorus (Isa 6:3; Rev 4:8). Both describe the dominion of God and its transfer to the Son/Servant. In Revelation, the glory and honor ascribed to the Father (4:9) is given to the Son (5:13). In Isaiah, the vision portrays this majesty (6:1-6) and then attributes it to the Servant (52:13—53:12).

40. Oswalt, *Isaiah 1-39*, 378; Carson, *John*, 449-50; Motyer, *Isaiah*, 424.

41. Oswalt, *Isaiah 40-66*, 378: "Even more so, it is not saying that the Servant will be a rich man. Rather, it is saying that he will both know and do the right things in order to accomplish the purpose for which he was called (Isa. 42:1; 49:2-3; 50:7-9). Whatever the intervening intimations of failure might be (49:4), the Servant and the world should know that he will not fail." Oswalt thereby links the Servant's success contextually with the realities I stated above.

42. Morris, *Gospel According to John*, 537.

43. Carson, *John*, 449-50; Köstenberger, *John*, 391-92.

44. Carson, *John*, 449-50; Köstenberger, *John*, 391-92.

Unity of Vision as Foundation for Biblical Theology of Vision

Thus, the innertextual connection within Isaiah becomes the very structure of John's vision. Could it be that John, closely following Isaiah's logic, knew he saw the same event as Isaiah? In any case, Isaiah indicates that his vision reflects the inauguration of the Servant and John recognizes this association.

We can apply a similar logic to Ezekiel's opening vision. Ezekiel helps the reader see the innertextuality of his vision by referring to his inaugural vision throughout the book (cf. Ezek 8:4; 10:15; 43:3). The last of these allusions, Ezek 43:3, seems to include all of the previous references. It claims that the final vision matches the first vision (1:1–2) and the one which resulted in the destruction of Jerusalem (8:4, 10:15). Accordingly, Ezek 43 provides the most complete significance or purpose of what the writer saw concerning his original vision when heaven was opened (cf. 1:1).

In this final vision, Ezekiel understands that God's presence certainly judges (8:4; 10:15) but will ultimately never leave God's people (43:3). The glory of God returns to the temple and remains there (43:7). Looking further at the details of this vision, we see substantial overlap with the visions of other biblical writers. In Ezekiel, God declares that the temple is now his throne and he will reside with his people forever (43:7). This corresponds to the throne imagery in Isaiah (6:1), Daniel (7:9), and John (Rev 4:2; 5:7).[45] God's glory fills the temple (Ezek 43:5b) just like in Isaiah's vision (6:1b). His glory (מִכְּבֹדוֹ, ἀπὸ τῆς δόξης) shines through the earth (Ezek 43:2) just as the angels proclaimed in Isaiah's vision (6:3b). This notion of filling the earth with glory may also correlate with Daniel's vision, where all glory (וִיקָר, πᾶσα δόξα) is given to the Son of Man amongst every people and nation (7:14). We see the same motif in Dan 2:35, a text that parallels Dan 7, where the mountain of God's kingdom fills the entire earth. John's vision features this motif as well. All creation acknowledges the glory of the Lamb (ἡ δόξα, Rev 5:11–13). Importantly, the motif of God's glory and/or dominion filling the earth runs through all the visions. In this way, the significance ultimately assigned to the chariot-throne of heaven found in Ezekiel's vision (cf. Ezek 1:1) matches the agenda of all the other visions.

Moreover, Ezekiel's vision is situated in the context of that Messianic individual. Commentators recognize the connection between Ezekiel 43 and the salvation oracles of chapters 34–37.[46] The return of God's presence and dwelling with his people is made possible by God's shepherding activity (34:11–22). Within this, God establishes his shepherd, a new David, who is associated with a new covenant granting peace (34:25). This results in the fruition of God's relationship with his people (34:30). The permanence of God's presence with his people in chapter 43 depends upon the inauguration of the new David (cf. the Prince in 44:3).[47] These

---

45. Allen, *Ezekiel 20–48*, 256. Allen recognizes the strong similarities of Ezekiel's language with Isaiah's own vision: "In language derived from the ark tradition, the temple is initially described as the exclusive royal residence of YHWH (cf. Isa 6:1; 60:13; Ps 99:5)."

46. Block, *Ezekiel*, 1:578.

47. Ibid., 301: "In short, he [the new David] symbolizes the presence of YHWH in the midst of

I Saw the Lord

innertextual connections are significant for harmonization. While Ezekiel's vision itself may concentrate on the chariot-throne and God's presence, its context still involves the inauguration of the Son (34:25) and a similar redemptive-historical situation as the other visions. Thus, the circumstances surrounding Ezekiel's vision match the content of those other visions.

Accordingly, the "what" of these passages seems quite similar. The visions and their innertextuality describe components of the same situation within and surrounding the visionary event. Specifically, they describe aspects of the sovereignty of God as it pertains to the occasion surrounding the inauguration of the Servant/Son of Man/Jesus. They portray how the Messiah receives dominion, rules over the world, and fills the temple and all the earth with the glory of YHWH. This unique motif in the visions points to their identical nature.

THE QUESTION OF "WHEN"

At this point, one could argue that the visions may share the same motif but that it is a repeated event throughout redemptive history. After all, God's glory fills the temple at various moments in history (cf. Exod 40:35; 1 Kgs 8:10). Could the prophets and apostles have witnessed an ongoing reality, or moments in history that directly relate to their situation? If this is the case, then biblical authors witness similar but distinct events because they occurred at different times. Thus, further analysis of the question of "when" can help allay this concern and make a stronger case for the unity of visions.

The immediate complication when dealing with a vision's timing is that the calling of the prophet or apostle involves two components: the "vision proper" (or, what the prophet or apostle saw) and the reaction of the prophet or apostle to what he has just seen. Because the "vision proper" is quite related to the prophet's response, scholars have assumed that what is described within the "visionary proper" occurs simultaneously with the rest of the prophet's experience.[48] Under such a presupposition, the events reflected in the vision occur multiple times, making it impossible to harmonize the visions. Yet this assumption does not necessarily have to be taken as true. Upon closer examination, I would contend that the biblical writers indicate that they see an eschatological event. The "vision proper" portrays something future, and that future reality drives and shapes the prophet's or apostle's present ministry as is discussed in the rest of their calling.

Dan 7:1–28 and Rev 4:1—5:14 both portray realities that will occur after the days of Daniel and John. The Son of Man's inauguration comes around the time when the fourth beast and its horn wage war against God's people (Dan 7:13–22).[49] The second

---

his people." See also Allen, *Ezekiel 20–48*, 163; Cooper, *Ezekiel*, 302. See later discussion concerning the prince.

48. Block, *Ezekiel*, 1:83; Allen, *Ezekiel 1–19*, 20; Oswalt, *Isaiah 1–39*, 176.

49. Collins, *Daniel*, 298–303; Walvoord, *Daniel*, 163; Goldingay, *Daniel*, 166–67. The chronology

chapter of the book provides a parallel vision in which Daniel explains that the timing of Nebuchadnezzar's dream is future (2:28–29). This establishes that the inauguration of the Son of Man occurs under the circumstances of the end of Israel's exile and the launch of God's kingdom (2:34–35; 7:7–14).[50] God reiterates that the book and vision are for a time beyond Daniel (12:7–9). The prophet's visions are ultimately fulfilled in the latter days (2:28 [בְּאַחֲרִית יוֹמַיָּא, ἐπ' ἐσχάτων τῶν ἡμερῶν], 29 [אַחֲרֵי דְנָה, μετὰ ταῦτα]): the climax of history.[51]

John's own vision ties directly into this framework. The book of Revelation follows the paradigm of the "things you have seen, the things which are, and the things which will take place after these things" (ἃ μέλλει γενέσθαι μετὰ ταῦτα) (Rev 1:19). Scholars acknowledge that John's visions reflect a future reality.[52] Beale also points out that John's wording of μετὰ ταῦτα parallels certain Greek versions of Dan 2:28–29.[53] Such intertextuality indicates that the timing of John's vision matches the timing of Daniel's prophecy. Both occur in the "latter days."

Another observation reinforces this suggestion. God instructs Daniel to seal his visions in a book (Dan 12:7–9). The timing of his visions is set for the end and not ready to happen yet.[54] However, he gives John opposite directions and tells him not to seal the words of the book (Rev 22:10). John's vision will occur soon.[55] Although the statements are contrastive, their highly similar language (about sealing a book) seems

---

of the vision presented to Daniel does not necessarily communicate the real order of events. Nonetheless, the context implies the existence of the fourth kingdom for the courtroom to make its decision. The fourth beast is slain and the Son of Man is proclaimed king (Dan 7:11). It appears that the heavenly courtroom event occurs in tandem with the demise of the fourth kingdom. Dan 7 recapitulates Dan 2, which provides a similar progression. God's kingdom is the rock that crushes all other kingdoms and becomes a great mountain (2:44). Daniel explains that he and Nebuchadnezzar live in the "gold" kingdom of Babylon and all the rest of the kingdoms are future. This provides an anchor to argue that Dan 7 predominantly refers to future events.

50. It appears that the fourth segment of the body (iron legs; 2:33) corresponds to the fourth animal in Dan 7:7–8. The feet of iron mixed with clay (2:33) seem to parallel the horn that supplants three other horns (7:8). This all takes place right before the stone not made with hands crushes the statue (2:34) and the Son of Man is inaugurated (7:9–14). This parallelism relates the end of the fourth modified kingdom, the establishment of God's kingdom (2:44), the end of Israel's exile, and the inauguration of the Son of Man.

51. Culver, *Latter Days*, 107.

52. Aune, *Revelation 1–5*, 105–6; Osborne, *Revelation*, 97. This is not restricted to purely a "futurist" reading of Revelation. Those in the amillennial camp will acknowledge that the cycle of events in Rev 6–20 repeats throughout church history, much of which is future to John. Preterists may view this as historical as opposed to a future reality.

53. Beale, *Revelation*, 216. This is particularly reflected in Theodotian's version.

54. Aune, *Revelation 1–5* 1216; Beale, *Revelation*, 1129–30. Aune holds the connection more loosely, saying that only similar language is used. However, Beale recognizes the contrast between the instructions of Daniel's day and the present day instructions. The contrast or change between the two presumes that they shared the same content but now, due to a change of situation, were required to handle it differently. This deals rightly with the intertextuality.

55. Beale, *Revelation*, 1129–30.

to make them parallel. Such wording evidences that God's instruction to John alludes to his exhortation to Daniel. The relationship between the two seems to be that while Daniel and his contemporaries must wait for his vision to be fulfilled, John's readers will experience the fulfillment of that vision soon. If this reading is correct, we can draw two inferences. First, Daniel and John overlapped in their revelation. Second, both awaited for a similar point of redemptive history. Put differently, why does God instruct Daniel differently than John? It appears that Daniel was further away from that moment in redemptive history, whereas John was much closer. However, this presumes that both are awaiting the same moment. The contrast seems to hinge upon that presupposition.[56] Thus, the differing instructions also strengthen the thesis of identical timing, and even identical revelation.

As noted, Isaiah's vision relates to the exaltation of the suffering Servant (52:13). In context, this occurs after the Servant sacrifices himself for his people (53:1–10) and redeems them from exile (54:1). Such timing is future (relative to Isaiah) and matches the circumstances of the end of exile found in Daniel. The Servant's transformation of Zion (54:1–17) appears to be a part of a series of "Zion texts" which discuss the eschatological renewal of Jerusalem. Isa 2:1–4 is one of these passages and explicitly states that this occurs in the latter days (בְּאַחֲרִית הַיָּמִים, ἐν ταῖς ἐσχάταις ἡμέραις, 2:2).[57] Thus, the event in Isaiah's vision seems to relate to that time period, which matches both Daniel's and John's visions.

This is also true of Ezekiel's vision. As we have noted, the full nature of his vision recounts God's eschatological presence in the temple, where he fills the world with glory (43:1–7). The fulfillment of this aspect of the vision follows Israel's exile (37:1–28), which matches the circumstances surrounding Isaiah's and Daniel's visions (Isa 54:1; Dan 2:34–35). Furthermore, filling the earth (as opposed to temple) with glory is distinctly eschatological in the OT (cf. Num 14:21; Ps 72:19; Hab 2:14).[58] Hence, if both Isaiah (6:3) and Ezekiel (43:2) discuss that reality, then both relate to the same

---

56. Ibid. The chronology in Daniel appears differently than Revelation. Daniel views the fourth beast as slain, the inauguration of the Son of Man, and then the victory of the saints (Dan 7:11–14). John views the inauguration of the Lamb and the consequent judgment and takeover of the kingdoms of the world. However, Daniel's vision does not assert a strict chronology. It only presents a sequence of events as Daniel saw them. Both visions seem to put the decision of the heavenly court as the source of the nations' downfall. The match in the relative chronology and scheme of causation shows similar timing.

57. See Watts, *Isaiah 1–33*, 41–42. Watts acknowledges the similarity of these Zion texts. For this reason, some have argued that this is actually an interpolation of Deutero-Isaiah. While I disagree with that conclusion, a similar motif binds texts like Isa 54:1–5 and Isa 2:1–4 together. The phrase "after these days" (2:2) indicates, "this is the Judah and Jerusalem of chs. 40 and following" (42). See also Motyer, *Isaiah*, 53–54, 445–46. Motyer draws additional comparisons between Isa 54:1–5 and other latter days texts. For example, the tent imagery may refer to Amos 9:11, which deals with the resurrection and culmination of the Davidic dynasty. Further evidence for a connection between Isa 2 and 6 will be offered in the next chapter.

58. All of the above texts anticipate the time when God will fill the earth with glory. Ps 72:19 frames this as a prayer request. Hab 2:14 describes this as God's agenda. Num 14:21 swears by the surety of that outcome.

eschatological moment. In addition, the context indicates that the event in Ezekiel's vision occurs in the "latter days" (בְּאַחֲרִית הַיָּמִים, ἐσχάτων τῶν ἡμερῶν, 38:16) similarly to Isaiah (2:2), Daniel (2:28), and John (Rev 1:19).[59]

One objection to the notion of timing is that in Rev 4:8, the angels do not cease singing their praise to the Lord. This makes the scene appear timeless. However, in addition to the evidence already discussed, John possibly has in mind an event within the constant worship of the living creatures. His wording in Rev 4–5 seems to indicate that this is not a timeless scene, but rather a specific moment. For example, John's use of ὅταν consistently describes a particular incident (cf. Rev 10:7; 11:7; 12:4; 17:10). Its use in Rev 4:9 probably then designates a unique event as opposed to a timeless scene. Accordingly, an eschatological viewpoint of the event can still be maintained.[60]

Overall, the visions of Isaiah, Ezekiel, Daniel, and John are all associated with the latter days. Beyond this general heading, the biblical writers provide further detail to indicate that their visions pertain to the same moment of redemptive history. The inauguration of the Son of Man takes place around the end of Israel's exile (Isa 54:1–17; Ezek 37:1–28) and relates to the demise of the fourth kingdom in Daniel (7:7–8). This future timing of the vision argues that these biblical writers did not see similar events that repeated throughout history. Instead, they all witnessed a single event at the climax of redemptive history.

THE QUESTION OF "WHO"

The visions revolve around YHWH (Isa 6:1; Ezek 1:1–2; Dan 7:9; Rev 4:2–3). They describe his glory with an overwhelming brilliance and compare it to precious jewels (Ezek 1:26–28; Dan 7:9; Rev 4:2–3). As noted above, he is positioned in the same location: the heavenly courtroom on a chariot-throne (Isa 6:1; Ezek 1:26–28; Dan 7:9; Rev 4:2–3). This similar characterization of the Lord could indicate an identical scene. One could even say that God is "dressed" for the occasion (cf. Ezek 1:27).

However, the Lord is not the only character involved in the visions. The Son of Man approaches the Ancient of Days in order to receive dominion over all creation. Daniel and John clearly mention this figure (Dan 7:9–10; Rev 5:1–10). Isaiah envisions God handing his-high-and-exalted-dominion to the Servant (Isa 6:1; 52:13). So he too includes this individual by implication. Ezekiel, by parallel logic, associates his vision with the work of the Shepherd (34:1–11) and Prince (44:3).

---

59. Alexander, "Ezekiel," 941–44. Later on, Ezekiel summarizes his messages by showing how he sent his people into exile but then brought them back and defeated the nations (Ezek 39:21–28). Following this, God will richly dwell with his people by pouring out his Spirit on the house of Israel (Ezek 39:29). This paradigm suggests that the fullness of God's dwelling in Ezek 40–48 occurs after his attack against Gog (Ezek 38–39) and thereby in the latter days.

60. Beale, *Revelation*, 333.

Other characters can be harmonized as well. The myriad angels found in Daniel 7:10 may be identified with the many angels in Rev 5:11.[61] While this angelic host is not explicitly mentioned in Ezekiel or Isaiah, their presence is easily harmonized with the silence in those descriptions. In the scope of progressive revelation, the earlier prophecies (i.e., Isaiah and Ezekiel) provide less detail, which later revelation (i.e., Daniel and John) further elaborates. Furthermore, God may unveil parts of this scene to a particular prophet for theological reasons.[62] A similar explanation can apply to the twenty-four elders (Rev 4:4).[63]

What is perhaps the most difficult discrepancy deals with the angelic beings known as seraphim (Isa 6:3–4) versus cherubim (Ezek 1:5–24; 10:1) versus the living creatures (Ezek 1:5; Rev 4:6–8).[64] They are described with different titles. Their descriptions also include differences in appearance. Isaiah records that the seraphim have six wings, whereas the cherubim in Ezekiel have four (Ezek 1:6) and the living creatures in Revelation have six (Rev 4:8). Ezekiel describes the creatures as having four faces, but John describes the "four faces as distributed amongst the four creatures, one apiece."[65] The creatures also may be in different positions, with one below the throne (Ezek 1:22) but the others above or around (Isa 6:2; Rev 4:6–8).[66]

Granted, we could resort to an "additive harmony" as a solution at this point. I could claim that the seraphim of Isaiah, cherubim of Ezekiel, and living creatures of Revelation are all separate angelic beings who all are present before God's throne. This solution runs into some difficulties, however. First, John's vision seems the most comprehensive, yet does not mention Isaiah's seraphs. An additive harmony does not seem viable in light of this discrepancy. Second, John seems to merge the imagery of Ezekiel and Isaiah's visions. The words from the living creatures' mouths in Revelation 4:8 match the seraphim's words in Isa 6:3. John's designation of living creatures matches how Ezekiel initially describes the cherubim in Ezek 1:5 but their number of wings corresponds to Isaiah's seraphim. Hence, it appears that John claims that the creatures he sees resemble those in the visions of Isaiah and Ezekiel.

In light of this, the biblical authors may have referred to the same creatures, but differ in description because of their theology, perspective, or emphasis. The issue is one

---

61. Aune, *Revelation 1–5*, 363; Beale, *Revelation*, 364.

62. Blomberg, "Limits of Harmonization," 141–44; Dillard, "Harmonization," 153. Blomberg and Dillard both observe that while additive harmonization can at times be a workable solution, other solutions, including redactionary or theological purpose, also exist. In this case, God has a specific purpose in revealing certain elements of a vision for theological reasons. This accords with their assertion.

63. Blomberg, "Limits of Harmonization," 141–44; Dillard, "Harmonization," 153.

64. Cf. Block, *Ezekiel*, 1:97. See quote above; Block argues that the difference in the number of wings serves as a major obstacle to harmonizing the visions.

65. Thomas, *Revelation 1–7*, 358 n. 73.

66. Ibid., 358. Thomas also argues that the creatures are full of eyes in Rev 4:6–8, but not in Ezekiel, but later on, Ezekiel records that they do have eyes (10:12). This illustrates how innertextuality can resolve some of the tensions within the accounts.

of agenda. Were Isaiah and Ezekiel purely trying to describe all that they saw, or were they selective in their presentation for the sake of their message? There is evidence that Isaiah and Ezekiel portrayed the angels equally on the basis of theology as well as on the physical characteristics they observed. For example, their use of certain language is more theologically or functionally oriented than physical. Ezekiel claims that he saw "cherubim" (10:1). However, "cherubim" in ANE iconography look a certain way. They have bendable knees and do *not* have multiple animal faces.[67] Ezekiel describes what he saw far differently. His cherubim have straight legs (1:7) and have four faces of different animals, a feature that actually has no ANE parallel. Similarly, Isaiah asserts he saw seraphim, but his descriptions are not like those of the ANE. The "seraphim" typically are winged serpent creatures.[68] While Isaiah's seraphim are winged, they do not appear to be snakelike at all. In these cases, the authors are not using the titles to denote the physical description of the angelic creatures. Rather, it appears that they utilize these words for different purposes, to describe the *function* of these beings and thereby a theology about them. This reflects that the prophets were not merely concerned about describing the physical appearance of the angels they saw, but were equally focused upon the theological message these angels (by their appearance) communicated. Based upon this observation, they arguably wrote these descriptions accurately, but not necessarily comprehensively. The biblical writers may have concentrated on certain aspects of the angelic beings instead of describing the whole in order to accentuate their message. Likewise, their terminology portrays theological ideas as much as physical characteristics. This facilitates the harmonization of certain supposed contradictions.

Hence, I would contend that the differences in the titles of seraphim, cherubim, or living creatures are more theological than actually indicative of different creatures. Isaiah may label the angels as seraphim due to his emphasis on holiness. Seraphim most likely relates to the term burning, which accords with God's holy presence.[69] The title may also denote his judgment, since seraphim were traditionally associated with the wasteland, which Israel was to become (cf. Isa 6:11).[70] Ezekiel's choice of the term cherubim reflects God's presence. In ANE culture, the cherubim are associated with bearing a deity's presence and throne.[71] Living creatures in Ezekiel or John reflect the dominion of God over all creation.[72] This corresponds with Ezekiel's theology of God's presence filling all the earth, as well as with John's theology that God's judgment and salvation will extend throughout the entire earth, ultimately in a new creation.

---

67. Ibid., 166–67; see also Allen, *Ezekiel 1–19*, 26–33.

68. Oswalt, *Isaiah 1–39*, 179; Hartenstein, "Cherubim and Seraphim," 171–72.

69. *HALOT*, 2:1359–60; Hartenstein, "Cherubim and Seraphim," 171–72; Oswalt, *Isaiah 1–39*, 179. See See also Exod 3:1–6; 13:21; 19:18; Num 11:1–2, which discusses other passages where fire reflects God's holiness.

70. Hartenstein, "Cherubim and Seraphim," 171–72.

71. Ibid.

72. Ibid.; Block, *Ezekiel*, 1:97.

We can account for the differences in the number of wings and faces as well by taking an approach used in harmonizing the Gospels. In those texts, we understand that an author may focus on one person over all the individuals who were present (Matt 8:28–34; Mark 5:1–17; Luke 8:26–37).[73] Because the accounts are not mutually exclusive, we can harmonize them. Mark does not claim that *only* one man was present in opposition to Matthew's description of two. Instead, they choose to focus on different aspects for theological purposes.

We can apply a similar logic in addressing the angelic creatures. Ezekiel utilizes the number four frequently in his account. He stresses four creatures (1:5), four faces (1:6), four sides (1:8), and four directions (1:17). The four wings correspond with each side, or face of the living creature and provide covering (1:8, 11). The repetition of the number four shows that the creatures in every respect testify to God's presence amongst and over all creation.[74] His presence is in all the cardinal directions.[75] The description does not necessarily mean that the beings had only four wings. They could have had more (i.e., six). Isaiah and John observe the full number of wings (six), whereas Ezekiel concentrates on four of those wings to reiterate his message.[76] A similar logic applies to the faces of the creatures. Ezekiel sees four faces on each creature, corresponding to his emphasis on God's omnipresence. John chooses to focus upon a distinctive face of each creature to show correspondence with Ezekiel, but also stress his own theological message. He makes allusions to both Isaiah and Ezekiel to claim that their theology and vision are fulfilled in his own. Thus, we can resolve the issues of differing appearance.

One final major discrepancy remains. The cherubim in Ezekiel carry the chariot-throne, while in Isaiah they seem to be above it (6:2, מִמַּעַל), and in Revelation they seem to be in the midst of and surrounding the throne (ἐν μέσῳ τοῦ θρόνου καὶ κύκλῳ τοῦ θρόνου; 4:6). The construction in Isaiah does not necessarily mean the angels were physically over God, but rather attending on God.[77] Hence, Isaiah's description does not speak to the issue of physical location discussed in Ezekiel and Revelation. Within

---

73. In Matt 8:28–34; Mark 5:1–17; Luke 8:26–37. Matthew records two demoniacs, but the other Synoptics record only one. The argument could be that Matthew presents the entire situation, whereas Luke and Mark focus upon one of them. Also, see the harmonization between Matt 28:2 and Luke 24:4, in that the former contains one angel, but the latter contains two. See Morris, *Gospel According to Matthew*, 735.

74. Block, *Ezekiel*, 1:97; House, *Old Testament Theology*, 327–30.

75. Block, *Ezekiel*, 1:97.

76. Oswalt, *Isaiah 1–39*, 179. Isaiah's presentation of the total amount of wings seems to bring out their covering function even more. This shows how the angels shielded themselves from God's holiness from head to foot. While Ezekiel includes this functionality (another indication of similarity and harmonization), his emphasis on four shows a distinct theological agenda on direction and presence. John seems to provide the full picture and the fulfillment of the vision. He thereby describes six wings like Isaiah.

77. Oswalt, *Isaiah 1–39*, 178; Young, *Book of Isaiah*, 240. See Gen 45:1; Judg 3:19; 2 Sam 13:9 for similar constructions.

those two latter books, the phraseology is actually quite similar. Notice Beale's own observation on this matter: "It is plausible that ἐν μέσῳ τοῦ θρόνου portrays the living beings as supporting the throne (as in Ezek 1:15–26)."[78] Thus, understanding the nature of Isaiah's claim can help resolve this issue, and more importantly, actually points to significant overlap between Ezekiel and John.

With that, we can go beyond resolving the differences and demonstrate that the various writers describe the angels with great similarity. They characterize the seraphim and cherubim as burning (Isa 6:1; Ezek 1:13). Seraphim and cherubim interact with the altar before God's throne and touch its coals (Isa 6:6–7; Ezek 10:2). Isaiah and Ezekiel depict the angels (with similar prepositions) waiting on the Lord for his command (Isa 6:2; Ezek 1:11, 23–24).[79] Both have hands (Isa 6:6; Ezek 1:8). Both use their wings for covering (Isa 6:2; Ezek 1:11, 23) and movement (Isa 6:2; Ezek 10:16). Both are covered with eyes (Ezek 10:12; Rev 4:4–6). These parallels point to their identity. Furthermore, the ANE audience had certain conceptualizations of the heavenly throne room. The iconography indicates that guardian angels surrounded the divine throne. These were commonly known as cherubim.[80] Seeing Isaiah's and Ezekiel's unusual usage of terminology, the original audience might have assumed that the prophets were being creative in their approach to describing these beings who accompany the heavenly throne. This posits a cultural basis that the angels in the various visions are one and the same. Watts agrees with this overall assessment, "such throne-room scenes regularly describe the heavenly 'host' but use different words."[81]

This explains why John claims that the living creatures with the faces matching Ezekiel's cherubim (Rev 4:6–7) actually have the wings and speech of the seraphim in Isaiah (4:8). They are all one and the same creature, but each author has concentrated on particular characteristics for the sake of their theological emphases. John's wording hints that what he saw merges the visions of Ezekiel and Isaiah together. All of this indicates that the visions involve identical characters and thereby supports the notion of a singular event.

---

78. Beale, *Revelation*, 329. This actually deals with quite a bit of confusion surrounding the description that commentators deal with. See Osborne, *Revelation*, 232.

79. Oswalt, *Isaiah 1–39*, 178. The collocation of עָמַד with עַל seems to communicate to wait or attend on an individual (cf. Gen 45:1; Judg 3:19; 2 Sam 13:9). Similar language is used with the compound preposition מִמַּעַל. In Isaiah, the angels may have been located "above" God in their location as they flew; however, they were waiting upon his command. However, this may denote their standing position as he was seated. Ezekiel contains a similar preposition (מִלְמָעְלָה) describing God's position in command of the cherubim (Ezek 1:26). They move with the Spirit's command (Ezek 1:12).

80. Hartenstein, "Cherubim and Seraphim," 171–72.

81. Watts, *Isaiah 1–33*, 106.

THE QUESTION OF "WHY"

In the immediate context of each vision, God reveals the heavenly courtroom scene in order to shape the ministry and message of the prophets and apostles. This fact may lead us to conclude that the visions are different in their purposes and therefore all separate. However, the vision proper of each prophet and apostle depicts an occasion(s) that relates to redemptive history. Do the visions reflect a similar purpose in that regard?

Isaiah's vision portrays how YHWH will bestow his dominion to the Servant (Isa 6:1–3; 52:13—53:12) and that His glory goes to the end of the earth (Isa 6:2). Ezekiel's vision has a similar import, as God's glory will fill the temple and earth forever (Ezek 43:1–7). The significance of Daniel's and John's visions relates to the inauguration of the Son of Man over all creation (Dan 7:13; Rev 5:1–10). Specifically, the outcome is that the Son receives dominion from all creation and his glory extends to the entire earth (Dan 7:14; Rev 5:13). It is critical to recognize that all the visions seem to relate to the same result of the culmination of history. Accordingly, the prophets and apostles relate this to the period of the latter days, the climax of God's plan (Isa 2:1–4; Ezek 38:16; Dan 2:28; Rev 1:19). Based upon this, the visions seem to have the same agenda. As opposed to some generic motif concerning YHWH's reign, they discuss the fulfillment of God's plan for all of the cosmos in his Son. This apex in redemptive history must be unique and unrepeatable. Thus, that shared purpose argues that the visions are one and the same.

PAUL'S CHRISTOPHANY ON THE DAMASCUS ROAD

I am indebted to Kim's work on the connection between the Damascus road and Pauline theology. His thesis is itself an examination of the innertextuality between vision and theology similar to what I am attempting to accomplish on a broader level. I will provide a summary of his argumentation as it is pertinent to this discussion, as well as how the unity of vision may provide further grounding for his observations and conclusions.

Kim argues that Paul's conception of Jesus as the image of God distinctly originates from the Damascus Christophany.[82] Based upon the apostle's own reflections of the event and his usage of the phrase "image of God" (cf. Rom 8:29; 1 Cor 15:49; 2 Cor 3:8; 4:4; Col 1:25; Phil 2:6), we can learn more about his original experience. Paul's language shares similarities with various texts stemming from Ezek 1, including Dan 7, *1 En.* 46, *4 Ezra* 13, and Rev 1.[83] It appears, then, that "Paul is describing his call vision in the form of the call vision of Ezek 1."[84] In even clearer terms, "On

---

82. Kim, *Paul*, 165.
83. Ibid., 165–66.
84. Ibid., 167.

the Damascus road Paul must have been convinced that the glorious figure on the divine throne whom he saw in the vision was Jesus Christ whose followers he was persecuting."[85] Accordingly, Kim contends that if Jesus is the Son of Man, he receives worldwide dominion per Dan 7. This formulates Paul's mission to the Gentiles.[86]

To be clear, I do not think Kim argues that Paul saw the exact same vision or event as Ezekiel or Daniel. Rather, Paul saw the glorified Christ and identified him through the tradition-history with the visions seen by his predecessors and with all the implications therein.[87] Nevertheless, Kim's observations provide substantial evidence for the thesis of this book. Kim agrees that Paul witnessed a person that he identified as the individual in Ezek 1 and Dan 7 (who). He also argues that Paul understood that this one had received dominion (what) and that the reality of his universal lordship, based upon Dan 7, shaped Paul's mission (why). In fact, Kim comments that the apostle's vision unveils an eschatological reality, a *"proleptic Parousia,"* that Paul awaited (when) (cf. 1 Thess 1:10).[88] These comments answer the questions of who, what, when, and why just as the other visions do. When examined through the lens of harmonization, the data suggests that the apostle saw a certain angle or aspect of what his predecessors witnessed. I would argue that Kim's argument moves in the direction of my own thesis.

Furthermore, the unity of visions can help bolster the epistemology of Kim's argumentation in two ways. First, the unity of visions accounts for the cohesive nature of the tradition-history Kim appeals to. With the tradition-historical approach, Kim fell under undeserved criticism for arbitrarily merging pieces of visions into a composite. Dunn accused Kim of the same activity and methodology of the history of religions school, which took different parts of the visions and redacted them into the notion of a "pre-Christian Gnostic redeemer."[89] Kim responded that he did not randomly pull from various visions to form a composite, but instead was appealing to linkages already linguistically and culturally present. He argued for the existence of an established tradition-history. The linguistic data from Paul indicated that the apostle viewed his experience in light of that tradition.[90] My thesis provides further support for Kim and counters Dunn's accusations. In fact, it essentially reverses Dunn's allegation. Fundamentally, the tradition-history is not some later man-made derivation. Instead, it stems from the intertextuality already present in the text. This argues for

---

85. Ibid., 187.

86. Ibid., 171.

87. Ibid., 176–77.

88. Ibid., 170–71, emphasis mine. "The ἀποκάλυψις of the Son of God from heaven on the Damascus road was a prolepsis of his eschatological ἀποκάλυψις and as such it provided Paul with the ground of hope for the latter" (Kim, *Paul*, 170–71).

89. Ibid., 176.

90. Ibid., 176–77.

intentional associations and harmonization that took place within the canon.[91] This also means that what Kim suggests does not arbitrarily take pieces of various visions and merge them together into a composite. The unity of the visions argues that the visions *as a whole* actually fuse together. This justifies the tight interconnectedness of visions and theologies. They integrate so closely because they are, in fact, one and the same. The tradition-history to which Kim refers reflects an underlying reality, that the visions are all angles to the same eschatological event. Kim's analysis of tradition-history supports my broader thesis (harmonization of visions) as well as the reality that Paul's vision is identical to the others.[92]

Second, the unity of visions also accounts for other allusions Kim sees as part of the Damascus Christophany. Kim notes a link between the mission of Isaiah, the Servant, and Paul.[93] After his Damascus road experience, the apostle proclaims his task to go to all nations in terms given to the Servant (Acts 13:47; cf. Isa 49:6). Kim states that the apostle must have understood his experience in light of Isaiah's call, the Servant's call, as well as the tradition-history surrounding Daniel and Ezekiel. Why would Paul do this? Surely the glory of God, along the lines of the *merkabah* would have linked with Daniel and Ezekiel per the tradition-history. However, what provoked Paul to recall Isaiah *and* the Servant? What compelling factor put all of these passages together in his mind? I do not disagree with Kim's remarks. Rather, I wholeheartedly concur and seek to point out that a unity of vision can account for the connection between Isaiah, the Servant, Ezekiel, and Daniel. I have already discussed the ways in which Isaiah's vision harmonizes Ezekiel and Daniel. Its innertextuality relates to the exaltation of the Servant. The Son of Man's inauguration in Daniel is thereby the Servant's exaltation in Isaiah. Hence, in seeing the exalted Christ on the divine throne, Paul could correlate the theology of Ezekiel, Isaiah's call, and the Servant, since they are all interconnected by the reality of a single vision. This explanation accounts for Paul's application of the Servant terminology to himself as well as his use of language from Ezekiel and Daniel when he alludes to his vision (cf. Acts 13:47; Isa 49:6 as well as 2 Cor 4:4–6; cf. Isa 6:3; 49:6; Ezek 1:26; Dan 7:13).[94] In essence, their callings and theologies become his own.

In addition to Kim's own analysis, further details in the Lucan account evidence Paul's parallel experience with the other prophets. Daniel 7 influences the context of

---

91. Collins, *Daniel*, 302: "The fiery wheels on the stationary throne, however, undoubtedly derive from Ezekiel's *Merkavah* vision (Ezek 1:15–21; 10:2)." Collins counters Halperin and Zimmerli, who argue that this is just incidental. Cf. Miller, *Daniel*, 205.

92. My analysis in this chapter and the previous does not cling to Kim's notion of tradition-history. Rather, it points at the exegetical reasoning that girds such an approach. That is arguably where the prophets and apostles intersect. The tradition-history provides a broader cultural perspective, which provides a backdrop for the apostles' claims in the NT as well as precedent that people understood the visions as one.

93. Kim, *Origin of Paul's Gospel*, 93.

94. See Harris, *2 Corinthians*, 336.

the Damascus road experience. Not long before Paul's conversion, Stephen witnesses the Son of Man at the right hand of God (Acts 7:55–56). This itself affirms Jesus' own claim that his death and resurrection would fulfill Daniel 7 (cf. Luke 22:69). Scholars recognize that the use of "Son of Man" has Daniel 7 in the background.[95] It appears that Stephen's vision concerns the victory of Jesus, who wins dominion over all peoples and rules against the enemies of God, as Daniel communicates.[96] Such a realization angers the Jewish leaders even more and leads to Stephen's death (vv. 57–60). Luke parallels Stephen and Paul immediately thereafter (8:1–4). He juxtaposes Paul's aggressive actions against the church with Stephen's death and burial. They are almost a foil to one another.[97] Could it be that Stephen's vision parallels Paul's on the Damascus road? At a bare minimum, Lucan theology contains elements of Daniel 7 and is even in the near context of Paul's vision.

In addition, the brief account in Acts 9:2–8 record parallels between the visions of Daniel and Paul. In Dan 10:1–8, the prophet sees a supernatural being similar to the one he saw in Dan 7:9.[98] This signals to Daniel that the messenger will bring news about the vision of Dan 7.[99] At the presence of this messenger, those around Daniel did not see the vision but sensed a great dread (Dan 10:7). Similarly, those around Paul during his vision could not see or hear the full vision but knew something was happening (Acts 9:7). Paul repeats this reality before a Jewish audience (22:9) but not the Gentiles (26:12–19). Perhaps the allusion would only make sense to those who had greater familiarity with the prophets.[100]

---

95. Bruce, *Acts*, 154–55: "This is the only New Testament occurrence of the phrase 'the Son of Man' outside the Gospels. Apart from this instance, it is found only on the lips of Jesus. It has its Old Testament roots in Dan. 7:13–14, where a human figure ('one like a son of man,' in the literal rendering of the Aramaic) is seen coming to the enthroned Ancient of Days 'with the clouds of heaven' to receive universal dominion from him. The un-Greek idiom 'the Son of Man' (more literally 'the son of the man') means 'the "one like a son of man"' who is to receive world dominion, but since it was not in current use as a technical term, Jesus could and did employ it freely of himself and fill it with whatever meaning he chose. The background in Dan. 7:13–27 links the 'one like a son of man' closely with 'the saints of the Most High,' whom the New Testament identifies with Jesus' disciples and their converts."

96. Bock, *Acts*, 310–11.

97. Ibid., 319; Witherington, *Acts of the Apostles*, 278. The juxtaposition between Saul and Stephen may have been because Saul headed the opposition against Stephen. If this is true, that puts them in further parallel with one another.

98. Goldingay, *Daniel*, 291; Collins, *Daniel*, 373. The description also has striking similarities to Ezek 1. If Dan 10 relates to Dan 7 by innertextuality, then this demonstrates further incorporation of Ezekiel's motifs and ideas into Daniel's own vision.

99. Goldingay, *Daniel*, 291. The angel's appearance probably demonstrates that his mission and message relates to the previous glorious vision Daniel had seen and was prophesied in Ezekiel. It does appear that these figures were known in that culture (cf. Ezek 14:14; see Block, *Ezekiel*, 1:449) so Daniel might have understood that both his own vision and Ezekiel's message would be advanced at this point.

100. This actually brings up a seeming discrepancy in Paul's recounting versus Luke's account. In Luke's record, the men could hear the voice (ἀκούοντες μὲν τῆς φωνῆς Acts 9:7) but could not see anything. In Paul's description, the men could see the light but could not hear the voice (τὴν δὲ φωνὴν οὐκ ἤκουσαν, Acts 22:9). Both accounts emphasize awareness (so that the vision is not just to Paul) and

Paul also falls to the ground like others who experience the same vision (Ezek 1:28; Dan 10:8–9; Rev 1:17).[101] This allusion could indicate that Paul also saw the same kind of glory and event as the other visions. Thus, even in the brief accounts of Acts, Luke provides contextual indicators and linguistic parallels to suggest a connection with Daniel 7 and thereby with the other interconnected visions.

I submit that my thesis fits well with Kim's findings. It picks up on his observations and provides further epistemological certainty to the tradition-history to which he subscribes. I have also tried to provide some additional observations that link the Lucan description to Daniel 7. As Kim has suggested, Paul saw Jesus as the one on the chariot-throne. This striking picture, as well as his parallel experience, alerted the apostle that he saw the same vision as his predecessors. He therefore knew that their theologies would also shape his own mission. My exegetical approach (as opposed to tradition-historical) accounts for the tight tradition-history Kim advocated and its diverse theological implications.

REINFORCEMENT BY CONTRAST

Certain visions of God's throne room do not harmonize with the visions of Isaiah, Ezekiel, Daniel, Paul, and John. Their contrast reinforces the unity presented above. For instance, 1 Kgs 22:19–23 is an accepted text of the throne-theophany tradition.[102] Considering this recognition, we might expect that the passage would harmonize well with the visions discussed. Initial observations would argue for this supposition. The text recounts a heavenly throne room scene. Micaiah describes the Lord sitting on his throne with similar wording as Isaiah.[103] There is also an angelic host, which coordinates with other visions. However, these beings are not described in any terms similar to the cherubim and seraphim we have discussed. In fact, they are merely called the host of heaven (צְבָא הַשָּׁמַיִם, 1 Kgs 22:19). Micaiah's vision also does not appear to include the Son of Man. These differences could arguably be harmonized, but other questions of what, when, and why make harmonization less likely.

There is no indication in this text (or in the innertextuality of Kings) that God hands his authority over to the Son of Man. Rather, God, in this situation, asks a

---

confusion. Luke may be more general in his description, whereas Paul provides more details of exactly what took place. However, the dissimilarities bring out an important point: the bystanders of this vision experience confusion. This observation correlates with Dan 10. While the exact mechanisms of such confusion are themselves convoluted and therefore do not need to be parallel between Acts 9 and Dan 10, the point remains the same.

101. Bock, *Acts*, 357. Bock also parallels Paul's fall to the ground with Ezekiel and Daniel.

102. DeVries, *1 Kings*, 268.; Collins, *Daniel*, 300; Allen, *Ezekiel 1–19*, 26–27. Scholars consistently assign Micaiah's vision as part of the heavenly throne room motif.

103. Micaiah's introductory statement (רָאִיתִי אֶת־יְהוָה יֹשֵׁב עַל־כִּסְאוֹ, 1 Kgs 22:19) corresponds to Isaiah's (וָאֶרְאֶה אֶת־אֲדֹנָי יֹשֵׁב עַל־כִּסֵּא, Isa 6:1).

specific question (what) about how to entice Ahab to battle (1 Kgs 22:20).[104] This makes the scene not about an eschatological moment but rather a historical event.[105] The decision in heaven does not result in the Son receiving the kingdom of the world or in God's glory filling the earth. Rather, the purpose of the event (why) relates to the death of Ahab (1 Kgs 22:36–40). These differences make it quite difficult to harmonize Micaiah's vision with the rest of the visions. They do, however, relate in similar language, setting, and characters. Thus, we can speak of this situation as part of the throne-theophany tradition of Israel.[106]

This brief discussion illustrates that we can identify and distinguish between the eschatological event seen by the prophets and apostles and other visions of the heavenly courtroom. Moreover, this distinction also accentuates the significance of certain forms of language and details that accompany the visions of Isaiah, Ezekiel, Daniel, and John. Micaiah's vision does not focus on the particulars of God's glory, as do the others. His vision does not emphasize God's holiness or dominion over all nations. His vision also does not bring out the specifics concerning the angels or the throne or the heavenly courtroom. The presence of these features brings the visions discussed above even closer together. They form a particular subset of the heavenly courtroom motif in Israel's thought and culture.

CONCLUDING THOUGHTS

This chapter has endeavored to demonstrate that the visions of Isaiah, Ezekiel, Daniel, Paul, and John are actually all angles of the inauguration of the Son of Man. Initially, the visions contain striking similarities that prompt us to ask whether they can be harmonized. Upon further examination, the interconnections and significant correspondences suggest that the visions are unified. They all, in their own way, reflect upon a reality upon a heavenly scene (where) with similar characters (who). Daniel and John witness the exaltation of the Son/Lamb, who receives glory from the cosmos. Isaiah, through his innertextual connection between Isa 6 and 52, sees the exaltation of the Servant and God's glory filling the temple and the earth. Ezekiel, through his innertextual connection between Ezek 1 and 43, sees that God's heavenly chariot-throne will fill the temple and earth with glory. The reality their visions all describe seems strikingly similar (what) as a moment that is distinctly eschatological (when) and serves as the culmination of redemptive history (why). If

---

104. DeVries, *1 Kings*, 268. Granted, the vision of prophets uniquely relates to their own situation. Nonetheless, in the structure of visions, the vision itself takes place before the biblical writer interacts with the characters of the vision. Thus far we have primarily compared the vision proper part of the biblical writers' visions. Since Micaiah does not do so at all, we may assume that 1 Kgs 22:19–22 is the entire courtroom scene, which we can compare with other visions.

105. Ibid. The context of the vision also argues for this reality. The question at hand is the outcome of Ahab's proposed battle with Arameans (1 Kgs 22:14–19).

106. See Collins, *Daniel*, 300; Allen, *Ezekiel 1–19*, 26–27; Keel, *Jahwe-Visionen Und Siegelkunst*, 190.

these visions all describe an event that happens in the same way, at the same time, in the same place, with the same people, and for the same purpose, it is likely that the visions are the same. For this reason, their visions do not merely employ a motif or tradition-history but refer to the same "event."

Through this discussion, I hope to have shown that there is substantial evidence pointing towards the unity of what Isaiah, Ezekiel, Daniel, Paul, and John saw. That being said, I view the evidence in this chapter as preliminary. It makes the unity of vision a *strong possibility*, which allows us to proceed in showing how the biblical writers build upon their visions and theologies. That discussion will provide more innertextual evidence for the eschatological nature of their visions and also show how the authors organically tie their revelation with previous visions and theologies. Seeing the visions develop in their "natural habitat" of progressive revelation makes this idea even more plausible and helps us better appreciate their theological beauty.

In that regard, we can address one final issue. The question remains as to whether the prophet or apostle seeing the vision would understand that he was seeing (part of) the same event as his predecessors. At a bare minimum, the biblical author knew his experience was parallel.[107] I would also suggest that as revelation progressed, the picture of a unified vision became clearer. Thus, at first, Ezekiel might have held some suspicion that his experience was identical to Isaiah's in certain ways. However, certainty remained lacking. By Paul and John's time, the unity of their visions with those that came before them had become apparent. John certainly evidences this recognition in his comments on Isaiah in John 12. Paul does so as well (per Kim's thesis) by correlating aspects of the mission of Isaiah, the Servant, Ezekiel, and Daniel into his calling. As discussed in the previous chapter, the presence of the language from the visions in the literature of their time also argues for contemporary culture's awareness of the unity of vision.

We may use the analogy of a puzzle to illustrate this development. Initially, we only have disjunctive pieces of the puzzle. Each of them has some sort of identifiable, if fragmentary, image. We do not know how all the pieces will fit, or even if they do fit (those with children know how puzzle pieces can become mixed up). However, there may be initial indications that two pieces fit together. As we put more of them together, we gain gradual confirmation that we have joined the initial pieces correctly. A unified picture begins to form, to which all the pieces contribute. Eventually, the entire picture becomes clear. Furthermore, its complete "message" also becomes apparent, and we understand it better after having studied every part of the whole. In similar manner, the prophets and apostles may have begun to put the pieces together. Their theologies and visions each describe in detail a piece of the whole. As the entire picture unfolds, later revelation confirms that their suspicions of connection or identity were correct, and their theologies combine to inform the reader of the full import of every angle of the vision.

---

107. The current consensus concerning the tradition-history attests that fact. If *1 Enoch* or other early Jewish writers saw that the visions were so similar, this probably reflects at least a cultural tradition.

This understanding forms the foundation for the rest of the book. Indeed, the answer to the "big question" has provided a conduit of studying the visions not only in the context of their respective books, but also with a view to each other. In this way, the intertextuality between the various visions actually binds them together. From here, we will explore how one event occupied the vision and theology of various biblical writers, how they uniquely describe that moment, and how all of those details compound upon each other to build the multifaceted significance surrounding the inauguration of the Son of Man. So it is that a biblical theology of vision is possible.

4

Isaiah's Vision
Vision of Salvation

TENSIONS INVOLVED IN ISAIAH'S VISION

IN EXPLAINING THE SUBSTANCE and significance of Isaiah's vision, the first issue concerns that vision's unique placement in the book. Typically, the calling of a prophet comes at the opening of his respective book (cf. Jer 1; Ezek 1). Five full chapters precede the vision in Isaiah. Scholars surmise from this arrangement that Isaiah's vision is the logical conclusion of the earlier chapters and serves as an introduction to what follows.[1] Such structural placement reinforces the notion of the vision as an innertextual encapsulation of the prophet's theology.

Under this understanding, the beginning of the book fundamentally shapes what Isaiah's call signifies. His experience not only interfaces with historical circumstances (e.g., the death of Uzziah, cf. 6:1) but also with the theological and redemptive-historical framework established by these opening chapters.[2] I would suggest that this theology revolves around three major tensions established in chapters 1 through 5. In the discussion, I will highlight terms and phrases that Isaiah later incorporates into his vision. These factors will become key issues, not only in Isaiah's message, but also in the entirety of a biblical theology of vision.

---

1. Liebreich, "Position of Chapter Six," 40; Bartelt, "Centrality of Isa 6," 316–35; Beale, "A Retributive Taunt," 257–78; Beuken, "Isa 6 Read Against the Background of Isaiah 1," 72–87; House, "Isaiah's Call," 207–22.

2. Cate, "We Need to Be Saved (Isaiah 1)," 145–46.

Isaiah's Vision

The Tension of Kingdom: Exile and Exaltation

Historically, Israel faced questions concerning its stability and longevity as a nation. While Isaiah may have penned these first chapters before Uzziah's death, the threat of the rising superpower, Assyria, would have been felt.[3] Particularly at the end of his reign, the northern kingdom began to collapse (2 Kgs 15:13–19). Only a matter of time remained before the southern kingdom would face the same fate. Hence, Israel would likely have been beginning to ask hard questions concerning how such looming danger harmonized with God's promises to Abraham and David of a great nation, peace, and a kingdom (cf. Gen 12:1–3; 2 Sam 7:8–14).[4]

In the first five chapters, Isaiah's approach to these questions centers on the city of Jerusalem. He indicates this emphasis as early as the opening verse. The prophet addresses not only the southern kingdom, but also its capital, Jerusalem (Isa 1:1).[5] He confirms Israel's worst fears: exile. Jerusalem was already susceptible to enemy attack, like a temporary shack under siege (1:8). The land had already begun to turn desolate (שְׁמָמָה, v. 7). Because of their sins, God will fight against Jerusalem, his adversary (1:24). He will trigger a collapse of their entire livelihood, economy, and leadership (3:1–7). Inevitably, God will burn the vineyard of Israel (5:5 ,בער) and the once-great city of Jerusalem will descend into death and destruction (3:8). The city once characterized by beauty and joy will be silenced (5:14). Darkness will overtake the land as God summons another nation to snatch his people away (5:26–30).

However, this is not the only portrayal of the kingdom Isaiah provides. Juxtaposed with this bleak description, the prophet paints another picture of Jerusalem: The Lord will restore Zion such that the corrupt city becomes one of righteousness (1:26). He will replace the city's oppressive governance with just leaders (v. 17). Moreover, Jerusalem, having been previously invaded, will become the city to which all nations would come. It will be the "the highest spot on the planet," the center of the world (2:2), the capital of the earth, and the location of God's reign (v. 3–4a).[6] Many nations will journey there to learn God's law (v. 3) and abide under his rule (v. 4a). As a result, Jerusalem's dominion will lead to world peace (v. 4b). Isaiah proclaims that the kingdom promises are just as glorious, if not more so, than his hearers had ever anticipated. Zion's metamorphosis promises to become the center of a golden age the likes of which the world had never seen. Contextually, Isaiah's call will interact with these two presentations of Jerusalem as exiled and exalted (and thereby Israel and the world).

---

3. Merrill, *Kingdom of Priests*, 348, 360, 367, 391–95.
4. Motyer, *Isaiah*, 80–81.
5. Oswalt, *Isaiah 1–39*, 83.
6. Motyer, *Isaiah*, 54; Oswalt, *Isaiah 1–39*, 117.

I Saw the Lord

The Tension of Presence: Holiness, Sin, Judgment, and Transformation

Isaiah defines the nation's guilt in ways that seem to anticipate the vision. For example, Israel refuses to know (ידע) its master (1:3; 5:13; cf. 6:9). The people's eyes carry proud (or "lifted up") looks (2:12, וְרָם וְעַל כָּל־נִשָּׂא) and they are called to hear but certainly do not (1:2, 10). Their lack of sensitivity probably links to God's later statements concerning Israel's own blindness, deafness, and lack of discernment (6:9–13). The prophet's language continues in describing the people's abandonment (1:4), mockery (5:19), and rejection of (5:24) the Holy One of Israel (קְדוֹשׁ יִשְׂרָאֵל; cf. 6:3). They have rebelled against God's glorious presence (3:8, כָּבוֹד; cf. 6:3) and instead filled the land with gold, silver, and idols (מלא, 2:6–7; cf. 6:3).

As a result, the Holy One will judge and show himself righteous therein (5:16–19). At this point, it could be argued that this becomes the main segue to Isaiah's vision. The writer mentions the title, "Holy One of Israel," at both the beginning of this section (1:4) and at the end (5:19, 24). This inclusio suggests Isaiah's attention to the notion of holiness and specifically God's holiness offended. Moreover, the repeated use of this appellation in close proximity builds a crescendo effect toward Isaiah's vision (5:19, 24). Israel has repeatedly violated God's holiness, and they are now going to meet him in Isaiah's vision.[7]

Before reaching that conclusion, the fourth chapter holds this notion of sin and judgment in tension. Granted, God's holiness overwhelmingly points to judgment in the opening chapters. In fact, the prophet *almost always* employs holiness (קדשׁ) to express the perfection of God and his hatred and judgment of wickedness in this section. However, there is *one* exception.[8] Isaiah describes Israel as holy in 4:3. Instead of Israel's punishment ending in its complete obliteration, God produces a nation in conformity with his holy self.[9] Furthermore, despite Israel's rejection of God's glory and its broken relationship with the Lord (3:8), God's glory (כָּבוֹד) will dwell in their midst as in the days of the Exodus (4:5). Accordingly, holiness and glory are not used entirely negatively in the book, but instead describe both a condemning reality as well as a transforming reality. To understand the vision fully, we will also have to examine this tension in terms of Israel's relationship with God.

---

7. Liebreich, "Position of Chapter Six," 39.

8. Cf. 1:4; 4:3; 5:16, 19, 24. Out of the five usages, only 4:3 applies to Israel, whereas the others apply to the Lord.

9. Motyer, *Isaiah*, 65; Dillard and Longman, *Introduction to the Old Testament*, 271. Cf. 1:25 as well. Conceptually, God cleanses his nation from the dross of their terrible leadership and sin.

The Tension of Time: Present and Eschatological

The final tension synthesizes the two topics of kingdom and presence with the flow of the first five chapters. Isaiah's portrayal of hope, whether in Jerusalem's political exaltation (2:1–4) or Israel's spiritual transformation (4:2–5), points to eschatological realities. In context, the use of the term "latter days" (2:2) anchors these texts to a future time for the consummation of God's plan.[10]

Those eschatological realities are juxtaposed with more proximate situations. In fact, structurally speaking, after God initiates a covenant lawsuit against Israel (1:1–18), there appears to be two cycles of a judgment oracle followed by a salvation oracle. The first deals with the kingdom reality I spoke of, wherein Jerusalem was a debauched city (1:19–31) but will become the central city of the world (2:1–4). The next covers the more relational tension also mentioned earlier. Even though Israel has God's promises of a future kingdom, its people still cling to idols instead of worshipping the glorious and holy God (2:5—4:1). Nonetheless, they will be changed so that the holy God can dwell with them (4:2–5). With this, Isaiah's oracles are balanced. Salvation counteracts judgment. However, a major question remains as to how the present links with the eschatological (if it even does). How can God work through the current situation to fulfill the future? Isaiah's vision and calling will deal with these factors as well.

This question becomes even more important in light of the negative conclusion to this section (5:1–30). Although previous passages are balanced between judgment and salvation, the fifth chapter offers no such assurance. Because Israel has condemned itself via the parable of the vine (vv. 1–4), a series of woes ensue (vv. 5–30). No light shines at the end of this passage, only darkness (v. 30). Considering how this text draws the opening chapters to so foreboding a close, readers might conclude that its magnificent future is suspect. What is the guarantee that it will occur? The outlook at the moment certainly appears more pessimistic.[11] Accordingly, not only does the vision connect past, present, and future, it also contextually may provide the epistemology of hope.

ISAIAH'S VISION AS CALL AND MISSION

I have already explained that Isaiah's vision will interact with the theological framework set up by the preceding context. In the first three verses, Isaiah seems to allude back to the tensions discussed above. Verse 1 appears to deal with the issues of kingdom and Jerusalem. God's reign, high and lifted up, may be compared with Jerusalem in Isa 2:2, which is also lifted up.[12] Similarly, verses 2–3, with their repetition of

---

10. Motyer, *Isaiah*, 54; VanGemeren, "Spirit of Restoration," 84–87; Ashley, *Book of Numbers*, 499.
11. House, "Isaiah's Call," 212.
12. Dumbrell, *End of the Beginning*, 8.

holiness and glory, mirror the discussion concerning God's judging and transforming holiness seen specifically in Isa 4:2–4.

In addition, the context of Isaiah's immediately following call (6:5–13) provides an interesting innertextual expansion on the vision itself. For example, the term for holy (קדשׁ) appears in the vision (v. 3) as well as in Isaiah's calling (v. 13). Isaiah's own purification experience may conceptually relate to the term also (vv. 5–7). These immediate associations also help us to better grasp the import of his vision, an understanding that I will develop in this section in relation to the context that both precedes and follows Isa 6:1–3. Such analysis will not only support our understanding of the substance of the vision, but also of its bearing on Isaiah's call and mission.

The Lord's Reign (v. 1)

The first verse contrasts the death of Uzziah with the Lord's unshakable reign. In the midst of these uncertain times, Isaiah comes face to face with the true king.[13] Every detail of the brief description attests to that reality. The use of the term אֲדֹנָי (Lord) emphasizes God's lordship[14] and unwavering sovereignty as he sits on his throne. He is supreme, high and lifted up (רָם וְנִשָּׂא). He possesses unmatched glory, as evidenced by the train of his robe filling the temple.[15] Isaiah's reaction confirms this impression. His eyes have seen the King, the Lord of Hosts (הַמֶּלֶךְ יְהוָה צְבָאוֹת) and he is undone (v. 5, cf. v. 1). Indeed, the opening verse presents the total dominion of the Lord. Isaiah has seen the only true king, the one who provides Israel's true security.

In light of this text's clear presentation of YHWH's dominion, scholars have traditionally concentrated upon God's character and his unrivaled sovereignty.[16] To them, the vision reflects the timeless reality of the Lord's kingship. It shapes the prophet's ministry because it impresses upon the prophet a sense of the Lord's supremacy over idols and his unshakeable sovereignty over the world.[17] While this emphasis is appar-

---

13. Merrill, *Kingdom of Priests*, 391–93. Historically, the death of Uzziah begins the nation's collapse into exile.

14. Oswalt, *Isaiah 1–39*, 177. See also *HALOT*, 1:12; Jenni, "36–234 ", הֵיכָל.

15. Contra Eslinger, "Isaiah Vi 1–5," 145–73; Oswalt, *Isaiah 1–39*, 178. Most likely שׁוּל refers to the hem of a garment similar to Exod 28:33. In fact, if one accepts a relative early dating of Isa 6, then the Exodus references would be primarily involved. Eslinger argued for the term's later association with the pubic region (148–55). That use may be metonymic instead of communicating the term's inherent semantic referent. Here it refers to Isaiah's limitation in truly seeing the Lord seated on the throne. Similar to Exod 24:10, the prophet can only catch a glimpse of the person of YHWH. This also denotes the grandeur of God. The smallest part of his "garment" can fill the temple. Thus, YHWH's temple or palace (הֵיכָל) possess true splendor as opposed to the various pagan temples. No other idol, person, or being can share in that power. This implies that every pagan will understand that God's house is the place of true glory. See ibid., 178.

16. Oswalt, *Isaiah 1–39*, 177–78; Motyer, *Isaiah*, 74–77; Harvey, "On Seeing: Isaiah 6:1–12," 97–104.

17. Motyer, *Isaiah*, 76–77; Oswalt, *Isaiah 1–39*, 173–76; Watts, *Isaiah 1–33*, 107.

ent, Isaiah might be seeing something far more particular than just a general presentation of the Lord's dominion. A major tension in context includes the present situation of Jerusalem's looming exile and its eschatological prominence. I would suggest that God's reign relates to this concern. Isaiah saw not only a portrayal of God's kingship, but saw it specifically in connection with the event wherein he will reign from Jerusalem as the prophet's previous vision (2:1, חָזָה) proclaimed. Instead of an abstract portrait, the prophet witnessed an eschatological, redemptive-historical reality.

Several lines of argument suggest this innertextual association:

1. Fundamentally, God's reign does not just pertain to heaven but also to earth. His robe fills the temple with glory, which presumably is in Jerusalem.[18] This being the case, Isaiah cannot be merely seeing the nature of God's authority in heaven, but is also seeing how it plays in time and space on earth. Arguably, that could be the present moment (as some commentators assert). Based upon the factors below, it could also be eschatological. Nevertheless, we probably cannot restrict the passage to a discussion on the abstract notions of God's perfection and complete dominion. It most likely holds implications for what he is doing in the world and history.

2. Along that line, Isaiah's vision is contextually tied to history. Uzziah's death provides the immediate circumstance surrounding the prophet's experience. Furthermore, God announces that the cities of Judah will be desolate when the exile occurs (Isa 6:11–13). All of that content pertains to Isaiah's own commissioning, which itself is a part of history. If the vision were so connected with time and history, it would make sense that verse 1 is as well, albeit eschatologically.

3. We may derive an eschatological perspective of Isa 6 within the context of the first five chapters. Isaiah's vision does not exist in a contextual vacuum. The writer has already crafted the context of the previous five chapters to build tensions that this vision presumably interacts with in some fashion. If he has made us familiar with the Lord's glorious reign in Jerusalem before, why would we expect him to refer to something else here? That should be the default concept. If we argue that Isa 6 comes later in the book because it binds together the issues and theology introduced in the previous chapters, then the present passage probably links with what has already been stated for consistently. In concluding his comments on Isa 6, Dumbrell links the chapter with Isa 2 and the grander context of the book:

> It is therefore not surprising that the eschatology of Isa 1–12 should be directed toward the re-establishment of Zion as the city of God world centre after its condemnation in chapter 1. In its positioning as responsive promise to the threat of the first chapter, the prophecy of 2:1–4 is critical and its detail unfolds the eschatological direction in which the book will move.[19]

---

18. Oswalt, *Isaiah 1–39*, 182; Lacheman, "Seraphim of Isaiah 6," 71.
19. Dumbrell, *End of the Beginning*, 10.

4. In addition, the immediate wording suggests an eschatological context. In Isa 6:3, the seraphim proclaim that God's glory fills the earth. As argued in chapter 3, such language is distinctly eschatological. The wording of God's glory filling the earth only occurs in three other texts (Num 14:21; Ps 72:19; Hab 2:14), all of which deal with a future reality.[20] This is an important observation in this discussion because the OT consistently does not speak of God's glory filling the earth as a present state of affairs, but rather as one that is anticipated. This makes it difficult to conclude that the announcement of the seraphim relates to the current moment (or to an ever-present reality). Instead, the phraseology is technical language, consistently used to refer to the eschatological outcome of God's plan.

5. The link between Isa 6 and 2 has linguistic and thematic merit. This point is also critical to the argument. The wording of Isa 6:1 parallels the portrayal of an exalted Jerusalem in chapter 2. In Isa 6:1, YHWH is high and lifted up (רָם וְנִשָּׂא) while his temple (הַהֵיכָל), the center of his kingly operation, completely reflects and emanates his majesty, presumably to the nations. In Isa 2:2, Zion is lifted up (וְנִשָּׂא) such that the house of God is clearly supreme as the center of the world.[21] All the nations stream towards it for governance (v. 3). Similar wording and activity tie these passages together. I am not the first to suggest the connection:

> YHWH is on a throne, "high and lifted up," already described metonymically, with the attributes of royalty and transcendence. It is set above the Temple and events, perhaps even about Mt. Zion, which will be "lifted up (נשא) above the hills" in the eschatological vision of 2:2.[22]

6. The semantic parallels suggested above are considerable in light of how Isaiah differs from other "heavenly courtroom scene" descriptions. For example, Micaiah's vision parallels Isaiah's (1 Kgs 22:19). Both describe seeing YHWH sitting on a throne with essentially identical wording. In light of their similarities, the differences stand out. Micaiah omits any mention of the house of God or the Lord being "high and lifted up."[23] This discrepancy attracts our attention to those

---

20. Ashley, *Book of Numbers*, 260; Kraus, *Continental Commentary*, 80. Ashley ties the oath statement with God's agenda depicted in the prophetic context of Hab 2:14. The statement in Ps 72:19 seems to express a doxology or expectation that God's glory will fill the earth. Kraus observes that this links with Israel's eschatological expectations about Jerusalem.

21. See Jenni, "2:234 ",הֵימָל. Compare also בֵּית־יְהוָה; cf. 6:4 as well as 2 Kgs 24:13; Ps 27:4; Ezek 8:16; Zech 8:9 where הֵיכָל and בֵּית־יְהוָה are parallel.

22. Landy, "Strategies of Concentration," 61. See also Beuken, "Isa 6 Read Against the Background of Isaiah 1," 79. Beuken discusses thematic versus semantic correlations. He notes that there is a strong thematic connection between Isa 6 and 2, even though the semantic parallel is restricted to the parallel between God's house and being "high and lifted up." Nevertheless, his observation acknowledges that an association between these chapters is likely.

23. Kee, "Heavenly Council," 259. Kee identifies a variety of passages as part of a typical heavenly courtroom scene. While they all have similarities, the wording of "high and lifted up" as well as "temple" in Isaiah would make the account stand out. Landy, "Strategies of Concentration," 61. Landy points out that such epithets set Isaiah's vision apart from Micaiah's.

descriptions and compels the reader to ask why Isaiah included such terminology. Arguably, he did so to allude back to Isa 2. Put differently, the semantic parallels of "high and lifted up" and the "house of God" are no small matter. The linguistic connection correlates items of unique importance in Isaiah's vision with his previous writings.[24]

7. From a broader viewpoint, Isa 6 as an eschatological event also matches the judgment-salvation pattern of the first five chapters. As stated earlier, unlike other pericopes, which contain judgment followed by salvation (1:19—2:5; 2:6—4:5), chapter 5 ends on an overwhelmingly negative note. Conversely, within the flow of the book, the beginning of chapter 6 could function as an oracle of hope to round out the fifth chapter akin to the other oracles.[25] This would make Isa 6 parallel with the second chapter.

8. This interpretation provides a reading of Isa 6 that ties together the entire prior context. The first chapters state that exile is inevitable (1:28–31) but that Jerusalem will still be exalted (2:1–4). Could Isa 6 parallel both of these ideas? The latter part of Isa 6 clearly relates to the notion of exile (6:11–13, cf. the use of שְׁמָמָה in both 6:11 and 1:7). Such an interpretation would make the first verse relate to Jerusalem's exaltation.[26] If this is correct, then Isa 6 presents this entire theme of kingdom. Such a reading would do justice to the vision as a synthesis of the first chapters and an introduction to the rest.[27] Thus, this reading of the echo in Isa 6:1 makes it fit well in context, providing "satisfaction" per Hays' criteria.[28]

These points provide *preliminary* indications (particularly points four and five) that the Lord appears before Isaiah to indicate that he will have complete dominion over the earth as described in Isa 2. More support for this conclusion will be added as the chapter progresses. Furthermore, the evidence above does not demand that Isaiah's vision be equated with the event of Isa 2, but only that it be associated with it.

---

24. This argument counters Beuken's suggestion that the semantic parallels are limited. This may be in quantity; however, Isaiah shapes his vision to make the restricted quantity quite substantial in quality. See Hays, *Echoes of Scripture*, 29–30. Hays comments upon the concept of "volume." Even when the semantic correspondence is limited, if it is distinct or otherwise unique, then such an association still is legitimate. The parallels between the unique terms "high and lifted up" as well as "house of the Lord" may fall under that rubric.

25. House, "Isaiah's Call," 207–10; Waltke, *Old Testament Theology*, 830–32.

26. Dumbrell, *End of the Beginning*, 8. Dumbrell concurs with my position, arguing that "Clearly, Isa 6 is concerned with presenting a contrast of staggering proportions. Implicitly, what is raised in verse 1 is the means whereby the future kingdom of Judah and the city of Jerusalem will find their salvation."

27. House, "Isaiah's Call," 214–23; Beuken, "Isa 6 Read Against the Background of Isaiah 1," 82–84; Bartelt, "Centrality of Isa 6," 319–24. Bartelt's analysis is particularly stimulating in this regard. He argues for a chiastic structure in Isa 2–12, with Isaiah's call as the center. This makes Isa 6 a literary bridge between judgment and salvation. It also contextually suggests that the oracles of salvation all speak of the same reality. The structure reinforces the notion that Isa 6 contains a mixture of all that is discussed in these chapters.

28. Hays, *Echoes of Scripture*, 30–31.

Later revelation will suggest the connection between the two is that Isaiah sees the Son of Man's inauguration, which will accomplish the outcomes of Isa 2.[29]

Accordingly, the death of Uzziah, loss of power, and instability in light of looming exile all are overcome by the reality of God's eschatological victory. Isaiah understands that God is not only sovereign, but also that his plan to climactically demonstrate his authority will happen in spite of the exile. The kingdom is not lost, because the majesty of the true King will prevail in the most spectacular way. Relative to the previous chapters, Isaiah's vision is a proclamation of the epistemology of hope—a hope already unveiled in the writer's introduction (cf. Isa 2:2–4).

The Lord's Holiness (vv. 2–3)

The vision continues by shifting our attention to the angelic attendants surrounding YHWH's throne. They are called seraphim, a description for angels only found in this account. Even later in the book, Hezekiah states that God is enthroned upon the cherubim (37:16). The description, then, is quite significant. The Hebrew term suggests the basic notion of burning.[30] In ANE iconography, seraphim are serpent creatures that harbor divine judgment and are associated with the wilderness.[31] This description corresponds with Isaiah's own use of the term, שרף. Isaiah has already paralleled the root, שרף, with destruction (שְׁמָמָה) in 1:7. In that text, God burned and left the cities as desolate wilderness.[32] Isa 6 seems to employ the same motif using the same terminology. The prophet records the seraphim (6:2, שרף) in the context of the desolation of Israel's lands (6:11, שְׁמָמָה). This pairing of terms suggests that the seraphim indeed signify Israel's condemnation in light of God's holiness.[33]

Not surprisingly, the angels shield themselves from the penetrating holiness of God (6:2) and proclaim the thrice-holy God (v. 3). They thereby present the basis of judgment. God is consummately perfect, and Israel fails to conform to such ethical distinctiveness, unlike the angels, who cover themselves.[34] This "judging holiness," as we may call it, resonates with the previous descriptions of the Holy One of Israel. He has been offended (1:4) and stands ready to judge (5:19). Now, Israel, through Isaiah, has met this awesome and able King (6:1, 3). Thus far, these verses correspond with the tension already established between the elements of God's holiness and Israel's sin.

---

29. This point was already argued in chapter 3. Daniel and John demonstrate that the inauguration of the Son of Man is in view. Nonetheless, see later discussions concerning the Son of Man's involvement in the enthronement ceremony in Isaiah.

30. *HALOT* 2:13, 60–61; Oswalt, *Isaiah 1–39*, 179; Lacheman, "Seraphim of Isaiah 6," 71–72.

31. Hartenstein, "Cherubim and Seraphim," 170–75; Landy, "Seraphim and Poetic Process," 60–714; Joines, "Winged Serpents," *Journal of Biblical Literature* 86, no. 4 (1967): 410–13.

32. Hartenstein, "Cherubim and Seraphim," 170–75.

33. Beuken, "Isa 6 Read Against the Background of Isaiah 1," 84.

34. Oswalt, *Isaiah 1–39*, 178–79.

Conversely, the use of "holiness" in the first chapters was not entirely judgmental, but also transformative (cf. Isa 4:3). If Isa 6 deals with that context, are the angels strictly proclaiming God's holy judgment? Does a "transforming holiness" have anything to do with their cry? A further factor in this discussion concerns the second line of the seraphim's announcement. Does it indicate whether the filling of the earth with God's glory is positive, negative, or neutral? Or does it merely refer to the reality that creation reflects the splendor of YHWH?[35]

The phrase "God's glory fills . . ." often refers to his relational presence with his people. For example, the primary way the terms כָּבוֹד (glory) with מלא (fill) occur is in the context of God's glory filling the temple. This denotes that he communes with them (cf. Exod 40:34, 35; 1 Kgs 8:11; 2 Chr 5:14; 7:1–2).[36] Consequently, the activity of God's glory filling the earth seems to cast the earth as a cosmic temple where God dwells in a relationship with all creation.[37] His glory does not just fill the temple in sovereignty (Isa 6:1) but also fills the entire earth as he rules, knows, and is known by creation. As Motyer points out, "it [glory] is not only the one thing that is capable of filling everything but the thing which actually does so."[38] This reiterates the message found in the fourth chapter: God's glory will fill a transformed Israel and restore their relationship (4:5). Not only do we have a thematic tie here, but the close proximity of the terms "glory" (כָּבוֹד) and "holy" (קָדוֹשׁ) provides a significant semantic concentration of terms, which further serves to posit Isa 6:3 as an echo of Isa 4.[39] To offer further evidence, as discussed above, God filling the earth is consistently linked with an eschatological reality of which Isa 4 is a part (Num 14:21; Ps 72:19; Hab 2:14).

Hence, the Lord's glory filling the earth seems to be positive. This should factor into our discussion of the thrice-holy God. To be sure, the context (both near and far) suggests that this holiness is one of judgment. At the same time, such condemnation must also relate to the next line of God's glory filling the earth, which is a proclamation of restored fellowship. Transforming holiness bridges this gap. The angels sing because God has displayed the complete nature of his perfection. His

---

35. Ibid., 181. Oswalt suggests this understanding of the verse, although he acknowledges the possibility of a more relational idea. Levenson, "Temple and the World," 289–90. Levenson suggests that the phrase should be rendered "his glory is the entire earth" as if the entire world is God's temple. While the conclusion matches the following discussion, the translation is suspect. The construct noun, מְלֹא, can denote the traditional translation. Cf. Num 22:18. The absolute noun(s) outside of the construct act as subject of the verbal action implied by the construct noun.

36. Usages outside of this include Num 14:21 and Ps 72:19, which mention God's glory filling the earth.

37. Beale, *Temple and the Church's Mission*, 49: "In the same way that God's glory (*kābôd*) filled both the tabernacle and temple at the conclusion of their construction, Isaiah 6:3 affirms with the same terms that God's glory fills the entire cosmos." Levenson, "Temple and the World," 288–90.

38. Motyer, *Isaiah*, 77.

39. Bartelt, "Centrality of Isa 6," 324–26. Bartelt seems to link Isa 4 with Isa 6 and the agenda of God to fill the earth with his glory in a relationship. See also Watts, *Isaiah 1–33*, 110. Watts connects Isa 6:13 (holy seed) with God's holiness and the remnant restoration motif in Isa 4.

holiness judges and transforms people to be holy so that his glory fills the earth (6:3).[40] This connection makes sense of the relationship between holiness and glory in the angels' proclamation and parallels the information in chapter 4. Isa 6, though it expands upon that prior context by stating that this relationship does not just extend to Israel, but to the whole world.

If this is the case, Isaiah does not merely witness a portrayal of the timeless character of God. Rather, he observes the eschatological celebration of God's work in punishing and transforming people in order that they may know him and his glory. This moment relates to the eschatological conversion of Israel presented in Isa 4. Naturally, this reflects God's ontological holiness and his sovereignty. Nonetheless, Isaiah sees these attributes dramatically manifested in time and space as a historical event to come in the latter days (2:1; 4:2).

Isaiah's Participation in the Vision (vv. 4–13)

Thus far, Isaiah's vision has dealt with the contextual issues of kingdom and presence (God's glory and holiness). The subject of time (exile versus eschatological) remains. Isaiah's mission, stemming from the vision, settles this tension and consequently brings further resolution to the others.

The vision itself concludes with a description of the temple shaking and filling with smoke. This begins a transition to Isaiah's declaration of his cursed state.[41] God's holiness causes a separation between him and the prophet.[42] Isaiah therefore cannot commune with the Lord because he is unclean. With this, the eschatological meets the present. In this moment, Isaiah is not transformed as the vision portrays. He is not fit to participate in the eschatological kingdom the vision portrays. Thus, judgment awaits him and he knows it. Interestingly, the prophet's statement that he is "undone" (נִדְמֵיתִי, v. 5) can also be rendered as "silent." This could be a play on words.[43] As the angels cry out, Isaiah is not ready to join them and is condemned.

In a shocking twist, the harbinger of God's holy judgment also becomes the messenger of salvation.[44] One of the seraphim gives Isaiah a coal to cleanse him. This act provides additional confirmation that a transforming holiness is implied in the angels' outcry. In fact, the entire situation makes little sense without this understanding. If the holiness the angels proclaimed was only God's character relative to his judgment,

---

40. Bartelt, "Centrality of Isa 6," 324. Bartelt argues that judgment and salvation must be part of God's holy presence, especially in light of 12:1–6.

41. Motyer, *Isaiah*, 77; Oswalt, *Isaiah 1–39*, 182. Note that verse 4 begins a series of *wayyiqtols* that link the temple's tremors to Isaiah's denunciation.

42. Motyer, *Isaiah*, 77; Oswalt, *Isaiah 1–39*, 182.

43. Roberts, "Double Entendre," 44–46. Although the English translations (and perhaps the LXX, κατανένυγμαι) communicate a "cursed" state, the Vulgate renders the term as "silence" (*tacui*).

44. Joines, "Winged Serpents," 415. Joines notes that this is a major deviation from the standard depiction of seraphim, which draws further attention to the notion of transforming holiness.

then why would the prophet be cleansed as opposed to judged? Some might argue this happened so that God could summon the man to ministry.[45] However, this interpretation does not deal with how Isaiah's own ministry testifies that he is not the only one who is transformed. The prophet's mission condemns and hardens Israel unto exile and also announces that a *holy* seed will emerge (Isa 6:13).[46] In context, this holiness seems to correspond to the thrice-holy God (6:3). Why would such holiness apply to the nation if God's perfection were only geared towards condemnation? Such innertextuality seems to confirm the notion of a holiness that both punishes and purifies. My suggestion of a transforming holiness (with a condemning holiness) allows the vision to relate to the whole of Isaiah's experience and mission.

Returning to the issue of resolving the present and the eschatological, Isaiah's purification demonstrates the linchpin between these two factors: salvation. While the prophet is initially unable to enter into God's eschatological presence, he is made worthy to participate. The paradigm of judgment to salvation provides the hinge between the present and eschatological, between the demise and later exaltation of Jerusalem, as well as between the sinful and ultimately holy people of God. Isaiah's name means

---

45. Oswalt, *Isaiah 1–39*, 184.

46. Schmidt, "Verstockungsauftrag Jesajas," 70–71; Robinson, "Motif of Deafness and Blindness," 176–77. See also Brownlee, "Text of Isaiah 6:13 in the Light of DSIa," 296–98; Beale, "A Retributive Taunt," 261–75. Textual critical concerns surround the phrase, קֹדֶשׁ מַצַּבְתָּה. DSIsa reads מצבת במה (sacred column of the high place). This has support with parallelism in the text itself, as well as with other passages (e.g., Josh 24:26; Judg 9:6; 1 Kgs 14:23). The LXX also omits the phrase. Such a reading eliminates the remnant idea from the text entirely. However, 1QIsa^a maintains the reading of the MT in this verse. Furthermore, Motyer points out that the LXX is not a good textual critical guide in this portion of the book (Motyer, *Isaiah*, 80). The MT reading, being the "harder" reading (yet with ample external support), should stand. We hesitate to accept a conjectural emendation that actually proposes to change the text without evidence. Iwry, "Maṣṣēbāh and Bāmāh in 1Q Isaiah," 225–32.

Beale comments that the phrase is more negative than positive. The מַצֶּבֶת refers to an idolatrous object based upon its similarity with מַצַּבְתָּה (cf. Exod 23:24; 1 Kgs 14:23). Accordingly, even the remnant will be completely idolatrous. The "holy seed" is an ironic use of the term. Oswalt and Motyer view this as a more positive reference. The context of Isa 6:13 does include both judgment, or idolatrous, and salvation elements. Nonetheless, the traditional notion of a righteous remnant still holds out better for the following reasons: First, the disjunctive clause probably is antithetical, showing a contrast to judgment. This is supported by the use of the particle עֹד. Hence, verse 13 discusses the ultimate salvation of God's people. Second, such basic structure follows the pattern established by the vision itself. Isaiah is unclean, but then is made clean by the coal. Third, the מַצֶּבֶת and מַצַּבְתָּה are not completely interchangeable and may not refer to the same item. The word in this text is consistently used for memorial stone without a cultic context (cf. 2 Sam 18:8). Thus, the cultic association may be slightly exaggerated for this term specifically. Fourth, the term מַצַּבְתָּה itself is used positively in the book of Isaiah. Egypt will set up a מַצַּבְתָּה to point to YHWH (Isa 19:19). This suggests the transformation of idolatry to true worship, which may actually correspond to the remnant of Israel itself. Fifth, innertextuality of the vision also pertains to this reality. The seed mentioned in Isa 6:13 is made righteous and enjoys the promises (41:8; 53:10; 65:9). The oaks, a cultic term and one mentioned in Isa 6:13 itself, are converted into oaks of righteousness (Isa 61:3). The innertextuality of the terms מַצַּבְתָּה and מַצֶּבֶת in Isaiah show such conversion. These reasons suggest that Isaiah refers to a small remnant that is refined, but saved, which matches the motif of the entire book.

salvation, and this concept is a well-recognized center to his theology.[47] The focus of the vision on this concept harmonizes well with the scholarly consensus surrounding the book as a whole.[48]

Thus, God has called Isaiah to urge the people of God toward the eschatological moment of the vision. This can only be accomplished through what that event signifies (from the prophet's perspective): the glory of God in salvation through judgment.[49] Hence, Israel will be condemned, just as Isaiah was. The prophet's ministry will facilitate the hardening of the nation (6:9–13).[50] Nonetheless, Isaiah's purification also links to Israel's experience. Israel will be a holy seed, as God is holy (v. 13b). Just as Isaiah is cleansed, so the people will be transformed to conform to the image of their God.[51]

In essence, Isaiah beholds a vision of eschatological salvation and hope. He looks forward to the moment in history when YHWH will rule in this world in an unparalleled visible fashion, when the earth will enjoy the fullness of his saving work. The prophet's mission participates in the vision in that he assists in moving the current circumstances towards that glorious future reality. This mission centers on the proclamation that the sovereign God will orchestrate history to bring about judgment and transformation that leads to his ultimate dominion. The prophet's theology will help us understand more detailed dynamics of how this vision will work out. The vision does not only impress upon Isaiah the notions of holiness and sovereignty, but actually becomes the very shape and *telos* of his mission. It is the motivation for and the outcome of Isaiah's work.

---

47. House, *Old Testament Theology*, 272.

48. Moreover, I would suggest that the vision itself is structured to that very end. How do the verses in Isa 6:1–3 relate to each other? Several possibilities exist. Isaiah first presents the Lord's supreme kingship, and then his holiness and glory. Hence, God's reign could be the basis or cause of his glory filling the earth. Alternatively, it could be that the opening verse presents the final outcome of God's working to extend his glory throughout the earth. Arguably, the verses might have only an incidental relationship. Since Isaiah is recounting an event in his life, perhaps there is no scheme of causation or relationship other than the fact that this is what he saw. Commentators typically take this view. However, the latter half of the chapter clarifies that salvation is the hinge on which all these theological realities turn. Isaiah and Israel's transformation testifies to this. The transition in verse 4 also supports this idea by stressing the separation between the holy God and the prophet. Based upon this, verses 1–3 seem to be arranged from solution to plight, or outcome to cause. The prophet concentrates on how the glorious outcome of the kingdom was accomplished—by the thrice-holy God who transforms the world and fills it with his glory. This paradigm will prove useful for the rest of the book.

49. Hamilton, *God's Glory*, 211. See particularly his discussion in fn. 146. See also Roberts, "Isaiah in Old Testament," 131. Roberts states that the appearance of the Holy One of Israel in the vision is the centerpiece of Isaiah's theology.

50. Schmidt, "Verstockungsauftrag Jesajas," 68–90; Evans, "Context of Isaiah's Theology," 144–46.

51. Motyer, *Isaiah*, 79–80; Watts, *Isaiah 1–33*, 110; Oswalt, *Isaiah 1–39*, 190.

ECHO AND RECAPITULATION OF THE VISION IN ISAIAH

Before analyzing these ideas further, I ought to address how this vision works out in the rest of the book. Scholars readily recognize that Isaiah is a wordsmith *par excellence* and makes brilliant puns.[52] Based upon this realization, my approach is to show how Isaiah weaves together words, phrases, and motifs derived from his vision into his discussions throughout the book. Given Isaiah's sophisticated literary ability, these allusions are probably not coincidental.

Furthermore, Isaiah appears to intentionally connect his eschatological presentation with the vision. In so doing, the prophet further explains the vision's import.[53] In this sense, such prophecies recapitulate the vision. One passage that provides a key illustration of this principle is Isa 11.

Scholars recognize that this text portrays the prophet's viewpoint of eschatological reality. They also observe its influence upon a variety of texts in communicating hope for Israel and the world (cf. 32:1–5; 49:1–3; 60:1–18; 65:13–25).[54] In a sense, Isa 11 acts as a backbone for Isaiah's presentation of the renewal of the world.

In that passage, a Davidic king reigns with the power of God's Spirit (11:1–5). The earth is changed as sin is restrained such that the child can play with previously dangerous animals (11:5–8). This is because no sin can occur on God's *holy* mountain (v. 9). Holiness has caused the eradication of sin and of death. Furthermore, this effect is indicative of the reality that the knowledge of God *fills* the earth as water covers the seas (v. 9b). Even from this brief survey, the chapter seems to resemble Isa 6. Some arguments for their parallelism include:

1. Initially, the passages' parallel wording is striking and significant. The terms "earth" (אֶרֶץ) and "filled" (מלא) do not often occur in the book (2:7–8; 6:3; 11:9). This argues for an association between 11:9 and 6:3. The collocation of terms in Isaiah are not an accident.

2. The substitution of "glory" with "knowledge" is not unreasonable. In Isa 6:3, glory denoted God's relational presence with his people. The knowledge of God in chapter 11 also refers to such fellowship.[55]

3. Other parallels between Isa 11 and 6 exist. The reference to "holy mountain" echoes two texts. The reference to mountain parallels Isa 11 with Isa 2:2, which seems to

---

52. Roberts, "Double Entendre," 39–48.

53. As previously noted, this does not demand that Isaiah's vision depicts the theological realities described in his book. Rather, there is an *association* between the two. Later revelation will clarify their precise relationship. Hence, the term "import" or "significance" refers to theology that is depicted by the event and its impact on redemptive history.

54. Bartelt, "Centrality of Isa 6," 323–24; Motyer, *Isaiah*, 120–21; Oswalt, *Isaiah 1–39*, 277–78; Watts, *Isaiah 1–33*, 207–9.

55. Oswalt, *Isaiah 1–39*, 284.

have connections with Isa 6.[56] The term "holiness" corresponds to 6:3. Furthermore, the flow of Isa 11 also matches chapter 6. Both begin with the reign of the king (6:1; 11:1–5), then discuss God's holiness (6:3; 11:9), and then detail his glory or knowledge filling the earth (Isa 6:3b; 11:9b). This suggests that Isa 11 is a fuller portrait of Isa 2 and 6. At a bare minimum, they both look to that moment when God's glory fills the earth, which, as discussed, is consistently eschatological in nature. That means that both texts relate to the same redemptive historical occasion.

4. Later use of the phrase by Habakkuk also provides confirmation of this parallelism. He states that the "knowledge of the glory of YHWH will fill the earth" (2:14). Could Habakkuk's combination of glory and knowledge indicate that he recognizes the correlation between the agenda presented in Isa 6:3 and 11:9? Hamilton acknowledges the association between these three texts.[57] He also comments on Isa 11:

> This [Isa 11:8] is a picturesque way of declaring that after the judgment on God's people, through which they are brought to salvation, there will be no more enmity between the seed of the serpent and the seed of the woman. And it culminates with God accomplishing his purpose, *stated in language that recalls the song of the seraphim* (6:3b; cf. Num 14:21) . . .[58]

Barker also affirms this notion:

> Habakkuk joined a prophetic chorus calling for more. God's glory should be recognized as filling the entire universe (Num 14:21; Ps 72:19; Isa 6:3), letting all the people of the world experience and respond to God's manifest, weighty presence. The prophet wanted the knowledge of God to be as pervasive as the waters that fill the seas.[59]

Based upon such evidence, Isa 11 seems to fulfill what was declared in Isa 6. Initially, these parallels affirm that Isa 6 pertains to an eschatological event. They also support the correlations between Isa 2 and 6. Moreover, if Isa 11 really is connected to a host of eschatological texts in the rest of the book, then those passages must also link back to the source text of Isaiah's vision. This suggests that Isaiah consciously links his theology to the vision and expounds upon its significance in later texts.

Both Isaiah's literary artistry and the important connection to Isa 11 serve as grounds for further discussion. The passages I have chosen below offer key links to the vision through either of these criteria or both. Accordingly, the rest of this chapter surveys how Isaiah expounds upon Isa 6:1–3. Such innertextuality will further confirm my original thesis of Isaiah's vision as eschatological event. It will also expound upon the details and beauty of the vision.

---

56. Motyer, *Isaiah*, 125.
57. Hamilton, *God's Glory*, 268.
58. Ibid., 197, emphasis mine.
59. Barker and Bailey, *Micah, Nahum, Habakkuk, Zephaniah*, 341.

GOD'S JUDGING AND TRANSFORMING HOLINESS

One might expect to cover the issue of kingdom first, since the vision presents that material before the issue of holiness and sin. However, for the flow of this chapter, I have elected to discuss the matter of holiness first. Since salvation is so critical to Isaiah's theology, I have deemed it appropriate to give primary attention to that subject.

Sin as Negative Transformation in Isaiah's Vision and Theology

Along that line, if the linchpin between the present and eschatological is the transforming salvation of God, then sin is Israel's central problem within the prophet's theology. Isaiah states as much. God's opening statement declares that Israel must come to the Lord in repentance so that its transgressions can be washed clean (1:18). In the vision, Isaiah's acceptance by the Holy One depends upon the forgiveness of his sins and the atonement of his guilt (6:7). When God synthesizes the argument of the book, he names sin as the primary problem (59:2). Israel's righteousness is like a soiled rag, and they are unclean (just as Isaiah was, cf. Isa 6:10; 64:6). The prophet's frequent use of terms for sin makes this meaning unequivocal (cf. 1:4; 3:9; 5:18; 22:14; 27:9; 30:1–2; 40:2; 59:6).

At the same time, the writer does not merely describe Israel's problems using the standard words for wickedness. Instead, he makes use of metaphor to portray such realities. This figurative language occurs in the immediate context of the vision itself. Isaiah parallels his problems with Israel on a variety of levels. The prophet's problems concerned what his eyes have seen (6:5) and that his lips are unclean (v. 5). After his sins are atoned for and removed, he can hear the voice of God commissioning him (v. 8). His people face the same problems. They cannot see and hear (v. 9) and Isaiah's mission is to preach these realities to these people even if they cannot respond. This will be their condemnation (Isa 6:10–13).

The innertextuality of Isa 6:10 with the vision provides the significance of this "blind and deaf" motif. God commands Isaiah to use his preaching to make the nation's ears heavy and dull (וְאָזְנָיו הַכְבֵּד, v. 10). This plays off the term "glory" found in the vision (v. 3).[60] The people's stubbornness is a perversion of God's glory, one that makes each of them resemble a deaf and dumb idol. For this reason, the latter part of chapter 6 equates the nation with an "oak" (כָּאֵלָה וְכָאַלּוֹן, v. 13), which alludes to Israel's idolatrous practice involving that tree (1:30; 2:13). In fact, the logic in 6:13 echoes the first chapter, when God likens the nation to an oak, presumably because of their idolatry (cf. 1:30). In a sense, they became what they worshipped.[61]

Overall, the vision provides the core reason (in Isaiah's theology) for why sin offends God's holiness. It is *negative transformation*. Sin takes the glory of God and

---

60. Landy, "Strategies of Concentration," 71.
61. Beale, "A Retributive Taunt," 257–78; Beale, *We Become What We Worship*, 38–49.

turns it into something that is far from his distinctive perfection, an impotent idol. As a result, sin degrades people into something the Lord cannot tolerate. In terms of the vision, the people inherently move in the opposite trajectory of God's perfection and plan. Like Isaiah, they are incompatible with the glorious kingdom God will ultimately establish in world history.

Two major sections within Isaiah deal with the blindness motif (28:1—35:10; 40:1—48:22).[62] Both units explicitly mention Israel's blindness (29:8; 42:20–21). Both also tie this blindness to the rejection of the Holy One of Israel (30:11–12; 31:1; 41:20).[63] This correlation of holiness and blindness parallels Isaiah 6. Arguably, Isaiah expands upon the theology of his vision in these texts.

In Isa 29–32, the people of Israel demonstrate their blindness in their reaction to God's imminent deliverance of Jerusalem from Assyria (29:9–15; cf. 36:1—37:38). Despite that this clearly testifies to YHWH's ability to save (29:1–8), the people suppress the truth. They see it, but do not understand (29:11–12; cf. Isa 6:10). They refuse to hear the words of the Holy One (29:10–12; 30:11–12) that would deliver them. Thus, God commands them to "be blind" (29:9, הִשְׁתַּעַשְׁעוּ). However, their blindness does not merely reject the Holy One of Israel. In context, Israel relies upon Egypt to save them from Assyria (30:1–2). They scorned the message of the Holy One of Israel to trust in political maneuvering (30:12). They look to Egypt because the nation appears mighty, but they fail to see the true strength of the Holy One of Israel (31:1). To them, God is no better than the nations he created. As the vision originally stated, Israel has so distorted God's glory as to become blind.

In the latter half of the book, God launches into a diatribe against idolatry (40:1—48:22). He aims to prove that the Holy One of Israel is not like any of Israel's idols (41:20). However, the nation cannot grasp that truth because its people are blinded on an unparalleled level (42:19). Historically, they have heard and seen the law of God but never actually listened, obeyed, or understood it (42:20–21). The language in those verses highly resembles Isa 6:13.[64] Furthermore, God brings up the oak tree, another item associated with the vision (44:18; cf. Isa 6:13). The people cultivate these trees in order to make an idol (44:14), which we are to understand as utterly foolish, since they burn one half and then worship the other (vv. 16–17). Nonetheless, they believe it can save them (v. 17). What causes them to be so irrational? God has done this. As the next verses state, he has caused the nation to go blind (44:18–19) just as he proclaimed in the vision (6:13). Such blindness was present at the very inception of the country (48:8). Once again, the theology of the vision resurfaces in Isaiah's

---

62. Robinson, "Motif of Deafness and Blindness," 178–81.

63. There are other parallels as well. For example, Israel's people give the appearance of godliness in the words from their lips (שׂפה, cf. 6:6) but their hearts are far from the Lord (29:13). The terminology of the vision and call is employed throughout these passages.

64. Oswalt, *Isaiah 40–66*, 131.

message to Israel. Israel's idolatry perverts the supremacy of YHWH, and as a result, its people become blind and dumb as their own idols.

In addition to these two passages, Isa 59:1–2 concisely and provocatively reiterates this negative transformation. In that text, the Lord summarizes his case against the nation presented throughout the book.[65] God chides his people for thinking he was blind and deaf as the reason for the catastrophe of exile (59:1). Instead, their sins have caused such separation that God ceases to respond to them (v. 2). The irony of these verses is telling. Israel is so blind that its people think God is like their idol, when in fact they are oblivious to their complete fault. Like their idols, they are the impotent ones; only YHWH is able to save them. Isaiah reiterates at the end what he had stated at the beginning: Israel's problem is one of negative transformation. As he provocatively states elsewhere, despite being the valley of vision (22:1), Israel cannot see anything: "Who is so blind as my servant?" (42:18–19).[66] The whole book testifies to this reality.

We may briefly examine this concept of sin as negative transformation from a different angle: the glory of God (cf. 6:3). Because of their blindness, Israel wrongly interacts with God's glory. They refuse to glorify God (43:23, לֹא כִבַּדְתָּנִי) and instead seek alternative glories, like wealth (10:3, כְּבוֹדְכֶם).[67] They *fill* the land with gold, silver, and idolatry instead of with the glory of the Lord (2:7–8, 13–14; cf. 6:3). Conversely, YHWH shares his glory with no one (42:8). Israel's arrogance and idolatry are not just "immoral" but in Isaiah's mind, compete with the Lord's agenda for his glory to fill the earth. This goes against the core reason for Israel's existence. The nation is supposed to reflect God's glory in bearing fruit (5:2) that would fill the entire earth (27:6; cf. 6:3). Israel has wandered far from that purpose and so has become an abomination to its maker.[68]

As a result, the nation is unable to repent. Its people have become incapable of doing anything, just like their idols. They could not respond to the crisis with Assyria, Aram, and the northern kingdom (9:13) even though the solution was so clearly presented: regard God as holy (8:13). Moreover, God concludes that Israel's blindness prevents them from ever having hope or salvation (59:9–11). Indeed, when God challenges Israel to demonstrate true repentance, he acknowledges that their leaders are blind (56:10), that they are without knowledge (v. 11), and that if they continue in their sinful delusion, they will see how their idols will deliver them. This, of course, will end in disaster (57:13a). As Isaiah says,

65. Ibid., 10–11.

66. Ibid., 130. Oswalt points out that the Servant needed to be one who could guide, yet was blind. This renders the nation unable to fulfill its role.

67. Oswalt, *Isaiah 1–39*, 258; Young, *Isaiah*, 1:357. The term "glory" in this context refers to wealth. See also Motyer, *Isaiah*, 111: "We should not forget the basic meaning, for it is not just a matter of cash but also all of the self-importance, pride of position and authority which that day will bring to nothing."

68. Oswalt, *Isaiah 1–39*, 409.

> For thus the Lord God, the Holy One of Israel, has said, 'In repentance and rest you shall be saved, In quietness and trust is your strength.' But you were not willing (30:15).

Judging Holiness in Isaiah

Though I have argued that the vision encapsulates transforming holiness and a positive glory that fills the earth, we cannot deny the judgmental aspect of God's perfection. Isaiah preaches that God will be exalted in judgment and thereby display his holiness (5:16). The vision portrays the seraphim as creatures burning with the destructive might of the Holy One of Israel to turn the land into a wilderness (6:2, 11–13; cf. 1:7). Throughout the book, Isaiah uses such imagery to describe impending punishment. Israel enters the wilderness of exile (40:3; 42:11). Its cities are burned, desolate, a wasteland (1:7, 31; 64:8–9), just as Isaiah's call predicts (6:11–13). The valley of Topheth becomes a pyre of God's judgment (30:33). All of this punishment stems from the fiery wrath of the Holy One of Israel (cf. 29:23; 30:11–12) and reflects that the holiness of God is a consuming fire (30:27, 30; 33:14; cf. Deut 4:24).

Additionally, in the vision, the temple shakes (וַיָּנֻעוּ) at God's holy presence (6:4) signaling Isaiah's unworthiness. So the entire earth shakes (24:20, תְּנוּעַ נוֹעַ) in the presence of God's holy wrath. This emphasizes that Isaiah's experience at his calling was a microcosm of the prophet's message to Israel and the world. The language of Isaiah's vision and calling also points out how God's holiness attacks wickedness in appropriate and ironic ways. Israel's unclean lips, like Isaiah's, merit the punishment of having its people sent into exile, where a people of unclean lips will speak to them (28:11). The punishment corresponds with the offense.

However, the most dominant aspect of God's judging holiness is his targeting of that which appears holy but is not. For example, in judging Moab, the Lord specifically allows its people to pray in their "holy places" (16:12, מִקְדָּשׁוֹ) to no avail. The failure of their sacred sites demonstrates that such locales do not compare to the Holy One of Israel.[69] Also, Isaiah proclaims that God will destroy the temple in Jerusalem, the holy place (43:28; cf. 64:10). This is because of Israel's persistent sin (43:27), including the fact that their offerings in the temple are more annoying than atoning (1:12–14). While the temple may be called holy, the Holy One of Israel declares that there is only one type of holiness: the one that matches his. Anything else will be condemned and will eternally demonstrate that Israel's people do not correspond with God's perfection (66:24).[70]

A similar logic extends to passages that discuss God's judgment in light of his glory. In shaming Israel for trusting in idols, God shows how he punishes the land

---

69. Ibid., 347; Motyer, *Isaiah*, 154.
70. Oswalt, *Isaiah 40–66*, 692–93.

filled with idols (2:8) and the influences of other nations (v. 6). In terrible fury, the Lord comes and exacts a cosmic judgment on the entire world, to the point where everyone recognizes the futility of idolatry (2:18). In their panic to flee from the fearsome wrath of God that shakes the world, the people cast their idols away (2:20–21). In this occurrence, we not only observe the awesomeness of God's glory and holy judgment, but also that he cannot share glory, and so destroys those things attributed false glory (42:8). Instead, he alone will be exalted (2:17). Hence, in the upcoming exile, Israel's glorious ones (their nobles, 5:13, כְּבוֹדוֹ) will be famished and humiliated. Its wealth and military might (both described as glorious, 2:8; 22:18) will be abandoned. In short, the glory of the leadership of Israel will fall apart (22:23–25).

Such deconstructive power amplifies the nature of the vision. Descriptions of God's glory filling the earth and the angels proclaiming his holiness are not exaggerated. Because his judgment eradicates false glories and false holiness, all glory is centralized in YHWH and his holiness prevails. There is no competition. The vision celebrates nothing less than the complete fulfillment and display of those realities to the world.

Transforming Holiness in Isaiah

For that event to take place, we do not just need to remove rival holiness and false glory (which are really abominations). Transformation is required. To be clear, the picture of such metamorphosis is not arbitrary or abstract. God's provision of holiness is not some baseless or magical act. In Isaiah's theology, such transformation stems from the satisfaction of God's justice. The prophet calls for Israel to repent so that its sins will be washed away (1:16–19; 44:22). God will forgive Israel's iniquity just like he atoned for Isaiah's guilt (33:24; cf. 6:6). Such judicial acts are based upon the substitutionary sacrifice of the Servant (52:13—53:12).[71] His sacrifice gives him the right to justify the ungodly and forgive them (53:11).[72] While "holiness," in a transforming sense, deals primarily with the outcome, it presumes that God has dealt with sin directly.

With that in mind, the rest of the book reinforces the notion that holiness is not just condemning, but also redeeming. This understanding is critically important, since the vision and its innertextuality has implied this concept, but not strongly. Of note are the juxtapositions of God's holiness and other titles for salvation. God calls himself "the Holy One of Israel, your Savior" (43:3). In the same context, he is also "your Redeemer, the Holy One of Israel" (43:14). In these texts, God's holy and redemptive nature drives his work to save Israel (v. 3). In his oracle of judgment against Babylon, God's victory to save Israel stems from the fact that he is the "Redeemer, the

---

71. Janowski, "He Bore Our Sins," 48–74.

72. The play on words in יַצְדִּיק צַדִּיק is significant. The Servant's accomplishments, which make him righteous, become the basis by which he justifies the many. See Oswalt, *Isaiah 40–66*, 404; Motyer, *Isaiah*, 441–42.

I Saw the Lord

Holy One of Israel" (47:4). Hence, even though Israel sins, God will save them because he is the "Redeemer, the Holy One of Israel" (48:17, 20). They will return from exile. The Lord bares his holy arm to the world to rescue his people (52:10). This results in the Lord's summons to his people to come home and not touch unclean things (52:11, cf. Isa 6:5 and the use of "unclean"). Those verses tie God's holiness with a power to make his people clean.[73] All of this evidences that God's perfection correlates with his determination to keep the covenant and transform his people in conformity with himself.[74] After all, it is none other than the Holy One of Israel who offers salvation to those who repent, even if they cannot at the time (30:15).

Accordingly, the Holy One of Israel radically counters Israel's negative transformation. As already discussed, Isa 28–35 comprise a major section that deals with Israel's blindness. However, the passage does not merely discuss the problem, but also its solution. The Lord promises a time when the people of Israel will hear his words and will see in the midst of the darkness of their exile (29:18). This promises to have dramatic results on Israel. Instead of being insensitive to the Lord, they rejoice in the Holy One of Israel (v. 19). Instead of perverting his uniqueness, they actually view him as holy (v. 23). Israel's conversion deals with the central problem of negative transformation Isaiah has portrayed, for they can see God for who he is and rightly attribute his worthiness to him.

Isaiah lays out the full context of this metamorphosis in chapter 32. In that text, a king reigns righteously (32:1) and the "eyes of those who see will not be blinded" and the "ears of those who hear will listen" (32:3). Does this not thematically parallel Isaiah's vision? Both begin with the reign of the king (6:1; 32:1). One (presumably) celebrates God's judging and transforming holiness (6:3). The other commemorates how God gave sight to those who had been blind to God's holiness (32:3). In addition to the flow of both texts, scholars recognize that the wording of 32:3 notably corresponds with 6:10.[75] Scholars also agree that Isa 32 correlates with Isa 11.[76] This ties it back to Isa 6, just as I have argued. Could all this evidence indicate that Isa 32 recapitulates Isa 6? In any case, the passage certainly shows that God transforms his people from blindness to conform to his holiness. Not only are their eyes opened, but they see the Holy One of Israel, their teacher (17:7; 30:20)! The nation may now look upon the holy God whom even Isaiah could never see without fear and trembling (6:6).

Further reversals occur. God's holiness exploits the unclean lips of Isaiah (and presumably Israel, 6:5); conversely, because of the Servant's work, God creates a people

---

73. Oswalt, *Isaiah 40–66*, 371. Oswalt acknowledges the transformational or delivering holiness sense, but also that the holiness may refer to God's unparalleled power.

74. Ibid., 139, 243. The pairing of names (particularly Savior) may correspond with God's saving work in the Exodus, and then his holiness at Mount Sinai. This reinforces his covenant-making and -keeping nature, especially in light of the second Exodus motif in this part of the book.

75. Oswalt, *Isaiah 1–39*, 581; Motyer, *Isaiah*, 257.

76. Oswalt, *Isaiah 1–39*, 581; Motyer, *Isaiah*, 257; Watts, *Isaiah 1–33*, 483.

with clean lips that can praise him (57:19). He puts his words in their mouths (51:16), even though they rejected them previously (30:11–12). This transformation relates to the powerful work of the Spirit, who guarantees that God's word will not depart Israel's lips (59:21; cf. 6:5). It extends not only upon that generation of Israel, but also to their descendants (59:21). The term offspring (זֶרַע) in that verse may parallel the use of "holy offspring" (זֶרַע קֹדֶשׁ) in God's commissioning of Isaiah (6:13).[77] This resonates with other uses of the word throughout Isaiah (41:8; 43:5; 45:25; 53:10; 59:21; 65:9, 23). The term refers to the remnant in Israel, returned from exile (43:5; 65:9), used by God (41:8), and thereby justified and transformed (45:25; 53:10). They will endure forever (66:22). Once again, the theology of the book works out what Isaiah witnessed in his vision and calling. God has healed Israel (30:26) though previously the hardening of Israel had prevented that outcome (6:10). He has formed a "holy offspring" (6:13) that matches his own holiness (v. 3).

The highway of holiness serves as another example of God's transforming holiness. The Lord establishes this roadway, on which only those who match God's standard can walk (35:8).[78] The unclean (cf. Isa 6:5) will not tread on it (35:8). Nonetheless, Israel walks on it on its sojourn back to Jerusalem (35:10). The nation, previously marked by complete disobedience and rebellion, now conforms to the perfection of their God. They are holy.

As a result, Jerusalem becomes a place of holiness (4:2–5; 48:2) because it is clothed in the holiness of God (52:1) as opposed to its own fabrications (cf. 1:12–14). Its inhabitants are holy people (62:12). God's judgment has purged the nation from false holiness and established a true holiness based upon his own character. Even its idolatry has been transformed. Before, Israel worshipped the oaks (1:29; 44:14; 57:15) and had been compared to those idols (1:30; 6:13). Now, the Servant proclaims that the nation is an oak of righteousness (61:3).[79] The stigma of idolatry has been removed, and the Servant has made people of Israel who had worshipped false idols acceptable before the Lord.[80] Accordingly, God will dwell with his people. The vision highlighted the massive separation between the present and eschatological. Sin cannot mix with holiness (6:4). However, God will save and transform his people. They will dwell with him, and he will commune with them because the barrier of sin has been removed (8:14). In the end, Israel's chorus will be "great in your midst is the Holy One of Israel" (12:6). The holy God has removed counterfeit holiness and instituted his own for his people. The people celebrate God's holiness, just like the angels in Isaiah's vision.

This discussion illustrates that holiness in Isaiah not only pertains to condemnation, but also to transformation. The juxtaposition of terms (e.g., holiness, seed, king,

---

77. Motyer, *Isaiah*, 80; Gignilliat, "Theological Exegesis as Exegetical Showing," 228.

78. Robinson, "Motif of Deafness and Blindness," 182. Robinson argues that the highway of holiness in context relates to the transformation of blindness to sight.

79. Gignilliat, "Theological Exegesis as Exegetical Showing," 228.

80. Ibid.; Motyer, *Isaiah*, 501.

and blindness) and motifs (e.g., king ruling, Jerusalem's exaltation) in these texts seems to allude back to Isaiah's calling. Hence, the book helps explain the completeness of God's holiness as it was proclaimed in the vision. His perfect character can tolerate nothing but his own true holiness to stand. He therefore purges the world of all counterfeits and transforms it to conform to his own perfection. He is "holy, holy, holy."

The transformation of Israel does not just revolve around God's three-fold holiness in the vision. The angels also proclaim that God's glory fills the earth. How does that proclamation play out in the book? As noted, God's judging holiness crushes all competing glory, for the Lord cannot share his glory with anything lesser. The same reason drives the display of his supreme glory. He acts to save his exiled people for the sake of his glory (48:11). God loves his people and has assigned his glory to them (43:4a). Thus, he will intervene on their behalf (43:4b) so that all will glorify him (61:3).[81] God's glory is the motivation for their redemption.

Furthermore, this saving activity is itself a display of God's glory. The second half of the book begins with God proclaiming his comforting work to redeem his people, which unveils the glory of God to the entire world (40:5). Specifically, God's majesty is revealed as he marches from the wilderness into Jerusalem (40:3), where he will dwell and reign (vv. 3–5).[82] This revelation affirms the association between God's glory filling the earth and a future redemptive-historical situation. Furthermore, it implies why God's salvation is glorious: it works out the ultimate reality of God's glory filling the earth.

However, God's glory is not just found in his person, motivation, or demonstration of his saving power. His glory *fills* the earth through his relationship with people who reflect that glory. As Isa 4 and 6 imply, God's glory dwells amongst his people, like in the Exodus (12:1–6). Israel worships the Holy One, who dwells in their midst (v. 6). In this way, God will become Israel's glorious protection instead of its judge (58:8). Israel glorifies the Holy One of Israel (41:6) even though they could not before (43:8). Just as the Lord removed all other glories but his own, so Israel now becomes the perfect mirror of its God. The decrepit vine (5:3) becomes one of beauty that "fills the whole world with fruit" (27:6) just as God's glory fills the earth in the vision (6:3). God glorifies Israel as a great nation (26:15) to the point that other nations recognize this unique status (60:9, 13; 62:2–11). Hence, those who doubted that God could ever transform the despicable nation will be put to shame (66:5).

This transformation goes beyond people. If God permits nothing to share his glory, it makes sense that he removes the light-bearers and instead allows his glory to illuminate the world (24:23; 30:26). All will know that glory is only found in YHWH. This innertextuality confirms our analysis of the vision and expounds upon the nature of the seraphim's proclamation. God's glory fills the earth in the sense that he

---

81. Ibid. While the term פאר is used in 61:3 for "glorify," it parallels כָּבוֹד in Isaiah. Cf. 60:13. The end result of his work was that YHWH would display his splendor.

82. Oswalt, *Isaiah 40–66*, 51–52.

accomplishes his saving purposes so that his people worship only him, acknowledge his unique splendor, and perfectly reflect that reality all over creation.

All the Earth: God's Plan for Gentiles in Isaiah

The descriptions above seem to involve the nations, and we should expect nothing less. After all, the seraphim state that God's glory fills *the whole earth*. Either this phrasing is hyperbolic, or it is precisely literal. Conversely, the perfection of God's threefold holiness has not been an exaggeration. Isaiah presented an exhaustive demonstration of God's unique ability to both judge and transform. Similarly, his glory filling the earth is by no means a platitude. His salvation not only reveals his glory, but also changes his people. The description relates to a time when God communes with the people of God and they worship and glorify him in turn. To extend this pattern, God's glory filling *the earth* is likely not an overstatement.

Isaiah's theology confirms these suspicions. Israel's iniquity (6:7; 27:9), which must be forgiven, is a problem shared by the entire world (13:11; 26:21). Egypt, like Israel, fails to recognize the true wisdom of God (19:11–12). Like Israel, the world also reveres the wrong kind of glory. As opposed to honoring the weighty majesty of YHWH, they are weighed down (וְכָבֵד) with iniquity (24:20). Thus, God must deal with the nations as much as with his own people. This necessity is particularly apparent in Isa 13–27 (cf. Isa 14:7, 25–26). In the midst of dealing with nations such as Tyre, God reveals that he will destroy "all the glory of the earth" (23:7, כָּל־נִכְבַּדֵּי־אָרֶץ). This phrase is strikingly similar to God's glory filling all the earth (6:3, כָל־הָאָרֶץ כְּבוֹדוֹ). The preparation for the reality of the vision is the de-glorification of the *entire world* such that all of creation will know that his glory alone fills the earth. Hence, nation after nation will be judged. The very structure of Isa 13–27 moves from east (Babylon) to west (Tyre) to demonstrate God's comprehensive control over the whole planet. Countries such as Babylon, Assyria, Philistia, Moab, Aram, Ethiopia, Egypt, and Tyre are listed to reiterate that "all the earth" is not a catchphrase but a precise reality. God's agenda includes each and every nation.[83] Thus, Israel should trust such a sovereign God, who will surely accomplish his intention to fill the earth with his glory.

The Lord provides specific and shocking examples of this intent to better reinforce his agenda to the reader. Egypt, a nation whose past has always been in opposition to God and his people, will speak Hebrew and pledge its allegiance to Israel (19:18–21). Egyptians will know YHWH and will be healed (19:22), as Israel needed to be healed (6:10). Their transformations are identical, for God equates Israel and Egypt as his own people (19:25). Even more shocking is that the Lord includes Assyria in this group (v. 25). Within the historical situation, Assyria was both the southern and northern kingdoms' worst enemy. In the end, they become part of God's inheritance.

---

83. House, *Old Testament Theology*, 281–84.

This stark contrast shows how far and deep the transformation goes. Even those nations that seem diabolically set against God can be made anew. Because there is no other God but YHWH, he calls all the earth to repent and be saved (45:22).

Isaiah ties this discussion back to the vision. He mentions a highway between Assyria and Egypt (19:23). He has already made note of this road in Isa 11:16. It appears that they are one and the same.[84] As Isa 11 was an expansion of the vision, so Isa 19 links back to the vision through that chapter. The two different contexts illustrate the important notion of God's glory filling the earth. Chapter 11 emphasizes the dominion of Israel and the peace that extends because of Israel's hegemony. A highway is constructed to facilitate Israel's fullness (11:16).[85] However, chapter 19 also shows that this highway facilitates the nations' (e.g., Egypt and Assyria) worship of God. God's glory fills the earth not only because Israel has dominion, but because all nations love and champion YHWH. This is not a "one-sided" filling; rather, it is reciprocal. God displays his awesome character and work to the world, and the world reflects it back to him. Just as God fills the temple to build relationship with his people, he fills the world with his glory to found an uninhibited relationship with all his creation.

Thus, the nations also reflect God's glory and amplify it in their worship (24:15–16; 25:3). Their worship results from their witness of God's glory in salvation (52:10). They also partake in the atoning work of the Servant, who justifies them (53:1–11).[86] Hence, their faulty knowledge is replaced with the true knowledge that YHWH alone is God (45:6). They in turn will see his glory (35:2), and every knee will bow before him (45:23). He will also dwell and commune with them in a way that mirrors his relationship with Israel (25:6).[87] His house will be a place for all peoples (56:7). In this way, the fullness of God's glory fills the earth without qualification. At the same time, these nations further recognize, reflect, and magnify God's glory by working with Israel as opposed to against them (55:5; 62:2–11; 66:19–20). Even the beasts of the field will respond to his glory (55:5). In this sense, God's glory *filling the earth* is quite precisely what happens. God floods the world, with all his acts proclaiming his majesty. Every nation, every person, and every creature witnesses and is amazed at the display.[88] Ultimately, God transforms them to reflect his glory and enjoy a relationship with the Holy One.

---

84. Oswalt, *Isaiah 1–39*, 380.
85. Ibid., 289.
86. Olley, "'The Many,'" 330–56.
87. Oswalt, *Isaiah 1–39*, 463; Motyer, *Isaiah*, 209–10.
88. This is not universalism by any stretch. Such a notion would contradict the judging holiness presented above and God's deconstruction of authority, which will be mentioned later. Rather, the scope of God's saving work is without qualification and extends to all creation.

Synthesis

The innertextuality of holiness and glory argue that the seraphim's cry is precisely what occurs in Isaiah's message. The book has described God's judging and transforming work in history to bring about the realities Isaiah witnessed in chapter 6. God's holiness reflects his own perfection and hatred of sin, because it perverts his person and plan. He therefore judges the people of the world for their counterfeit and competing idols and glories. All of this removes false notions of holiness and glory to prepare the world to see and know what is truly only holy and glorious: YHWH himself. In the end, his transforming holiness changes Israel and the world to conform to his perfection. He can dwell with them and thereby fill the entire earth with his glory to the exclusion of any other entity. He has unveiled his salvation before all, and they give all honor and worship to the only true God, who now shares fellowship with every nation, tribe, and tongue. Isaiah's vision celebrates this reality, which God will accomplish. The vision has presented the resolution to the tension of God's holiness and worldly sin with the power of his transforming salvation.

GOD'S HIGH AND LIFTED UP REIGN

Our discussion thus far has already covered some material pertinent to this topic. When the knowledge of God fills the earth (11:9; cf. 6:3), a descendant of Jesse reigns on the throne (11:1–5). Israel's blindness will be removed in the context of a king's dominion (32:1–6). The nations will commune with the true God and journey to Jerusalem to worship YHWH (18:7; 19:20–21). They will make political treaties with Israel (19:18). These eschatological depictions of transformation include portrayals of YHWH's central authority. This observation moves us from examining how the cry of the seraphim reverberates in Isaiah's theology (6:3) to considering how that theology shapes our understanding of the opening of Isaiah's vision (6:1). What does it mean that Isaiah saw God ruling high and lifted up?

God's Judgment as an Attack on False Sovereignty

Just as Isaiah used terms (e.g., holiness and glory) to explain his theology in light of the vision, he also uses phrases from Isa 6:1 to expand upon this aspect of his vision. For example, the phrase, "high and lifted up" can refer to YHWH (57:15); however, the combination of terms also refers to proud looks (2:11). This, along with other repetitions of words found in the vision, such as Lord (6:1), throne (v. 1), glory (v. 3), king (v. 5), or Lord of Hosts (v. 5), begin to demonstrate a pattern. Israel, and the world, sin against God by attempting to set up entities that compete with God's exclusive authority.

This notion rings true in Isaiah's discussion of idolatry and human pride. He describes how God judges the "high and lifted up" idolatrous oaks, hills, and fortifications (הָרָמִים וְהַנִּשָּׂאִים, 2:13–17; cf. 6:1). In the same text, YHWH likewise aims to bring down the "high and lofty" looks of man (2:11). Later, YHWH upbraids the king of Assyria for raising his voice and lifting up his eyes (קוֹל וַתִּשָּׂא מָרוֹם עֵינֶיךָ הֲרִימוֹתָה, 37:23, emphasis mine). Thus, pride and idolatry are wrong, because they both encroach on God's unique sovereignty. For that reason, God judges the idolatrous hills and people such that they will throw away their idols (2:20). YHWH soundly defeats the king of Assyria, who ends up dying right in front of his idol (37:36–38). In these texts, God does not merely show his ability to judge or save, he also exhibits his intent to be the only one who is high and lifted up on the throne (6:1). For the same reason, pagan kings who thought they could be equal to the Most High (14:14) are brought down to nothing and mocked (14:1, 15).

The Lord's criticism of Israel's self-sufficiency falls under similar logic. The nation had engaged in aggressive projects that allowed them to enjoy seemingly glorious (כָּבוֹד) fortifications and military might (17:3, 22:18). This replaced their trust in YHWH, who actually is glorious (22:8–13).

God's condemnation of false sovereignty pervades his interaction with the Davidic dynasty. Rather than submit to him, Israel's leadership competes with God's lordship. In the very chapter following Isaiah's vision, the prophet confronts King Ahaz with his complacency to follow the Lord (7:1–3). The repetition of אֲדֹנָי may indicate an antipathy between King Ahaz, who "reigns" over Judah (7:1), and King YHWH, who reigns on his throne (6:1).[89] Though God has promised any sign Ahaz desired (v. 3, 11), the human king refuses to rely upon his heavenly master. As the "Lord" over Israel (see the use of אֲדֹנָי in vv. 13, 20), God declares that the Davidic dynasty will be brought down (7:13–18) and that another nation will actually overtake the kingdom (v. 20). God's king must respect his authority and not subvert it.

Similarly, God also judges Israel's leadership (and the entire nation) for not conforming to his rule. His standard is one of justice and righteousness. He enforces this standard when the vision is fulfilled in his high and lifted up reign (cf. 1:26–27; 32:16).[90] Accordingly, God demands that his human regents rule in justice and righteousness (1:21, cf. 1:26–27; 5:7; 9:7; 16:5; 28:17; 56:1). However, these people perverted God's authority with their own version (Isa 5:7).[91] Isaiah shows that the Judean rulers opposed what was announced in the vision.

---

89. Bartelt, "Centrality of Isa 6," 332. Bartelt also parallels the difference between Isaiah's humility before God and Ahaz's contempt.

90. 1:26–27 is in the context of 2:2–4, which intertextually links with Isa 6. We have already discussed how Isa 32 may parallel Isa 11, and thereby the vision. 32:16, in that case, shows how YHWH's rule will occur from Zion. Further discussion on this point will follow.

91. Isaiah does this by way of a pun. The term "justice" (מִשְׁפָּט) sounds like "violence" (מִשְׂפָּח). Similarly, the word for righteousness (צְדָקָה) resembles an "outcry" (צְעָקָה). God holds Israel's leadership and people guilty for their perversion of his perfect authority.

Isaiah's Vision

Hence, judgment follows (5:8–30). One way Isaiah articulates this demise is through the person of Eliakim. God assigns Eliakim the task of securing the Davidic dynasty (22:20–21). He is the "throne of the glory of his father's house" (לְכִסֵּא כָבוֹד לְבֵית אָבִיו, v. 23; cf. Isa 6:1). However, he collapses, taking the entire royal house down with him (v. 25). Such judgment relates back to the vision. No throne or leadership can rival the glory of YHWH. He alone will sit on the throne high and lifted up. God banishes all false sovereignty in the exile.

This judgment does not focus on Israel or its leadership alone. As we have noted, God targeted Assyria for its hubris (10:12; 37:23). He will also wage war against Babylon for similar reasons (13:11).[92] This punishment results in the desolation of their temples (בְּהֵיכְלֵי עֹנֶג, v. 22). In contrast, YHWH's glory fills his temple in the vision (6:1), and he later proclaims his victory from that temple (66:6). The empty pagan temples point to the one temple that is filled by the true king of the universe. Furthermore, as the vision portrays, YHWH fills not only the temple, but also the world (cf. 1, 3), such that his sovereignty extends over all creation. The glory of the entire earth fades in light of God's judgment (24:4–10) and he tears apart all supposed authority structures, whether hosts of heaven or earthly kings (v. 21; cf. 40:23).

These examples show how Isaiah uses wordplay based upon his vision to demonstrate the nature of the lordship of God and the nature of sin. In Isaiah, God often views sin as antithetical to his person and his agenda to reign. It poses as a competitor or counterfeit to the true nature of his sovereignty and contradicts the glorious outcome portrayed in the vision. Thus, God judges Israel and the nations for their insult to his kingship. Such punishment brings down (2:11) that which was "high and lifted up" and thereby paves the way for the revelation of the only one who truly is "high and lifted up" (33:10).

Re-centralized Authority in YHWH

This revelation indicates that all authority should go to the one who always possessed such power, YHWH. The eschatological portrayals in Isaiah connected with his vision (e.g., 11:1–16; 32:1–8; 54:1–10) all point to such a reality. After God has judged the nations and humbled them, the Lord reestablishes his authority in a restored Davidic dynasty (11:1; 32:1). The dynamics that exist between YHWH and the Davidic house merit a separate discussion and will be covered in a subsequent section. Nonetheless, what characterizes this king is the pervasiveness of justice and righteousness under his rule (9:7; 16:5; 32:16). Although Israel's leadership had previously perverted God's authority, the Davidic king mirrors the righteousness of YHWH's rule.

---

92. Although the terms גָּאוֹן זֵדִים וְגַאֲוַת עָרִיצִים are different than the use of נשא and רום, they are semantically related and refer to the competition of man for what belongs to God. See Oswalt, *Isaiah 1–39*, 306.

This transformation extends from the leadership to the people. The inhabitants of Jerusalem care about justice and righteousness. The entire city is characterized by this uprightness (33:5). The inhabitants actually are humble, which is significant. God declares that the Holy One who is high and lifted up will dwell with those who are humble and lowly (57:15). I can make two major observations about this text: First, it alludes to Isa 6:1–3. The terms "high and lifted up" (רָם וְנִשָּׂא) as well as "holy" (קָדוֹשׁ) are found in Isaiah's vision. Second, the prophet has used the verb "made lowly" (שׁפל) to refer to God's activity to what he does to those who presume to be "high and lifted up" (2:9, 11, 12, 17; 13:11). These two observations help us understand why the holy God in the vision can dwell with his people in Isa 57:15. They have been made low by judgment so that they can acknowledge the only one who is distinct, perfect, and exalted. Israel's humility points to the fact that only the Lord is high and lifted up.

Jerusalem plays a key role in Isaiah in demonstrating God's exclusive sovereignty. The vision has already established this idea through its connection to Isa 2:2 and its depiction of Jerusalem as "high and lifted up." Thus, Isaiah's emphasis on Jerusalem's restoration makes sense. God will bring his people back from exile to Jerusalem (7:3; 10:21; 27:13; 37:31–32; 65:9). This will involve a second Exodus (41:18; 43:18–20) and judgment against other nations (43:4–20). Those nations will also participate in aiding this return from exile (43:6; 49:22; 60:4; 66:20) as well as the rebuilding of the city (60:10; 61:4), which indeed begins to make the city the center of the world as a demonstration of God's sovereignty.

The nations thoroughly recognize this reality. Not only does their participation in the rebuilding of Jerusalem evidence this, but also the fact that they worship in Jerusalem (19:23), contribute to its economic wellbeing (16:1; 18:7; 23:17–18; 60:5), join with it politically (19:18), and seek refuge there (16:4). This is not because Israel is superior to the nations or more prized by God. Rather, God's house, his holy mountain (cf. 2:2), is for all people (56:7), and his glory fills the *entire earth*. So it is that the nations recognize that the God of Israel in Jerusalem is the only one who is high and lifted up. The nations have ceased exalting themselves, their kings, and their temples in favor of seeking out the one true king, YHWH, at his temple on Mount Zion. The centralization of all political and economic transactions in Jerusalem underscores the centrality of YHWH to the whole world. They know that Jerusalem is "the city of the LORD, the Zion of the Holy One of Israel" (60:14). Ultimately, Israel and the world now recognize God as their sole king in all his beauty (33:17, 22) and proclaim "Glory to the Righteous One" (24:16a).

However, God's high and lifted up reign does not extend merely to Israel or the Gentiles, but rules over the entire cosmos. The passages that discuss YHWH's reign from Jerusalem (cf. 2:2; 4:2–5; 11:1–10; 24:1—27:13; 32:1–5; 65:18–25) also detail massive changes in creation. We already have a glimpse of this in Isa 2:4, which describes world peace. The rest of the book describes a situation that goes beyond world peace. Animals, who normally would not live in peace, live in harmony with each other and humanity (11:6–9; 65:18–25). The consequences of sin are quashed by God's holiness (11:9), supernatural powers are defeated (24:21; 27:1), and death itself is swallowed up (25:8–10; cf. 11:8–9). Life overcomes death, both for the nation corporately and for individuals over all creation (26:19; cf. 65:20).[93] At this moment, all creation reflects the exhaustive reign of God as creator; sin, Satan, and death cannot even rebut his rule.

Synthesis

Once again, the vision of the Lord seated on his throne high and lifted up is no understatement. The innertextuality shows that God rids the world of any other entity that presumes to be "high" or "lifted up" so that he alone has sovereignty. His glory fills the palace in Jerusalem even as all other palaces remain empty. Both Israel and the world recognize that God alone reigns through the physical act of going to Jerusalem. He removes any other thrones or authority and replaces them with a Davidic king who reigns as a perfect reflection of the Lord's character. This transforms the world, bringing widespread peace and victory over sin and death. All this reinforces the notion that Isaiah does not just see an abstract idea of God's sovereignty, but rather one that makes an impact on history in time and space. Isaiah sees the time when the earth recognizes that YHWH alone has all authority and power and that there is no other.

WHO IS THE "LORD" ON THE THRONE?

We have already covered the sovereignty of the "Lord" (אֲדֹנָי) on the throne. However, *who* is the person who rules and accomplishes the transforming salvation? Isaiah has already identified this individual on the throne in two ways. First, if the oracles of Isa 2 and 4 correlate with Isa 6, then YHWH is the Lord on the throne. Second, Isaiah's reaction to the vision reaffirms this. The prophet states that he has seen the king, the Lord of Hosts (6:5). Thus, we might conclude the matter of the identity of אֲדֹנָי at this point.

Is it really that simple though? The chapter immediately following Isaiah's vision may cause us to think further on this issue. The use of the term "king" (מֶלֶךְ) for Ahaz, Rezin, and Pekah (7:1), introduces an additional dynamic into the discussion. Not only does YHWH rule on his throne, but such sovereignty also interacts with that of human king(s). Because of Ahaz's unbelief, God will cause the Davidic dynasty to

---

93. Motyer, *Isaiah*, 218–20. Scholars have argued that these passages strictly refer to national resurrection. Motyer provides an excellent argument that corporate resurrection requires the reality of individual resurrection over sin and death. That factors the context of 25:6–10a and the language in the text itself. For YHWH's reign to extend over new nations and a renewed earth, surely the people within those nations must have victory over death.

collapse (7:13); however, there is hope. A child will be born into the exile eating curds and honey (vv. 15–16; cf. v. 22).[94] He will signify that God is with Israel (v. 14).

The identity of this child is traditionally messianic.[95] Some suggest him to be Mahler-Shalal-Hash-Baz, Hezekiah, Josiah, or a variety of other historical kings.[96] This also raises the issues surrounding the virgin birth and the use of Isa 7:14 in Matthew.[97] While evidence exists challenging the traditional interpretation of this text, there are also arguments to counter such allegations.[98] The debate illustrates that the text is not as clear as we would like it to be. For the purposes of this discussion, chapter 7 raises an interesting dilemma. While Isa 6 clearly makes YHWH the king, Isaiah surprisingly introduces the element of a Davidic human king. Is the ruler an earthly or heavenly king? How do they relate?

This tension continues through chapters 7–12. Isaiah 9:6 is a good example of this. Scholars agree that the passage is messianic.[99] Oswalt observes the interconnectedness of Isa 7:14 with 9:6 and 11:1–3. He says of 9:6:

94. Ibid., 86. Cf. vv. 20–21. Curds and honey are the food of poverty, which people eat because their land is desolate from the exile. This child will be born into such conditions.

95. Feinberg, "Virgin Birth," 251–58.

96. Hamilton, "The Virgin Will Conceive," 228–47; Schreiner, *New Testament Theology*, 71–73; Carson, "Matthew," 79–80; Motyer, *Isaiah*, 86–87; Watts, *Isaiah 1–33*, 136.

97. Walton, "Isaiah 7:14" 289–306; Wegner, "How Many Virgin Births," 467–84.

98. Walton, "Isaiah 7:14" 289–306. Walton challenges the traditional interpretation with lexical and contextual argumentation. He contends that the term "virgin" more aptly means "young woman." He also suggests that a non-messianic interpretation accounts for the immediate historical or contextual situation. See also Oswalt, *Isaiah 1–39*, 195–96; Wegner, "How Many Virgin Births," 468. However, the idea of a young woman who is marriageable and thereby presumably a virgin is defensible. See Wegner, "How Many Virgin Births," 471–72, as he critiques Walton's construal of the evidence for a helpful discussion. I disagree with Wegner's methodology of including Isa 7:14 in the discussion. If Isa 7:14 is the verse in question, bringing it as evidence of a certain lexical definition is circular reasoning. See also Feinberg, "Virgin Birth," 251–58; Niessen, "Virginity of the עַלְמָה," 133–41. Two passages also bring attention to this issue, including Isa 54:4, where the term is supposedly used with a barren woman, as well as Prov 30:19–20, where an adulterous woman is mentioned in the context. Reading Isa 54:4 as synonymous parallelism is misleading. Lexically, if עלמה refers to youthfulness, we are dealing with antithetical or merismatic parallelism. In the latter case, it demonstrates that Israel has been shameful in the context of her youthfulness as well as her adulthood. Seeing other prophetic appeals to Israel's youthfulness as a sexual promiscuous woman (cf. Hos 1–2) as well as the immediate context which talks about how God will be the faithful husband and make her glorious (Isa 54:5–12). Zion's perversity as the shame of her youthfulness reinforces the notion of virginity rather than counters it. Similarly, if one takes Prov 30:19–20 as the adulterous woman perverting the purity of relationship between man and עלמה, then it implies the chastity and purity of the עלמה. That too harmonizes with the notion of implied virginity in the term. Furthermore, on a contextual level, the person of Shear-Jashub (the remnant returns, 7:3) also needs to play an important role in the discussion. Immanuel not only involves the immediate issue of the aggression from the north, but also the end of exile. Grammatically, the sign relates directly to the prophecy in 7:14 and not to the destruction of the northern nations threatening the southern kingdom. Also, the construction ילד + הרה probably denotes a miraculous birth, something akin to reversing barrenness (cf. other parallel uses, Gen 16:11 and particularly, Judg 13:5). See also Kidner, "Isaiah," 639; Motyer, *Isaiah*, 90. Kidner and Motyer make good arguments against the identification with Mahler-Shala-Hash-Baz, which seems to favor the traditional interpretation.

99. Oswalt, *Isaiah 1–39*, 239. Oswalt states, "But this person will also be a child, and it is inescapable

Somehow a virgin-born child would demonstrate that God is with us (7:14). Now he says "to us a child is born" (Isaiah including himself with his people in their deliverance as he did in their sin [6:1]) and this child has those traits that manifest the presence of God in our midst. Surely this child (also described in 11:1–5) is presented to us as the ultimate fulfillment of the Immanuel sign.[100]

To further solidify these associations, I can point to the "child-redeemer" motif established when Isaiah mentions a child, or a young shoot, who becomes the vehicle of deliverance and sovereignty for the nation and the world.[101] This motif overlaps with what Isaiah saw in the vision. In the prophecy of Isa 9:6 and 11:1–3, the child becomes the foundation of the government and the one whose reign has no end. However, in the vision, YHWH reigns exclusively over the world. How can both be true? The tension is even more deliberate if Isa 11 is an expansion of Isa 6, as I have argued. A simple resolution might be to argue that YHWH reigns *through* the Davidic monarch. After all, in Isa 11:1–5, the Spirit of God empowers this individual, and he is characterized by the attributes of the Lord. The human king and the heavenly king, then, are not distinct so much as they are confluent.

That harmonization, however, has its own challenges in the details of Isa 9:6. While the ruler in that prophecy is clearly of human origin (he is a child), he is also assigned titles of divinity.[102] Wegner has pointed out the difficulties with taking such appellations as adoptionism.[103] At the very least, the names seem theophoric, or use the child to point to certain attributes of YHWH. Another alternative is that the child is himself divine.[104] This raises further questions; could the child and YHWH be the same individual?

Isaiah leaves the reader in further suspense. The human king accomplishes everything in the vision that is ascribed to YHWH's reign on the throne. The human king reigns in righteousness and justice (16:5) and is also associated with giving sight to the blind (32:1–3). Later on in the book, the Servant, another title for this individual, fulfills details of the vision.[105] He opens blind eyes (42:7) and makes people

---

that the childish aspect of the deliverer is important to Isaiah, for it appears again in 11:6, 8 (as it is, of course, implied in 7:3, 14; 8:1–4, 8, 18)." See also, Kaiser, *Messiah in the Old Testament*, 158–64; Motyer, *Isaiah*, 101–2.

100. Oswalt, *Isaiah 1–39*, 247.

101. Ibid., 239.

102. In addition to explicit titles such as "Mighty God," other terms in Isaiah only apply to the Lord. For example, no one is a "counselor" except YHWH (40:13).

103. Wegner, "Re-examination of Isaiah," 106–7. If this were a text communicating God's adoption of a human as a king, the text would include a declaration and/or be in the active. However, neither of these elements is true of this passage. No examples of ילד occur in adoption texts in the ANE, which also rules heavily against 9:6 being interpreted that way.

104. Ibid., 110–11. Motyer, *Isaiah*, 104–5. Motyer provides persuasive lexical evidence that the noun, אֵל, does not communicate divine likeness or divinity but rather means being God himself.

105. To further examine the parallels between these individuals, compare the following: The king and the Servant are both empowered by the Spirit (11:1; 42:1). They both extend justice and

righteous (53:11). He returns the remnant back to Jerusalem (49:8) and his atoning work (52:13—53:12) causes Jerusalem to lose its stigma of wickedness (54:1). His presence signals the end of God's judgment against the capital (49:14-26; 51:17) and its transformation into holiness (52:1).[106] The Servant extends God's salvation and justice *to the ends of earth* (42:4; 49:6; cf. 6:3). All authority goes to him, as kings and princes bow to him (49:7; cf. 52:15; 53:12). Thus, God's sovereign judgment to tear down all authority and to re-centralize it in YHWH is actually assigned to the Servant. We must ask once again, is YHWH himself so distinct or distant from his Servant?

The connection between the two heightens when we consider how the Servant accomplishes those tasks related to the vision that YHWH reserves for himself. The Servant saves the people, though YHWH is the only savior (43:11). The Servant makes intercession (53:12), even when God states that no one could or did but him (59:16). Moreover, the Servant displays God's glory (49:3), even though God will not share it with another (42:8).[107] Could all this indicate that YHWH and the Servant are one and the same?

At the same time, the Servant's humanity and solidarity with Israel forms a major part of Isaiah's argument. This individual contrasts descriptions of the rest of Israel in both the terms and concepts derived from the immediate context of the vision account. The Servant is not blind, as Israel is. His ears are open (50:4b-5), unlike Israel's (cf. 6:10; 48:8). No deceitfulness is found upon his mouth (53:7, 9; cf. 6:7). Rather, his tongue can sustain his people (50:4). Isaiah depicts the Servant as the perfect Israelite; the one who fits in the eschatological kingdom where Isaiah himself (and the rest of Israel) did not. This gives him the right and ability to redeem the nation. Not surprisingly, Isaiah calls the Servant "Israel," perhaps for this reason (49:3). Yet even in depicting his humanity, Isaiah still posits the Servant as the one who fulfills the vision. At this point, the prophet shows how the Servant is at least highly associated with YHWH (if not the same person), even as he is highly associated with humanity and Israel, and highly associated with the vision. How does all of this fit together? Does the Servant represent God in accomplishing the theology of the vision, or is he YHWH himself?

Isaiah resolves all of these questions in the final song of Isa 52:13—53:12. The prophet lays it before us plainly. The one who is "high and lifted up" (52:13 ;רָם וְנִשָּׂא; cf. 6:1) in the vision is none other than the Servant. He is the Lord on the throne. Kings shut their mouths at him in shocked submission (52:15) and he inherits the

---

righteousness over the earth (2:2; 9:6; 42:1–3). They both are weak, yet strong (42:3–4, 14; 50:4-5; cf. 11:1–3). They are characterized by how they grow up (9:6; 11:1; 53:1). For these reasons, scholars recognize a connection between the two. See also Chisholm, "Christological Fulfillment," 387–404. Other scholars observe significant parallels between Isa 2:2, 11:1–5, and 42:1–4.

106. Oswalt, *Isaiah 40–66*, 359. The Lord summons Jerusalem to "arise" twice in this section. In 51:9, this removes God's wrath from his people. In 54:1, this clothes them in the joy of his holiness.

107. Motyer, *Isaiah*, 386: "This is never said to any prophet or individual, or to Israel or any group within Israel. Isaiah says a unique thing about a unique person." While Isa 49:3 uses the term פאר, the word does overlap with the term "glory" (כָּבוֹד). See Isa 60:13 for an example of this.

portion of the strong (53:12). He transforms Israel by his sacrificial death and justifies them based upon his own righteousness (52:15; 53:11).[108] He is the perfect Israelite; he makes other Israelites perfect, and not just Israel, but the Gentiles as well. Because the Servant is successful and so showcases God's glory (Isa 52:13; cf. 49:3), he takes his rightful place as the one to whom all authority and glory is due. He is "high and lifted up" (52:13). This accounts for why the child/king/Servant acts like YHWH and accomplishes the vision. This also accounts for how he can empathize with Israel and substitute for God's people in his sacrifice.

This final component becomes essential for our understanding of the vision. Isaiah witnesses the culmination of history that celebrates the transforming work of God so that he might reign over and have a relationship with the entire world. However, this is not just a celebration, but also a coronation. It is the moment where the Servant takes the throne because he has wrought salvation, and God has placed all authority in his hands. He now receives his just reward for his work in bridging history with the eschatological. He has earned the right to be the sovereign over the entire cosmos, high and lifted up. However, Isaiah makes it clear that he can do this because he is not merely a man, but YHWH himself. Such tensions bring out that in Trinitarian terms, the event is not just about the Father, but equally, if not more so, about the Son.

ISAIAH'S CONTRIBUTION TO A BIBLICAL THEOLOGY OF VISION

Our discussion does not exhaustively cover the theology of Isaiah. Instead, it primarily surveys key ideas within his theology through the organizing principle of his vision to help refine our understanding of what Isaiah saw. I have outlined three major categories of tensions found in Isaiah's vision that point to three major areas of emphasis in his theology. First, Isaiah balances a tension of a kingdom in exile against eschatological hegemony. Second, he also shows the tension of God's holy, glorious presence against Israel's former sinfulness. This all contributes to the third tension between the present and the eschatological. Though future hope awaits, the present somehow must work itself out to that time.

While our discussion has analyzed several different verses pertaining to each of these subjects, Isaiah weaves all of them together for specific purposes within his book. Hence, Isaiah's present distress concerning the reign of the Davidic dynasty paves the way for YHWH to rule through an ultimate Davidic king in fulfillment of the vision (7–12). He will transform Israel, and world in the process, to perfectly reflect his glory as knowledge of him fills the earth (11:13). God's plan will work out from present to future,

---

108. Oswalt, *Isaiah 40–66*, 415–17; Motyer, *Isaiah*, 441–42. The hiphil of צדק presumes the status of an individual often expressed by a cognate (cf. 1 Kgs 8:32; Prov 17:15). This argues that the Righteous One justifies based upon his righteousness. The parallelism in Isa 53:11 confirms this. The Servant justifies as well as bears his people's sins or guilt (וַעֲוֹנֹתָם הוּא יִסְבֹּל). His work plays into forgiveness as well as justice.

because he has a plan for every nation (13–27). This includes the reality that he will bring down every authority structure and recentralize power in his rightful king. However, such domination is not tyrannical. Rather, God also transforms the nations (even Egypt and Assyria) to know and worship him. In this way, we can see that his glory filling the earth is not an understatement. The immediate interactions of Judah and Egypt (28–35), as well as Hezekiah's encounter with Assyria, serve as an initial indicator that God does rule upon the cherubim (37:16) and he has the power to save (vv. 21–28; cf. 34:1—35:8). At the same time, the judgment the King declares about exile is still true, as Babylon now gains ascendency (38:1—39:8). However, the blindness of Israel will be transformed, and a new king will come to establish righteousness (32:1–8).

God is committed to the agenda of transforming holiness and displaying his glorious sovereignty and salvation before all the world (40–48). He displays this ultimately in his Servant (49–56), who opens Israel's blind eyes and brings all the nations under his rule (42:1–9; 49:1–13). The Servant is the catalyst of what was revealed in Isaiah's vision, and in fact, the vision specifically celebrates his achievements (Isa 52:13). Hence, God confronts Israel a final time over the nation's folly in believing an idol could ever accomplish what he has promised in the vision (58–66). Israel must be blind to think that YHWH is no better than an idol, when their sins are in fact the problem (59:1–2). Instead, the Servant will restore and transform the nation, rule exclusively, and his glory will be recognized within the nation, through the nation, and by the world (61:1–11) just as the vision portrayed in microcosm. This survey shows that the role of the vision does not just provide major theological ideas for the substance of Isaiah's writing, but also gives direction to such content. From a variety of angles, Isaiah shows that God will fulfill his agenda as it is described in the vision.

This provides further confirmation and details about the nature of the vision itself. As opposed to a more generic view of God's timeless reign, the innertextuality of Isaiah positions this vision as the reality of a certain point of redemptive history. This does not mean that God is not sovereign or that he is not holy at other times. Rather, Isaiah witnesses the moment when these attributes become fully visible to all creation, when the reality of heaven completely meets earth. The visionary event commemorates the Servant's work in judging and transforming. Having accomplished such a great salvation, he then is enthroned as the exclusive ruler of all the earth, and his glory goes forth for every nation to experience and worship.

Isaiah, being the first one to see this scene, provides us a fundamental framework through which we can view the various angles of other visions. In particular, the tensions of kingdom and presence (i.e., God's holiness versus Israel's sinfulness) will be notable. Also, the logic of Isaiah's mission as active participation in moving the present forward to the eschatological will become significant in other call visions. In this way, Isaiah has laid the foundation for us to comprehend the vision and theologies of those who follow. As many have noted, he is a central prophet in biblical theology.[109]

---

109. House, *Old Testament Theology*, 272: "Few Old Testament books match Isaiah's ability to use

5

Ezekiel's Vision
Vision of Presence

COMPARING ISAIAH AND EZEKIEL

A PRELIMINARY COMPARISON BETWEEN Isaiah and Ezekiel helps demonstrate the latter's unique contribution to a theology of vision. I have already argued for the unity of their visions in chapter 3. Nonetheless, this unity does not mean their perspectives are uniform. Isaiah has set the foundational eschatological scene, one that Ezekiel builds upon by focusing on the throne central to Isaiah's vision. While Isaiah describes the throne accompanied by seraphim with relative simplicity, Ezekiel goes into exquisite detail about this chariot-throne and little else. The chariot-throne is undoubtedly the signature element of Ezekiel's vision. Consequently, it appears that the prophet "zooms in" on a specific aspect of Isaiah's vision in describing his own vision of heaven (cf. Ezek 1:1).[1]

Ezekiel's message also seems to "zoom in" on Isaiah's theology. Out of the two points of emphasis in Isaiah of kingdom and presence (i.e., God's holy presence and glory versus Israel's sinfulness), Ezekiel focuses upon the latter. While we might expect the prophet to discuss the notion of kingdom in relation to his focus on the chariot-throne, Ezekiel consistently describes that chariot-throne as the glory of God (1:28; 8:4; 43:2).[2] This suggests that his emphasis picks up on Isaiah's description of God's glory and holiness.

---

received biblical theology while introducing new theological concepts." See also Dillard and Longman, *Introduction to the Old Testament*, 276: "Many regard Isaiah as the theologian of the Old Testament."

1. Recall the previous discussion in chapter 3 concerning Ezek 1:1. All the innertextuality of Ezekiel will amplify the nature or agenda of the heavenly chariot-throne.

2. It is important to note that both visions contain references to God's throne (Isa 6:1; Ezek 1:26), the temple (6:1; Ezek 43:2–7), a restored Jerusalem (Isa 2:2; 6:1; Ezek 40:2), and the glory of God filling

A simple lexical search corroborates this conclusion. A search for specific words from Isaiah's vision within the book of Ezekiel turns up a greater frequency of Isaianic terminology for sin, holiness, and glory than expressions concerning kingdom.[3] Ezekiel describes Israel's problems in terms of God's holiness (22:26). Moreover, the prophet uses the same blind and deaf metaphors that Isaiah employed in describing the nation (12:2; cf. Isa 6:10). God's holiness judges Israel and the nations (28:22, 25; 36:20–23). His holiness also transforms, sanctifying the people (37:28; cf. Isa 4:3) and providing them with a holy temple (40–43; cf. Isa 6:1–3). At the same time, the Lord will be glorified in the midst of both Israel and the world (28:22–25; 39:21; cf. Isa 49:3). This culminates in the final vision, where his glory does indeed fill the temple and shine throughout the earth (43:2–7; cf. Isa 6:1, 3). These examples suggest that Ezekiel amplifies Isaiah's depiction of how God's holiness triumphs over sin to fill the world with his glory.

Such analysis is purely based upon lexical similarities between Isaiah and Ezekiel. If we broadened the discussion to the thematic or conceptual overlap between the two visions, the evidence would show Ezekiel's pervasive stress on the Isaianic concepts of God's holiness and glory in the midst of his people (cf. 8:5–18; 16:1–63; 22:1–31; 23:28–29). As Block observes:

> Second, although Ezekiel avoids the title "Holy One of Israel" (qĕdôš yiśrāʾēl), so common in Isaiah, the attribute of YHWH's holiness is high in his mind. From the form and radiance of the inaugural vision to the concentric gradations of holiness built into the design of the temple in the final vision (chs. 40–43), everything about YHWH's character and actions proclaims "Holy! Holy! Holy!"[4]

In addition, even in the cases where Ezekiel recounts kingdom descriptions found in Isaiah, those texts contextually serve to amplify God's relationship with his people. For example, in Isaiah, the Lord's throne was linked to his intent to have complete dominion over Israel and the world (cf. 11:1–15). In Ezekiel, God establishes his throne so that Israel would never be defiled again and so the Lord would dwell amongst them (43:7). In Isaiah, God punishes Israel's leadership for being high and lifted up, when he alone merits such status (2:11). In Ezekiel, God condemns Israel's leaders for making idols in their hearts (14:3). As a final illustration, in Ezekiel, the Lord establishes a new David as shepherd over Israel so that God might dwell with his people (34:24) in contrast to Isaiah's emphasis that the root of Jesse rules to extend the authority of YHWH (11:1–5; 42:1–4). Kingdom, in Ezekiel's theology, appears to facilitate God's presence and fellowship with his people.

---

the temple and earth (Isa 6:1, 3; Ezek 43:2). At this time, Israel will serve God on his holy mountain (Ezek 20:40; cf. 11:9; 27:13) and YHWH will dwell with his people (Isa 4:4–6; Ezek 48:35). Ezekiel, like Isaiah, associates the vision with redemptive-historical events and realities. This indicates that their visions and messages speak to the same storyline and agenda of God.

3. In comparing the frequency of terms from Isa 6:1 (e.g., כִּסֵּא, מֶלֶךְ) with terms from Isa 6:3 (e.g., קָדוֹשׁ, כָּבוֹד, מלא) the latter turns up around twice as much in Ezekiel.

4. Block, *Ezekiel*, 1:47–48.

All this supports that Ezekiel overlaps significantly with Isaiah in terms of both vision and theology. Ezekiel's vision more fully describes the throne Isaiah witnessed, and his message further explains the significance of that entity. This seems to revolve around Isaiah's notion that God will transform the world in holiness to fill the earth with his glory. Accordingly, we may initially characterize Ezekiel's vision as a vision of God's presence, a theme central to this book and widely recognized by biblical theologians.[5]

STRUCTURE AND DEVELOPMENT OF VISION IN EZEKIEL

How does Ezekiel develop the theology of his vision in the book? Herein lies another distinction between Isaiah and Ezekiel. Isaiah worked to expound upon his vision by repetition and innertextual allusion. His method was subtle and demanded more linguistic and thematic analysis. Ezekiel, by comparison, is quite explicit. Scholars notice three major passages where the prophet essentially sees the same vision (1–3; 8–11; 40–43),[6] which makes the innertextuality of his book more apparent.

That being said, Ezekiel has its own complications. For one, we encounter difficulties in determining which passage correlates with which vision. In Isaiah, all the relevant theological data went back to amplify the vision at his calling. Conversely, Ezekiel has multiple visions. How do we know whether particular material in the book relates to one vision as opposed to another? In addition, we run into problems surrounding the *nature* of such associations. Why does Ezekiel repeat the same vision? How do these reoccurring visions interrelate (if at all)?

In answering these questions, we can better formulate how Ezekiel develops the concept of the chariot-throne in his theology. The structure of Ezekiel can help us collate a certain part of the book with a corresponding vision. Ezekiel has clearly set the organization of the book using a series of discourse markers on both the macro and micro levels.[7] After organizing the book according to these indicators, we observe

---

5. House, *Old Testament Theology*, 327–28; Waltke, *Old Testament Theology*, 842–43.

6. Beale, *Temple and the Church's Mission*, 336–38; Hartenstein, "Cherubim and Seraphim," 173.

7. Scholars divide the book into four essential parts: Ezekiel's calling (1–3), Jerusalem's condemnation (4–24), the nations' condemnation (25–32), and the restoration of Jerusalem (33–48). Ezekiel's dating formulas, the parallel calling of the watchman (3:17–20; 33:1–9), and the linkages of key themes and words support this accepted structure. Technically, the structure perhaps breaks down into three parts, since chapters 25–32 concerning the judgment on the nations accompanies Jerusalem's own destruction. Such analysis also allows for a clear parallel structure between the second two parts of the book, in which God calls Ezekiel to be a watchman of his judgment and then later again for his restoration. See Alexander, "Ezekiel," 744.

Within this, Ezekiel provides other introductory formulae (e.g., "the word of YHWH came to me", 1:3; 7:1; 11:14; 21:1; 38:1) that further break down the book into subunits on a micro-level. After applying these discourse markers to the text, we derive the following flow: After Ezekiel's call (1–3), he provides a series of initial messages of judgment (4–7). He then sees God's presence leave the temple (8–11) and a series of detailed condemnations follow (12–19). God then proclaims the final judgment of Jerusalem (20–23), begins to accomplish it (24), as well as judges other nations (25–32). However,

that chapters 8–11 serve as a transitional section in the book. The passage concludes Ezekiel's opening warnings and inaugurates his declaration of the upcoming exile.[8] Chapters 8–11 include another account of Ezekiel's vision, which also seems to facilitate this transition. In Ezek 8:4, the prophet describes his vision as being like the one he had on the *plain* (cf. 3:22–23). The reference to the plain is curious, since his original experience was at the river Chebar (1:1–3). However, it appears that Ezek 8 concludes one section of the book that began with the vision on the *plain* in 3:22–23.[9] Similarly, 9:1—11:25 begins a new motif by which God's presence leaves the temple, setting up for his return in the final vision of 43:2–7. Thus, part of the reason that 8–11 transitions from one section of the book to another is because Ezekiel's visions actually conclude one unit of the book and start another.

This helps us to arrange the material around the visions. A vision begins and ends certain sections of the book. Ezekiel's vision on the plain marks the beginning of one section (3:22–23), which ends when he has another vision just like it (8:4). Another section begins right after as Ezekiel sees the glory of God departing from the temple (9:1—11:25). That unit concludes when God's glory returns to the temple (43:2–7). Thus, the material within 3:22–23 and 8:4—11:25 corresponds to those visions, and the material between 9:1—11:25 and 40–48 corresponds to those two visions.

Having collated segments of the book with their respective visions, I can move to answer how the visions (and their corresponding material) relate. We might perceive them as completely independent oracles with no developmental relationship to each other.[10] Block's suggestion is better; namely, Ezekiel engages in *resumptive exposition*. That is, Ezekiel introduces a concept at one point in the book and then elaborates upon it later. Block's first and primary example of this actually is the visions.[11] However, other instances also exist.[12] If this is the case, Ezekiel designed the book such that each set of visions expands upon the previous, with the final being the fullest explanation of them all. This allows the reader to progressively wade through the depth of Ezekiel's dense vision and theology.

Such a suggestion has exegetical merit. In Ezek 43:3, the prophet records that his vision was "like the vision which I saw when he came to destroy the city. And the visions *were* like the vision which I saw by the river Chebar." This phrase appears

---

even after Jerusalem's fall (33:1), God summons Ezekiel to watch again as God works to restore his people (33–39). This culminates in a vision of God's glory filling the temple (40–48).

8. Block, *Ezekiel*, 1:272–73.

9. Zimmerli, *Ezekiel*, 277.

10. Allen, *Ezekiel 1–19*, xxv; Zimmerli, *Ezekiel*, 40–50. Such may be the viewpoint of those who engage in an elaborate compositional-history scheme.

11. Block, *Ezekiel*, 1:23.

12. Ibid.; Block lists as examples "the charge to the prophetic watchman (3:16–21; 33:1–9), Ezekiel's muteness (3:26–27; 33:22), security in Jerusalem portrayed as a pot (11:1–12; 24:1–14), the harlotries of Israel presented in allegorical form (chs. 16, 23), the problem of hubris (28:1–19; 29:1–8), and the doctrine of personal responsibility for one's fate (18:1–32; 33:10–20)."

to trace back through the book. It mentions the vision in chapters 8–11, when God came to destroy the city, as well as chapters 1–3, when he appears at the river Chebar. Hence, this verse implies that Ezekiel's final vision encompasses the previous ones, thus illustrating the concept of resumptive exposition.

Moreover, the vision in Ezek 43 mirrors what happens in those previous experiences. Ezekiel falls on his face (43:3) just as he did previously (1:28; 3:23). The Spirit lifts Ezekiel up (43:5) like before (3:14; 11:1). The proclamation is also similar. Earlier, God declares that the Lord is blessed in his *place* (3:12). In this passage, the Lord proclaims that this is the *place* of his throne (43:7). Thus, not only does 43:3 claim to be resumptive, the context of the passage demonstrates that this is the case. The recapitulation of prior visions in the final vision shows that it is the fullest portrayal of the theological significance of the visions. Block's suggestion of how passages build upon one another is a solid model for how the visions relate to each other.

Putting all of this together, Ezekiel develops his theology of divine presence almost like a layered cake. His call vision forms the foundational layer (1:1—3:13). The subsequent two layers each begin with the appearance of the chariot-throne and end with a corresponding vision (3:14—8:18; 9:1—48:35). These layers build on top of each other to formulate the entire significance of the heavenly chariot-throne. In this way, these theological layers provide us a framework to ascertain Ezekiel's thoughts about his vision as he develops it throughout his writing. This chapter will trace his theology of vision based upon this paradigm.

CHARIOT-THRONE AS COSMIC PRESENCE

The opening of the book introduces the reader to Ezekiel's fundamental symbolism. To the modern reader, this chapter can seem cloaked in mystery. However, there are certain factors that help us grasp its meaning. The structure is actually quite clear. Ezekiel first describes the "engine" of the chariot, or the angelic creatures (1:5–14).[13] He then shifts his attention to the chariot itself (vv. 15–21) and the throne upon the chariot (vv. 22–27). Each piece of this portrait contributes to the notion of divine presence. Furthermore, examining each element of the description through the lens of ANE culture proves to be illuminating.

The basic idea of this chariot is the mobile and unhindered presence of God. Verse 4 presents the chariot speeding toward Ezekiel as a cloud from the north. Since the enemies of Israel were located in the north, God's presence evidently overcame that obstacle to reach Ezekiel.[14] God's presence cannot be stopped by foreign powers; he goes where he wishes. The lightning flashes accompanying this chariot signal that

---

13. The angels are technically not the engines of the vehicle. As we will see, they do not move the chariot, but instead follow the Spirit's movement (1:12).

14. Block, *Ezekiel*, 1:92, contra Cooper, *Ezekiel*, 63.

God's glory is indeed in view (cf. 1:27 for the same wording) but needs further definition and confirmation.

As the chariot draws near, Ezekiel begins to describe the chariot in terms of the living creatures that "pull" the divine throne. In the ANE, such beings were divine guardians and an extension of a god's power to war against his enemies.[15] Thus, the creatures in their appearance not only facilitate the movement of God's presence, but also reflect a message about his glory. The end of this section actually emphasizes that purpose. Ezekiel reveals that these creatures do not technically move the chariot-throne. Their wings are not for locomotion, but rather for covering. Their legs are straight and unmoving (vv. 7, 11).[16] Instead, the Spirit moves, and the creatures can seamlessly follow (v. 12). Accordingly, all their qualities are not to move the chariot, but rather to mirror the nature of God's unhindered presence.

With this in mind, the *four* living beings each have *four* faces, *four* wings, and hands on all *four* sides (1:5–8). The repetition of the number four corresponds to the four cardinal directions. Because the creatures face every side, they always go straight (v. 9). This portrays how God's presence can go directly in any trajectory he chooses. Additionally, the wings shield the angels from God's holiness on every side. His holiness is as pervasive as his presence.

The four faces of a man, lion, bull, and eagle all represent these creatures' different qualities (v. 10). They bear the wisdom of a man, the strength of a lion, the power of a bull, and the swiftness of an eagle.[17] As they move, they "carry" God's presence with corresponding grace, might, and skill. They do so with incredible speed, like a bolt of lightning (v. 14), for God's presence is incredibly mobile.

However, these specific characteristics are held in tension with the creatures' overarching function, as communicated by their title. They are called "living creatures" (1:5). The title stresses their place in creation.[18] In doing so, the imagery discussed above begins to imply a parallel idea. Not only is God's presence swift and unrestricted, it also inherently extends over the earth. The physical appearance of the angels depicts the creatures that rule over earth and sky. Thus, they seem to function collectively as a microcosm of creation.[19] God's throne is above these creatures, signaling his dominion over heaven, earth, and all that is in them—the entire cosmos. This compliments the notion of God's omnipresence and conceptually matches Isaiah's idea that God's glory will fill the earth (cf. 6:3).[20]

---

15. Hartenstein, "Cherubim and Seraphim," 173–74; Block, *Ezekiel*, 1:94–95; Allen, *Ezekiel 1–19*, 31.

16. Barrick, "Straight-Legged Cherubim," 543–55.

17. Block, *Ezekiel*, 1:96.

18. Wacholder, "Creation in Ezekiel's Merkabah," 14–18.

19. Ibid., 14–32. Wacholder's essay points out numerous points of overlap between the creation account and Ezekiel's vision.

20. Cooper, *Ezekiel*, 66–67.

Ezekiel continues to describe the chariot itself with particular attention to the wheels (vv. 15–21). Once again, there are four of them, indicating omni-directional capabilities (v. 15). The wheel within a wheel may also contribute to that notion, since one wheel could move backward and forward, while the other could move left and right. This would allow the chariot to move without turning, just as Ezekiel observed (v. 17). The wheels amplify the unrestricted presence of God. Consequently, they are filled with eyes, which may indicate the Lord's all-seeing presence. The description also could denote a jewel shaped like an eye, which would be quite dazzling. This interpretation also reflects the majestic glory of God.[21] The Spirit animates the wheels, and thus the wheels directly represent the nature of God's workings. He can move and work in any direction he chooses instantly; he is omnipresent.[22] In fact, his presence is also in the midst of the wheels (v. 20). If the chariot reflects the cosmos, the workings of the wheels emphasize God's omnipotent immanence over all creation.

Such a notion finds further support in the next verses, which begin the discussion concerning YHWH's throne (vv. 22–27). Ezekiel mentions a רָקִיעַ above the angelic creatures (v. 22). The expanse or firmament is reminiscent of Gen 1:6. We have already observed a creation motif apparent in the angels' title and faces. Here is another: the chariot seems to represent all of creation as it is filled by God's dominion and presence. This is perhaps why the angels hide themselves behind their wings (v. 23); God's presence comes from heaven and extends throughout all the cosmos.

In addition, the chariot-throne as a microcosm of creation makes it actually quite similar to the temple. Some have observed that the temple ornaments and decorations are meant to resemble Eden and the world (cf. 1 Kgs 6:32; 7:44).[23] This imagery positions the chariot as something of a temple on wheels. This association will be confirmed later (cf. 8:4; 9:1—11:25) and so we will save it for further discussion (as Ezekiel does). Nonetheless, we can understand where Ezekiel is going. The connection between the temple and chariot-throne will also help us identify other ways Ezekiel later ties his theology to the vision. In this context, the prophet has already declared that the temple is not just a building, but also the place where God's presence dwells; that is, the whole earth. The assertion that Isaiah viewed the world as a cosmic temple (6:3) is picked up explicitly by Ezekiel, which some scholars consider as God's heavenly or cosmic presence.[24]

---

21. Block, *Ezekiel*, 1:99–100.

22. Ibid., 100–102; Cooper, *Ezekiel*, 68–69. Block observes that the Spirit of the living creatures ties the Spirit back to the angels. The angels reflect the Spirit's power as well as that of the chariot and wheels.

23. Beale, *Temple and the Church's Mission*, 36–37.

24. Ibid., 343–44. This is not just demonstrated visually, but also audibly. The angels' wings sound like abundant waters, an army, or even the voice of God himself, reflecting his thunderous noise. However, that cannot even compare with the voice of God, which comes from above the firmament. That itself causes the angels to cease their sound so that his voice can be heard (vv. 24–25). If the angels serve as a symbol of God's intention with all creation, the world must magnify and point to the glory

The description of the throne reinforces the connection between God's presence and the temple (vv. 26–27). God's throne is characterized by lapis lazuli, a precious stone (סַפִּיר, v. 26). The rare term is found in Exod 24:10 to describe what surrounded God's presence at Sinai. The allusion may show that the chariot-throne in Ezekiel parallels how God manifested himself on Sinai to give the law, to commune with the elders of Israel, and then to dwell in the tabernacle. The chariot-throne may share a similar functionality to Sinai and the tabernacle in mediating God's presence.

We also see further evidence that the chariot-throne links with creation and represents God's cosmic presence in the prophet's description of him who sits on the throne. At the end of his first vision, Ezekiel sees one with the appearance of a man (v. 26b). This could be an anthropomorphic accommodation.[25] However, could this also further connect the chariot-throne with the creation account that concludes with God making man in his own image?[26] Considering the description under that context, God creates man in his image in order that he might rule and fill the earth (Gen 1:26–28). Man would thereby mediate God's authority and presence to the world. Coupled with the creation motif in Ezekiel's vision, could God's appearance as a man signal that in the end, he will ultimately be the one who fills the earth with his glory?[27]

While God appears to resemble a man, he certainly cannot be equated with man. Every part of his "body" is characterized by light. While the portrayal of the individual on the throne is brief in comparison with previous descriptions, Ezekiel has rhetorically anticipated this moment. Starting from verse 4, the prophet makes mention of light and fire in the midst of the chariot. This continues into verse 13, when he describes the living creatures. With each use, this motif of light heightens the sense of mystery in the account. That which is hidden is now revealed. The terms glowing metal (חַשְׁמַל), light (נֹגַהּ), and fire (אֵשׁ) in verses 4 and 13 are now all ascribed to God, who is shown seated on the throne in verse 27. He alone makes up the mystery and the brilliance that surrounds the throne. His unspeakably holy self is unveiled in splendor.[28] Ezekiel struggles to adequately describe the blinding radiance of the Lord, for he is limited to mere comparisons, and ultimately concludes that he has seen the glory of the Lord (v. 28). With that, he falls on his face, evidence of the overwhelming presence of God.

In concluding this way, Ezekiel expresses the main import of the chariot-throne, which is that it displays the complete, unique glory of God. Every part of this vision contributes to two major complimentary ideas in our understanding of God's presence. First, God is not spatially restricted. Contrary to those who thought God's presence was confined to the temple of Jerusalem, God reveals to Ezekiel that his

---

of YHWH in every regard.

25. See Allen, *Ezekiel 1–19*, 35; Cooper, *Ezekiel*, 70–71.
26. Ibid.; Wacholder, "Creation in Ezekiel's Merkabah," 25–32.
27. Beale, *Temple and the Church's Mission*, 82–84.
28. Block, *Ezekiel*, 1:104; Allen, *Ezekiel 1–19*, 35; Cooper, *Ezekiel*, 70.

glory goes directly wherever he wishes, with inexorable speed and without restraint.[29] Ultimately, he is omnipresent.[30] Second, it is revealed that God intends to exhibit his omnipresence over all creation. Creation is the temple where he will dwell. The entire account mirrors Gen 1, with its animals (the living creatures) and firmament, and ultimately one like a man who reigns over and fills it all.

EZEKIEL'S CALL: GOD'S INDWELLING PRESENCE

Ezekiel's calling offers interesting innertextuality with the vision he has just witnessed. These dynamics will be pivotal in understanding the theological development of vision for the rest of the book. Like Isaiah, Ezekiel's experience is formative for his ministry; in fact, his calling will be a microcosm of what he will proclaim to Israel. This embodies both Israel's problem and solution, which all relates to the presence of God presented in the first chapter.

Israel's Problem as Being Relationally Dead

Initially, Ezekiel's call demonstrates the basic nature of Israel's problem in the book. Upon seeing the glory of the Lord, he falls on his face and is incapable of standing, contrary to the Lord's command (2:1). He is almost like a dead man. The problem is solved when the Spirit enters Ezekiel and brings him to his feet. Accordingly, the prophet devoid of God's presence is an essentially lifeless man.

In this passage, God characterizes Israel's difficulty as analogous to Ezekiel's. He shows that the nation's dilemma is an internal problem that corresponds with the need for the Spirit to come *into* Ezekiel. The Lord declares that the people of Israel are rebellious (2:3–7) but specifically that Israel has a "strong heart" (הזק, v. 4). This plays off of Ezekiel's name, which means, "God strengthens" or "God is strong."[31] Israel resists God from within. This notion becomes critical in Ezekiel's theology. Israel cannot love God because of their calloused nature (cf. 3:9).

This inner coldness translates into an external reality. Along with Israel's hard heart comes a hard face, often translated as "stubborn" (קְשֵׁי פָנִים, 2:4). Israel's face is likened to the toughness of a rock (cf. 3:9), depicting the nation more as a statue than a living being.[32] Israel's corrupt heart has made its people completely unresponsive, a stone unable to interact with God. Later, God re-characterizes his people as having unintelligible speech and difficult language (3:5). The words for "difficult language"

---

29. Cooper, *Ezekiel*, 64–65.
30. Ibid.; Allen, *Ezekiel 1–19*, 27; House, *Old Testament Theology*, 329–31.
31. Block, *Ezekiel*, 1:129.
32. Note how the terms "hard" and "strong" parallel God's comparison of Ezekiel's face to a rock (3:9). Cf. Block's discussion on how Ezekiel is a "living human idol" versus what Israel worships and becomes, dead idols, in ibid., 157–58. See also Beale, *We Become What We Worship*, 38–49.

(כִּבְדֵי לָשׁוֹן) actually are a "heavy" or "glorious" tongue. As in Isaiah, God shows how the people have perverted his glory and become dull. Unlike Isaiah, this change does not seem to stress negative transformation (falling short of God's glory) but rather emphasizes that the people are incapable of responding to God. In context, the Lord explains that even though Ezekiel ought to communicate easily with Israel, its people cannot talk or listen and thus are relationally dead (3:6–7). Their deadness parallels Ezekiel's reaction to God's glory in this regard—those who are devoid of God's presence are incapable of having a relationship with the God who dwells over the cosmos. As noted, Ezekiel needed the Spirit to come within him to properly respond to God's presence (Ezek 2:2–3). Accordingly, Israel and Ezekiel share the same problem of being relationally dead. Those devoid of God's presence are incapable of having a relationship with the God who dwells over the cosmos.

God's Indwelling Eschatological Presence

However, Ezekiel does not remain paralyzed. The Spirit of God enters him and causes him to stand and respond to God (2:2–3). While Isaiah concerns himself with transforming holiness, Ezekiel focuses on death to Spirit-empowered life (cf. Ezek 36:26–27; 37:1–14).[33] The Spirit's indwelling is particularly significant to Ezekiel's theology of vision. This is not the first appearance of the Spirit. Rather, he is the one who drives the chariot-throne (1:12, 20, 21). Now his presence dwells in Ezekiel. This establishes an important aspect of the message surrounding the chariot-throne. I have argued that the chariot-throne depicts a microcosm of creation. God's presence reigns over all creation and the world serves as a sort of cosmic temple for him to reside within. The Spirit's intimate communion with Ezekiel clarifies that God's filling of the earth is not only extensive but also *intensive*. His glory does not only cover the breadth of the entire universe; it extends into internally into man's own person.

One may object to this suggestion by claiming that this communion relates to Ezekiel alone. Certainly that is the bare minimum; however, two arguments indicate that the application is broader. First, the logic between Isaiah's call vision and theology was that the prophet served as an example of what would take place corporately. That could be happening in this instance. Second, later parts of Ezekiel confirm that this is indeed the case. Ezek 36:26–27 show that God's Spirit will dwell within individual Israelites. Therefore, Ezekiel's calling introduces us to the full nature of God's eschatological presence. He will dwell from the inside (of his people) out (to the entire cosmos). This will solve Israel's predicament, as it did Ezekiel's.

---

33. Block, *Ezekiel*, 1:114; Alexander, "Ezekiel," 761. Scholars note that Ezekiel is the prophet of the Spirit. House, *Old Testament Theology*, 341; Schafroth, "Exegetical Exploration of 'Spirit' References," 61.

Ezekiel's Present Mission as God's Temple

Therefore, in a sense, the prophet himself becomes a temple of God, able to do his will just like the chariot-throne.[34] This notion becomes central in the prophet's ministry. The Lord frames Ezekiel's work around two sets of commands: to not fear Israel in preaching the word (2:6–7; 3:4–10), and to listen to the word, unlike the nation itself (2:8—3:3, 10–11).[35] Both of these instructions directly relate to Ezekiel as God's human temple. They also help us understand the subtleties of God's presence better in Ezekiel's theology.

God's initial command to Ezekiel to be fearless actually posits the prophet's mission as a "battle of presences." In essence, God pits his presence, mediated by Ezekiel, against Israel. God tells the prophet to not be dismayed before the presence of Israel (2:6–7). He also declares that he will make Ezekiel's "face" harder than Israel's (3:8). I should make three observations about this latter statement. First, the word "face" is actually the same word as "presence" in 2:6. Thus, Ezekiel's face being harder than Israel refers to this battle of presences. Second, *God* makes Ezekiel's face harder than Israel's. This is not, then, merely a battle between the prophet and the people, but actually concerns God's workings through the prophet against the people. Third, the notion of "hardness" alludes to the "hardness" (חזק) of Israel's heart (2:7), which implies that God will use his prophet to ultimately crush the people's internal resistance. Overall, God's command not to fear relates to God's presence. Ezekiel's boldness will allow him to represent God's presence and so overcome the nation's defiance.

Thus, instead of fearing the people, God commands Ezekiel to speak his message to the people (2:6–7; 3:11). How does speaking the word work against fearing their presence? Once again, the innertextuality of Ezekiel's call with the opening vision may provide an answer. The prophet earlier associates the "word of the Lord" with God's chariot-throne (1:3). Hence, the word represents, in some way, the very presence of God.[36] Thus, speaking the message to the people was a way to extend God's presence to them.[37] Consequently, the fact that they refuse to listen to the message is tantamount to saying they reject his presence. This rejection reiterates their relational deadness. The Lord already hints at this concept in describing his people as those who transgressed not only against his law, but also *against him* (2:3).

The association between God's word and presence actually helps explain the second set of commands. The Lord commissions Ezekiel to not be like rebellious Israel, but rather to fill his being with the word (3:1–3) and to listen carefully so as to put the

---

34. Odell, "You Are What You Eat," 229–48. Parallel to this idea, Odell points out that imbibing the scroll represents Ezekiel becoming the embodiment of the priesthood.

35. Cooper, *Ezekiel*, 74–80; Block, *Ezekiel*, 1:113.

36. Robson, *Word and Spirit in Ezekiel*, 24–25. Robson argues convincingly that word and spirit are intertwined in Ezekiel.

37. This may explain the repeated use of the phrase "the word of the Lord came to me" within the book. Ezekiel mediates God's presence in his word to the people.

word upon his heart (3:10). Why so much emphasis on the word? Such is certainly the mark of a godly minister.[38] Moreover, in light of the above discussion, the emphasis on the word may be another way to stress God's presence. Ezekiel's transformation in 2:8—3:3 seems to confirm that idea. God commands Ezekiel to eat the scroll and to fill himself with the book. This activity seems to parallel the Spirit's work in Ezekiel. The act of eating internalizes God's word, corresponding to the Spirit's indwelling (2:2). The scroll *fills* the writer's stomach just as God's Spirit *fills* the chariot (1:18) and later *fills* the temple (43:5). Once full of the scroll, the prophet is sympathetic with God's purposes. The judgments and woe that should have been bitter become sweet to him (2:10; 3:3b), which corresponds to how the Spirit empowered Ezekiel to follow God (2:2b). These parallels argue that the Spirit is highly connected with his word. Word and Spirit engage in the same kind of activities in Ezekiel. Thus, God calls Ezekiel to demonstrate that he is filled with the divine presence just as he is filled with his word, for that is how he will specifically exhibit God's presence amongst the people.

All of this evidences that God's interaction with the prophet makes him like a temple to represent God's presence to the people. Ezekiel speaks God's presence amongst them and is controlled by the word as evidence that God dwells in him.[39] Once again, this reaffirms that God's presence extends not only throughout the cosmos, but also intends to dwell in the human heart.

From Present to Eschatological

Ezekiel's call experience concludes with what he first saw: God's glory.[40] The Spirit lifts him up (3:12) and he hears God's blessing upon "his place" (3:13) (מִמְּקוֹמוֹ).[41] Commentators note that doxology seems out of place in the prophet's call and emend the text to read "when the glory rose."[42] However, external textual critical evidence still favors a doxology, and so the MT reading should be retained.[43] As such, it may parallel

---

38. Alexander, "Ezekiel," 763.

39. Other associations between Ezekiel's presence and YHWH's presence exist. For example, the prophet's purpose in ministry is also linked to God's presence. The Lord commands Ezekiel to speak his words and explains that whether Israel listens or not, its people will know a prophet has been amongst them (2:5). The use of "know" (ידע) is particularly interesting. A repeated refrain in the book states that Israel and the nations will know that YHWH is the true God (7:27; 11:10; 13:23; 20:44). In fact, this is the main use of the verb "to know" in the book. There may be an association between the two. The prophet's ministry would result in the people knowing God's representative had been in their midst, which brings about their knowledge of the true God himself. This supports our suspicion that Ezekiel represents God's presence to Israel as a Spirit-filled human temple.

40. Alexander, "Ezekiel," 764; Allen, *Ezekiel 1–19*, 43. Alexander rightly considers this as an inclusio, further demonstrating that this concludes a structural unit.

41. Cooper, *Ezekiel*, 82.

42. Block, *Ezekiel*, 1:133–34.

43. No other source supports the emendation. Block supposes this comes from an early corruption. However, without evidence, this is quite speculative.

the final vision in which God declares that the temple is the *place* of his throne and dwelling (43:7). If this is the case, then Ezekiel's initial vision not only includes the beginning of the book, but also anticipates the ending. Furthermore, it shows, like Isaiah, that Ezekiel's vision is not just an abstract picture of God's omnipresence, but one associated with an eschatological event. This connection will become apparent as Ezekiel develops the theology of his vision.

Like Isaiah, Ezekiel's commissioning is a microcosm of his message. Namely, that God intends to show in the chariot-throne that his presence is unlimited, and in fact, will fill the entire earth. This will take place in spite of Israel's recalcitrance, because the Lord will dwell within its people and transform them into individual temples to be a part of his cosmic temple. Ezekiel's own experience evidences this intent. Ultimately, God will change the nation's defiance into doxology. They will acknowledge that God's glory is blessed in his place. The prophet's mission specifically participates in this scheme as a representative of God's presence to Israel. In this way, he works toward the actualization of the vision in history. Like Isaiah, the vision is the *telos* of Ezekiel's ministry. It relates to the fulfillment of God's particular theological agenda in redemptive history.

THE CRISIS OF PRESENCE: THE QUESTION OF GOD'S CORPORATE PRESENCE

Confusion of the Eschatological with the Present

After the call vision, Ezekiel begins his ministry by exhibiting the nature of God's presence to Israel. The next "layer" of information starts from the context of Ezekiel's vision on the plain (3:14–27) to the next vision, which is like the one on the plain (8:4–18). Ezekiel focuses on Israel's need for God's life-giving Spirit in light of the current redemptive-historical situation. This is particularly important because Israel simply did not believe that there was a problem within their relationship with God. They assumed that God's presence would always dwell with them. Jerusalem was YHWH's chosen city (Pss 87:1–7; 132:13) because God had placed his temple there (1 Kgs 8:44, 48, 11:13), leading them to believe that the capital was therefore inviolable.[44] Their essential equation was that God's presence was an automatic guarantee of protection and blessing. For him to do otherwise would be betrayal or abandonment. Jeremiah rebukes this mentality by declaring that Israel should not repeat "the temple of the Lord" as a catchphrase for their security (Jer 7:4).

The problem with Israel's thinking is that God's promises of presence do not *always* mean that all would be relationally well or that Jerusalem would be safe. They failed to understand that while the Lord may have guaranteed a certain outcome to his promises (Isa 2:2; Ps 68:15–16, 29) a tension remains with the current system of

---

44. Block, *Ezekiel*, 1:7–8.

covenant blessings and curses (cf. Deut 28:15–68). These were not the eschatological people of God transformed by the Spirit. Instead, they were still intent on sinning and offending the Lord, which would result in the exile according to the covenant (Deut 28:63–65). In essence, their mistake was in confusing the eschatological with the present. The people's false theology needed to be challenged and properly redefined, which the upcoming collapse of Jerusalem (cf. Ezek 33:21–22) would make quite clear.

Hence, Ezekiel intends to revamp Israel's false theology of presence. The people must be made to understand the current negative status of their fellowship with God. Contrary to popular opinion, their relationship is actually at a breaking point in light of their sin. The following section will expand on why this is the case.

Vision on the Plain as Symbolic of the Problem of Presence

Ezekiel's vision on the plain introduces the reader to the problem of God's presence. In context, the call vision has ended, and the Spirit transports Ezekiel back to the exiles (3:13). After seven days, the Lord tasks Ezekiel to be the watchman for Israel (3:16–21). His message will contain warnings from God himself (3:17). This reinforces Ezekiel's mission of representing the Lord's presence. However, Ezekiel is angry and resists his calling, which is natural, yet somewhat surprising. God's assignment to the prophet is difficult, and so anyone might resent the commission.[45] At the same time, the entire point of Ezekiel's call was to demonstrate an internal transformation. How can this be if he resists?

The rest of the passage seems to resolve this issue. Hence, he not only states that the prophet rages, but also that God's hand is strong upon him (3:13). Ezekiel has already used the phrase "hand of the Lord" as another way to summarize the entire vision (1:3). The term "strong" plays off of Ezekiel's name, and also on how God's presence would be stronger and harder than the hard heart of Israel (cf. 3:9). It appears that God's "battle of presences" with Israel is now depicted between the Lord and Ezekiel. The prophet resists God the same way Israel has. Presumably, God's hand will have the victory over the prophet.

The vision on the plain accomplishes this task (3:22–27). The "hand of the Lord" compels Ezekiel to go to the plain (v. 22). Ezekiel sees the same presence of God he witnessed on the river Chebar and is completely incapacitated (v. 23). The Spirit again dwells within Ezekiel and overpowers him to stand (v. 24). God commands the prophet to undertake his mission by going back to his home (v. 24) and speaking to Israel whether they listen or not (v. 27). From this point forward, God will directly control Ezekiel's mouth to say exactly what the Lord desires him to say (v. 26). This would occur for the next seven years until the fall of Jerusalem (cf. 1:1; 33:21). If, at this moment, Ezekiel represents rebellious Israel, the vision shows that God's presence

---

45. Cooper, *Ezekiel*, 82; Block, *Ezekiel*, 1:135–37.

will overcome resistance. However, the duration of Ezekiel's "muteness" corresponds to the days when he was angry: a year for each day.[46] The vision, then, also serves as a demonstration that God's presence is not necessarily a blessing. Rather, he overpowers Ezekiel's defiance in order to accomplish his will and consequently will *judge* the prophet for his stubbornness.

Ezekiel's Consequent Message to Israel

Accordingly, Ezekiel enacts what God showed him in the vision on the plain. The way Ezekiel interacts with Israel corresponds to God's interaction with Ezekiel. Thus, when Ezekiel locks himself in his home (3:24), he demonstrates that God's presence is now inaccessible to the people even though he is present.[47] The prophet is to bind himself with the aid of the people (v. 25). This seems to signify that the disconnection of God's relationship with his people is mutual. They reject him ("bind him") as well. Ezekiel's mouth is shut so that he cannot speak as an אִישׁ מוֹכִיחַ (v. 26). The phrase, commonly translated as "rebuke," actually denotes legal mediation.[48] The Lord has cut off communication with his people; there is no more intercession, only judgment.[49] The vision reveals an aspect of God's presence that Israel has not been willing to contemplate: God's presence does not always bring with it all the positive benefits of a covenant relationship. His presence in a relationship can be offended and bring down punishment.

The prophet visibly reinforces this reality. As he acts out the siege of Jerusalem, he places the city "before him" or "in his presence" (פָּנֶה, 4:1, 3). He sets his face against the city (v. 7). The use of "face" or "presence" reminds readers of the very words associated with God's presence in the vision (1:6–8) as well as in Ezekiel's call (3:8). In this scenario, the Lord is present amongst his people, but against them. In fact, God instructs Ezekiel to put an iron plate between the city and himself to show that God's decision is final; no one can intercede to alter the course (v. 7). The outbreak of wrath is imminent. This indeed is a crisis of presence.[50]

Sin and Judgment in Relational Terms

This crisis stems from the reality that sin itself is relational. As Ezekiel's calling portrays, Israel is relationally dead. The discussion in chapters 3–7 expands upon this notion. Ezekiel connects Israel's wickedness with the theology of his vision by showing how its people treat God's temple. We have already noted that the chariot imagery

46. Block, *Ezekiel*, 1:158.
47. Cooper, *Ezekiel*, 87; Block, *Ezekiel*, 1:154–56.
48. Cooper, *Ezekiel*, 87; Block, *Ezekiel*, 1:154–56.
49. Allen, *Ezekiel 1–19*, 61.
50. Ibid.

is associated with the temple concept. As such, in Ezekiel, God's presence does not merely pertain to the cosmos or the heart of an individual, but also to the corporate nation via a physical temple.

This being the case, Israel's actions toward the temple exhibit their attitude towards God's presence.[51] God points out Israel's unfaithfulness to him in having defiled his house with idols (5:7). In fact, God later labels such idolatry as adultery from the heart, which offends him (6:9).[52] This reiterates that corporate sin is still an *internal problem*, as Ezekiel's call demonstrated (cf. 2:1–2). Such descriptions illustrate an additional perspective of idolatry in terms of God's presence. In contrast to Isaiah's concept of negative transformation, in Ezekiel idolatry is wrong because it constitutes infidelity to what is sacred, trades the true presence of God for another, and thereby insults him.

Interestingly enough, God designs Israel's judgment to bring out this reality. Israel's people receive exactly what they deserve. God will allow the temple and its beautiful relics to be profaned by foreigners (7:22–24). In Ezekiel, that punishment unveils the true nature of the relationship between God and the nation. Just as the foreigners desecrated the temple, so God shows that Israel's harlotry violated their relationship.[53] Similarly, during the siege and after, Israel will be unclean amongst the nations, as the prophet would provocatively portray (4:13–14). The use of the Levitical term "unclean" (טָמֵא) again exhibits Israel's status relative to God's temple and presence.[54] If Ezekiel is a representative of God's presence, then perhaps the prophet's disgust and abhorrence of being unclean reflects God's own viewpoint towards his people (cf. 4:14). Overall, Israel's actions have made them repulsive, as the exile will demonstrate.

God will also slaughter the Israelites "in the presence of" their idols (6:4). These "false presences" would be exploited, as Israelites would die right in front of idols that could not save them. Ultimately, the nation would learn and know that YHWH is the true God (6:10; 7:9). He had not abandoned them but was present, and because of his presence, their actions had consequences. They would come to comprehend the true demands of God's presence the hard way.

---

51. Allen, *Ezekiel 1–19*, 75. See also Cooper, *Ezekiel*, 103. Cooper notes that 5:11 is the first time God discusses the temple, to be further defined in 8:1–8, when God's presence is in the temple itself. Cooper recognizes how Ezekiel associates God's presence, Israel's relationship, and the temple. A theology of presence develops from the vision in how the prophet shapes the way sin impacts Israel's relationship with God.

52. In context, God claims that the remnant will recognize and loathe their "idolatrous/adulterous heart." They too will understand the true nature of their sin; it comes from the heart. This may point to later passages in which the Lord provides a new heart through which they can recognize the depravity of their old one. In any case, Ezekiel begins to plant initial groundings about the nature of sin in his work, specifically, its adulterous and internal nature. See Block, *Ezekiel*, 1:231.

53. Allen, *Ezekiel 1–19*, 110–11.

54. Block, *Ezekiel*, 1:185.

The Confirmation of the Concluding Vision

This all moves to the concluding vision of this section in chapter 8. The chariot-throne vision appears again, rounding out the prophet's experience on the plain (8:4; cf. 3:22–23). However, this time that presence is in the temple (8:3), which substantiates the notion that the way Israel treated the temple relates to Ezekiel's original vision. The two are explicitly related, as chapter 8 reveals. The question concerns how the inhabitants of Jerusalem will regard the Lord's presence amongst them.[55] To put it in terms of the vision at Chebar, will Israel declare the glory of God in his place (cf. 3:12)? Is Israel's corporate relationship with God on par with that eschatological reality? Is it really as grave as Ezekiel has portrayed it to be?

God reveals the depth of Israel's adultery in the temple. They have set up an idol of jealousy (vv. 5–6). The term "jealousy" often relates to adulterous practices (cf. Num 5:14; Ezek 16:42). By setting up this idol in God's house (cf. 5:11), the people of Israel are being unfaithful to their God in his own home. Their leaders are also involved in these abominable acts. They even pretend that they can hide their actions from the all-present God (8:10–12). In addition, the Lord shows that the women join in. Their act of "weeping for the Tammuz" implies that they thought God had forsaken them. Every segment of society has used the temple to commit whoredom. Finally, the ultimate insult comes. God points out how prominent leaders bow eastward to the sun. Such posture inherently turns their backs to God in the holy of holies in overt rejection.

This picture stands in complete contrast with the original vision at Chebar. The temple was supposed to radiate God's glory as a place of blessing (cf. 3:12). Israel's activity before God's presence was anything but this. God's people had filled the temple with idolatry and spiritual adultery.

Accordingly, Ezekiel reinforces that the present situation cannot be confused with the eschatological. Israel is far from blessing God's presence. From the inside out, they are spiritual harlots. Though God's agenda is clear, at this time, only judgment can come in response to such insulting wickedness. Nonetheless, the Lord will overcome these obstacles to fulfill the agenda set forth in Ezekiel's vision on the river Chebar.

THE FULFILLMENT OF GOD'S COSMIC, CORPORATE, AND INDWELLING PRESENCE

Initial Vision as God's Full Presence in Judgment and Redemption

The problem, in sum, is that Israel is not the eschatological people of God. They are devoid of the Spirit, relationally unresponsive, and spiritual adulterers. How will God resolve this crisis? Thus far, the Lord has shown that his glory will dwell on three

---

55. Ibid., 782.

levels. His presence will *extend throughout the cosmos*. He will also reside *in the human heart*. Finally, his glory relates to Israel nationally through the *temple in Jerusalem*. The final layer of visions expresses how those factors and the present situation interfaces with God's eschatological plan (9:1—11:25).

Ezekiel's vision continues right where the previous section left off. He concentrates on God's interactions with the temple and thereby his corporate relationship with Israel. Ezekiel brings further attention to this facet of God's presence by describing the living creatures as cherubim (9:3; 10:1). The change of name probably relates to his explicit association between these creatures and the temple. The cherubim were associated with God's temple presence in Israel's own worship system (cf. Exod 25:19; 1 Kgs 6:23). Thus, the issue of the rest of this section (9:1—11:25) primarily concerns how God will relate to his people.[56]

At the moment though, that very aspect of God's presence presents tremendous challenges. He cannot dwell with his people, considering their sins. The current abysmal state of Israel's corporate relationship does not match God's eschatological agenda of presence. Thus, the same chariot-throne seen at the river Chebar moves from the inner sanctuary of the temple to the threshold (v. 3). This first stage of departure culminates in 10:22.[57] Will God's departure end his relationship with his people? The prophet asks that very question (11:13).

The Lord explains that the departure of his presence signals upcoming judgment. He commands for angels to *fill* the temple with unclean corpses (9:1–2, 6–7) to show Israel how they have *filled* the land with their iniquity as opposed to the glory of God (v. 7). They will see firsthand how corrupt their relationship had become. God has revealed this before (7:22–24). Nonetheless, he also sends another angel to mark certain people for preservation (9:4). These individuals have bemoaned how Israel has treated both the temple and God himself. This demonstrates that while God's judgment is warranted, he will still be faithful to preserve the remnant with whom he can have a relationship. These select Israelites care about how they associate with him.[58] All of this evidences that God's departure balances judgment with redemption.

God provides an additional response that explains this further (11:14–21). This answer shows how his cosmic and indwelling presence work together with his corporate presence. He states that though people may have thought the exiles were the outcasts, God actually will be their sanctuary in their sojourn (vv. 14–16). God's presence is not limited to Jerusalem but instead is mobile, as the original vision portrayed. Hence, he can and will act as a temple to the people far away from the land. He will be present to gather his people, bring them home, and aid them in removing all the detestable things that caused the separation in the first place (11:17–18). As a result, the corporate relationship will be restored. To further solidify this, God will grant Israel a

---

56. Ibid., 744.
57. Ibid., 786.
58. Block, *Ezekiel*, 1:307; Alexander, "Ezekiel," 786.

new spirit and a new heart to replace their previous heart made of stone (11:19; cf. 2:4; 3:9). This alludes to what Ezekiel's calling revealed: the work of internal transformation by God's indwelling Spirit. While the prophet does not state it explicitly here, he soon will (36:26).[59] Such internal presence will also allow Israel to have a positive relationship with God (cf. 11:20a). Thus, cosmic and indwelling presence facilitates God's corporate presence. This section shows how he will forge his eschatological people.

Therefore, even though the presence of God leaves the temple and Jerusalem (11:22–25), it does not mark an end, but rather a beginning. God will fill the world in every way so that he will have the most glorious relationship with his people. They will be his people and he will be their God (11:20). God's eschatological agenda will win out. The rest of the book will detail the specifics of how all this will come to pass.

Deconstruction of Relationship: Corrupt Heart Produces Corrupt Temple

As soon as God's presence leaves Jerusalem in the vision, a series of judgment oracles ensue (12–24). They all target Israel's adultery, which stemmed from its people's corrupt hearts and rejection of God's word—problems already seen in Ezekiel's calling and vision (cf. 1:3; 2:1—3:5).[60] Israel believes the charlatans who proclaim peace and safety when the opposite is true (13:1–16). These include prophetesses who attempt to encourage Israel's sin through false oracles (13:7–23), which actually results from their rejection of his word (12:22–28). In this way, Israel has cut off communication with God. If placing God's word on the heart is indicative of his presence (cf. 3:10), then Israel has ceased relations with God and is devoid of God's presence within them.[61]

The prophet brings our attention to this state of affairs more explicitly in chapter 14. He reveals that at the core of the communication problem is Israel's heart, which is actually a temple, filled with idolatry. The elders of Israel, though they have consulted the false prophets, still come to inquire of YHWH (14:1–2). God refuses to talk with them. He states that they have "set up idols in their hearts" (14:3). This use of "heart" is quite significant, as it portrays the human heart almost like a temple where idols reside. This idea gains further legitimacy when we consider the parallels between this passage and chapter 8. Block observes a great deal of similarities between the two texts, including a community of elders desiring to consult YHWH (8:1; 14:1), the presence of elders demanding a divine response (8:2; 14:2), and the Lord subsequently refusing to heed the cry of the elders (8:17; 14:3b).[62] If these parallels are valid, then

---

59. This illustrates that the rest of the book expands upon the framework above.

60. See discussion above and also Schafroth, "Exegetical Exploration of 'Spirit' References," 61. As Ezek 37 will make clear, the Spirit operates in the word, as the prophetic word brings in the Spirit to give life, and the Spirit thereby gives effectiveness to the word spoken.

61. Allen, *Ezekiel 1–19*, 209. Allen notes that this section defines the eschatological community of God as those who would listen exclusively to him.

62. Block, *Ezekiel*, 1:421–22.

Israel's idolatry in the temple (8:3–16) corresponds to Israel's idolatry in the heart (14:3).[63] So it is that the external temple reflects the inner temple of the heart.

This highlights the level of disconnection between God and the people, not just on the level of the physical temple, but also within the temple of man's heart. Israel's heart is an abomination. As a result, Israel has lost the ability to commune with God. In context, God leaves the temple and ceases speaking to his people as a mirror to what Israel's people have already done to him within their own hearts.

If Israel's heart-temple is filled with idols, it is inherently an adulterous heart. The nation shows a singular disposition to act unfaithfully toward their God. For that reason, Ezekiel describes Israel's whoredom on a whole new level.[64] They have used God's blessings to facilitate their adultery, even paid to be unfaithful (16:15–20, 33). Equally shocking is how Israel then slaughters God's children on altars to idols (16:21). Such depictions in this section reinforce that Israel is completely dysfunctional in its covenant relationship, both on the religious level in that the nation whores after idols (16:24–25), as well as the political level in that they align themselves with other nations instead of YHWH (23:1–49). This harlotry has filled their past (20:1–49) and their present (22:1–31). This is indicative of the northern kingdom's name, Oholah (her tent), designating Israel's pagan worship. Tragically, such whoredom occurs even though the southern kingdom is supposed to be Ohlibah (my tent is in her) to signify that God dwells in Judah's midst. Overall, God has attempted to have a relationship with his people, but they have scorned him in every way, at every place, and at every time. As God stated at the very beginning, the people of Israel have rebelled and rejected YHWH from the days of their ancestors until now (2:2). They have lustful hearts (16:30) in dire need of transformation (18:31).[65] So it is that Israel's problem of indwelling presence is central to Ezekiel's theology.

God's resultant judgment reflects this issue. The Lord commands the prophet to cry out against God's holy place (21:1). The Lord even kills Ezekiel's wife (24:15–19) to bring Israel's attention to how he would remove the prize of its eyes, the sanctuary (24:21). Once again, Ezekiel's life becomes an interactive stage of God's presence. In fact, God calls him a sign to Israel (24:24–27). YHWH will abandon "her tent" and "my tent is in her" in turn, just as they did to him. This emphasis on the temple's judgment is far from incidental, for God links it to the theme of his presence. He proclaims that the covenant relationship has become so corrupted that the temple is in essence an empty shell, a place of profanity (23:38–40). So he proceeds to profane the temple to illustrate the ruptured relationship between the nation and its God (24:21).

---

63. Ibid.

64. Recall that adultery has already been used in Israel's relationship to God's presence in the temple (5:10; 6:9). This discussion continues that motif relating to the vision.

65. Zimmerli, *Ezekiel*, 345. Some have argued for a variant reading concerning God's anger based upon a related Akkadian root. Such a reading is argued to fit better in context. Zimmerli contends the opposite: that the MT reading seems to be acceptable and fits with the whole motif of adultery in the section. God works from the external reality to expose the internal problem, which fuels a host of other sins.

These dramatic measures do not stem from a hateful God. He may be jealous, as one rightfully is over an unfaithful spouse (cf. 16:38, 42), but he has explicitly repeated his purpose behind these actions. He desires Israel to know him (15:7; 21:5; 24:27). At this point, God's wrath would show Israel the true and holy God (13:21; 20:12; 22:16). They would further know him by turning away from their idols (6:13) to commune with him in a relationship (12:15). Thus, even as the Lord predicts judgment, there are hints of restoration to this very purpose (cf. 16:49–63). Overall, God has used Israel's depravity to justify exile and affirm its inevitability. God does tear down the temple, which signals the dissolution of his presence with national Israel. Nonetheless, all of this is necessary in order that it might be rebuilt anew. As the opening vision of this section articulated, this is not the end, but rather a beginning.

Reconstruction of Relationship: Re-Creation of Indwelling to Corporate Temple

Ezekiel's second call as watchman introduces a new stage in the argument of the book (33:1–33). While the first call came in the context of God's judgment against Jerusalem, this one seems to point to the nation's restoration. Much of this revolves around the innertextuality with Ezekiel's vision.

Central to this reconstruction is Ezek 36:25–27. Terms such as "heart," "clean," and "stone" found in this text have been used to discuss the dynamics of God's presence starting from Ezekiel's calling (cf. 2:1–3; 6:9; 11:19; 18:31). The phrases in that passage parallel 11:19, which itself is directly associated with one of Ezekiel's visions of the chariot-throne. Similarly, the motif of a people with a new heart continues in this latter section and serves as the basis for God's national restoration of his people (cf. 37:6–9; 39:29). That is to say, linguistic evidence supports that 36:25–27 is a major connecting point for Ezekiel's theology of vision from the beginning of the book to the end of his writings.

In this text, God sprinkles clean water on the nation (36:25). The language is Levitical, relating to Israel's ceremonial state. Their idolatry has rendered them completely unpresentable before the Lord, thereby cutting them off from his presence.[66] God cleans up his people by removing the stigma of idolatry, as well as the idols themselves, from the land (36:25b) so that communion can take place.

Conversely, such external actions cannot ultimately facilitate God's dwelling with man. After all, Ezekiel has already posited that man's heart is a temple, and Israel's heart is one filled with idols (14:3) and adultery (16:30). So it is that God provides Israel with a new heart and a new spirit, bringing forth an entirely new disposition, which is essential since Israel could never love God in its infidelity. The specific transformation from a heart of stone to one of flesh reminds readers of the nation's hard heart as mentioned at Ezekiel's calling (2:7). There, God characterized the nation as

---

66. Cooper, *Ezekiel*, 316–17.

impervious to God's word. Now, the nation that refused to listen to God in favor of false revelation will be sensitive to his decrees (36:26–27). Furthermore, readers will recall that I originally argued that Israel's hard heart made its people like statues, unable to interact with their God. The description of a heart of stone used in 36:26 can also refer to an individual who has died (cf. 1 Sam 25:37).[67] In light of this connotation, the transformation of stone to flesh means that for the first time, the people of Israel are not just spiritually dead statues, but have become living people. A relationship can now take place. Such language hints at creation terminology, as God makes the remnant new so that his presence can dwell with them. God's chariot-throne presence will fill the cosmos, a new one he is creating from the inside out.

Up to this point, Ezekiel 36:26 parallels 11:19. In Ezek 36:27, God reveals an additional and climactic reality: God will house his Spirit within each Israelite.[68] With this revelation, the metamorphosis is complete. Through the new covenant, each person transforms from having an idolatrous heart-temple to become the temple of the living God. They are thereby empowered to commune with him.

These ideas, which have been latent within our discussion thus far, become quite pronounced in 37:1–14. God equates Israel's exile with dry bones, which are inherently unclean and unable to live (37:1–3). Hence, Israel's (and Ezekiel's) state of being dead, defiled, and statue-like is all too real. To make the bones live, God initially joins the bones with flesh (vv. 7–8). However, they are not yet alive, since "there was no breath in them" (v. 7). This point underscores the need for internal rejuvenation for true life. The Lord provides this by fulfilling Ezekiel's prophecy with four winds that rise to fill these bodies with life. The word of God and "wind" or "spirit" (רוּחַ) are associated together once more. The number four in this description may correspond to the other primary use of that number in the book: the omnidirectional presence of God (cf. 1:5, 6, 8, 10, 15). Accordingly, the miracle points out that Israel has life when God's Spirit dwells within its people. God explicitly states this interpretation of the miracle in 37:14. Furthermore, such life is linked with knowing God, as he repeatedly states throughout this chapter (37:6, 13, 14). Ezek 37 confirms that Israel was dead and therefore hopeless (37:11), but God's presence is one that gives life and transforms Israel to form a relationship with him.

The rest of the chapter explains that when Israel becomes God's temple internally, then they can be his people corporately (37:15–28). The Lord has now dealt with the central problem highlighted at Ezekiel's calling and reiterated throughout the book. God has remade the idolatrous heart-temple into one where he dwells. Since this is the reason the symbol of his corporate presence collapsed (the temple), now Israel's national relationship with YHWH can be restored. This is how God's indwelling presence relates to his corporate presence (cf. 11:20). Hence, Israel will return to the land

---

67 The heart of flesh refers to that which is alive.

68. Cooper, *Ezekiel*, 317; Block, *Ezekiel*, 2:355. Block sees further confirmation of this, as individual bodies all have the Spirit to animate them to life in Ezek 37.

(v. 21), be united (v. 22), have one king (v. 24), and one covenant (v. 26). The climax of this restoration is that God sets his sanctuary in their midst and makes his dwelling with them forever (vv. 26–27). The entire chapter of Ezek 37 details how God will make his sanctuary among his people, who have his sanctuary within their heart (37:6–9; 23–28).[69] At that moment, all the nations will witness his presence and know that he is the Lord (36:23).

Preparation for God's Cosmic Presence

That last statement brings up an essential point within a theology of presence that has been somewhat sidelined in our discussion. I have tried to make clear how God's personal presence in the human heart correlates with his corporate presence in the temple. However, God's agenda for his glory to fill the earth is not lost in Ezekiel. To be sure, the Lord states that his omnipresence facilitates his communion with the exiles and the restoration of the remnant (11:16). However, the prophet devotes an entire section to discussing God's presence relative to the nations (25–32).

He will remind nations such as Ammon about the nature of his sanctuary, which they had mocked (25:3). They would learn that YHWH was the true God. They would also discover that he still is with his people even as he exacts judgment against their enemies (25:6–7). Likewise, Tyre believed that it would have Israel's fullness but instead would find that God would empty them because he had a relationship with Israel (26:2; 28:22). Those who set up their own temples in competition with God would find out that only God's glory would fill the earth (28:1–10). Such pronouncements climax in the Gog and Magog prophecies of Ezek 38–39. This epic battle will force the nations to know YHWH (38:16), to see his glory (39:7), and to understand his renown (39:13). The ultimate outcome is that God spreads his glory amongst the nations (39:21–22). Block comments on the weight of this phrase:

> The employment of *nātan bĕ* (lit. "to put in place") with the substantive *kābôd*, "glory," treats the latter almost as if it were an objective, concrete reality, like the Shekinah glory that went before the Israelites during their wilderness wanderings and rested over the tabernacle (Exod. 40:34–38), and that later took up residence in Solomon's temple (1 Kgs 8:10–12). Ezekiel had witnessed the departure of this glory in visionary form himself (Ezek. 8–11), and he will announce its return to the rebuilt temple (43:1–5). As the glorious Shekinah had symbolized the presence of YHWH among his people in the past, so the new vision of his glory would declare his presence among the nations.[70]

Thus, Ezekiel hints at God's concerns for his presence before the world. The prophet also highlights how the Lord will take action in his holy name (39:7, 25) to vindicate his presence before the nations. As a result, he will establish his glory

---

69. Zimmerli, *Ezekiel*, 277.
70. Block, *Ezekiel*, 2:480–81.

throughout the entire earth. The cosmic agenda evident in Ezekiel's vision at Chebar is still part of his theology.

Contextually, all of this takes place to reassure Israel that God still cares for them. After the battle, when God's glory fills the earth, Israel will "know that I am the Lord their God from that day onward" (39:22). Hence, just as indwelling presence established God's corporate presence with his people, so the Lord's cosmic presence also solidifies that relationship. This harmonizes with the agenda of the vision in 11:17–20, for God will dwell with his people in the temple. The Lord will work in their hearts and throughout the world to accomplish that task.

Final Vision as God's Fulfilled Presence in Redemptive History

This brings us to the final vision in 40–48. The chariot-throne that left the temple returns, unquestionably demonstrating that God will dwell with his people corporately. He has worked through redemptive history to transform his people and the world so that he can fulfill his relationship with them. That is the full significance of all other visions (cf. 43:3).[71] Similar to Isaiah, Ezekiel ultimately associates his vision with the culmination of redemptive history. The chariot-throne does not stand merely for an abstract portrayal of God's presence, but rather as a means of enacting that presence in the world; he will fill the earth with his glory. While the overall message is clear (and will be helpful to remember as we proceed to the more controversial discussion below), several critical matters remain for us to consider before we can grasp the full import of Ezekiel's theology of vision.

Foremost among them is the question of whether Ezekiel 40–48 envisions a physical building in Israel. Some argue in the affirmative, but others contend that the text portrays the heavenly temple, or an ideal temple.[72] Others argue that this refers to a spiritual or non-structural temple that would be a part of redemptive-history in the latter days.[73] Those who argue in support of a physical structure draw upon the exacting details of dimensions, structure, and function, which are meaningless if purely spiritual.[74] Conversely, others point out that these facts are not in accordance with current geographical limitations, and thus may be an indication of the temple's non-localized nature. They point to a cosmic temple, the place where God's presence dwells through-

---

71. See above discussion for how Ezek 43:3 ties all elements of previous visions together. See also Halperin, *Faces of the Chariot*, 41: "The lesson of this solemn withdrawal appears to be that God is not bound to the Temple of Jerusalem. When he pleases, he can abandon it to its destruction, taking the cultic apparatus that expresses his holiness and his power with him to his people in Babylonia (11:15–16). But there is more. Chapters 40–48 describe in meticulous detail the rebuilt and purified Temple of the future. To this Temple it will someday please God to return, reversing the procession with which he once departed."

72. Block, "Gog and the Pouring Out of the Spirit," 269–70.

73. Beale, *Temple and the Church's Mission*, 335–36.

74. Cooper, *Ezekiel*, 50; Rooker, "Evidence from Ezekiel," 129.

out the entire earth.[75] In the midst of these hermeneutical issues, other systematic and biblical theological factors arise, including data from the NT, the nature of sacrifices in this temple, and the need for a physical temple, since Christ fulfilled the sacrifices (cf. Heb 10:10) and believers are a temple (cf. 1 Cor 3:16–17; 6:19; Eph 2:20–21).

Those theological issues seem to drive the hermeneutical debate. Apart from such considerations, it appears that the prophet (and his original audience) would have perceived the temple in 40–48 as a physical building in the future, restored nation of Israel. Block explains:

> The view I take in this commentary is that, while the NT often recognizes fresh significances in its reading of OT texts (the church is heir to the spiritual promises of God to Israel), Ezekiel's own understanding of his oracles must be determinative in our interpretation. If one could ask Ezekiel whether he expected a literal regathering of his people, their return to the land of Israel, their spiritual rejuvenation, and the restoration of a Davidide on the throne, one would expect an unequivocally affirmative answer.[76]

Nonetheless, the theological questions listed above are still significant, and I would contend that the book of Ezekiel actually answers them, particularly on the matter of believers themselves being the temple. Does the Spirit's indwelling cancel the need for a structural temple? Some may use the data amassed in this chapter to argue against such necessity. After all, God's presence in Ezekiel does render the human heart as a temple (2:1–2; 36:27), and the eschatological agenda relates his presence throughout the entire cosmos. Considering these two possibilities, the "middle level" of an architectural temple may seem irrelevant. Furthermore, temple and Levitical language applies to both God's cosmic presence as well as his presence in the heart. Perhaps the temple presence is simply relegated to those other aspects of God's presence.[77]

However, the analysis of this chapter seems to curb such argumentation. The prophet holds God's cosmic presence in tension with his indwelling and corporate (temple) presence. For example, they are introduced as related but separate entities. God displays his cosmic presence in the chariot-throne in the opening chapter, but then introduces the reality of his indwelling presence in the next. There is also a mention of a physical temple structure in 8–11. So while God's presence exists on each of these levels they are associated with each other, that does not mean they are perfectly equated.

Along that line, the symmetry within Ezekiel also supports the notion of a real physical structure. We have argued that a vision begins and ends each section within the book. This last section deals with Ezekiel's vision of the departure of God's glory from

---

75. Beale, *Temple and the Church's Mission*, 335–37.
76. Block, *Ezekiel*, 1:56–57.
77. Beale, *Temple and the Church's Mission*, 336–40. Beale in essence argues for that position.

the temple in Jerusalem with the concluding vision of his return. What does he return to? Arguably, if he left a physical structure, he probably would return to one as well.[78]

This actually highlights how God has a unique agenda for each of these aspects of his presence within the book (even if there is some overlap). His cosmic presence ensures he will be a sanctuary to the exiles, which facilitates their restoration both physically and spiritually (11:16–17). That is partly why the chariot-throne leaves the temple in Jerusalem. This also relates, in the same chapter, to his indwelling presence, which will transform his people (11:19–20). God will put his Spirit in people's hearts (36:26). Later in the book, Ezekiel states that when God dwells in the people's hearts, he will also dwell in a sanctuary amongst them (37:27) such that the nations will see it (v. 28). Accordingly, the cosmic and indwelling presence of God do not rule out his presence in a physical temple. Instead, the cosmic and indwelling presence work in harmony to establish Israel's restoration, which includes a physical temple. In the end (40–48), the cosmic presence communicated by God's chariot-throne joins with a physical temple as God's glory returns to the temple. This is indicative of the fact that God already dwells within the hearts of his people. At that moment, God's glory fills the earth in its entirety; he communes with his people on every possible level.

Hence, the assertion of a physical temple does not deny legitimate observations that God's glory seems to extend far beyond Jerusalem to the entire world. Much of the temple's size (40:1—42:20), geography (45:1–9), Edenic likeness (40:22; 41:18–22), and location within Israel (48:8–10) proclaim those realities.[79] Indeed, this accords with God's agenda for his cosmic presence indicated in the vision at Chebar, which is confirmed by the return of that chariot-throne to the temple.

At the same time, perhaps the physical building helps to reflect the reality of God's cosmic and indwelling presence rather than those realities negating the existence of the building. This is where a theology of vision is useful. Isaiah's own vision provides the context for the suggestion above. Arguably, Ezekiel desires the reader to have such a framework in mind, as suggested by the parallels between Ezek 43:4–7 and Isa 6. Like Isaiah, Ezekiel witnesses God's glory shining throughout the earth (43:4–5; Isa 6:3). In both visions, God also fills the temple with his presence (43:4–5; cf. Isa 6:1). Finally, both prophets see the temple becoming the place of God's throne (Ezek 43:7; cf. Isa 6:1). This argues that Ezekiel is not alone in seeing a structural temple. Even more, such close similarities between the two argue that the visions share the same

---

78. Rooker, "Evidence from Ezekiel," 128; Zimmerli, *Ezekiel*, 326; Childs, *Old Testament as Scripture*, 367.

79. Beale, *Temple and the Church's Mission*, 340–43; Block, *Ezekiel*, 2:505–7; Alexander, "Ezekiel," 952. The size and location of the holy district demonstrates how God's holiness extends to the entire nation, and thereby becomes the center of the country. God's presence, then, is not spatially limited to the temple, but is centralized there as Isaiah depicts. The sanctuary's large size also accentuates that the nation and the world will see and know that God dwells with his people (cf. 37:28) in keeping with the logic behind the tabernacle in the wilderness.

significance. They relate to the same complex of eschatological events. Ezekiel alludes to Isaiah to bring his theology of vision to bear upon this final vision of the temple.

Consequently, as we have established, Isaiah views the temple as the centralized location of God's dominion and glory. The nations will show that God's glory fills the earth through their pilgrimages to the temple (Isa 2:3), which demonstrate that God alone reigns in the earth and that he alone is worthy of honor and worship. These aspects of Isaiah's vision help to explain the purpose of the temple in Ezekiel. Just as Isaiah's temple worked as a visible demonstration of God's glory amongst the nations, so Ezekiel's structural temple is intended to be a visible demonstration of God's presence before the world. It shows that God has fulfilled his relationship with people, in contrast to the state of the previous structural temple. Its large design also tangibly and internationally projects the reality of what Isaiah said: God's glory will fill the temple as well as the entire earth (6:1, 3).[80] In this way, Isaiah's vision helps us sharpen the significance of Ezekiel's vision.

We can observe another important parallel between the two. Ezekiel and Isaiah both view Jerusalem as a "high and lifted up" hill (Isa 2:2; Ezek 40:2). Some argue that the high hill in Ezekiel's vision means that the temple cannot be an actual building, since Jerusalem is not a "high hill."[81] However, such a description does not disqualify the temple or the vision from referring to physical realities. Instead, it draws the reader to see that Ezekiel's vision relates to the same redemptive-historical significance that Isaiah envisioned in Isa 2:2.[82] In this way, the unity of vision points to what God will do in the world at a certain point of redemptive history, rather than to something more abstract.

Comparing Isaiah's vision with Ezekiel's not only clarifies issues such as these, but also amplifies Ezekiel's unique perspective, specifically with regard to Ezekiel's concept of cleansing. In the prophet's vision, the Lord informs the prophet that Israel will never defile his holy name, but that he will dwell in their midst forever (43:7). God repeatedly uses the Levitical term "defile" in this book to describe Israel's disassociation from God (cf. 20:22–24; 22:4–8; 23:30). However, he cleansed them from such corruption and made them individual temples of the Spirit (36:27). Because of that transformation, he communes with them on a scale never before experienced. This emphasis helps us to appreciate the distinct perspectives that Isaiah and Ezekiel's visions offer. God's dominion and glory will be fulfilled in the end, as Isaiah saw it.

---

80. See also Zimmerli, *Ezekiel*, 277. In commenting upon Ezek 37:28, Zimmerli states, "In the citing of the nations, however, it is made clear that the realization of the מקדשי בתוכם ('my sanctuary in their midst'), which is described in chapters 40–48 without any reference to the nations, is to be understood as the central event in which YHWH is acknowledged throughout the world." This corresponds to Isaiah's vision and theology and is akin to what occurred in Solomon's day.

81. Beale, *Temple and the Church's Mission*, 336.

82. Ibid.; Block, *Ezekiel*, 2:501. Both Beale and Block acknowledge the connection but discount its significance. In fact, Beale perceptively links this to Dan 2:35, which will impact the discussion of Daniel's vision in the next chapter.

At the same time, Ezekiel helps us see specific nuances of that glory that will fill the earth. God's presence and relationship with his people (and the entire world) will be consummated exhaustively.

This concept of fulfillment of presence and relationship helps to resolve the difficult issues of the need for a temple and the existence of sacrifices at the time. In Ezekiel's theology, these entities exhibit the consummation of Israel's relationship to God both to the nations as well as to Israel itself. For the first time in redemptive-history, the nation would be able to commune with the Lord as it was always supposed to. In contrast to Israel's former spiritual adultery, they now will bless God in his place (cf. Ezek 3:12), as the first vision predicted.

Hence, the sacrifices are much more than just commemorative of our Lord's work.[83] Rather, they participate in the worship and consecration scheme similar to that of Leviticus. However, they are by no means identical to that system. Of note is the complete omission of the Day of Atonement in Ezek 40–48, even though other holidays exist in this section (cf. 44:24; 45:17; 46:9, 11). This implies that a greater work of atonement has been exacted.[84] The transformation of the Spirit has reflected that atonement (36:26). The internal temple of the heart facilitates the physical, corporate dwelling. Thus, this system in Ezek 40–48 appears to recognize Christ's ultimate sacrifice.[85]

Instead of dealing with sin, in the eschatological temple, atonement (כפר) actually pertains to sanctifying the altar for use in God's holy presence (43:20, 26). Likewise, this also ensures that the house of God is clean (45:20). This coincides with Leviticus' portrayal that כפר can denote either atonement for sin (which Ezekiel does not seem to appeal to) or the notion of consecration. After all, an altar does not sin, yet requires atonement (Lev 16:18–19) in order to be made holy. This is the notion of setting something apart for God's service. That idea is the background behind how כפר and certain combinations of sacrifices are used in relation to cleansing for sacred objects (Lev 16:16) as well as for the ordination of the priesthood (Lev 9:1–24).[86] That latter concept is particularly important. Ezekiel describes the use of sin, grain, burnt, and peace offerings to "atone" for the people (45:15, 17). However, when these sacrifices are made together, they are actually for the consecration of the

---

83. Contra Alexander, "Ezekiel," 946–48. See Cooper, *Ezekiel*, 49; Whitcomb, "Animal Sacrifices in Israel," 201–17.

84. Alexander, "Ezekiel," 947–48.

85. Schmitt and Laney, *Messiah's Coming Temple*, 114–19, 141–52. Schmitt and Laney cite additional differences in the temple structure that indicate this as well.

86. Hartley, *Leviticus*, 241. See also Averbeck, "כפר," in *NIDOTTE*, 2:700. The forgiveness of sin is not always in view, since atonement can be made for objects. Rather, it denotes the purification or cleansing of those entities. Critics might object that the altar is cleansed from impurities for holiness. However, the term "impurities" does not refer necessarily to sin, but rather to being ceremonially presentable (or unpresentable) before God. Hence, the contrast is not between sin and righteousness as much as between being normal and consecrated. See Wenham, *Leviticus*, 19 for a helpful distinction.

priests (Lev 9:7), which in context relates to priests being set apart to lead worship and not to the forgiveness of sin per se.[87] If the parallel is valid, then Israel functions as God's prized possession, a priesthood to the nations (cf. Exod 19:6), which fulfills Isaiah's declaration that all Israel will be called a priest (Isa 61:6). Hence, the sacrifices in Ezekiel do not seem to atone for sin but instead display Israel as a worshipping community of priests before the watching world.

Thus, every part of the temple testifies that God's presence is consummated for Israel and also for the world. Israel's original problem was in confusing the present with the eschatological. Ezekiel, however, assures Israel that such confusion does not negate the eschatological. Ultimately, God will never leave the people of Israel or his temple, as his presence comes into the building and shuts the door behind him (44:2). The cherubim found in the temple show that the mobile chariot-throne is now fulfilled so that it may dwell permanently in the eschatological temple (41:18–25). The priests serve in perfect holiness in their intended ceremonial capacity (44:15–31).[88] His presence transforms creation, as seen in the Dead Sea (47:1–12).[89] As a result, all of Israel communes with him as a priestly nation (45:13–17), and as Ezekiel concludes, "The Lord is there" (48:35).

Halperin's comments sum up this entire discussion well:

> The destroyed Temple is rebuilt, the departed glory has returned; the sin of the Israelites is purged, the wounds of their punishment healed. The action of the Book of Ezekiel, which began at the river Chebar, is concluded on the mountain of the Temple to come (40:2), and its rhythms are marked by the comings and goings of God's glory and the *ḥayyot*-cherubim that carry it [12b,13]. The initial vision of God and his entourage, which once seemed so purposeless, now appears as a foreshadowing of the grand cycle that underlies the rest of the book.[90]

---

87. See Hartley, *Leviticus*, 123: "This practice differs from that prescribed for a high priestly purification offering in 4:5–7. There are many ways to account for this variation. Possibly the practice in 4:5–7 was a later development. Wenham, however, suggests that the altar of incense at this time did not need atonement, for Aaron had not yet entered the Tent of Meeting (149). It is more *likely that this purification offering differs from the one prescribed in chapter 4, for it is being offered on a high day, rather than to expiate a specific sin committed by Aaron*. Since the altar of incense and the sanctuary have not been polluted by a specific sin, they do not need to be cleansed by a blood rite performed inside the holy place" (emphasis mine). Earlier, Hartley notes that what is in view here is not forgiveness of specific sins, but rather the state of uncleanness in coming directly into the presence of the holy God (*Leviticus*, 121). All this demonstrates that the combination of offering relates to priestly ordination and that ordination relates not to sin as much as to consecration. Applying this same scheme to Israel makes them a kingdom of priests. If Israel is a kingdom of priests, then the sacrifices also distinguish it as a theocratic nation. See also Whitcomb, "Animal Sacrifices in Israel," 211–12. Whitcomb correctly argues for a difference between ceremonial cleansing versus true spiritual cleansing. This notion of consecration for God's service is the best way to view the sacrifices. See also Wenham, *Leviticus*, 19. Wenham argues persuasively for the categories of the unclean, clean, and holy. The rituals above consecrate the clean as holy.

88. Cooper, *Ezekiel*, 394–96; Block, *Ezekiel*, 2:633–46.

89. Block, *Ezekiel*, 2:701.

90. Halperin, *Faces of the Chariot*, 42.

With that, Halperin reaffirms much of what we have discussed. He agrees that Ezekiel portrays a physical temple and identifies the significance of this relative to Ezekiel's visions. The final vision in Ezek 43:1–5 displays the *telos* of Ezekiel's original vision, when heaven was opened before him (1:1). God's works through his chariot-throne to consummate his presence with his people on every level: cosmic, corporate, and indwelling. Ezekiel's vision ultimately pertains to that eschatological outcome.

One final note remains. The presence of the prince is integrated into Israel's restoration and the final vision. He, as the new David and the Shepherd, mediates God's presence (34:24).[91] The same individual is set apart in the temple to maintain the communion between man and God (cf. 44:3; 45:7). Like the messianic figure in Isaiah who accomplishes Isaiah's vision and theology, so too does this individual fulfill the consummation of God's presence with his people. He leads the way for them to know him.[92]

EZEKIEL'S CONTRIBUTION TO A THEOLOGY OF VISION

Overall, Ezekiel's visions combine to form a composite picture. God's chariot-throne demonstrates his agenda to fill the earth with glory. However, Israel resists this agenda because of its adulterous heart. Its people cannot relate to God in any of the right ways and are more like statues than people. Thus, God rides out in his chariot-throne to cast his people into exile. However, he also rides out to be with them in their sojourn so that he might bring them back to himself. His presence will dwell in them, giving life to his people so that they may truly know him. He transforms their hearts from an idolatrous temple to his own dwelling place. Consequently, he then takes up permanent residence in a physical eschatological temple, which signals to Israel and the nations that his presence has truly filled the world. That is the fullest understanding of Ezekiel's original vision, when he saw heavens opened at the river Chebar.

---

91. Ezekiel proclaims that since all of Israel's leadership failed, God will become their shepherd (34:1–22). The prior political establishment had guided the nation into further debauchery and spiritual adultery (23:1–49), but God removed them (19:1–14; 34:10) in order to establish a new David (34:23) in whose reign God will "dwell with his people" (34:24). That phrase corresponds to God's agenda of his vision in 11:1–20, for the outcome of the chariot-throne's departure would be that God would become Israel's only God and they would be his people. God replaces false political leadership with one true leader who brings fidelity and communion instead of harlotry. This too signals that the corporate relationship has not ended permanently; God's presence will dwell with them.

92. Contra Alexander, "Ezekiel," 974; Cooper, *Ezekiel*, 389. The common arguments against the prince being the Messiah include the fact that he is not depicted as a priest, but instead has priests under him, as well as the fact that he "atones" for himself. Conversely, the prince could be the head of the priests as seen in Israel's history (cf. 2 Sam 8:18 with 1 Chr 18:17, where the parallelism appears to be that David's sons were chiefs over the priests). In addition, if the term "atone" refers to consecration as demonstrated above, then the second argument offers no difficulties. See Block, "Bringing Back David," 167–88; Johnston, "Messianic Trajectories," 181–83. This may even signal a link between the one on the chariot-throne and the Shepherd. Such a link will be confirmed by later descriptions of the resurrected Christ.

Ezekiel's Vision

How does the innertextuality of Ezekiel's vision contribute to the intertextuality of a biblical theology of vision? Initially, Ezekiel helps us better understand the significance and impact of the visionary event. Like Isaiah, Ezekiel relates his vision to the climax of redemptive history. In doing so, the prophet expands upon Isaiah's framework and shows that God's glory filling the earth includes the consummation of presence. His majesty not only extends in breadth—compelling all nations to worship him, but also in depth—filling the heart of man with his Spirit to create true worshippers. Accordingly, the vision not only pertains to the Servant's work of salvation, but also the fulfillment of relationship.

Along that line, Ezekiel's explanation of the chariot-throne sharpens our understanding of the visionary event itself. It helps us unpack the significance of that object within the visionary event. Ezekiel does see a vision of heaven (1:1), and Daniel includes the throne in that heavenly courtroom scene (Dan 7:9). What is the throne doing there? While that moment certainly commemorates the saving work of the Son (as Isaiah envisioned), the presence of the chariot-throne in the scene reminds us all how God rode that chariot throughout redemptive history to fill the earth with his glory from the inside out. At this moment, heaven celebrates God's final consummation of his relationship with his people.

6

Daniel's Vision
Vision of King and Kingdom

THUS FAR, ISAIAH HAS provided the foundational framework for the nature of the vision. His vision pertains to two major realities. First, God will reign exclusively, high and lifted up. Second, he will dwell with his transformed people. Ezekiel's vision expands upon the latter notion of how God will commune with his people. Daniel's vision pertains to the former aspect of Isaiah's vision: God's kingdom and rule. Even a brief perusal of this book indicates that God's rule and kingdom form the emphasis of the vision (cf. 2:44; 4:3; 7:14, 26). Daniel will add further detail to Isaiah's paradigm of God's sole dominion.

Along that line, Daniel synthesizes his predecessors' visions into an eschatological framework. Both the visions of Ezekiel and Isaiah heavily imply an association with the culmination of history (Isa 11:1–16; Ezek 44:1–5) and the Messiah (Isa 52:13; Ezek 44:3), though such associations are based upon context and innertextuality rather than categorical statement. Hence, the exact relationship between the event in heaven and God's eschatological work on earth remains somewhat unclear. Daniel's vision clarifies these issues. Whereas Ezekiel's vision "zoomed in" on the throne in Isaiah's vision, Daniel's vision "zooms out" to show the full context of the visionary event.

As such, the writer integrates the visions of previous prophets with the coronation of the Son of Man.[1] What God announces in heaven about the Messiah will then be wrought out on earth. This framework is essential to our discussion of a biblical theology of vision. Interestingly enough, as previously noted, the writers of *1–3 Enoch* and *4 Ezra* also placed Isaiah and Ezekiel's visions into Daniel's eschatological

---

1. Technically, the individual in Daniel is not labeled by that official title. Rather, he is one like the son of man. A further discussion of what that phrase means will follow. Nonetheless, since scholars do describe the individual using both the phrase found in Daniel as well as the later appellation that derives from it, I will use them interchangeably throughout the chapter.

paradigm. Again, a biblical theology of vision is not a novel idea. Although differences exist, this chapter walks in the footsteps of a rich tradition-history.

RECAPITULATION OF VISION IN DANIEL

Recapitulation within Daniel

Isaiah and Ezekiel make use of unique strategies in expounding upon the theological substance of their visions. Isaiah's central vision is explained by his later writing through repetition and allusion. Ezekiel had multiple visions, each layering on top of the other to reveal the full picture of the vision's message. Daniel's approach is a hybrid of the two.

Daniel is full of visions. Nearly every other chapter contains some sort of dream or vision (2, 4, 7, 8, 9, 10–12). However, scholars recognize that these visions are not disconnected, but are interrelated. The rest of this chapter will embark upon a fuller discussion of the innertextual connections the book contains. At this point, a brief listing of overlap can adequately support the scholarly consensus.

Each of the visions begins with a date formula (which actually mirrors both Isaiah and Ezekiel).[2] Chapter 7 picks up on the imagery in the second chapter. The iron teeth of the fourth beast (7:7) correspond to the iron in the statue (2:33). That beast's ten horns (7:7) may correspond with the ten toes of the statue as well (2:33).[3] In addition, the descriptions of the second and third metals/creatures in Dan 2 and 7 correspond with Daniel's vision in chapter 8. The ram with two horns matches the bear with uneven sides and the statue's two arms of silver (7:5; 8:3; cf. 2:32). The goat, which eventually has four horns, corresponds with the leopard that has four heads (7:6; 8:8). The visions in chapters 9–12 also link with the previous chapters. The prophecy in chapter 9 may allude to the fourth kingdom mentioned in Dan 2 and 7.[4] Scholars also conclude that Dan 10–12 deal with the issues surrounding Greece, the referent of the goat in chapter 8 and the third kingdom described in chapters 2 and 7.[5] This provides only initial evidence of what scholars widely accept: the visions in Daniel are all angles of the same eschatological vision.

Hence, like Ezekiel, the development of Daniel's own theology of vision is tied into a series of visions. However, how exactly do the visions interact with each other? Do they work as they do in Ezekiel, where each vision reveals more of Ezekiel's theology (resumptive exposition) with the final vision being the fullest expression of them all? Is the final vision in Daniel central to all the various visions in his book? What is the central vision in Daniel?

---

2. Nicol, "Isaiah's Vision," 502.
3. Miller, *Daniel*, 98.
4. Ibid.; Beale, "Influence of Daniel," 414–15.
5. Beale, "Influence of Daniel," 415; Kratz, "Visions of Daniel," 93.

Daniel differs from Ezekiel in this regard. Arguably, the principal vision is found not at the end of the book, but rather in the middle: Dan 7. The structure of the book supports this formulation. Scholars propose two possible structures for the book.[6] Some suggest that Dan 7 links with chapters 8–12 because they all share a visionary report genre.[7] Each of them deals with how Daniel witnessed divine revelation in a dream (cf. 7:1; 8:1; 10:1). Furthermore, in content, they deal primarily with the future of the people of Israel as opposed to the Gentile nations. The connection of the ram and goat in chapter 8 with the second and third animals in chapter 7 also ties these chapters together.[8]

However, an equally intriguing structural understanding places Dan 7 as the end of the first section (as opposed to Dan 6). This is consistent with the use of language throughout these chapters. Dan 7, written in Aramaic, would conclude the Aramaic section of the book (2–7). This structure actually generates a chiasm. Dan 2 and 7 deal with the prophecies concerning four nations. Dan 3 and 6 describe how Daniel and his friends triumph over foreign rulers. Dan 4 and 5 record the humiliation of two foreign rulers.[9] In essence, both of these proposals have solid evidence and both differ in how they place Dan 7. Does Dan 7 belong with the following material, as the genre suggests? Or does it belong with the previous material, forming a chiasm?

This tension in Daniel's structure posits Dan 7 as a pivotal chapter for either half of the book. This makes it central in Daniel's vision and theology. Patterson explains:

> The key role of chapter 7 to the book of Daniel is thus readily apparent. Its central location and close correspondence with the two major portions make it evident that Daniel 7 is in many respects the key that unlocks the door to the problem of the unity, as well as the understanding, of the book.[10]

Accordingly, the structure of Daniel situates chapter 7 as the culmination of prior discussion and as the foundation for the rest. Baldwin confirms this estimation:

> Looked at in relation to the Aramaic section, this chapter constitutes the climax, and it is the high point in relation to the whole book; subsequent chapters treat only part of the picture and concentrate on some particular aspect of it.[11]

Baldwin's observation leads us to another reason why Dan 7 is the central vision. In terms of content, Dan 7 provides the most inclusive framework for the other visions. The text is the broadest common denominator of the visions. Dan 7 incorporates the four kingdoms mentioned in chapter 2 and the two specific kingdoms that appear in chapter 8. Dan 7 also includes the metaphor of "horns" to be further

---

6. Patterson, "Key Role of Daniel 7," 252; Goldingay, *Daniel*, 159; Walvoord, *Daniel*, 151.
7. Ford, *Daniel*, 28–29.
8. Miller, *Daniel*, 51; Lucas, *Daniel*, 31.
9. Patterson, "Key Role of Daniel 7," 250.
10. Ibid., 252.
11. Baldwin, *Daniel*, 137.

expanded in the visions of Dan 8 (cf. vv. 5, 8, 9) and Dan 11–12 (cf. 11:3–4). Dan 7 provides a complete description of the saints' victory and the eternal kingdom that is anticipated in Dan 2:35 and echoed in Dan 9:24 and 12:1–3. Although the visions surrounding Dan 7 may expand upon the details or certain nuances of the vision in Dan 7, that chapter includes the fundamental elements of each of the other visions in the book. Such observations have led scholars to conclude that Dan 7 is the controlling vision in the book.[12]

Hence, the way Daniel's vision develops within the book almost mirrors the way the visionary event is developed between books. Just as various prophets see different aspects of the same event, different visions in Daniel give insight to different parts of Dan 7. In this way, the innertextuality of vision in Daniel resembles Isaiah's recapitulation strategy. Just as Isaiah has a central vision that the rest of his book elaborates upon, Daniel also features a central vision that his other visions anticipate or explain.

While Daniel is full of visions, it also offers other content. The book contains familiar narratives (Dan 3–6). They also include dreams (cf. 4:5) that may link the narrative with the visions, but other factors point to the connectedness of dream or vision and story. Certain repeated phrases or words, such as "people, nations, tongues" (עַמְמַיָּא אֻמַּיָּא וְלִשָּׁנַיָּא), are found both in the narratives (3:4; 4:1; 5:19; 6:25) and in Dan 7:14. These elements show that every part of the book contributes to the development of Daniel's theology of vision.

Understanding recapitulation and innertextuality in Daniel helps us recognize his theology of vision. Initially, it confirms that Daniel has a theology of vision. While Daniel is a book full of visions, these visions are not disparate dreams, but instead focus on one central vision. This unity within the book forms the foundation for the innertextual connections I will point out within the book as we trace theological significance within Daniel. The content of the book highlights important theological concepts by contributing to the full picture presented in Dan 7.

These innertextual connections influence how I will structure this chapter. Two major innertextual threads run through the book. One concerns the image of the statue (2:31) or beasts (7:1–4; 8:2–5) found throughout Daniel, which directly relate to the history of kingdoms and the kingdom of God.[13] The other concerns the motif of various kings who struggle against the rule of YHWH (cf. 3:1–15; 4:29; 5:3–4). Daniel's own reaction to God's revelation confirms the existence of these themes (2:20–22). He acknowledges that God controls all history (עִדָּנַיָּא וְזִמְנַיָּא) and both raises and displaces kings (מְהַעְדֵּה מַלְכִין וּמְהָקֵים מַלְכִין). In doing so, Daniel introduces the reader to the two major themes of his book. However, these themes are not mutually exclusive.

---

12. Patterson, "Key Role of Daniel 7," 252; Goldingay, *Daniel*, 151–52; Baldwin, *Daniel*, 137.

13. Beale, "Influence of Daniel," 413; House, *Old Testament Theology*, 504–6. Beale argues for three major themes in Daniel: historical and cosmic eschatological judgment, which sets up for God's historical reign or divine earthly kingdom, God's absolute sovereignty and kingdom, and the saints' suffering under an ungodly reign.

Both of these threads intersect at different points of the book, but ultimately find their fullest expression in Dan 7, when God, at the culmination of history, decrees the end of all kingdoms but his own and places all authority in the hands of his king, the Son of Man. This chapter will follow the themes of kingdom and king in Daniel and see how they intertwine in his vision in Dan 7.

Integration of Previous Innertextuality in Daniel's Vision

I should note one further observation before delving into Daniel's theology of vision. Recapitulation in Daniel extends beyond just the material within his book to include *intertextual* recapitulation as well. I have already suggested that Daniel expands upon Isaiah's notion of God being high and lifted up. Indeed, even the opening dream in Dan 2 suggests such an idea. The statue, as impressive as it may be (Dan 2:31), could not withstand the power of the stone not made with human hands. In the end, this statue, which represents various kingdoms, shatters and God's kingdom fills the earth (v. 34–35).

Conceptually, the shattering of the statue reiterates Isaiah's theme that God alone reigns over every nation and that, in the end, they will all recognize his authority (Isa 2:1–4; 11:1–16). However, that connection is not merely thematic in nature. Dan 2 alludes to Isaiah and Ezekiel. Verses 34–35 are of particular note in their description of a stone crushing the statue and becoming a great mountain. The description of the stone alludes to its supernatural origins (vv. 44–45).[14] Such language surrounding a stone may echo Isaiah's own description of the messianic figure in Isa 28:16, who is also metaphorically described as a stone. As we have discussed, that individual was incorporated into Isaiah's own vision as the individual who was "high and lifted up" on the throne (cf. Isa 53:12).

The stone crushes the statue's feet, with the result that it becomes like chaff (Dan 2:35). Goldingay observes that such language reminds readers of Isaiah, when God enables Israel to destroy the nations like chaff (Isa 41:12–16).[15] This was a part of God destroying all other authorities so that his own reign would alone be high and lifted up (cf. Isa 6:1). Such an allusion further indicates that Daniel had Isaiah in mind, thereby strengthening the connection of the "stone" in Daniel to the "stone" found in Isaiah. It appears that Daniel describes the triumph of God's kingdom in light of the outcome tied with Isaiah's vision.

These potential associations have greater certainty when we consider a series of clearer allusions between Daniel and his prophetic predecessors. In Nebuchadnezzar's dream, the stone becomes a great mountain and fills the earth (Dan 2:35). Both the visions of Isaiah and Ezekiel relate to a great mountain in Jerusalem (cf. Isa 2:2; 11:9;

---

14. Miller, *Daniel*, 91; Lucas, *Daniel*, 74; Ford, *Daniel*, 86–87. Lucas acknowledges that "rock" is an epithet commonly used for God in the OT (Pss 18:2; 42:9; 71:3), which may also be behind the image of the stone in the first place.

15. Goldingay, *Daniel*, 49.

Ezek 40:2). Commentators commonly point out this allusion and even identify the mountain in Nebuchadnezzar's dream as Zion because of the association.[16] Furthermore, the mention of "filling the earth" also occurs in the visions of Isaiah and Ezekiel. Both of them see God's glory filling the earth in their visions (Isa 6:3; Ezek 43:2). The description of the mountain and God's glory filling the earth in Nebuchadnezzar's vision offers considerable evidence that the visions and theologies of Isaiah and Ezekiel have intersected in Daniel.

What occurs in chapter 2 is quite significant for Daniel's contribution to a theology of vision. Initially, it demonstrates that Dan 7 is not the only place where the prophet draws previous visions together. Such intertextuality takes place throughout the book, providing even more evidence of the visions' unity. Furthermore, Daniel not only associates Nebuchadnezzar's dream with the visions of Isaiah and Ezekiel, but also with the texts linked with their respective visions. For example, he links Isa 2 and 6 together with his description of the mountain (Isa 2:2) filling the earth (Isa 6:3). In essence, Daniel's vision takes the innertextual relationships between the visions of Isaiah and Ezekiel and their theologies and incorporates them into his vision.[17] This confirms the previously suggested connections between vision and theology within Isaiah and Ezekiel. It also demonstrates an important aspect of Daniel's strategy. His visions bring to the foreground what was implicit in his predecessors' writings. As such, he begins to more clearly unveil the nature of the visionary event and the theological significance that his predecessors had more subtly indicated. This is nowhere more apparent than in the central vision of Dan 7, when the visions converge into their full context and theological significance.

KINGDOM: GOD'S EXCLUSIVE ESCHATOLOGICAL REIGN

Kingdom as God's Final Reign over World History

With this in mind, we can observe how Daniel builds his own theology of vision while incorporating, confirming, and expanding the work of his predecessors. We can begin with the first dream of the book, which is found in the second chapter. The motif of this text echoes the visions found later on (cf. Dan 3:1; 4:11–12; 7:2–8). Accordingly, Dan 2 is foundational to one of the major strands of a theology of vision in the book.

Chapter 2 primarily focuses on God's reign over the breadth of history. The progression of metals in the dream resembles Hesiod's *Works and Days*, as well as other works that link the progression of history with various metals.[18] It is difficult to argue

---

16. Lucas, *Daniel*, 74; Goldingay, *Daniel*, 49; Miller, *Daniel*, 91; Collins, *Daniel*, 165; Goswell, "Temple Theme in the Book of Daniel," 515–16.

17. Granted, God revealed these dreams/visions to Daniel and others. However, it is the way that Daniel communicates what has been revealed that is at issue. He recounts the vision in such a manner so as to allude to the innertextuality within Isaiah and Ezekiel.

18. Collins, *Daniel*, 162. Collins cites this as well as the Persian account of *Bahman Yasht*.

that Daniel depends on these works, but he may present metaphors and paradigms familiar to the culture of his time.[19] Daniel's own interpretation affirms that the statue represents the progression of human history (cf. Dan 2:37–39), which is why the stone strikes the statue's feet rather than any other part. God's kingdom succeeds the fourth kingdom and thereby all other earthly dominions.[20]

However, how far does this scope of history extend? Some would argue that the four kingdoms are Babylon, Media, Persia, and Greece. If this were the case, it would refer to the immediate future for Daniel, or some sort of prophecy *ex eventu* contemporaneous with the writer.[21] Alternatively, some have suggested a scheme (e.g., Babylon, Medo-Persia, Greece, Rome [with a future hybrid component]) that is more eschatological.[22] Does Daniel deal with near history or with its totality?

The eschatological scheme is preferred. While Dan 2 only establishes that Babylon is the first nation, it does leave some clues that this refers to the entirety of human history. The mystery pertains to what will occur in the latter days (2:28). This expression may refer to simply the future, but it also denotes the culmination of history.[23] Furthermore, contextually, the obliteration of the statue would be odd if other kingdoms were to arise (e.g., Rome) afterwards. Rather, the extreme contrast between human authority and God's sovereignty signals that an eschatological scheme is present.

Moreover, Daniel develops the initial dream as the book progresses. Certain elements of the dream in Dan 2 are picked up in Dan 7 and Dan 8. As already discussed, the two animals in Dan 8 seem to correspond with the second and third beasts in Dan 7 and the second and third metals in Dan 2. The interpreting angel explicitly names these entities as Medo-Persia and Greece, respectively (8:20–21). Such an identification of the hybrid nation, Medo-Persia, tightly matches the image of various pairs: two arms of silver (2:32), two uneven sides (7:5), and two horns (8:3).[24] It makes good sense within both the context and imagery in the book. However, if the third beast is Greece, then the fourth kingdom cannot be Greece, but a later kingdom instead (i.e., Rome).[25]

In addition, various descriptions in these accounts hint at an eschatological element in Daniel's vision. Dan 8 states that future events pertaining to Greece occur to parallel the events of the end (8:17, 19). In this way, immediate history corresponds

---

19. Daniel does not completely abide in either Hesiod's framework or that of *Bahman Yasht*. For example, he talks about iron mixed with clay, which is foreign to either account.

20. Miller, *Daniel*, 94–95; Lucas, *Daniel*, 75–76; Wood, *Commentary on Daniel*, 73.

21. See Collins, *Daniel*, 166–67; Lucas, *Daniel*, 74–77; Goldingay, *Daniel*, 50. Goldingay is not as dogmatic, since he recognizes that if a different source composed the latter part of Daniel, an entirely different scheme might be present than that which is discussed in chapter 2.

22. See Miller, *Daniel*, 93–94; Walvoord, *Daniel*, 74–75; Patterson, "Key Role of Daniel 7," 248–50; Barker, "Premillennialism in the Book of Daniel."

23. Beale, "Influence of Daniel," 415–16; VanGemeren, "Spirit of Restoration," 87–89; Ford, *Daniel*, 93.

24. Miller, *Daniel*, 94; Patterson, "Key Role of Daniel 7," 248–50.

25. Ford, *Daniel*, 40.

with eschatology.[26] The juxtaposition of the "horns" imagery in Dan 7:8 and 8:3–9 also confirms this correlation. In Dan 7:8, the fourth beast/kingdom has a horn that supplants other horns and makes great boasts. In Dan 8:9, another horn acts similarly; however, this horn belongs not to the fourth beast but to the third. On one hand, disharmony exists, since two different animals and kingdoms are in view. On the other hand, a striking similarity exists between the imagery and actions. Dan 8:3–19, in connecting immediate history and eschatology, may provide a simple explanation for this device: the differences and similarities between the two different "horns" refer to two different epochs of history that will resemble each other.[27] This juxtaposition may also explain the ending in Dan 11:36—12:3, for scholars cannot find a correlation between that text and the historical situation of Antiochus Epiphanes.[28] Perhaps the paradigm in Dan 8:17 of immediate history corresponding with the end time (לְעֶת־קֵץ) aligns with Dan 11:40, which also discusses the end time (בְּעֵת קֵץ).[29]

Finally, Dan 9:24–26 also seems to have the culmination of history in view. The famous "seventy-weeks prophecy" may provide insight to the statue/stone motif of the second chapter. In Dan 2:35, a mountain arises to destroy all other nations. This likely refers to Jerusalem, based upon Daniel's allusion to Isa 2:2 and Ezek 40:2.[30] Dan 9 also concentrates on the mountain of Jerusalem. The writer describes Jerusalem as God's holy mountain (9:16). The prophecy itself concerns Israel and the holy city, Jerusalem (9:24–26). These factors indicate that the seventy-weeks prophecy addresses the same issues that the statue, mountain, and stone spoke to in Dan 2.

If this passage expands upon chapter 2, the seventy-weeks prophecy reinforces the broad sweep of history involved in the dream of the second chapter. Scholars conclude that the seventy-weeks concern the fulfillment of all history. The realities of dealing with evil as well as establishing Jerusalem speak of a state that only comes at the completion of God's plan.[31] Overall, Daniel seems to take an eschatological view of history.

26. Miller, *Daniel*, 232; Porteous, *Daniel*, 125. Porteous recognizes the connection of the horn between these different kings.

27. Miller, *Daniel*, 232; Wood, *Commentary on Daniel*, 212.

28. Miller, *Daniel*, 304; Collins, *Daniel*, 387; Goldingay, *Daniel*, 304.

29. Miller, *Daniel*, 308; Wood, *Commentary on Daniel*, 308. Various scholars make the connection between the two texts (e.g., Collins, Goldingay), but do not see the connection as near history to eschatological, but rather just as the resolution of the situation.

30. Collins, *Daniel*, 165; Goldingay, *Daniel*, 49; Lucas, *Daniel*, 74; Miller, *Daniel*, 91; Goswell, "Temple Theme in the Book of Daniel," 516. This stems from the rich intertextual imagery found in Isa 2:2. Goswell states it plainly: "the 'mountain' of the vision is most likely a metaphor for God's future universal rule centered on Zion and its temple (2:34–35, 44–45), given the use of this image more generally in the OT (e.g., Isa 2:2–4: 'the mountain of the house of the LORD')." See also Evans, "Daniel in the New Testament," 500: "To be sure, the kingdom of God is apocalyptic in the sense that its coming is *revealed* (ἀποκαλύπτειν), but its continuity with the four kingdoms and its identification with Mount Zion (to which surely the 'great mountain' refers), strongly imply that his kingdom is of *this world*." This not only supports our suggestions above, but as will soon be discussed, the earthly quality of God's kingdom as well.

31. Miller, *Daniel*, 259; Wood, *Commentary on Daniel*, 248–49; Baldwin, *Daniel*, 169.

For a reader of Daniel, these debates may quickly become tiresome. In fact, could such discussions be completely misguided? After all, the main message of God's control over kingdoms is clear regardless of viewpoint. Why not merely emphasize the strength and value of each metal, showing that God's reign is the most powerful and beautiful of them all?

Conversely, I suggest that our above discussion falls within Daniel's intended purview. Goldingay rightly observes that Dan 2 is more ambiguous in identifying the referents of the metals. This invites the reader to begin to search for those answers, which takes place within the book itself. Daniel initiates this investigation by labeling the head of gold as Babylon (2:38). Our pursuit for answers actually helps to formulate a theology of kingdom within the book. Along this line, the entire interpretive process has an important intended effect, for "in encouraging his reader to match symbol with historical reality he is drawing him into assent to the schema of history which the author himself has unfolded."[32] Daniel leads the reader to understand that the kingdom is the culmination of world history.

That reality makes three substantial contributions to the nature of Daniel's theology and vision. As the summation of *world* history, the statue in Dan 2 does not signify abstract or invisible authority, but rather the impressive might of human power in the world. Equally, the stone's dominance is even more terrifying, because its authority is not merely intangible, invisible, or spiritual, but is both physical and global. God's kingdom appears to have every bit of (and even more) political authority and visible dominion as the nations it dispossesses. This is what intimidates Nebuchadnezzar.

The physicality of the kingdom is made apparent in the broader discussion of God's supreme reign over all humanity and history. Daniel's eschatological presentation of history reminds the reader of the absolute nature of God's kingdom. As opposed to representing more immediate world powers, the statue actually depicts the *totality* of all human authority and achievement, illustrating that God's majesty outweighs the sum of man's power. Similarly, the dream in Dan 2 communicates the *finality* of God's kingdom. A time will come when history will give way to the presence of a single nation, God's own nation. As Daniel states, it will not go to another people, but remain forever (2:44). No other kingdom will exist. This reiterates Isaiah's precise message of God's "high and lifted up" reign, and that is not coincidental, considering the intertextuality discussed above. Daniel has brought Isaiah's innertextuality into his own vision with new metaphors that affirm that theology with clarity and vividness. In this way, Daniel's theology of kingdom details how God's dominion will triumph in this world, for all time, without any rival whatsoever.

All of this culminates in the central vision in Dan 7. Since the four metals in Dan 2 become four beasts in that vision, this discussion on what they signify forms the context of the central vision of the book. The visionary event takes place at the end of human history. Mankind has displayed its might through a series of kingdoms;

---

32. Davies, "Book of Daniel," 44.

nonetheless, God will crush them all, and his reign will be supreme. In this way, Daniel's theology of vision clearly portrays what other visions had only implied: that the visionary event is eschatological and forms the climax of kingdom and history.

Kingdom Related to the Fulfillment of God's Agenda in Vision

We have briefly discussed Daniel's seventy-week prophecy above. However, it deserves further and separate discussion, as it mentions the phrase "to seal up vision and prophecy" (וְלַחְתֹּם חָזוֹן וְנָבִיא). What exactly does this mean in context, and how (if at all) does the phrase contribute to an overall theology of vision? Since this prophecy appears to expand upon Daniel's idea of kingdom (cf. Dan 2:25; 9:16), this discussion will enhance our understanding of Daniel's theology of kingdom as well.

Daniel's concern in Dan 9 is the end of exile as predicted by Jeremiah (v. 2; cf. Jer 25:11–12).[33] While the content of the seventy-week prophecy describes what is involved before the end of exile, Gabriel first explains what will take place when Israel's exile is complete (Dan 9:24). In that verse, the angel lists six infinitives to summarize the nature of the culmination of history.[34] My goal in this section is to explore the echoes (or at least conceptual associations) between the theologies and visions of Isaiah and Ezekiel, as well as to see how such intertextuality plays into Daniel's statement concerning the fulfillment of vision and prophecy.

The first three infinitives deal with how God will put an end to sin.[35] He will end rebellion against his rule (לְכַלֵּא הַפֶּשַׁע) as well as sin in general (וּלַחְתֹּם חַטָּאוֹת) to free the world from spiritual uncleanness.[36] These acts seem to be based upon the third infinitive, in which God atones for guilt (וּלְכַפֵּר עָוֹן). These descriptions may conceptually remind readers of Isaiah's themes of salvation and the transforming holiness by which God will end sin and rebellion to make a people who conform to his perfection. A linguistic tie may show that this connection is not merely thematic. The collocation of כפר with עון only occurs ten times in the OT, with three of those occurrences in Isaiah (6:7; 22:14; 27:9). One of those instances in Isaiah describes how God atoned for the prophet's iniquity in the context of his calling. Just as Isaiah was transformed, so Israel will be made holy as well (cf. Isa 6:13). Daniel may be referring to this reality. Kingdom must include the "linchpin" of salvation and holiness.[37]

---

33. Goldingay, *Daniel*, 239.

34. Ibid., 258; Miller, *Daniel*, 259; Collins, *Daniel*, 353; Wood, *Commentary on Daniel*, 248; Young, *Prophecy of Daniel*, 198. Collins notes that this depicts an eschatological ideal.

35. Certain textual critical issues are at hand. See Goldingay, *Daniel*, 229; Miller, *Daniel*, 259. The MT reading of כלא could just be another way to spell כלה. In any case, their meanings are quite similar in context. Strong evidence also supports the reading of תמם instead of התם. For this study, the difference of wording is not substantial.

36. Miller, *Daniel*, 259; Wood, *Commentary on Daniel*, 248–49.

37. Gentry, "Seventy Weeks," 31. Gentry steeps his entire argument in Isaiah. "Isaiah indicates that the return from exile entails two separate stages: (1) return from Babylon to the land of Israel, and

The next three infinitives also follow suit by offering possible intertextuality. An additional outcome of the kingdom is the establishment of "everlasting righteousness" (וּלְהָבִיא צֶדֶק עֹלָמִים). This seems to refer to the institution of a world made right in conformity with God's righteous ruling standard.³⁸ Such a description corresponds to eschatological portrayals in Isaiah as well. In fact, some have even used Isa 11, a text connected with the vision in Isa 6, to illustrate the nature of this righteousness.³⁹ Although the exact phrase "everlasting righteousness" is not found anywhere else in biblical literature, Isaiah uses a similar phrase to refer to salvation that brings about righteousness (cf. Isa 45:17, 53:10–11; 60:21; 11:4–5).⁴⁰ Others claim to have identified an echo of Jer 23:5, which describes a righteous branch (צֶמַח צַדִּיק) that rules by implementing righteousness and justice in the land. This makes sense as well, since Daniel has Jeremiah in mind in context (cf. Dan 9:2).⁴¹ Conversely, the term "branch" in Jeremiah alludes back to Isa 11:1. Thus, even interpretations that ground understandings of "everlasting life" in Jer 23:5 still tie the prophecy to Isaiah's theology and vision. All of the above may also relate to how the Servant justifies (יַצְדִּיק צַדִּיק) the many (Isa 53:11). This too finds validity, especially in the context of the Messiah being "cut off" (Dan 9:26), which alludes to his violent death as it is described in Isa 53:8.⁴² Tanner agrees with this analysis, citing Isaiah as the predominant background to Daniel's concept of "everlasting righteousness."⁴³ Brownlee's comments further reinforce my observations surrounding both atonement and everlasting righteousness:

> Dan. 9:24–27 is particularly important as an interpretation of Is. 52:13—53:12. The 'seventy weeks of years are decreed ... to atone for iniquity, to bring in

---

(2) return from covenant violation to a right relationship to God so that the covenant relationship is renewed and restored (see Isa 42:18—43:21 and 43:22—44:23 respectively) ... Daniel's prayer is focused upon the physical return from Babylon—the first stage in redemption, but the angelic message and vision of the Seventy Weeks is focused upon the forgiveness of sins and renewal of covenant and righteousness—the second stage in return from exile" (Gentry, "Daniel's Seventy Weeks," 31). Gentry's observation is significant for two reasons. First, it shows the linchpin nature of the forgiveness of sins in redemptive history. Second, it shows that the Isaianic background to Daniel, which will be crucial in understanding Dan 9:24. See also Tanner, "Is Daniel's Seventy-weeks Prophecy Messianic?," 323–27. Tanner also notes the intertextuality of the term "Messiah" as part of Isaiah, which pulls an Isaianic context to the entire seventy-week prophecy. See also Goldingay, *Daniel*, 259. Notice Goldingay's statement, "The oracle might then be a response to Daniel's confession of Israel's sin, promising cleansing and relief from the afflictions that have come as sin's punishment; it would then parallel Isa 40:1–2 ..."

38. Lucas, *Daniel*, 242.

39. Ibid.; Tanner, "Is Daniel's Seventy-weeks Prophecy Messianic?" 330; Wood, *Commentary on Daniel*, 250. While Lucas describes a situation like Isa 11, Tanner explicitly states the connection.

40. Young, *Prophecy of Daniel*, 200.

41. Walvoord, *Daniel*, 222. Walvoord also mentions Isa 11, however.

42. Miller, *Daniel*, 267.

43. Tanner, "Is Daniel's Seventy-weeks Prophecy Messianic?" 330. Tanner forcefully argues for this. After citing Isa 1:26, 2:1–4, 11:1–10, 32:1, and 62:1–2, he states, "when Daniel wrote that one of the purposes for the seventy weeks is 'to bring in everlasting righteousness' (Dan. 9:24), this would have been freighted with meaning for the Jews, for they were looking forward to what the Messiah, Son of David, would accomplish for Israel as a nation and for the world."

everlasting righteousness, to seal both vision and prophet, and to anoint the most holy.' The atoning suggests the servant's work in Is. 53, and the bringing in of 'everlasting righteousness' reminds one of 53:11.[44]

If this is the case, then Daniel has the result of Isaiah's vision and eschatology in mind.

Another infinitive deals with the anointing of the holy place (וְלִמְשֹׁחַ קֹדֶשׁ קָדָשִׁים). This probably does not refer to a person, but rather the temple or holy sanctuary, which has been in view throughout the context (cf. Dan 9:16–17).[45] If this infinitive refers to the inauguration of an eschatological temple, could this relate to Ezekiel's final vision, in which God's presence is realized throughout the cosmos via the temple in Jerusalem? Scholars acknowledge the connection.[46] Miller makes this precise argument:

> If a future temple is intended, which seems the best view, then it would be the edifice described in Ezek 40–48. Daniel would have assumed that his readers were familiar with the prophecy of their contemporary, Ezekiel. This temple will be built and consecrated for service at the onset of the millennium.[47]

Hence, Dan 9:24 also seems to refer to the outcome of Ezekiel's vision.

This discussion has attempted to show how Dan 9:24 is associated with different elements of the respective visions and theologies of Isaiah and Ezekiel. Considering Daniel's intertextual strategy, he may again be incorporating the innertextuality within Isaiah and Ezekiel into his own theology. However, even if this apparent strategy is not "intentional," scholars have recognized that Daniel's statements describe a summary of eschatological prophecies of his predecessors.[48] At a bare minimum, what Daniel describes in Dan 9:24 appears to coincide with what prior texts have depicted.

In their parallelism, these six infinitives mutually compliment and fulfill one another. Contending with and removing sin facilitates the inauguration of the sanctuary, and atoning for iniquity is the judicial basis to end transgression.[49] This observation helps us better understand the infinitive phrase "seal up vision and prophecy." The descriptions in Dan 9:24 appear to reference the eschatological out-

---

44. Brownlee, "Servant of the Lord in the Qumran Scrolls," 13.

45. Collins, *Daniel*, 354; Goldingay, *Daniel*, 259; Miller, *Daniel*, 261; Lucas, *Daniel*, 242. All these scholars recognize that the verse refers to the temple. The debate concerns whether this temple is eschatological or exists during the time of Antiochus. If we recognize that the context is eschatological, then the former is preferred. Furthermore, if we see a near to eschatological connection between chapters 8 and 9, then the restoration of the temple in 8:13–14 corresponds to the eschatological inauguration of the temple in 9:24.

46. Miller, *Daniel*, 261; Wood, *Commentary on Daniel*, 250–51.

47 Miller, *Daniel*, 262.

48. Collins, *Daniel*, 354; Miller, *Daniel*, 259; Lacocque, *Book of Daniel*, 191; Keil and Delitzsch, *Old Testament*, 349; Baldwin, *Daniel*, 169. All of these commentators argue that Dan 9 sums up world history in light of how it was described in past revelation.

49. Miller, *Daniel*, 241.

comes depicted in prior visions. Arguably, vision and prophecy are authenticated and fulfilled because the other five infinitives, tied with Isaiah's and Ezekiel's vision and theology, are fulfilled. Collins states it well: "'Vision' here is interchangeable with 'prophecy.' The immediate referent is Jeremiah's prophecy, but the allusion probably includes all prophecy that is construed as eschatological."[50] Put differently, Dan 9:24 claims that vision and prophecy will be fulfilled because all the major elements of past visions and prophecies (like those in Isaiah and Ezekiel) are found in this verse and will be simultaneously fulfilled at the culmination of history. They are all tied to the same *telos*. In this way, Dan 9:24 seems to communicate something quite close to the biblical theology of vision that I have posited.

Relative to Daniel's own theology of kingdom and vision, this entire discussion shows that kingdom and eschatology involve much more than just God's definitive rule or any political outcome. Isaiah's stress on the necessity of dealing with sin and holiness is still present in Daniel. Also, the agenda of God's presence and ship, as described by Ezekiel, is a part of YHWH's rule. We can tie this back to Dan 7, to the scene where Daniel's concept of kingdom is fulfilled. Why does Daniel mention Ezekiel's chariot-throne and allude to Isaiah (Dan 7:9)? In the flow of the book, Dan 9 seems to remind the reader that what is accomplished in Dan 7 is the fulfillment of God's entire agenda, depicted from different aspects of past visions and prophecies.[51] Kingdom cannot be divorced from the totality of God's plan and all it entails. Instead, those elements are equally and essentially a part of God's kingdom. This too magnifies the epic nature of the visionary event and supports the thesis of a biblical theology of vision.

Kingdom as the Victory of the Saints (Present versus Eschatological)

The tension between the present and the eschatological is central to the visions and theologies of Isaiah and Ezekiel. This too carries over to Daniel. While Dan 7 deals with the glory of the kingdom and culmination of history, Dan 8–12 immerses the reader into the details of history, both near and more distant. As such, Dan 8–12 remind readers that while God will have final dominion, the present is laden with kingdom delay and suffering.[52] God's people still live in the time of the statue, before the

---

50. Collins, *Daniel*, 354.

51. Ibid. Recall Collins' comment on an eschatological ideal. See also, Baldwin, *Daniel*, 169. Baldwin labels this the "accomplishment of God's purpose for history." As already discussed (and as will be discussed further), Dan 7 and 9 interconnect. Initially, both deal with the culmination of history. Moreover, both involve the number three and a half (cf. Dan 7:25; 9:25–26) as well as a messianic figure (Dan 7:14; 9:25). Hence, Dan 9 explains the outcome of Dan 7. Both chapters seem to cover the fourth kingdom as well, which further unifies them. Overall, these chapters seem to cover the same entities at the same time and even in the same types of circumstances. In this way, Dan 9 seems to contribute to Dan 7.

52. Beale, "Influence of Daniel," 414; Goldingay, "The Stories in Daniel," 114–15.

stone destroys all other kingdoms and becomes a great mountain. Nonetheless, God is still in control throughout. In Daniel's words, the Lord sets both the "times" (עִדָּנַיָּא, individual circumstances) and the "epochs" (וְזִמְנַיָּא, eras of history). Thus, although suffering exists in the present, God's sovereignty paves the way to eschatological victory. In this section, I will first discuss the nature of suffering, and then how it relates to this eschatological salvation.

Daniel details how kingdom delay causes turmoil from the current time to the distant future. In Dan 8, the presence of the ram and goat, corresponding to the second and third metals/beasts, indicates that God's final reign has not yet commenced. Instead, Israel will be subjected to the kingdoms of Medo-Persia and Greece (8:21). Although the symbolism of Dan 8 directly corresponds with historical events, understanding the metaphorical depiction is equally valuable in seeing the intent behind the vision.

The violence inflicted by both animals against other nations (v. 4) and towards each other (vv. 6–7) enhances the vivid turmoil presented in chapter 7 (vv. 3–8). Tremendous viciousness occurs as one animal kills the other only to have its horn broken into four (8:7–8). This leads to further suffering as a small, but quite boastful horn tramples on the hosts of heaven and the stars (v. 10), a significant metaphor for the saints (cf. 8:24; 12:3) before desecrating the temple (8:11). The emphasis on the temple is significant. We have observed that the temple correlates with the establishment of God's kingdom (cf. Dan 2:35; 9:24). Its desecration reinforces the disgrace of the people and that they are far from the stability and peace that the kingdom offers.[53]

At the same time, the Jewish people themselves are far from being right with God. Their transgression brings about their woe (8:12).[54] Delay of kingdom and suffering relate to the people's need for transformation in conformity with God's holiness. In this way, the Danielic depiction of exile intertwines both political and spiritual elements to demonstrate that this is a dark time for Israel. While these descriptions of tumult may perhaps seem stale and distant to a modern-day reader, in Daniel's firsthand experience, this revelation caused him to be sick for days (v. 27). All of this affirms that the suffering his people were about to encounter was immense.

This oppression does not merely pertain to the immediate time, but also extends to the end time. As noted above, the angel relates the current time of wrath (8:19) with the end time (לְעֶת־קֵץ; 8:17–19). The horn imagery ties the discussion of the horn of the third kingdom with the horn of the fourth kingdom. In fact, both share quite a few similarities in their boastful character (7:8; cf. 8:4), brilliant minds (וַאֲלוּ עַיְנִין 7:8, כְּעַיְנֵי אֲנָשָׁא; cf.), and persecution of the saints (7:21).[55] As discussed before, Daniel seems to make an analogy between near history and far history.

---

53. Goldingay, *Daniel*, 206.
54. Ibid., 211; Miller, *Daniel*, 227; Anderson, *Daniel*, 96.
55. Miller, *Daniel*, 283; Steinmann, "Antichrist in Daniel" 201–9.

The seventy-weeks prophecy also seems to bridge these two time periods. Some consider the events described therein as references to the work of Antiochus Epiphanes. The destruction of the temple and persecution in Dan 9:26 seem to parallel Antiochus Epiphanes' boastful and violent activities mentioned in 8:13–14, 25.[56] However, two factors point out that the events in Dan 9:24–26 go beyond the events surrounding Antiochus Epiphanes. First, Dan 9:24 describes realities that are far broader than just the intertestamental period. Rather, the summation of all history is in view.[57] This gives the content of the seventy-weeks prophecy a more eschatological bent. Second, this explanation can account for the similarities between Dan 9:26 and 8:13–14, 25. If what occurs in that near time prefigures what will happen later, we would expect to see some similarities. However, instead of repeating what chapter 8 expresses, the seventy-weeks prophecies show the "far distant" future that Dan 8 anticipates. Such a reading does justice to the contextual factors presented. Not surprisingly, it is also the traditional reading of the text, stemming from the early church.[58]

In light of this interpretation, the seventy-weeks explain that the turmoil of the present will extend to the distant future. Jerusalem and the temple will be destroyed, prolonging exile (9:26–27). Israel's hopes will be dashed again as a ruler (Antichrist) makes a covenant with the people but then breaks it (v. 27). His duplicity culminates in disrupting the entire worship system and causing absolute abominations that are designed to persecute the people.[59]

Daniel continues to expand upon his description of the nature of kingdom delay in the final chapters of his book. Notably, Dan 10–12 reinforce a connection between the discussion of near and far history and the arrival of the eschatological kingdom depicted in Dan 7. The messenger in Dan 10:5–6 initially seems to draw all these factors together. In this passage, a heavenly being appears, resembling the glory described in Dan 7:9–13.[60] This likeness indicates an association between the angel's message and

---

56. Goldingay, *Daniel*, 259; Collins, *Daniel*, 356.

57. Baldwin, *Daniel*, 169.

58. Parry, "Desolation of Temple," 485. Although Parry takes a different view, he acknowledges that the reading above is traditional. He cites Hippolytus and Jerome as examples of those who upheld a future Antichrist view in Dan 9.

59. Miller, *Daniel*, 267; Goswell, "Temple Theme in the Book of Daniel," 519. Goswell connects all the temple violations together in his article. He rightly argues that this is a motif in the book. Contra Gentry, "Seventy Weeks," 38–40. Gentry views this as a prophecy of what takes place in the first advent period and immediately thereafter (e.g., 70 a.d.). Nonetheless, his interpretation is not widely accepted. Dan 9 seems to have a more expansive scope than only Christ's first advent.

60. Goldingay, *Daniel*, 283–85; Hamilton, *God's Glory*, 334; Kim, *Origin of Paul's Gospel*, 209. Contra Miller, *Daniel*, 281. Miller argues that this is a Christophany because of the overwhelming presence of this individual, as well as the notable similarities to Ezek 1:26–28. If this is the case, then this strengthens the case that I make above. If not, then at a bare minimum an affiliation between this angel and Dan 7 (as well as Ezek 1:26–28) exists, as Goldingay observes. In any case, some caution here might be best, especially since this individual appears to be a messenger (10:11) who requires angelic assistance (v. 13). However, identifying this individual as a theophanic Angel of the Lord may be problematic, since that being previously swore by himself directly (Gen 22:16) as opposed to God (Dan 12:7).

Dan 7.[61] At the same time, the angel explains to Daniel what will take place soon and what will take place at the end (cf. 11:35). Synthesizing these observations, the angel's message in Dan 11–12 connects with the inauguration of the Son of Man. The angel thereby signals that the present will meet the eschatological.

Dan 11–12 explains how this meeting occurs. As noted, the paradigm of near to far future is in play. The wealth of details in Dan 11 concerning the interactions of the Ptolemies and Selucids impress readers with the instability and violence of the immediate future, paving the way for the final section of chapter 11, which seems to portray the eschatological persecution of God's people. As noted above, this interpretation takes the fact that scholars have not found a historical referent for 11:36—12:3 into consideration. Linguistic data also supports this interpretation. The Jewish struggle's failure foreshadows a time still yet appointed (לַמּוֹעֵד, 11:35) which occurs at the end (וּבְעֵת קֵץ, 11:40; cf. 8:11–17). Such terminology was used in chapter 8 to suggest the near to far history analogy in the first place. It probably functions similarly here.

Consequently, evil and war beyond anything in history will take place. An ultimate evil king will use his unmatched military and economic power to pull the world under his allegiance (v. 38). He will engage in overwhelming military conquest and conflict, and nations will fall (vv. 39–44). In the center of this aggressive campaign is the Holy Mountain (v. 45). The mountain of God's kingdom has not yet filled the earth (cf. 2:35). Instead, it is still in exile and is threatened (11:45) as it has been in the past (cf. 8:13; 9:18–19).

How does this set up for the scene in Dan 7? That chapter describes an evil king who boasts (v. 8) and speaks out against the Most High (v. 25). This establishes the context for the heavenly court to convene (vv. 9–14). Interestingly enough, the king of 11:35–45 is also first described as one who speaks monstrous blasphemies against God (11:36). This commences a period of unparalleled distress (12:1), just like Dan 7:25 implies. Arguably, Dan 11:34–35 parallels what Dan 7 describes. If this is the case, Dan 11–12 moves the reader from near history to distant history, which is the very situation of Dan 7:9–14. The saints' turmoil extends to the time when the present will be resolved in the eschatological of Daniel's central vision.

Hence, the people of God do not merely anticipate kingdom delay and suffering. Scattered throughout chapters 8–12 are indications of hope. Near history does

---

61. See above note. See also Goldingay's fitting observation: "The man in linen is described in more awesome terms than have been used of Gabriel previously, like those used of God himself in Ezek 1. But they need not indicate that the person *is* God, or represents God (like the messenger of YHWH, e.g., Gen 16), only that the passages have this literary connection... The figure in v. 11 has the task of speaking, not acting, and the description of his role in v. 12 corresponds to that of Gabriel in 9:20–23; so also v. 14. Whether or not he *is* Gabriel, he has a role like Gabriel's. There is no reason to link any of the figures here specifically with the humanlike figure of 7:13. Like chapter 7, the scene has the allusiveness that often characterizes vision reports and the visionary experience itself, and exegesis must preserve this allusiveness. It heightens the awesomeness of what is described" (Goldingay, *Daniel*, 291). By this, the messenger actually signals a connection between Dan 10–12 and the fulfillment of the vision in Dan 7.

not only relate to far history in suffering, but also in salvation. In the near history surrounding Antiochus, God reveals that Antiochus will die, but not by the hand of man (8:25, וּבְאֶפֶס יָד יִשָּׁבֵר). This verse reminds the reader of the stone, not made with hands, that crushes all the kingdoms. God's sovereignty to end Antiochus' rule without human agency will mirror the time when he will also end human rule through an individual of supernatural origin (not made by hands).[62] God ordains one situation to show what will take place in the other, all of which hinges on the scene in Dan 7.

We can further observe how these events of the near future give way to the distant future. Antiochus' demise assures that indeed the horn of the fourth kingdom, or the king of the north, will come to an end (11:45; cf. 7:11). Similarly, the reinstitution of the temple at the time of Antiochus (8:14) foreshadows that the holy place will be consecrated at the end, as described in Daniel's seventy-weeks prophecy (cf. 9:24), and marks the completion of Ezekiel's vision and theology.

In addition, those who led others to righteousness will receive the eternal righteousness previously promised (Dan 12:3b; cf. 9:24b).[63] These individuals will also awaken from their sleep to everlasting life (12:2). This arguably refers to resurrection and the saints' victory over death, including Daniel, who will receive his due at the end time (12:13).[64] The imagery of waking from dust and receiving life echoes Isaiah's wording in 26:19.[65] In that text, God's exclusive reign in Jerusalem ends death and reflects his "high and lifted up" status. Dan 12 echoes Isaiah in other ways as well. For example, the saints in Daniel seem to parallel Isaiah's Servant. The wording "those who are wise" (וְהַמַּשְׂכִּלִים, Dan 12:3) matches the wording of the Servant's success (יַשְׂכִּיל; Isa 52:13). Leading people to righteousness (Dan 12:3b) likewise matches how the Servant has justified the many (Isa 53:11). Accordingly, Daniel seems to draw from the Servant's victory and resurrection as the basis for the saints' triumph. As I will discuss, such solidarity is implied between the saints and the Son of Man in Dan 7:13–27. If all of this is true, Daniel ties the victory of the saints with the Servant *and* with the Son of Man (another connection that will be discussed further). He also relates all of this to a future moment of the Servant's rule over the world. In so doing, Daniel seems to import Isaiah's theology of vision into his own. They envision the same outcome.[66]

---

62. Miller, *Daniel*, 236; Goldingay, *Daniel*, 218.

63. Block, "Beyond the Grave," 136; Miller, *Daniel*, 319; Baldwin, *Daniel*, 206; Collins, "Apocalyptic Context."

64. Miller, *Daniel*, 317–18; Collins, *Daniel*, 392. Collins here is emphatic: "Resurrection language is certainly used metaphorically in the Hebrew Bible (e.g., Ezekiel 37; Hos 6:2*), but there is virtually unanimous agreement among modern scholars that Daniel is referring to the actual resurrection of individuals from the dead, because of the explicit language of everlasting life."

65. Collins, *Daniel*, 392; Goldingay, *Daniel*, 307; Miller, *Daniel*, 318; Bailey, "Intertextual Relationship of Daniel 12," 305–8.

66. Barry, *Resurrected Servant in Isaiah*, 4–5; Levenson, *Resurrection and the Restoration of Israel*, 188.

Daniel provides one final description of God's people in Dan 12. The saints will shine like the bright stars of heaven (v. 3). The image of the star had previously been associated with the saints (cf. 8:10). In Dan 8, that image appeared in the context of how Antiochus would trample the people of God in persecution. Considering that the metaphor only occurs in chapters 8–12, it appears to be another innertextual wordplay. The suffering of the saints under one ruler is conquered as they transform spiritually in righteousness, overcome false kingdoms, enter into God's kingdom, and triumph over the final foe, death. The stars that suffered now shine. The kingdom, in this way, marks the complete victory of the saints.

Relative to Dan 7, this entire discussion fills out God's depiction of the horn's war with the saints and their final victory (7:21–22). Kingdom delay and suffering mark the present period, which itself provides precedent for even greater persecution to come and prefigures an eschatological showdown when the persecution against God's people reaches its peak. Nonetheless, God's historically repeated deliverance of his people foreshadows an ultimate deliverance as well.

The solution of exile, suffering, and persecution lies in the event of Dan 7:9–14 (cf. Dan 7:26–27). The saints, in the midst of the most horrid persecution of all time, will meet with glorious deliverance when they are granted the kingdom and dominion over every enemy, including the horn of the fourth beast and death itself (Dan 7:21–22, 26–27; cf. 12:2–3). The heavenly court's decree will prevail over the entire cosmos for God's people. This not only fulfills Daniel's theology, but also Ezekiel's message, since Daniel discusses the reconstruction of the temple (Dan 8:14; 9:24). It also accomplishes Isaiah's message, since Daniel alludes to that prophet's description of righteousness and eternal life (Dan 12:2–3; cf. Isa 26:19). Once again, Daniel imports the innertextuality of his predecessors into his own theology because the outcome of the kingdom fulfills all vision and prophecy. This section reminds us that the culmination of history and kingdom does not merely relate to the world at large, but also to the saints' hope and desire. The vision of Dan 7 resolves the tension of the present suffering and the eschatological kingdom, the moment the people of God are waiting for.

KING: GOD'S EXCLUSIVE REIGN IN THE SON OF MAN

How will the saints have victory in the kingdom? What assurances do we have of this outcome? According to Dan 7:13–14, this assurance comes through the saints' association with the Son of Man.[67] This introduces us to another essential pillar of Daniel's

---

67. See the parallel with Dan 7:24–26, a point which I will expand upon. See also Collins, "Son of Man," 50–52; Dunn, *Christology*, 68–69. Collins offers several explanations for why some actually equate the two together. He qualifies these with a number of objections. It is best to see a corporate solidarity between them. Dunn also equates the two based upon the parallels between the individual beasts representing kingdoms. Nonetheless, Dunn acknowledges that there is something latent in the text that points to an individual as well.

theology of vision: the king. In fact, the discussion of kingdom in Daniel naturally leads to a discussion of the ruler. Kingdoms in Daniel often serve as a metonymy of their representative. For instance, Daniel refers to the "golden" kingdom of Babylon as Nebuchadnezzar (2:38). The four kingdoms in Dan 2:32–33 actually are referred to as four kings (מַלְכִין) in 7:17. In Daniel, a tight correlation exists between king and kingdom. As will be shown, God's unique authority is not merely demonstrated in his comprehensive reign but also in its concentration in one individual.

Statue Versus Stone

Although Dan 7 most vividly introduces this individual to the reader, the innertextuality of the Son of Man's inauguration are prevalent throughout the book. The foundational text again is in Dan 2, in the metaphorical contrast between statue and stone by which all of human might throughout history is matched against God's supernatural agent, and the latter wins. This struggle plays out throughout the book. We encounter a series of narratives in which various kings who attempt to exalt their own power or even to usurp divine authority fail. This section will focus on how these kings strive against God, whereas the next will deal with the significance of their failure.

In describing these kings' struggles, Daniel intertwines the motifs and descriptions of Nebuchadnezzar's original dream throughout the book to illustrate the conflict between statue and stone. Certain words and phrases also anticipate wording in Dan 7:14 concerning the Son of Man's reign. Nebuchadnezzar serves as the first example. God provides the king with the "kingdom, power, strength, and glory" (מַלְכוּתָא חִסְנָא וְתָקְפָּא וִיקָרָא, 2:37). He is the head of gold on the statue (2:38). However, other nations and kings will replace him (vv. 39–40). The opening of the next chapter describes Nebuchadnezzar challenging that entire agenda. He constructs an impressive statue (3:1). The statue alludes to Nebuchadnezzar's dream, but offers a twist. Instead of following the pattern God had established, the king crafts the image entirely of gold.[68] He wishes to reign over all of history, as opposed to any other kingdom or even God. For this reason, the king demands that all "peoples, nations, and tongues" (אֻמַיָּא וְלִשָּׁנַיָּא עַמְמַיָּא) fall down and worship (תִּפְּלוּן וְתִסְגְּדוּן) the image (3:4–5). Nebuchadnezzar thus assumes all human might and challenges his place within God's agenda in history.

Similarly, Nebuchadnezzar's later dream reiterates this challenge. This time, a tree reaches to the sky instead of a statue (4:11). Nonetheless, the metaphors are highly related. Both figures are large and tall (2:31; 3:1; 4:10–11). Both the golden head and the tree serve as a refuge for the birds of the air and beast of the field (2:38; 4:12–14). In this way, the tree repeats the paradigm of claiming all human might against the Lord. In fact, instead of recognizing and submitting to God's control, the tree is visible to the ends of the earth (4:11), echoing the activity of the stone, which becomes a mountain

---

68. Goldingay, *Daniel*, 69; Miller, *Daniel*, 105.

that fills the earth (2:38). The dream depicts Nebuchadnezzar's hubris in assuming the place of God for himself.[69] As opposed to the third chapter, in which Nebuchadnezzar opposes God's plan, this chapter shows the Babylonian king challenging God himself.[70]

Belshazzar follows in his father's footsteps. He, like his father, challenges God's authority by flippantly drinking and eating from the utensils and plates of the temple. He exalts the gods of gold, silver, bronze, iron, wood, and stone (5:3–4). Those materials may echo the composition of the statue.[71] If this is the case, Belshazzar recapitulates the same paradigm of his father, whose rebellion was described in terms of the statue/tree motif. Along this line, Daniel reiterates the similarities between the two (5:19–23). Like his father, Belshazzar had dominion over peoples, nations, and tongues (cf. 3:4; 4:1) and acted proudly.

Other kings in the book also follow suit. Darius sets himself against God by attempting to compel his servants not to pray (יִבְעֵה בָעוּ) to God. Although he tries, the king does not have the ability to deliver Daniel from the lions' den (6:14), though Daniel's God clearly can (v. 22).[72] Later in the book, the horn of the goat grows throughout the land (8:9), imitating the way the mountain fills the earth (2:35). This horn also reaches the sky, just like the statue and tree in Nebuchadnezzar's dreams (8:10; cf. 3:1; 4:11). Like the kings before him, this one exalts himself as equal to God (8:11). In later descriptions, this horn seems to correspond with the king of the north, who possesses a great dominion and military. Daniel's descriptions of his power actually use identical terms of "largeness and greatness" associated with the statue (בְּחַיִל גָּדוֹל וּבִרְכוּשׁ רָב, 11:13; cf. 2:31). This one, as others before him, exudes the might of human authority as originally portrayed by the statue in Dan 2.

This pattern of recapitulation prefigures the final king in 11:36–45. Daniel describes him as one who does not parallel his fathers (v. 37). He breaks the mold, not because he follows the true God, but because of the unsurpassed intensity of his pride and rebellion. He does not honor the false gods, as Belshazzar did, but rather the new god of the fortresses (11:37–38). Even more than the horn of the third beast (8:11), he will glorify himself and speak blasphemies against the true God (11:36). The final description depicts this ruler warring against the Holy Mountain. The term "mountain" does not occur often in the book. It refers primarily (if not exclusively)

---

69. Goswell, "Temple Theme in the Book of Daniel," 517.

70. The rest of the chapter confirms this interpretation. Nebuchadnezzar explicitly claims that he was solely responsible for Babylon's greatness (4:30). God's response stresses how he removed the king's sovereignty (v. 31). He will learn what the watchers state: the Most High gives authority and takes it away (4:14). In the end, Nebuchadnezzar recognizes how the Lord humbled his pride (v. 37) and has exclusive authority (v. 3).

71. Collins, *Apocalyptic Vision of the Book of Daniel*, 44; Goswell, "Temple Theme in the Book of Daniel," 515. Contra Goldingay, *Daniel*, 113. I am merely proposing an echo to the same ethos of the statue, which is contextually present in any case.

72. We can see a similar situation with the king's officials as well (cf. 6:24)

to Jerusalem (cf. 9:16, 20) and most likely alludes to Nebuchadnezzar's dream (2:35).[73] The employment of that image here suggests that this man attempts to challenge the ending and outcome of the vision. In this way, this king embodies the pinnacle of what the statue represents in terms of human authority, might, kingdom, and rebellion in its opposition to the stone/mountain.

In discussing these texts, I have endeavored to describe a pattern in Daniel. Various kings attempted to transgress the boundaries of the power and might that God had assigned to them. Daniel describes their efforts using terms found in the visions. In a sense, their efforts attempt to overthrow the vision, but in the end, only serve to confirm it. Human kings may have human might but will never rival God's authority. They all fail. Nebuchadnezzar cannot overcome Shadrach, Meshach, and Abednego in the furnace (3:23–26), and that Babylonian king becomes no better than the beast that lodged in the tree (4:33). Belshazzar dies, and Medo-Persians take over in accordance with God's plans (5:30; cf. 2:26–27). Darius finds out that God can deliver Daniel (6:22). The horn of the third beast will perish by divine agency (8:25). Even the final evil king will come to an end (11:45). All of these examples show how history falls into God's plan concerning the statue and the stone communicated in Dan 2. Within this, the finiteness of the human kings shows that they are not the stone, but rather part of the statue, which is ultimately pulverized by the stone

The Stone as the Son of Man

This transitions the discussion from the hubris of human kings to what the Lord reveals in their defeat. A specific question on this subject concerns the identity of the stone. As already discussed, the stone may be an Isaianic allusion to the Messiah (cf. Isa 28:16).[74] In light of the intertextuality of theology and vision between Isaiah and Daniel, could this element be interwoven into Daniel's narrative as well?

The kings' reactions in their downfall answer favorably. Nebuchadnezzar, who attempted to usurp worship from all people, nations, and tongues, now commands that worship to go to the only one who is worthy: Daniel's God (3:29). He also proclaims God's wonders to all people, nations, and tongues (4:1). He acknowledges God's eternal dominion, which no one can resist (v. 35). As a result, he praises and honors God (v. 37). Darius shares similar sentiments. He too writes to all people, nations, and tongues, declaring that God's kingdom will not be destroyed (6:25). The Lord alone can deliver and do wonders throughout the cosmos (v. 26). These exclamations acknowledge that God alone has a perpetual dominion and that he has not extended such power to any of these human kings.

---

73. Goldingay, *Daniel*, 60.
74. Evans, "Daniel in the New Testament," 507–9.

However, the kings do not merely recognize God's exclusive authority, but also that he assigns it to whom he pleases.⁷⁵ Daniel explicitly states as much to both Nebuchadnezzar (4:25) as well as to Belshazzar (5:21). In fact, the prophet does not merely proclaim this truth, but actually exemplifies it. Daniel, like the prophets before him, actually functions as a microcosm of his message. This theme emerges as the kings consistently give honor and promotion to Daniel and to his friends. The king admits that God had not given him unique insight or power, but rather bestowed such upon Daniel (2:45). Nebuchadnezzar bows and pays homage (סְגִד) to Daniel (v. 46). The act probably signifies giving honor to Daniel's God and implies that Daniel is the one through whom God mediates his authority.⁷⁶ He then places Daniel, along with his friends, over the province of Babylon and over the wise men (vv. 48–49). In the narrative, these characters serve as a foil to the king. In this way, the narratives show how God takes away a king's presumed power and assigns it to godly individuals. Daniel thereby positively reflects God's dominion. Goldingay concurs:

> But this highlights the symbolic significance of each of these elements in the story. They are witness to the fact that pagan powers do put believers under pressure, but that they are destined to be defeated, and ultimately to bow before the name that is above every name (Isa. 45.23; Phil. 2.10–11).⁷⁷

This hints that while human kings are ultimately unworthy or unable to possess divine authority, there will be one who does. Daniel's development in the narratives suggests this reality. Daniel and his friends begin in the court (1:19–20) but receive a series of promotions through which Darius intends to put Daniel over the entire kingdom (6:1). Only the Son of Man ultimately is put in charge of the kingdom (7:14). Furthermore, Nebuchadnezzar assigns honor to Daniel, who provides the dream and its interpretation (2:6). The word "honor" (יקר) occurs only seven times in Daniel. Five of those occurrences concern Nebuchadnezzar, on whom God bestows honor before taking it away (2:37; 4:27, 33; 5:18, 20). Daniel is the only positive recipient of glory other than the final instance: the Son of Man in Dan 7:14. For that matter, the term "son of man" only occurs twice in Daniel as well; once referring to Daniel (8:17) and the other to one *like* a son of man (7:13).⁷⁸ Daniel may very well foreshadow the Son of Man's inauguration in Dan 7:9–14.

---

75. Goldingay, "Daniel in the Context," 644. Goldingay's observation corroborates my own. In reference to Dan 3, he states, "God delivers, but not by taking action in person; God delivers by sending someone else." Goldingay notes a repeated pattern of mediated authority throughout the book and links this with Dan 7. See also Evans, "Daniel in the New Testament," 501. Evans notes the exact same pattern in Nebuchadnezzar, Belshazzar, and finally, the Son of Man.

76. Bruce, "Discourse Theme," 182–83. Bruce's discourse analysis is useful in showing how the narratives are to be read in an eschatological framework. He comments that Daniel's victories are indicative of the fact that, in the end, the saints will achieve the kingdom. This of course only occurs through the Son of Man. In this way as well, Daniel can be used as a signifier to that messianic individual.

77. Goldingay, "The Stories in Daniel," 102–3.

78. Schmid, "Daniel Der Menschensohn," 192–221.

These factors bring Dan 3:25 to the forefront. I have already shown how the kings acknowledge that God alone possesses ultimate authority. I have also shown that God can positively assign this power to individuals. These two ideas come together in the story of the fiery furnace. Nebuchadnezzar points the reader to a fourth mysterious person in the furnace. On one hand, the king refers to him as a man (3:25, גֻּבְרִין). On the other hand, he also describes him as a "son of gods" (בַר־אֱלָהִין, v. 25) in reference to his divine nature.[79] The narrative presents the reader with an individual to whom God can assign ultimate sovereignty, for he is both a "human" individual, yet simultaneously divine. Perhaps this person is the Son of Man, the Messiah.[80]

However, some scholars object to this identification.[81] After all, Nebuchadnezzar later refers to him as an angel (3:28, מַלְאֲכֵהּ). Perhaps this man was merely a supernatural being as opposed to divine. Several observations argue against this supposition:

1. These statements are from Nebuchadnezzar's perspective. The king may not know who the person is (and thereby confuse his function) but may still be able to identify what kind of person he is. Hence, the phrase "son of the gods" as a reference to divinity is significant. Nebuchadnezzar knew this was not any ordinary person, recognizing him as belonging to the divine pantheon.

2. Nebuchadnezzar's recognition most likely rules out a "lesser supernatural being" such as an angel. As such, from Nebuchadnezzar's perspective, this individual is the son of the gods, not one of the gods' servants, and thereby partakes of divine nature.[82]

3. In that regard, "angel" may not necessarily refer to a lesser being. Even in Jewish literature, an angel could actually be God himself (cf. Gen 22:15–16). Montgomery points out that "angel" could, in western Semitic literature, refer to the appearance of a god.[83] Hence, Nebuchadnezzar's statements are not necessarily contradictory, but rather point to a divine being.

4. The phrase "one like a son of the gods" (דָּמֵה לְבַר־אֱלָהִין) sounds quite similar to "one like the son of man" (7:13, כְּבַר אֱנָשׁ). In fact, the construction of preposition + בר in the singular only occurs in these two texts. The linguistic similarity may point to their connection. Finally, the divinity of the "son of the gods" may also link to what is communicated by "son of man" in Dan 7. Boyarin argues that the phrase "son of man" actually refers to divinity rather than humanity.[84] If this is the case, the divinity of the individual in Dan 3 observed by a pagan likely prefigures the divine individual in Dan 7 seen by an Israelite.

79. Collins, *Daniel*, 190; Miller, *Daniel*, 123; Goldingay, *Daniel*, 71.
80. See Collins, *Daniel*, 190. Christian scholars have traditionally taken this position.
81. See Goldingay, *Daniel*, 71.
82. Miller, *Daniel*, 125.
83. Montgomery, *The Book of Daniel*, 214–15.
84. Boyarin, *Jewish Gospels*, 83–87; Boyarin, "Daniel 7," 139–62.

5. The vision of Dan 2 is in the immediate background. Not only is it in close proximity, but Nebuchadnezzar has also challenged that entire vision by making a statue completely out of gold. In light of this, Dan 3 could be a sort of recapitulation of the previous chapter.[85] The account, then, not only shows the hubris of the statue (and king) but also subtly reveals the stone God will use to conquer all kings.

If these observations are valid, then the series of events in Dan 3 serve as a microcosm of Dan 2 and by extension, Dan 7. The episode of the fiery furnace reminds all that the entire might of the statue cannot topple God. Rather, the stone, which is associated with the divine figure in the fire and ultimately, the one like the son of man, will overcome.

One final passage plays into this discussion: Dan 9:24–26. Gabriel seems to further describe the Son of Man (Dan 7:14) in the seventy-weeks prophecy. The angel refers to him as "Messiah prince" (מָשִׁיחַ נָגִיד). The term "prince" does not denigrate his kingly position. Rather, it matches the entire theology of Daniel, as Murray notes:

> In our texts the *melek* is one who sees his power from YHWH as susceptible to his own arbitrary manipulation, who obtrudes himself inappropriately and disproportionately between YHWH and Israel, and who treats Israel as little more than the subjects of his monarchic power. The *nāgîd*, on the other hand, is positively portrayed as one who sees his power as a sovereign and inviolable devolvement from YHWH, who acts strictly under the orders of YHWH for the benefit of YHWH's people, and holds himself as no more than the willing subject of the divine monarch.[86]

Hence, the title "prince" actually is conceptually consistent with the Son of Man in Dan 7. It communicates the endowment of divine authority corresponding to what takes place in Dan 7:14, when the Most High grants the Son of Man all authority and sovereignty. In fact, "prince" can denote a Davidic figure as well as a messianic individual (cf. Isa 55:4). This consequently precludes the identification of Onias III, who is a priest and not a royal figure.

Other connections between Dan 9:24–26 and 7:14 exist. Both contexts deal with the culmination of history. Gabriel associates the Messiah prince with the fulfillment of the purposes behind the seventy weeks.[87] As discussed, those dealt with the consummation of God's plan. For that reason, Oswalt claims that 9:25–26 is the most unambiguous reference to Messiah as eschatological figure in the OT.[88] The individual

---

85. Young, *Prophecy of Daniel*, 83–85.

86. Gentry, "Seventy Weeks," 33; Murray, "Divine Prerogative," 299.

87. As discussed, 9:24 deals with ideals that fulfill vision and prophecy. The Messiah prince is involved in that process. Even though this passage discusses suffering as opposed to the exaltation seen in Dan 7:9–14, my point is that they are both implicated in eschatological realities.

88. Oswalt, "משח," 2:1126.

in Dan 7:9–14 also relates to the fulfillment of history. Hence, both characters, by their contextual description, seem to share a similar purpose.

Further details of the texts also point to this conclusion. Both contexts refer to a period of three-and-a-half. In Dan 7:25, an evil king makes changes to the law during a period of a "time, times, and half a time" (three-and-a-half units). In Dan 9:27, an evil prince also abolishes certain laws, such as offerings, at the halfway point of a "week" (a period of seven, half of which is three-and-a-half), which corresponds to a period of three-and-a-half years. In light of this association, the king in Dan 7:25 and the prince in 9:26–27 most likely refer to the same individual.[89] In the same way, the good ruler (the Son of Man) in Dan 7:14 most likely corresponds with מָשִׁיחַ נָגִיד in 9:25.

Accordingly, Dan 9:25–26 may very well expand upon the function of the figure in Dan 7:13–14. The seventy-weeks reminds the audience that the Son of Man does not merely rule and have dominion, as stated in Dan 7:14 and implied in Dan 9:24–26. He also functions like a priest who who suffers in atonement for sins (9:26). As discussed, such a motif echoes Isaiah's description of the Servant (Isa 52:13—53:12).[90] At this point, Daniel positively identifies the Son of Man as the same individual as Isaiah's Servant. This is not the only time Daniel does this. As discussed, Dan 12:3 also seems to relate the Servant, the saints, and the Son of Man.[91]

This connection has several important implications for Daniel's discussion of the Messiah as well as a broader discussion concerning a biblical theology of vision. By linking Isaiah's Servant with the Son of Man, Daniel merges the vision and theology of Isaiah into his own vision. After all, in Isaiah, I argued that the Servant ultimately is the one high and lifted up (Isa 52:13). By stating that the exalted individual of Dan 7:13–14 is the same as the Servant (cf. 9:26), Daniel acknowledges this same fact, which serves as yet another example of how Daniel brings out the innertextuality of

---

89. Miller, *Daniel*, 267; Collins, *Daniel*, 356; Young, *Prophecy of Daniel*, 259–60. Contra Gentry, "Seventy Weeks," 39; Parry, "Desolation of Temple," 499. Gentry and Parry view this individual as Christ, and the desolation as his positive work of healing and dissolving the temple. While this is possible, it is less likely, given the way the visions relate innertextually. It would make an exception to the negative notion of the term "abomination" as it appears in the book (cf. 11:31; 12:11) in connection to these texts. A further connection that associates the prince of Dan 9:26–27 with evil as opposed to Christ is the participle, הַבָּא. It is used in reference to this prince as well as to another evil prince (Ptolemy V) who, in context, is compared with Alexander the Great (11:3) and the unidentifiable king in 11:36. See Chisholm, *Handbook on the Prophets*, 320; Collins, *Daniel*, 357, 380. Again, the interpretation I give above is traditional and widely accepted. See also Goldingay, *Daniel*, 262: "The hostility of Jason's action may well be indicated by the expression 'to come' (הבא): the verb is used frequently of an aggressive 'coming' in ch. 11 (e.g., v. 10, with the term 'flood' [שטף] as here; cf. NEB here). 'His end' and 'the end' are closely related." Although we may disagree over the identification of the prince, Goldingay makes the same correlation about the participle and further anchors the association with more lexical connections.

90. Miller, *Daniel*, 267; Collins, *Daniel*, 356; Young, *Prophecy of Daniel*, 250–55; Brownlee, "Servant of the Lord in the Qumran Scrolls," 13.

91. Barry, *Resurrected Servant in Isaiah*, 3–5; Levenson, *Resurrection and the Restoration of Israel*, 188. See above discussion for parallels.

prior vision and theology into his own vision. More to the point, Daniel depicts the Son of Man as the same individual who completes the visions and theologies of Isaiah and Ezekiel. He is the Servant who is cut off and atones for his people (Dan 9:24, 26a). Moreover, his work, described in the seventy-weeks prophecy, contextually takes place so that the holy place can be anointed per Ezekiel (Dan 9:24). This reinforces the unity of vision. Daniel demonstrates that the *same* person is involved in each of the visions, which supports that the visions are also describing the *same* event. All of this amplifies why the Son of Man receives all honor in the end of Dan 7. He fulfills all aspects of vision and prophecy.

Synthesis

This entire discussion details the significance of a single verse in Dan 7. Verse 14 illustrates how the Ancient of Days bestows dominion, glory, and a kingdom upon one like the son of man. All peoples, nations, and tongues should worship and serve him, as he alone has an eternal reign. Daniel records how kings previously attempted to compel people, nations, and tongues to worship and serve them. They mocked or doubted the legitimacy of serving the true God. They attempted to usurp all authority and glory for themselves. However, in the end, they realized that they could never have any of those attributes. They are the statue and not the stone, and so God will grant such dominion to another. Their failures pave the way for the presentation of the true king. He is the only one who can receive all of these honors, because he fulfills vision and theology.

DANIEL 7: THE INAUGURATION OF THE KING

Thus far, we have understood the significance of Daniel's vision in part, but now we will grasp the whole. Our entire discussion has helped to sharpen the setting, nature, and significance of the central vision in Dan 7, and that vision provides the essential framework for us to see the significance of its parts. Hence, Dan 7 works as a synthesis to reveal the complete nature of the vision and theology in Daniel. As will be discussed, Dan 7 is not merely a summary presentation of the culmination of history, the fulfillment of God's agenda (vision and prophecy), or the victory of the saints. Instead, this chapter shows how kingdom, history, vision, and prophecy all hinge upon the Son of Man. His inauguration marks the climax of all that God's agenda entails. Such a synthesis makes a substantial contribution to a theology of vision of not only *what* the visionary entails but also *who* it centers upon.

Kingdom Contingent upon King (Dan 7:1–8)

The opening of the vision echoes the dream of Nebuchadnezzar in Dan 2. As such, the beasts represent the flow of history as represented by four major kingdoms. Additional details in Dan 7:1 affirm this reading. The prophet sees the four winds of heaven stirring up the sea. These winds may represent God's workings in the world and history.[92] The number four may also correspond to the entire progression of history itself, similar to what the *four* metals/beasts represent. This reinforces the nature of the visionary event. Daniel's central dream concerns the climax of history and kingdom. The context of Dan 7 is ultimately eschatological in nature.

However, certain details in verses 2–8 show that the vision also pertains to a more particular issue. The specific characteristics of the beasts mimic stories we have already read. For example, the lion is cast down, but then made to stand on its feet like a man (7:4). This echoes the humiliation of Nebuchadnezzar.[93] Also, the four-headed leopard anticipates the four horns that spring out from the single horn of the third beast in 8:8. The image refers not to a kingdom but to a king: Alexander the Great. The imagery of the beasts specifically represents kings rather than kingdoms, which the angel explicit affirms in 7:17.

To be sure, we cannot make a categorical separation between the two.[94] Throughout the book, king is juxtaposed with his country (cf. 2:38–39). That is the precise point of the association here. The emphasis is that the success and power of the kingdom hinges on the power of its king. History, then, is a struggle not only of kingdoms against God, but as the previous narratives have explained, kings against God. The success of any kingdom hinges upon its king. Thus the progression of beasts in this vision is not merely told from the standpoint of kingdoms found in Dan 2, but also in terms of the struggle of statue versus stone found in the narratives.

Accordingly, the authority, agility, intellect, ferocity, dominion, and sheer terror of these beasts dramatically describe the struggle of the kings against God and his agenda.[95] They retell what Daniel and his friends had experienced throughout

---

92. Collins, *Daniel*, 296. Collins argues against a mythological backdrop concerning the winds (not the sea). He does not see a connection with Gen 1:2 and the creation account. See also Goldingay, *Daniel*, 160. Goldingay argues that the winds do communicate God's activity over the world and that the number four corresponds to the four major directions on the compass. Such an interpretation fits with the overarching picture of God's work in world history. Miller concurs, "In this context, however, the figure seems rather to denote factors of all kinds that produce turmoil among the earth's nations throughout history. This must be the case, for the winds continually stir up the sea during the rise and fall of all four empires" (Miller, *Daniel*, 196).

93. Kratz, "Visions of Daniel," 95–96.

94. Dunn, *Christology*, 67–69; Schmidt, "'Son of Man.'"

95. See discussion in Goldingay, *Daniel*, 160–62; Collins, *Daniel*, 297–99. These attributes seem to reflect the three beasts. The lion possesses characteristics of authority with wings that denote agility. The bear denotes ferocity, and the leopard receives dominion over other nations (v. 6). The final beast is described as terrifying (דְּחִילָה וְאֵימְתָנִי).

the book, which also foreshadows the final climactic showdown of the might of humanity against God and his chosen one. For this reason, the fourth beast exceeds the rest and tramples them down (v. 7). What takes place in the fourth kingdom eclipses what has already taken place in prior kingdoms. The events of the near time only are a shadow of the end.

However, the vision not only focuses upon the unparalleled viciousness of the beast, but also its horn (vv. 7–8). Our discussion has already shown that the horn represents kings (cf. 7:17). Once again, the vision hones in not just on kingdom, but also on king. History climaxes with the battle of kings. In this final showdown, the horn utters great boasts (רַבְרְבָן, 7:8) a term used originally for the majesty of the statue and then picked up by Nebuchadnezzar (4:27) and Belshazzar (5:1). As stated before, those historical kings attempted to wield the full strength of human might, only to fail. The horn of the fourth beast surpasses them and embodies the might of the entire statue combined. As noted, he challenges whether there will even be a mountain to overtake the statue (cf. 11:45).

The opening of this chapter sharpens the focus of the vision. While the vision deals with the climax of history and kingdom, the linchpin of this is upon the king. Daniel has established that in the end, kingdoms rise or fall based on how God deals with their rulers. Kingdom and history are equally a story of statue versus stone. The ending of this first section makes this point quite poignantly. A ruler has arisen who is representative of all past efforts to usurp God's exclusive authority. This leaves readers with the sense that the destiny of history and kingdom hinges upon the final king. Who will it be? That is the ultimate question in Daniel's theology and vision of history.

Fulfillment of Vision and Prophecy in the King (Dan 7:9–14)

At this point, a familiar scene unfurls before Daniel. The Ancient of Days takes his seat on the chariot-throne, just as Isaiah and Ezekiel described (7:9). I have already mentioned the similarities between Daniel, Isaiah, and Ezekiel and will not belabor their connections here but will rather point out a likely reason behind the convergence of the visions. Daniel establishes that what he reveals is the same event as his predecessors and that they all share the same significance. The merging of the visions in Dan 7:9 therefore reflects how Daniel has merged the theologies of Isaiah and Ezekiel into his own work. Thus, Ezekiel's chariot-throne is present to remind Israel that God will complete his agenda concerning the anointing of the holy place (cf. Dan 9:24). The Ancient of Days seated on a throne reminds all that God will save and reign sovereign over the world. He will atone for Israel's sins, redeem them, and grant them eternal life and righteousness as Isaiah proclaimed (cf. Dan 9:24–26; Dan 12:2). As noted earlier, Daniel integrates the innertextuality of vision and theology of other books into his vision proper. This moment is the culmination of history and the fulfillment of vision and prophecy (9:24).

Consequently, this moment definitively deals with the question specifically posed in Daniel: who is the real king? When the court convenes, they destroy the boastful horn (7:11). Initially, this evidences that the visionary event does not merely pertain to heaven, but also to earth. This moment marks when heaven meets earth and its history. Accordingly, the court has declared to the world that the climax of history and kingdom belongs to no mere mortal. Not even one as powerful as the horn of the fourth beast, who had surpassed the power of all other rulers, can reign in the end. The other "beasts" (nations) are also made subservient. If not the horn or any of the other beasts, who is the real king?

At this juncture, one like the son of man appears on the scene (v. 13). Although I have used the term "Son of Man" as the title of this individual, technically the phrase describes one *like a son of man* (כְּבַר אֱנָשׁ אָתֵה). In what way is he comparable to a man? Initially, some suggest that this refers to his human-like appearance.[96] Similar phrases apply to angelic creatures in Daniel (cf. Dan 8:2; 10:5).[97] However, it goes far beyond this in both theological usage and context. The phrase implies not only similarity but also dissimilarity (or a lack of identity). The individual's appearance makes him comparable with other human individuals. Consistently, one area of overlap could be that like a man, God intended the Son of Man to bear his image and rule (Gen 1:28). This concept seems to be at play in this text, which has a creation backdrop. The very metaphor of various beasts that come out of the sea reminds one that God's creation is in view (Dan 7:1–8). Hence, Gen 1:28 and Adam could also be in the background of the idea of one like a son of man.[98] In further support of this reading, scholars acknowledge that the contextual use of "son of man" terminology in this text does not pertain to man's humility, but rather to royalty (cf. Ps 8:4).[99] This would also coincide with similar terminology in the context of Ezekiel's opening vision (1:5–12; 26–28).[100] Hence, the notion of authority seems to be a legitimate parallel between man and one like a son of man. However, the comparison between human authority and the Son of Man's dominion breaks down. In the broader context of Daniel, certain human rulers had attempted to exert their power unsuccessfully. In contrast, Daniel depicts the Son of Man as an immense ruler in receiving all dominion and authority (7:14) and overcoming the fourth beast (v. 26).

For these very reasons, the one like the son of man is different than every other human. Unlike previous kings who attempted to grasp all of God's authority but failed,

---

96. Collins, *Daniel*, 304; Kim, *Origin of Paul's Gospel*, 208; Dunn, *Christology*, 68–69.

97. Goldingay, *Daniel*, 167; Collins, *Daniel*, 309.

98. Lacocque, "Creation in Daniel 7," 126–28.

99. Collins, *Daniel*, 304–5; Schmidt, "'Son of Man,'" 22–26.

100. Note in Ezekiel that we have creational background with the four living creatures and then one like a man who sits on the throne. We discussed that this person probably has similarities with Adam, but exceeds him because he is God who fills the earth with his glory. That may be happening here. If this is true, this also strengthens the tie between the visions of Ezekiel and Daniel. See chapter 5 for details.

this "man" actually succeeds. This distinguishes him from (and above) the human kings of previous narratives, Daniel, and the angelic creatures as well.[101] Accordingly, the one like the son of man becomes the perfect image-bearer of God that man failed to be; he is divine.[102] I can draw upon further contextual support for this idea. The Son of Man, in this chapter, rides on the clouds, a description associated with divine theophanies (7:13; cf. Deut 33:26–28; Ps 18:10–11; 97:2; 104:3).[103] Previous discussion has already established his connection to the divine individual in the furnace. Similarly, Daniel's later identification of this individual with the Servant of Isaiah (9:24) reinforces his Messianic nature. Moreover, the authority he receives is one that is exclusively reserved for God himself (7:14; cf. 3:33; 6:27).[104] Overall, the one like the son of man shows that this individual takes on the role of man to rule. However, the description in context implies that he fulfills this role in a way that no mere mortal can.[105] He is God's perfect image-bearer, a new Adam, so to speak.[106]

For this reason, the language in 7:14 is quite poignant. The Son of Man receives glory, dominion, and a kingdom (שָׁלְטָן וִיקָר וּמַלְכוּ). Kings in past narratives attempted to possess and retain these attributes; however, they could not (cf. 2:37; 3:33; 4:22, 25). Instead, God takes their glory away and gives it to his chosen one, the Son of Man (cf. 4:25). Similarly, the Son of Man receives worship from every people, nation, and language (עַמְמַיָּא אֻמַּיָּא וְלִשָּׁנַיָּא). Again, past kings attempted to usurp that position. They too demanded worship from every people, nation, and language but in the end realized that all had to give honor to the Most High who gives it to one person alone, the Son of Man. Finally, God grants the Son of Man a kingdom that does not pass away. Other kings attempted to gain power and retain their kingdom but realized that only God has an eternal kingdom and he has given that to the Son of Man (7:14). He has full divine authority for he is the perfect image of God and thereby will rule forever.

---

101. Schmidt, "'Son of Man,'" 22–28; Kim, *Origin of Paul's Gospel*, 208; Morgenstern, "'Son of Man' of Daniel 7," 64–67.

102. See Boyarin, "Daniel 7"; Boyarin, *Jewish Gospels*, 83–87; Morgenstern, "'Son of Man' of Daniel 7," 76–77; Kim, *Origin of Paul's Gospel*, 207; Johnston, "Messianic Trajectories," 187. The logic here may be similar to what we observe in Ezekiel. Kim states, "when Ezekiel says he saw God in the form or likeness of man he is describing the reverse side of the great statement in Gen 1.26f that man was made בצלם כדמות of God." In Dan 7, the Ancient of Days hands over all of his authority and dominion to one like the son of man, in effect declaring that this individual is divine. He is the perfect image-bearer of God.

103. Miller, *Daniel*, 207; Goldingay, *Daniel*, 167; Montgomery, *The Book of Daniel*, 303–4; Wood, *Commentary on Daniel*, 193. Goldingay sees a parallel with Ezek 1, which ties the visions even closer together.

104. Goldingay, *Daniel*, 168.

105. This point is strengthened when we consider that Nebuchadnezzar's reign is described with Adamic terminology. God gives him charge over beasts and birds similarly to Adam (Dan 2:37–38; cf. Gen 1:28). See Goldingay, "Daniel in the Context," 644.

106. Lacocque, "Creation in Daniel 7," 128. While some may not accept all of Lacocque's suggestions, the motif of creation does seem to run in the background of Dan 7, casting "one like a son of man" as an "Adam-king."

As commentators recognize, this is the fulfillment of what was depicted in Dan 2:44.[107] The statue and stone conflict has ended with the victory going to the stone.

Therefore, in Daniel's theology, the central vision and its innertextuality unveil that history is a contest to determine who is the high king. Dan 7 reveals that despite the power and might displayed in world history, no one can match the Son of Man. How can we see God's ultimate and exclusive authority? Dan 7 testifies that God most visibly exhibits this power in the fact that he reserves it for one individual out of all history alone: the Son of Man.

However, we cannot forget that this all occurs at the intersection of the visions of Isaiah and Ezekiel. Daniel "zooms out" to bring us the full picture of what takes place. This is not the fulfillment of merely Daniel's message, but also of the visions and theologies of Isaiah and Ezekiel. Daniel revealed that the Son of Man is the same person as the Servant and facilitates the anointing of the holy place (cf. Dan 9:24–26). His arrival on this scene, variously described by prior visions and theologies, marks the celebration of what he has done and is about to do in reference to those themes. This moment is the fulfillment of vision and prophecy in the Son, which further demonstrates why there is no one like him.

The Victory of the Saints in the Son (Dan 7:15–28)

One further element remains in Daniel's theology of vision. The writer was not merely concerned with the breadth of history, but also with its impact upon God's people. Accordingly, the interpreting angel explains that, in the end, the *saints* (קַדִּישֵׁי עֶלְיוֹנִין) receive the kingdom (v. 18). This seems to parallel when the Son of Man receives dominion (7:14). Based upon this connection, some argue that the angel's claim construes the Son of Man as merely a symbol for the people of God. He is not an individual, but rather a corporate whole.[108] However, as already discussed, the immediate and innertextual context suggests an individual because of Daniel's emphasis on kings.[109]

That being said, Daniel seems to invite the reader to make an association between the Son of Man and the saints. The juxtaposition of one over the other signifies *corporate solidarity*, where the king intimately represents his people. In this case, the Son of Man's victory and dominion means that his people will also receive that same

---

107. Collins, *Daniel*, 311; Miller, *Daniel*, 210; Wood, *Commentary on Daniel*, 193–94.

108. Goldingay, *Daniel*, 170; Dunn, *Christology*, 68–69; Montgomery, *The Book of Daniel*, 323–24.

109. The term "son of man" seems to point to an individual in other biblical texts, including the book of Daniel (cf. Dan 8:17; Ezek 2:1). In addition, unlike the symbolism of the beasts and horns, the "one like a son of man" does not seem to function in the same way. After all, his appearance is in a slightly different scene, one with the non-symbolic individual, the Ancient of Days. Even more, in context, the "one like a son of man" would symbolize a king rather than anything else. Once again, the immediate context of kings as well as the potential innertextuality with Daniel's exaltation points to that function. Instead, just as king and kingdom overlap, could not the people of the kingdom overlap with their king? That is contextually acceptable, and such linguistic and contextual factors have grounded a solid, longstanding tradition against a corporate interpretation of the Son of Man.

success. Hence, he receives the kingdom and authority, and so do the saints (Dan 7:13–14, 26–27). This results from the true king overcoming the ultimate evil ruler who oppresses the saints (7:25–27). Like other elements of Daniel's theology of kingdom, the victory of the saints is found squarely in the Son.

I should mention one other observation here. Daniel's vision includes both Jew and Gentile in relation with the Son of Man. The phraseology surrounding "saints" appears to refer to Israel. For example, the phrase לְעַם קַדִּישֵׁי עֶלְיוֹנִין in verse 27 and the contrasting phrase of other "dominions" (שָׁלְטָנַיָּא) seem to cast the former as Israel and the latter as the Gentiles. Nonetheless, in Dan 7:14, those who surround and worship the Messiah are individuals from various peoples, nations, and languages. They are Gentiles. As Isaiah and Ezekiel established, God's reign and agenda relate not only to Israel, but also to the entire world (cf. Isa 2:2–4; 11:1–16; Ezek 39:21).[110]

DANIEL'S CONTRIBUTION TO A THEOLOGY OF VISION

Daniel makes a substantial contribution to a theology of vision in several ways. To begin with, Daniel enhances the motifs already discussed. He specifically amplifies Isaiah's theology of God's dominion. For Daniel, the Lord's reign is the climax of all world history. The kingdom of God will crush all other earthly kingdoms to fill the entire earth, just as Isaiah envisioned (Dan 2:35; cf. Isa 6:3). The visionary event unveils the triumph of God over nations and history. It provides the saints hope and resolution for their suffering. The vision concerns the exclusive glory of God's kingdom.

In addition, Daniel provides an important synthesis of vision and theology up to this point. Daniel integrates the innertextuality of his predecessors into his kingdom theology. He takes a variety of connections Isaiah and Ezekiel make between vision and theology and integrates them into his own vision. In so doing, Daniel confirms not only the innertextuality I suggested within those books, but also reinforces the

---

110. Another possible allusion to Isaiah is found in the term "saints." The term "holy ones" may refer to the fulfillment of Isaiah's agenda. Daniel uses the term "holy" (קדש) to refer to the divine distinctiveness (cf. 4:8; 5:11) as well as to the moral uprightness required by God (cf. 9:16). In fact, part of the outcome of redemptive history is the anointing of the holy place and the forgiveness of sin (9:24). The saints would be resurrected and characterized by a brilliant holiness and righteousness (12:2–3). Isaiah discusses his vision partially from the standpoint of transforming righteousness. Unholy Israel would be made holy. Daniel may see the outcome of that reality in his own vision. If this is the case, then Isaiah's vision and theology again dovetails with Daniel's. The saints receive the kingdom because they have been made holy and are ready to receive it. This all comes from the work of the Servant, the Son of Man, who is cut off to atone for his people (9:24–26). However, there are some significant problems with this suggestion because "saints" or "holy people" is used elsewhere of non-eschatological Israel (cf. Dan 8:24). Thus, the only way the allusion would work is if the harmonization of vision and theology relates the "holy ones" with those who are transformed in righteousness (12:2–3). The conceptual agreement with Isaiah is not, then, based upon the term "saints," but on who the people are, as discussed by Daniel. Thus, the allusion is not as strong. Daniel, however, still affirms that transforming holiness and atonement are critical, as Isaiah stresses (cf. Dan 9:24).

unity of all their visions. As a result, the visionary event also pertains to the fulfillment of vision and prophecy.

Daniel's synthesis focuses all these ideas upon the king. The struggle of kingdoms against God's agenda is actually that of their rulers, who attempt to claim divine sovereignty. This results in the persecution of the saints, both in the immediate future and its heightened display when a king of unparalleled power and evil arises (11:36–45). Nonetheless, each king in history, past and future, testifies that God always has the victory and grants his dominion to whomever he chooses.

All of this sets the stage for Dan 7. The major kings of redemptive history wage war against God and his saints, but in the end, God ultimately displays his definitive might by handing all authority over to the Son of Man. He is one like the son of man in that he surpasses all of mankind in his ability to reign. Consistently, this coronation officially inaugurates the rule of the Son of Man over all authorities, powers, and kingdoms. It also incorporates other visions, because their significances are also fulfilled at that moment. While other visions have emphasized God's centrality and implied the involvement of Messiah, Daniel puts the Son of Man in full focus. Daniel's synthesis brings background issues into the full forefront, a major contribution to a biblical theology of vision. In context, the prophet calls upon the saints to persevere, knowing that their victory is sure in that ultimate king. They are to look forward in the present to that eschatological moment (cf. Dan 12:13).

Hence, Daniel has provided us with a clear definition of the significance of the visionary event. It marks the eschatological moment when God gives glory and honor to the Son of Man to rule over all the earth. This coronation in heaven is likewise wrought upon the world. However, the moment also relates to when God's purposes (as depicted in prior visions) reach their climax because of the work of the Son of Man (cf. 7:13–14). He is the one who fulfills kingdom and king. He is the one who fulfills salvation. He is the one who fulfills the presence of God and the holy place. He is therefore the fulfillment of vision and prophecy.

7

Paul's Vision
Vision of Inauguration and Anticipation

VISION AND PAUL'S CALL AND MISSION

BIBLICAL THEOLOGIANS HAVE WRESTLED with identifying the center of Pauline theology. Some maintain it is justification while others insist it is salvation.[1] Reconciliation, as well as being "in Christ," are other suggestions. Schreiner notes a two-fold problem with these proposals (and the notion of a center at all). First, center implies that other themes or concepts are tertiary or inconsequential. Second, suggested centers risk falling outside of Paul's thought and imposing upon his writings rather than taking a more inductive approach.[2]

This chapter cannot resolve such concerns. Nonetheless, Paul's calling on the Damascus road at least plays a part in forming a framework (rather than center) to the apostle's theology. After all, Jesus tells Paul on the road to Damascus to bear witness to all that he has just seen and heard (Acts 26:16). Ananias repeats this commission (22:15). Such statements make the Damascus road experience a significant component of Paul's ministry. They indicate that the "innertextuality" between Damascus road and Pauline theology is real and quite formative.[3] In considering Paul's calling,

---

1. See discussion in Schreiner, *Pauline Theology*, 16–18. Kasemann, "God's Righteousness in Paul," 100–110.

2. Schreiner cites as examples Sanders, *Paul and Palestinian Judaism*; Schweitzer, *Mysticism of Paul the Apostle*.

3. I put innertextuality in quotes because while Paul technically references the event (cf. Gal 1:16), the event is not exhaustively or systematically described in his writings. Rather, we derive the experience from Luke's record in Acts. This connection does not strictly fit into the definition of innertextuality, but parallels the way a prophet's vision (recorded by that prophet) interfaces with the rest of his writing(s).

we can see where Paul's theology (partly) comes from and its goal, as opposed to a controlling idea. The Damascus road addresses those types of issues.

The apostle's personal reflections on the matter are limited, and at times we must infer such sentiments from discussions on other issues. To help us begin to grasp the nature of the Damascus road, we may examine the book of Acts to see how the event of the Damascus road impacted the apostle and his purpose. This background enhances our understanding of his personal statements surrounding his conversion and calling, which provides us the foundation to explore how the Damascus road shaped his theology. This is the approach of the chapter.

Thus, the opening section will deal with how Acts depicts the Damascus road. Some critics may object to my investigation of Acts to determine the workings of Pauline theology. Luke wrote Acts, and so the book contributes to a Lucan theology rather than Pauline thought.[4] This may smack of imposing a foreign paradigm upon Paul. Nevertheless, Luke records the history of what took place, which (as an event) communicates the original circumstances that influenced the apostle's mission. At times, Luke records Paul's own sentiments concerning his experience (Acts 22:4–10; 26:12–18),[5] which indicates that Luke is a reasonable source of insight into Paul's understanding of his calling and mission. Furthermore, since Paul was presumably Luke's primary source for the Damascus road account, the apostle's perspective on the matter may have influenced (and been reflected in) Luke's account. For these reasons, Acts can offer us insight into how Paul thought through the connections between his calling, commission, and mission.

Isaianic Elements of Paul's Calling

Luke alludes to Isaiah in describing Paul's experience, beginning with the vision itself. I have argued that Isaiah's vision pertained to the exalted and glorified Servant. The apostle seems to see that exact picture. Ananias tells Paul that he saw the Righteous One (Acts 22:14), a distinct title for the Servant in Isaiah (53:11).[6] The apostle describes this individual as glorious. In fact, he was blinded by the "glory of the light" (τῆς δόξης τοῦ φωτὸς ἐκείνου, Acts 22:6, 11). The wording suggests that Jesus unveiled God's glory to Paul. Thus, the apostle saw the glorified Servant, just like Isaiah. In fact, the use of "light" terminology corresponds with how Isaiah characterizes the Servant (φῶς ἐθνῶν; cf. Isa 42:6). Pervo also notes that Paul's depiction recalls Isa 6:3.[7]

---

4. See Bock, "Theology of Luke-Acts," 28–30.

5. Peterson, *Acts of the Apostles*, 298. Peterson states, "So important is the event that Luke gives three versions of it (cf. 22:3–21; 26:9–18). The second and third are autobiographical in style, forming part of Paul's defense before a hostile Jewish crowd in one case, and before a bemused King Agrippa in the other."

6. Ibid., 135; Bock, *Acts*, 170.

7. Pervo, *Acts*, 562.

The apostle does not merely see something similar to Isaiah's vision, he also begins to experience the theological significance of that vision. Paul is blinded in the same way that Isaiah described Israel in Isa 6:9. Israel has eyes to see but cannot (Isa 6:9; 43:8), and Paul opens his eyes but cannot see (Acts 9:8). However, just as the Servant transforms Israel to restore the nation's sight, so Ananias heals Paul's blindness by the power of Jesus (Acts 9:17). Ananias also associates the Righteous One with the healing of Paul's blindness (Acts 22:14). Just as the Righteous One cleanses and justifies the many in Isaiah, so the Righteous One now appears to Paul to cleanse him from his sin (Acts 22:14, 16).

These associations are far from incidental. Luke casts Paul's experience as the substance and purpose of his entire ministry. Ananias proclaims to Paul that he will open the eyes of the blind (Acts 26:18). The wording comes from Isa 42:7 concerning the mission of the Servant to blind Israel. This statement demonstrates that Paul's blindness was not just a physical result of the light, but rather a statement of his spiritual condition. He was spiritually blind, just as Israel is. Even in Acts, Paul seems to pick up on this paradigm, as he uses Isa 6:9 to describe the people of Israel (cf. Acts 28:26).

Furthermore, Ananias' words show that others will receive the same saving experience Paul just underwent. The apostle is supposed to open the eyes of Jew and Gentile alike. The statement comes from the Servant's mission, and thus the Servant's mission becomes Paul's mission. Just as Paul received sight from the completed work of the Servant, so he works to extend the benefits of the Messiah's victory to others (Acts 26:18). This includes the forgiveness of sins, a reality prophesied in Isaiah (Acts 26:18b).

Acts 26:18 contains another potential connection with Isaiah. The apostle's ministry also encourages individuals to join with those whom God had sanctified (τοῖς ἡγιασμένοις, Acts 26:18). The term "sanctified" is based upon the root, "holy," a key idea in Isaiah. Isaiah's vision prophesied a time when Israel would be judged by God's holiness and transformed to conform to his holiness (cf. Isa 4:2; 6:13).[8] God's perfect holiness would then be displayed (Isa 6:3). Paul's ministry contributes to that precise endeavor of transforming holiness as God makes his people holy.

A significant part of Paul's ministry extends to the Gentiles. This relates to the Damascus road and its connection with Isaiah. At his calling in the vision, Jesus commands Paul to go to the Gentiles (Acts 26:17). Paul reaffirms this commission in Acts 13:47–48 and states that Jesus told him to bring light and salvation to the ends of the earth. The phraseology echoes Isa 42:6–7, which refers to the Servant's mission. In Isaiah, the Servant was to spread salvation to the ends of the earth so that God's glory would be able to fill all the earth (cf. Isa 6:3). Paul takes up the mantle of the Servant and proceeds to go to the Gentiles so that God's light (or glory) would indeed spread to all the world. Luke describes Paul's mission in terms of Isaiah's theology and vision.

---

8. Hamm, "Paul's Blindness and Its Healing," 63–72.

So it seems that Paul sees the Righteous One on the Damascus road. The presence of the glorified Servant alerts Paul that Jesus is the One who has accomplished redemption for his people, as the vision scene in Isaiah indicates. As such, Paul experiences in microcosm the salvation predicted in Isaiah. He personally understands the problem of Israel, as well as its solution in their Messiah. Consequently, the salvation commemorated in Isaiah's vision has been inaugurated. Nonetheless, Paul is commanded to continue to extend the Servant's work to prepare for the time when all the world can receive and behold God's glory in Christ.

Ezekielian Elements of Paul's Calling

Ezekielian elements are also present at the Damascus road. All of the accounts of the Damascus road describe a light brighter than the sun (cf. Acts 9:3; 22:6; 26:13). Such light is indicative of theophanies, of which Ezekiel's vision is the prime example (cf. Ezek 1:4, 26–28).[9] Conversely, Paul does not merely see a light, but rather a human individual who proclaims his human name, Jesus the Nazarene (Acts 9:5). This combination of humanity and divine glory resembles Ezekiel's description of the divine appearing like a man (Ezek 1:26).[10] Bruce notes, "There are affinities between his conversion experience and Ezekiel's inaugural vision, in which the prophet saw the 'likeness' of the heavenly throne and above it 'a likeness as it were of a human form' (Ezek. 1:26)."[11] Paul's reaction also mirrors Ezekiel's experience. Both fall to the ground when confronted by the vision (Acts 9:4; cf. Ezek 1:28) and both are commanded to arise (Acts 26:16; cf. Ezek 2:1).[12] These similarities tie the visions and callings of Ezekiel and Paul together.

Just like the apostle saw Isaiah's vision and experienced an inauguration of Isaiah's theology, so Paul also sees Ezekiel's vision and encounters the partial actualization of Ezekiel's message. Ananias states that Paul will be filled with the Holy Spirit (Acts 9:17). Part of Ezekiel's message concerned the internal temple, where God's Spirit would dwell in the human heart (cf. 36:27). Ezekiel himself demonstrates this aspect of God's presence when the Spirit enters and empowers him to stand and to minister amongst God's people (2:1–3). That aspect of Ezekiel's theology and vision now comes into fruition in Paul's life. He sees the same vision and experiences part of its significance. I may qualify these observations by noting that Ananias' statement relates to a unique Spirit empowerment of the apostle.[13] Nonetheless, this all takes

---

9. See Peterson, *Acts of the Apostles*, 303; Conzelmann, *Acts*, 71; Witherington, *Acts of the Apostles*, 317. Although the word φῶς is not used in Ezekiel's vision, a variety of synonymous terms are, including ἐξαστράπτον, φέγγος, and πῦρ.

10. Kim, *Origin of Paul's Gospel*, 254–57.

11. Bruce, *Acts*, 183.

12. Bock, *Acts*, 357.

13. Pettegrew, *New Covenant Ministry*, 137. The construction of πίμπλημι with the Spirit

place in the context of the Spirit's new covenant work in Acts (cf. 2:1-4). Paul's special anointing relates to how the Spirit dwells amongst both Jew and Gentile, as described by Luke (cf. Acts 10:44; 19:1-6). Hence, we observe that Paul's vision connects with Ezekiel and that he experiences the inauguration of the theological significance of Ezekiel's vision.

Danielic Elements of Paul's Calling

Daniel's vision intersects with the Damascus road in a variety of ways. Since Daniel employs the imagery of Ezekiel and Isaiah, support for their association with the Damascus road also evidences a connection with Daniel. For instance, the appearance of a divine-human figure not only refers to Ezekiel, but also to one like a son of man in Daniel.[14] In addition, other circumstances indicate Paul's vision's conformity with Daniel's experience. As discussed earlier, Paul's companions sense that something unique is happening, but cannot completely understand what takes place (Acts 9:7; 22:9). This mirrors the reaction of those around Daniel when he encounters a vision (Dan 10:7).[15] Luke has already included allusions to that passage in his work.[16] It should not shock the reader to find echoes of it at Paul's calling and conversion. The vision of Dan 7 plays a part in the Damascus road, Paul's calling, and his theology and mission.

The reality of the connection between Dan 7 and the Damascus road may be partly responsible for how Paul views Christ and the church. Before, Saul presumably viewed Jesus as a blasphemer and cursed by God, only to discover that Jesus is actually the direct opposite. Christ's glory testified that not only was he exalted, but also the nature of that exaltation. Conceptually, Paul realized that Jesus was God's perfect image-bearer, since the divine glory radiates from him (τῆς δόξης τοῦ φωτὸς ἐκείνου, Acts 22:6-11). Only one like a son of man in Dan 7:13-14 could possess such majesty. As discussed, that description referred to the individual who perfectly bears God's image and authority as God intended in Adam.[17] Paul, seeing such unmistakable magnificence, most likely identified Jesus as the Son of Man and thus as the new Adam.[18] This connection will be expounded upon later. Nonetheless, the contrast suggests that Paul reconfigured Christ from cursed to the true divine king shown in Dan 7:13-14.

---

communicates the Spirit's unique working (Acts 2:4; 4:8, 31; 9:17; 13:9) as opposed to πληρόω (cf. Acts 13:52).

14. See previous discussion on "one like the son of man." See also Kim, *Origin of Paul's Gospel*, 235-47.

15. Bock, *Acts*, 357-58; Conzelmann, *Acts*, 71.

16. See Peterson, *Acts of the Apostles*, 266; Bock, *Acts*; Conzelmann, *Acts*, 59; Polhill, *Acts*, 207-8. See Luke 22:69 and Acts 7:54-56 for major examples.

17. Miller, *Daniel*, 207; Baldwin, *Daniel*, 142; Goldingay, *Daniel*, 167-68.

18. Kim, *Origin of Paul's Gospel*, 260-62.

In addition, Jesus' statement to Paul will reshape his view of the church in terms of Daniel's vision. The Lord reveals that Saul had actually persecuted Christ rather than merely the church. Fundamentally, this indicates a union between the two, and thereby establishes corporate solidarity between Christ and his people. This concept is a critical part of Paul's theology.[19] Such a relationship also recalls the connection between the Son of Man and the saints in Daniel's vision. In Dan 7:14–27, the saints and the Son of Man are essentially equated, since both receive the same kingdom and authority. In light of this, it appears that the relationship of corporate solidarity between the Son of Man and the saints parallels Christ and his church. Accordingly, assuming Dan 7 as a theological background, Paul would not only have realized on the Damascus road that Jesus is the Son of Man, but also that the church is connected with the saints in Dan 7:27. In Daniel's vision, the nations are to worship and serve the Son of Man (7:14). Paul's mission to the Gentiles may relate to this end as well, insofar as Daniel and the Damascus road influenced Paul's viewpoint of Christ and the church.

This in turn forms Paul's mission. Fundamentally, these realizations on the Damascus road change Paul from a man who hated Christ to one who declares him to be God's Son (Acts 9:20–22). Having formerly persecuted the church, he now champions the church and Gentiles (9:24–28). In addition, Ananias relays that Paul must open blind eyes in order to turn people from the dominion of Satan to the kingdom of God (Acts 26:18). The word "dominion" (ἐξουσία) occurs often in Daniel (cf. 3:2; 4:17; 7:14, 27) and is what the Son of Man ultimately possesses (7:14). This further suggests that divine authority is in view in the vision, as I have suggested. Jews and Gentiles, like Paul, are in rebellion against the Son, but the apostle's mission is to bring people under the lordship of Christ so as to move redemptive history closer to the time when the Son of Man possesses all authority and when all the saints receive his victory. They will be amongst those who receive an eschatological inheritance (κλῆρον, Acts 26:18) like Daniel (εἰς τὸν κλῆρόν σου εἰς συντέλειαν ἡμερῶν, 12:13). This too fuels Paul's mission to the Gentiles, who are present in Dan 7:14 to serve the Son of Man.

Synthesis: Present and Eschatological

The Damascus road intertwines the theologies and visions of Paul's predecessors. These echoes suggest that Paul saw an angle of the same visionary event as those before him. In contrast to Isaiah, who sees the general scene, or Ezekiel, who focuses on the throne, or Daniel, who zooms out on the broader context of the visionary event, Paul hones in on the central individual of this moment: Christ. The apostle understands that Jesus is the Servant and Son of Man. His resurrected glory declares that he is the one who is the center of the visions and consequently fulfills vision and theology.

---

19. Ibid., 252–56; Schreiner, *Pauline Theology*, 158.

Accordingly, Paul experiences the inauguration of the vision's theological significance. He receives both the sight and salvation proclaimed in Isaiah. He receives the Spirit prophesied in Ezekiel. He submits to the Son of Man as depicted in Daniel. However, the visionary event has not taken place, and its theological significance is by no means complete.[20] For this reason, Paul is commissioned to extend the work of the Messiah so as to move redemptive history towards the culmination found in the vision. All the earth must see the salvation of God, the presence of God must fill the earth, and the rule of God must go over all other kingdoms. Paul's work is to testify to what he has seen and heard to further that end. His vision is one of inauguration and anticipation.

Thus, the apostle's calling matches other prophets' calling in that they are all a microcosm of their message. However, the apostle's call at this stage of redemptive history goes beyond his predecessors. Where they only prophesied eschatological realities to come, Paul now begins to experience them. The present for Isaiah, Daniel, and Ezekiel was meant to go toward the eschatological, but by Paul's time, the eschatological has begun to come into the present. Hence, Paul's mission and message will show how the various theologies of Isaiah, Ezekiel, and Daniel all come to bear upon the life and ministry of the church in preparation for the culmination of history still to come (but which will come soon).

As I close this opening discussion, I want to stress that the findings above are *suggestive* rather than *definitive*. Such analysis is not *prima facie* evidence for the proposed scheme. Rather, they grant us some bearings to help us make sense of Paul's own sentiments. The allusions under discussion lead us in this general direction, and further analysis in Paul's epistles, to which we now turn, will solidify these ideas.

CHRIST AS THE ESCHATOLOGICAL GLORY IN THE VISION

Paul's own perspective does not undermine our observations surrounding Acts. His writings uphold the entire framework of inauguration of the theology of vision with an anticipation of the vision's fulfillment. However, it is important to hear Paul's own words regarding the Damascus road. Not only does this provide affirmation of what I have discussed, it also adds a personal dimension to his thinking on his conversion and calling. His own accounts shed light on what this event meant for his life and ministry. Thus, this discussion forms a bridge from the suggested paradigm above to the language and theology of Paul.

To Paul, the Damascus road was nothing short of revolutionary. As he states in Galatians, the Damascus road transformed a man zealous for the law and a persecutor of the church into one who would go to the Gentiles with the true gospel

---

20. Further discussion on this will take place in the next section. Paul arguably sees a *proleptic Parousia*.

(Gal 1:12-16). It became not only the origins of his gospel (Gal 1:11-12) but also the motivation for his mission (1:23—2:7).

So what, to Paul, was the impetus of the Damascus road? In the apostle's mind, his vision was about one person: Christ. Paul's references to that event concern how he saw "Jesus our Lord" (1 Cor 9:1) and how Jesus appeared to him (1 Cor 15:8). His writings do not speak of falling to his face (cf. Acts 22:7) or other details, but only how God revealed his Son (Gal 1:16). This highlights Paul's own viewpoint of his calling. For Paul, the Damascus road is summed up in what it communicates about Christ. He is the driving force behind all of Paul's thinking and work. This not only affirms what I observed in Acts, but also begins to show how the Damascus road connects with Pauline thought.

So how did Paul perceive the Lord on the road to Damascus? What did that event reveal about him? To answer this question, I will examine certain texts in which Paul alludes to his calling (cf. 1 Cor 15:8; 2 Cor 3-4; Gal 1:16; Eph 3:1-10).[21] In surveying these passages, Paul fundamentally understood that Jesus possessed a unique glory and position. The apostle claims to have seen the glory of the resurrected Lord (cf. 1 Cor 15:8). This majesty is akin to his ascension glory (cf. 1 Tim 3:16).[22] However, what does that exactly entail? Knight notes other texts in which Christ ascends into heaven in glory. Such texts describe Jesus' exaltation by God (Phil 2:10-11) and how he is seated above every authority and power (Eph 1:20-23).[23] Both of those texts allude to the visions and theologies of Paul's predecessors. Phil 2:10-11 quotes from Isaiah, explaining that all will bow before YHWH (Isa 45:22-23). Eph 1:20-23 echoes Daniel in saying the Son of Man is exalted (presumably) in order to sit on a throne above all authorities, rulers, and powers.[24] To Paul, Jesus' glory relates to the Son of Man in Daniel and God's victory in Isaiah.

This notion is affirmed by 2 Cor 3-4. While the apostle speaks more generally to his audience about the new covenant and the glory of Christ, various scholars have detected the influence of Paul's own conversion experience on his descriptions.[25] Hence, we may infer that the glory of Christ described in this text alludes to what Paul saw on the Damascus road. In essence, this passage argues that the new covenant ministry is superior to the law because it is one not of condemnation, but of transforming glory. God's glory is seen through Jesus, who bears God's image (2 Cor 4:4, 6). Such glory is

---

21. One text excluded from this discussion is 2 Cor 12. The timing of fourteen years would put Paul's experience of the third heaven far too late to describe his conversion experience. See Martin, *2 Corinthians*, 399.

22. Mounce, *Pastoral Epistles*, 46:226.

23. Knight, *Pastoral Epistles*, 186.

24. Lincoln, *Ephesians*, 75-77; O'Brien, *Letter to the Ephesians*, 145. See Dan 7:14 (Theoditian) ἡ ἀρχὴ καὶ ἡ τιμὴ καὶ ἡ βασιλεία . . . ἡ ἐξουσία and compare with Eph 1:21 (πάσης ἀρχῆς καὶ ἐξουσίας καὶ δυνάμεως καὶ κυριότητος). O'Brien notes the notion of an Adam Christology present in Paul's argument in Eph 1:21, which probably stems from Dan 7:13-14. See Kim, *Origin of Paul's Gospel*, 260-68.

25. Kim, *Origin of Paul's Gospel*, 229-39.

characterized by light (2 Cor 4:4). Some are blind to this proclamation (2 Cor 4:4-6), but the Spirit allows people to see, and he also transforms Christians into Christ's image as they behold his glory (2 Cor 3:18). Based upon this, we can deduce that God made Paul see Jesus, who is God's perfect image-bearer, and therefore the ultimate display of God's glory.

I can offer four observations based upon this. First, I should reiterate that 2 Cor 3–4 relates to Paul's experience on the Damascus road. There is a personal element to the apostle's descriptions. For example, the mention of light (2 Cor 4:6) may allude to Paul's own encounter with the overwhelming light of Christ's glory (Acts 9:3). Moreover, the notion of blindness to the gospel in this context (2 Cor 4:4) is reminiscent of Paul's own blindness and sight (cf. Acts 9:8). Kim lists several other factors pointing to this assertion.[26] The apostle's description of the new covenant and the glory of Christ stems from his personal experience on the Damascus road.

Second, with this in mind, 2 Cor 3–4 alludes to the visions of Daniel and Ezekiel. Christ as the image of God is tied with their visions. For one, Kim has persuasively argued that the language of glory and likeness relate to the vision passages which describe "one like a man" or "one like a son of man."[27] This phraseology is similarly repeated throughout Second Temple literature. Thus, contemporary culture would have understood that when Paul speaks of Christ as God's glory and image (cf. 2 Cor 3:18; 4:4-6), he alludes to Daniel and Ezekiel.[28] Paul sees Jesus' glory and recognizes that this is the same unique glory described by Ezekiel and Daniel. Jesus bears identical majesty to Daniel's Son of Man and the one upon Ezekiel's chariot.

Third, these ideas from 2 Cor 3–4 seem to relate to an Adam Christology in Paul's theology. The language of "image" recalls how Adam was made in God's image, but now Jesus is the perfection of that image. That was part of the Danielic concept of "one like a son of man" discussed earlier, and Paul seems to have the same connection in mind.[29] This idea finds support in 2 Cor 3:18. The verse states that believers are conformed into Christ's image, which implies that Jesus is the second Adam, who begins a new humanity.[30] This notion is further evidenced by 1 Cor 15. It also affirms that believers will ultimately bear Christ's image (1 Cor 15:49).[31] In that same verse, the apostle contrasts the "heavenly" image of Christ against the "earthly" image of Adam.

---

26. Ibid. In addition to what I listed above, the wording of 2 Cor 4:6 also reminds us of Gal 1:16. The former states that God shines his light into our hearts (ἐν ταῖς καρδίαις ἡμῶν) and the latter details how God revealed his Son in Paul (ἐν ἐμοί). The reference to Christ's face (2 Cor 3:18) also may refer to how Paul beheld Jesus physically, since believers do not actually see his face today. These factors suggest that Paul's own conversion plays into the more general description in 2 Cor 3–4.

27. Hafemann, "Glory and Veil of Moses"; Martin, *2 Corinthians*, 72; Harris, *Second Epistle to the Corinthians*, 275.

28. Kim, *Origin of Paul's Gospel*, 205–23.

29. Ibid., 260–67.

30. Harris, *Second Epistle to the Corinthians*, 315; Barnett, *Second Epistle to the Corinthians*, 207.

31. Garland, *1 Corinthians*, 736.

This corresponds with Paul's explicit statements that Jesus is the second Adam (1 Cor 15:22, 45). Thus, the context of 1 Cor 15 associates the notion of "image" with Jesus as a new Adam. Interestingly, Paul appears to relate all of this discussion in 1 Cor 15 back to the Damascus road. The believer's resurrected body is based upon the glorified Christ Paul witnessed at his calling (1 Cor 15:8).[32] Hence, both 2 Cor 3–4 and 1 Cor 15 connect Paul's "image" language with the Damascus road, Daniel's Son of Man, and the apostle's concept of a second Adam.

I offer one fourth and final observation about 2 Cor 3–4. That text does not merely include language that alludes to Daniel and Ezekiel, but also to Isaiah. The notion of blindness and Christ's glory as light recall how God presented Isaiah's Servant (cf. Isa 6:3, 9; 49:3, 6).[33] Moreover, this coincides with Paul's appeal to the gospel (2 Cor 4:4) and new creation (2 Cor 5:17), concepts tied to Isaiah's vision and theology. The reference to new creation may also tie into our discussion of Christ as a new Adam. These allusions also harmonize with Paul's claim that he saw "Jesus our Lord" (1 Cor 9:1). "Lord" (κύριος) does not merely refer to Jesus' authority, but also to his divinity. The title alludes to his position as king over all. Such a picture parallels with how the Lord reigns high and lifted up in Isaiah's vision. Ciampa and Rosner allude to this connection:

> The conjunction of ideas suggests that the reference to Jesus as 'our Lord' may not simply reflect Paul's common use of the title as elsewhere, but reflects the fact that his vision was precisely that of Jesus reigning in glory as Lord.[34]

All of this affirms that Paul saw the glory of the Servant and recognized that he indeed saw the Lord, as Isaiah had (cf. Isa 6:1). Overall, 2 Cor 3–4 is an important text in this discussion. It echoes the language of past visions and theologies and ties them with the Damascus road. As such, 2 Cor 3–4 exhibits how Paul's vision resonated with that of his predecessors and how their theology integrates into his own.

So far, we have discussed Paul's identification of Jesus in terms of past visions. However, while he has "zoomed in" on Christ, the apostle still seems to understand the visionary event in the same way his predecessors had. Arguably, the Damascus road demonstrated to Paul that all of redemptive history is shaped around the Lord. Christ's glory in context of the vision mandates a Christotelicity in Paul's thinking. In Gal 1:16, Paul describes his conversion as how God "revealed Christ in him" (ἀποκαλύψαι τὸν υἱὸν αὐτοῦ). The words initially point out that God worked in Paul's heart to allow

---

32. Kim, *Origin of Paul's Gospel*, 263.

33. In Isaiah's initial vision, Israel's problem was that they were blind to God's glory (Isa 6:3, 9). However, the Servant would come to give light to those who were blind (cf. Isa 49:6). That is how he would reveal God's glory (ἐν σοὶ δοξασθήσομαι, 49:3).

34. Thiselton, *First Epistle to the Corinthians*, 667; Ciampa and Rosner, *First Letter to the Corinthians*, 398. What further evidences this mentality is Paul's application of YHWH texts with Jesus (cf. Phil 2:5–11 and Isa 45:23).

him to truly perceive the identity of Jesus.³⁵ Nevertheless, even this concise language contains echoes of previous visions and theologies. The word "reveal" may allude to the way mysteries were unveiled to Daniel (cf. 2:22). Like Daniel, Paul now had clear insight into what was hidden. Could it be that he also had insight into the same eschatological realities concerning God's plan to exalt his Son as Daniel portrayed?³⁶

Such a suggestion finds merit in a wider reading of Pauline literature. Eph 3:3–5 is a key text in this discussion. It too refers to the Damascus road event by which God's mystery was revealed to Paul (κατὰ ἀποκάλυψιν ἐγνωρίσθη μοι τὸ μυστήριον, v. 3).³⁷ Commentators recognize the similarities between this text and Gal 1:16.³⁸ Accordingly, the Ephesians text can shed some light on Paul's thinking about Gal 1:16 and the Damascus road.

What mystery was revealed to the apostle upon his conversion? Paul's use of "mystery" is quite important in describing his own calling. In Ephesians, the word "mystery" seems to connect with Daniel. O'Brien comments, "'Mystery' translates the Aramaic equivalent, frequently found in the book of Daniel (2:18, 19, 27, etc.), and this provides several parallels with its use in Ephesians: it connotes God's purpose, which is a unified plan with eschatological and cosmic dimensions."³⁹

Accordingly, Paul's vision of the exalted Christ on the Damascus road does not only pertain to a clearer perception of Jesus, but also to his role in the eschatological paradigm of Daniel. God reveals to Paul that Christ is the central person of the vision and as such, represents the climax of redemptive history. To put it in Pauline terms, the mystery is that all things would be "summed up in Christ" (Eph 1:10). On the Damascus road, this mystery surrounding the future climax of history is revealed presently to Paul. The apostle therefore sees *part* of a "*proleptic Parousia*," the moment when that summing up would take place.⁴⁰ That is the precise nature of the visionary event as we have discussed.

This notion of mystery brings us back to the tension between the present and the eschatological. The Damascus road unveils this mystery to Paul. What was hidden in former generations is now revealed (cf. Eph 3:5). Hence, certain realities surrounding that visionary event have come to be, such that the theological significance of the vision is inaugurated. Christ's resurrected glory signals this. Nonetheless, Paul still looks forward to when the mystery will ultimately take place. He looks forward to the

---

35. Fung, *Epistle to the Galatians*, 64; Bruce, *Galatians*, 93.

36. Fung, *Epistle to the Galatians*, 64. Fung supports this idea by arguing that Paul's conversion and apostleship originate from the Damascus road and from recognizing Jesus as the Son of God (notice the wording in Gal 1:16 ἀποκαλύψαι τὸν υἱὸν αὐτοῦ ἐν ἐμοί). See also, Longenecker, *Galatians*, 31.

37. O'Brien, *Letter to the Ephesians*, 229.

38. Thielman, *Ephesians*, 195; Bruce, *The Epistles to the Colossians, to Philemon, and to the Ephesians*, 312; O'Brien, *Letter to the Ephesians*, 228; Lincoln, *Ephesians*, 175.

39. O'Brien, *Letter to the Ephesians*, 169. See also, Thielman, *Ephesians*, 195; Lincoln, *Ephesians*, 26–30, 174.

40. Kim, *Origin of Paul's Gospel*, 228.

fullness of times, when all things will be summed up in Christ (Eph 1:10). The notion of mystery, with its connection to Paul's commission (Gal 1:16; Eph 3:3–5), indicates that his vision is one of inauguration and anticipation.

With this understanding, we can see how Paul's own descriptions of the vision do not undermine our findings from Luke. They work harmoniously. Paul does view Jesus as Isaiah's Servant, as Daniel's Son of Man, and as the one on Ezekiel's chariot-throne. He does view all of redemptive history culminating around the Messiah. He does see an inauguration of the vision's significance, but awaits its eschatological completion.

However, Paul has his own way of communicating these views. Primarily, he does so by expounding upon the magnificent glory of Christ. While I have teased out different allusions to Isaiah, Ezekiel, or Daniel, the apostle does not make any such divisions. The echoes merge to generate the unmatched splendor of Jesus. His glory is unique because it is the aggregate of the glory displayed in all previous visions and theologies. It is this glory, which alone belongs to the central figure in prior visions, that radically altered Paul. Thus, Christ becomes the central core of the apostle's thinking and motivation. His glory and significance in redemptive history become the framework of Paul's mission. It starts with Christ and ends with him.

Paul's language used in this discussion becomes the gateway by which we can start to discuss how that inauguration and anticipation works itself out in the rest of Paul's theology. The mystery that has been unveiled will also help us understand certain realities about Daniel (cf. Eph 3:3–5). Jesus as the head of a new creation, a new Adam, will be crucial in his logic (cf. 2 Cor 4:4; 5:17). Jesus as the Servant will show the influence of Isaiah on Paul's soteriology (cf. 2 Cor 4:4). The Spirit's new covenant work, per Ezekiel, will also be part of the apostle's pneumatology (cf. 2 Cor 3:3, 18). The summing up of all things in Christ will tie visionary language with Paul's eschatology (cf. 2 Cor 4:4; 1 Thess 4:17). These major staples of Pauline theology relate back to the Damascus road and a biblical theology of vision. Again, for Paul, all of this stems from the vision of the glorified Christ. Although we may not claim a center, the centrality of Christ in Paul's thinking and motivation is without question.

SALVATION AND TRANSFORMATION: ISAIAH IN PAUL

Servant and Salvation

With that, we can further explore the "innertextuality" that exists between Paul's vision and significant portions of his theology. Assuming the legitimacy of the above analysis, what ramifications might it pose for Pauline theology? The apostle's view of salvation is an appropriate place to begin such a discussion. Some scholars have argued for the centrality of soteriological ideas in Pauline theology. Although it may not be central, the apostle does write frequently on the subject. He discusses the forgiveness of sins (Eph 1:7; Col 1:14), atonement (Rom 3:25), justification (Rom 3:20–30; 5:1, 9;

Gal 2:16; 3:11; Tit 3:7), and reconciliation (Rom 5:1; 2 Cor 5:18–19; Eph 2:16). These Pauline notions form the backbone of traditional systematic theological discussions, and those references stem from Isaiah.

This also relates to Paul's recognition of Jesus as the Servant on the Damascus road. Based upon that realization, the apostle then applies other Servant texts directly to Jesus. Jesus was in the humble state of a man, just as the Servant was in lowly form (Phil 2:7; cf. Isa 53:3).[41] Paul describes the Lord's humble obedience to death, just as the Servant subjected himself to insult (Phil 2:5–8; cf. Isa 50:6). He was handed over on account of transgression (Rom 4:25; cf. Isa 53:12) and died for sins as the Servant (1 Cor 15:3; cf. Isa 53:2–8). Consequently, he made peace between man and God by his death, as Isaiah predicted (Col 1:20; Isa 53:5). His resurrection secures justification (cf. Rom 4:25), as discussed in Isa 53:11.[42]

Accordingly, Jesus' work as the Servant helps to define Paul's soteriology.[43] Isaiah then becomes an anchor to understanding how Paul views sin and salvation. Both Paul and Isaiah identify the same problem of humanity and the world: disobedience to God (Isa 1:1–18; 59:2; Rom 1:18—3:20).[44] In addition to a more conceptual overlap between the two, Paul describes mankind's problem using Isaianic jargon. For example, I have already noted that the apostle discusses the blindness of unbelievers (cf. 2 Cor 4:4; Rom 11:8). Isaiah too noted this same problem (cf. 6:9; 29:9). Likewise, the apostle claims that unbelievers fall short of God's glory (Rom 3:23). This notion recalls the negative transformation discussed in Isaiah. There, Israel and the nations set up competing glories and subsequently, degraded God's glory into an idol (cf. Isa 6:9–10; 44:18).[45] The world thus lies under judicial condemnation for its sins (Isa 24:1–5; Rom 3:20).[46] Paul uses other Isaianic texts to depict man's depravity (Rom 2:24; 3:15; cf. Isa 52:5; 59:7).

This agreement also extends to the solution for such a dilemma. Christ's sacrifice is not merely about victory or healing, but fundamentally concerns penal substitutionary atonement. This is not only due to the overarching narrative of sin to

---

41. Schreiner, *Pauline Theology*, 47.

42. Dunn, *Romans 1–8*, 38A:224; Moo, *Epistle to the Romans*, 289; Hofius, "Fourth Servant Song in the New Testament Letters," 180–82.

43. Moo, *Epistle to the Romans*, 898. Moo, in commenting upon the connection of Isa 52:12 and Rom 15:21, states, "Third, it alludes to the content of Paul's gospel. For Isa. 52:15 is part of the famous fourth 'servant' passage, and the 'him' concerning whom these Gentiles have not been told is the Servant of the Lord. Paul's pioneering church-planting ministry among the Gentiles is fulfilling the OT prediction about Gentiles coming to see and understand the message about the Servant of the Lord."

44. Schreiner, *Pauline Theology*, 101, 128–33; Smith, *Isaiah*, 15B:589; Oswalt, *Isaiah 40–66*, 513.

45. Moo, *Epistle to the Romans*, 226: "And just as this sharing in God's 'glory' involves conformity to the 'image of Christ' (Rom 8:29–30; Phil 3:21), so the absence of glory involves a declension from the 'image of God' in which human beings were first made." For Isaiah's concept of negative transformation, see Beale, "A Retributive Taunt," 177.

46. Oswalt, *Isaiah 1–39*, 444–45; Schreiner, *Romans*, 165–66.

salvation, but also because Paul puts Jesus' death in direct terms of the Servant.[47] Isa 53 puts the Servant's death in terms of sin (v. 5), sacrifice (vv. 6–8), substitution (vv. 5–6), God's wrath (v. 10), and restoration (v. 10).[48] Paul, by asserting that Jesus is the Servant, imports these concepts into his own soteriology. Jesus' work was to bear the wrath of God for the sins of his people, which resulted in the forgiveness of sin (Rom 3:25; 5:8; 2 Cor 5:17; Gal 3:13; Eph 5:2; Phil 2:7–8; Tit 2:14). He satisfied God's justice (Rom 3:26).[49] Moreover, Paul states that God sanctified (ἡγιάσθητε) believers (1 Cor 6:11). They find their sanctification (ἁγιασμὸς) in Christ (1 Cor 1:30). Such language recalls Isaiah's concept of transforming holiness. Although Israel faced God's judging holiness (5:16), in the end, they would be brought to conform to God's holiness and act accordingly (ἁγιάσουσιν, cf. Isa 29:23). The salvation depicted in Isaiah's vision and theology now emerges in Paul's mission.[50]

Consequently, we can develop some observations to the discussion of justification.[51] Some scholars contend that justification primarily regards the horizontal notion of covenant membership and the way one participates in God's blessings, whereas others argue that it mainly concerns judicial standing before God relative to sin and righteousness.[52] While the debate over the historical issues of Paul's day are important factors in considering his intent, the apostle also grounds his views on the work of the Servant. Such intertextuality is quite important, since the Servant, the righteous one, justifies the many (יַצְדִּיק צַדִּיק עַבְדִּי לָרַבִּים; δικαιῶσαι δίκαιον εὖ δουλεύοντα πολλοῖς; Isa 53:11).

Paul seems to reference this particular verse in a variety of places. For example, in Rom 5:19, Christ accounts the many as righteous (δίκαιοι κατασταθήσονται οἱ πολλοί) echoing the result of how the Servant justifies the many (δικαιῶσαι δίκαιον εὖ δουλεύοντα πολλοῖς). The combination of "justify" (δικαιόω) and "sin" (ἁμαρτία) in Isa 53:11 does not occur often throughout the NT, but does appear in two noteworthy incidences within Paul's ministry. In Acts 13:38, Paul discusses how Christ's sacrifice justifies believers from sin, a feat that the law could never accomplish. Also, Rom 6:7 explains that the resulting state of justification mandates freedom from sin's

---

47. Schreiner, "Penal Substitution View," 73–78. Schreiner appeals to the flow of Scripture to establish the problem that salvation through atonement solves. This is certainly a legitimate argument. I would suggest that an additional anchor would be how Paul appeals to the Servant and imports Isaiah's theology into his own.

48. Averbeck, "Christian Interpretations," 53–60.

49. Schreiner, "Penal Substitution View," 82–93; Moo, *Epistle to the Romans*, 242–43; Dunn, *Romans 1–8*, 38A:175.

50. Granted, this refers to one's status as holy as opposed to becoming perfectly holy in all practice. Nonetheless, the transformation has begun.

51. I do not intend to answer all the questions surrounding justification here. Rather, to show how a biblical theology of vision brings some perspective to the matter.

52. Moo, "Israel and the Law in Romans 5–11," 186–87; Dunn, "Justice of God," 1–22; Dunn, "Echoes of Intra-Jewish Polemic," 459–77; Dunn, "Justification by Faith," 85–101; Wright, *Justification: God's Plan*, 120–22; Schreiner, "Perfect Obedience," 151–60.

dominion.⁵³ Justification leads to sanctification. Finally, the combination of the adjective δίκαιος with the verb δικαιόω in Isa 53:11 does not appear anywhere else in the NT other than in Paul's writing (Rom 2:13; 3:26; Gal 3:11). Within this, Rom 3:26 mentions how God's work in Christ presents him as just and the justifier. These examples suggest that Paul uses unique wording to allude to Isa 53:11 in his writings. Other instances of intertextuality between Paul and Isa 53:11 exist as well (cf. Rom 4:25; 2 Cor 5:21; Phil 2:7–8).⁵⁴ All of this indicates that the apostle claims Jesus is the Servant and appeals to the Servant's work as the backdrop of certain discussions of justification.

As such, grasping the notion of justification in Isaiah helps us to better comprehend Paul's understanding. In the context of Isaiah, the issue is still sin and God's wrath. The Servant is pierced for his people's transgression (Isa 53:5) and is crushed by God (v. 10). This hints that justification in Isaiah pertains to judicial rightness in relationship with sin, with one's correct standing relative to the law. The various uses of צדק in the OT affirm this idea.⁵⁵ Moreover, Isaiah links the Servant's sacrificial work towards sin with the notion of justification in Isa 53:11. The prophet states that the Servant justified the man by his knowledge (בְּדַעְתּוֹ). In context, that knowledge relates to his sacrificial work.⁵⁶ Hence, the Servant's work of justification is oriented around the issue of sin. The parallelism in Isaiah 53:11 also confirms this. The Servant justifies

---

53. Schreiner, *Romans*, 319; Cranfield, *Epistle to the Romans*, 311; Moo, "Israel and the Law in Romans 5–11," 376.

54. Harris, *Second Epistle to the Corinthians*, 452; O'Brien, *Letter to the Ephesians*, 222–28; Moo, *Epistle to the Romans*, 288.

55. The qal stem denotes the state of being righteous. It is a law court status, but indicative of conformity to a standard (morality). See *HALOT*, 2:1003–4. Hence, Judah admits that Tamar, in the eyes of the law, actually did what was more appropriate or correct than he had done in view of the cultural standard (Gen 38:26). She thereby is not punished. The piel is factitive, denoting the proof that one has this status. Even though Elihu declares Job not to be right (33:12), through his speech he can correct Job such that ultimately Job *comes* into a right state before God. However, the hiphil (the form in Isa 53:11) is declarative. It denotes the judge's declaration, or verdict, and enforcement of a person's vindication before the court. Solomon prays that God would rightly judge such that those who are wicked would be condemned and that he would justify the righteous *according to that individual's righteousness* (וּלְהַצְדִּיק צַדִּיק לָתֶת לוֹ כְּצִדְקָתוֹ, 1 Kgs 8:32, emphasis mine). Thus, the hiphil of justification seems to presume that the person in court has some sort of righteousness or conformity to the legal standard. Cf. Waltke and O'Connor, *IBHS* §24.2 (400). Waltke and O'Connor list צדק as a primary case example of qal intransitive, piel factitive, and hiphil causative. See also Clines, *Job 21–37*, 18a:741; Matthews, *Genesis 11:27—50:26*, 723; Wenham, *Genesis 16–50*, 369.

The above discussion clarifies the logic of Prov 17:15. God detests those who justify the wicked and condemn the righteous. To do so misevaluates the way people truly stand before the law. A correct justification instead enforces people's proper status. God calls on human judges to rule fairly by justifying even the poor of society (Ps 82:3). Consequently, these righteous people are to have the full force of the law on their side (Ps 82:4). This declaration is not superficial, but instead results in the judge treating the person accordingly and siding with him. See Waltke, *Book of Proverbs*, 84–85. "As for one who pronounced the wicked person . . . innocent denotes a corrupt judge who esteems and declares the behavior of the guilty as conforming to the divinely established moral order and so acquits them from the punishment of wrong doing" (84).

56. Oswalt, *Isaiah 40–66*, 403.

and bears the people's sins or guilt (וַעֲוֹנֹתָם הוּא יִסְבֹּל). This antithesis positions justification as dealing with judicial guilt rather than covenant membership or standing. All of this evidences that Isaiah views justification as dealing with God's judgment against sin and the vindication of God's people from condemnation.

I will offer one further comment on Isa 53:11. What is interesting is the wordplay between the Servant, who is the Righteous One (צַדִּיק), with justification (יַצְדִּיק). It seems that the Servant is the judge who declares that the people are righteous, not because of an innate righteousness they possess, but because of his own righteousness.[57] He is the basis for the people's justification. This may parallel the substitutionary nature of his atoning work in context. Justification, then, is a declaration that a person stands before the Judge without sin and with the court's full vindication because he is in conformity to the law; he possesses the status of the Servant.

Does Paul abide by Isaiah's paradigm? We may particularly ask the question of the texts in which the apostle alludes to Isa 53:11, as well as of other passages about justification that allude more broadly to Isa 53 (cf. Gal 2:16; 3:11; Phil 3:7–9). In Romans, Paul's echoes of Isa 53:11 relate to contexts dealing with sin and judgment. Adam's disobedience led humanity into sin, but through Christ, many will be made righteous (Rom 5:19). Rom 3:26 discusses how God is unquestionably correct in his dealings with sinners by Christ's propitiating death. Rom 6:7 also discusses justification in the context of sin. Admittedly, however, there is a slight difference. Rom 6 deals with how people may be freed from sin's power so as to live righteous lives. Rom 6:7 links justification with that reality. This does not negate the fundamental reality that justification is God's declaration of one's righteousness. Instead, it demonstrates that such a declaration entails much more than a statement; it has results.[58] The perfect tense of δεδικαίωται, as well as its collocation with the preposition ἀπό, distinguishes the use of the verb here from the previous examples in Romans.[59] The state of being justified actually means one is freed from sin.

All in all, Paul remains consistent with Isaiah's depiction of the Servant and justification. Christ's death brought about a right standing of believers before God. This is primarily relative not to covenant membership per se, but rather in terms of sin, guilt, and death.[60] This has ramifications for believers' ability to live for God, a paradigm that Isaiah actually shares with his notion of transforming holiness (cf. Isa 4:3; 63:18).

Dunn, however, brings up two other texts related to the Damascus road that support a more ecclesiastical emphasis of justification. Galatians presents justification

---

57. Motyer, *Isaiah*, 441–42; Oswalt, *Isaiah 40–66*, 415–17.

58. Schreiner, *Romans*, 319.

59. Ibid.; Moo, *Epistle to the Romans*, 376; Dunn, *Romans 1–8*, 38A:320. On the use of ἀπό see Gathercole, "Justification of Wisdom."

60. Sin impacts one's covenant standing before God. However, the question of justification is what is primary versus what is consequence. Justification primarily solves the issue of sin and therefore has implications for covenant membership.

(2:16) in the overarching context of Paul's conversion on the Damascus road (1:16). In this epistle, Paul deals with issues of table fellowship (2:11–13) and Jew and Gentile relations as opposed to strictly soteriological matters.[61] Similarly, Phil 3:7–9 associates what Paul discovers at conversion with his discovery of righteousness through faith in Christ.[62] That epistle also deals with avoiding the Judaizers and keeping the unity of the church. Dunn argues that Paul, when referring to the Damascus road, does not use repentance or guilt language, which is required for a vertical understanding of justification. Instead, he emphasizes his calling to go forth to the Gentiles (cf. Acts 22:15; 26:17–18; Isa 42:6). That synthesizes well with these contexts, which deal more with horizontal or ecclesial issues.[63]

A biblical theology of vision may aid us in answering some of Dunn's critiques. For example, in contrast to Dunn's presentation, Paul's depiction of the Damascus road is expansive enough to encompass both the mission to the Gentiles as well as soteriological issues. Most certainly, Paul's calling to the Gentiles is a part of Paul's commissioning and a vital part of the inauguration of Isaiah's theology in Paul, as I will later discuss. However, we have observed that Luke links Paul's calling with the forgiveness of sins (cf. Acts 22:16; 26:18), as does Paul himself (cf. Gal 1:4). Accordingly, the entire notion of justification as pertaining more to forgiveness and sin can still be tied with the Damascus road. The evidence is there. A biblical theology of vision helps us see that the Damascus road is intertwined with far more theology than just the call to the Gentiles.

Furthermore, even in the passages Dunn cites, there is room for the traditional definition of justification to exist, even if Paul appeals to its implications. If one has completely right standing with God in Christ, then that has ecclesial repercussions. No one can set up alternative standards by which one can be fully accepted into table fellowship.[64] Paul may argue this way in Galatians. By negating the implications of the gospel, one can damningly distort the gospel itself (cf. Gal 1:8).[65] This accounts for how Paul depicts the false teaching as beginning in the Spirit and ending with the

---

61. Dunn, "Justification by Faith," 92–94.

62. Ibid.; Hawthorne, *Philippians*, 188; O'Brien, *Letter to the Ephesians*, 384.

63. Dunn, "Justification by Faith," 93.

64. Witherington, *Grace in Galatia*, 175. Witherington offers an especially helpful explanation: "Paul's primary concern in this letter is with how the Galatians will go on in Christ, and indeed he even discusses the possibility of their going out of Christ, committing apostasy. The language about how they entered the Christian community is used in the service of this larger discussion, reminding them how they got in, but also discussing how they should now walk in Christ. Justification is not the main subject of this letter, it is brought into the discussion about how the Galatians should behave as Christians and whether they should 'add' obedience to the Mosaic Law, to their faith in Christ. Paul's response is that precisely because they did not come to be in Christ by obeying the Law (initial salvation and justification was by grace through faith), they should *not* now add obedience to the Mosaic Law to their faith in Christ. Rather they should continue as they started in Christ, walking in the Spirit and according to the Law or Norm or Example of Christ."

65. Ibid.; Nanos, "Peter's 'Eating with Gentiles,'" 267–81; Piper, *The Future of Justification*, 146–61.

flesh (Gal 3:1–4). It also takes into consideration that the apostle argues to Peter that he has been justified but now acts differently and inconsistently with that justification (Gal 2:14–16).[66]

Likewise, Phil 3:7–9 does not immediately address the issues of restrictive covenantal membership. Dunn acknowledges this.[67] Rather, Paul explains how he once "boasted in the flesh" but now trusts in Christ's righteousness. The context suggests that the apostle contrasts his personal achievement with what he "gains" (κερδαίνω) in Christ.[68] Such boasting makes it appear that the issue is not covenant membership as much as accomplishment before God. Moreover, Paul having "his" (Christ's) righteousness reminds us of the play between δικαιῶσαι and δίκαιον in Isa 53:11. Just as the Servant's righteousness becomes the basis for the justification of the many, so Paul now has Christ's own righteousness before God (Phil 3:9). The apostle upholds the Servant's work throughout his writings after all.

Paul's recognition that Jesus is Servant carries tremendous implications for the apostle's soteriology. However, all of this presumes that the salvation prophesied by Isaiah has come into the present day. Paul does not speak of the Servant's work as something future, but instead as something that was accomplished. He discusses justification and forgiveness as received realities rather than merely anticipated (cf. Rom 5:1; 13:11; 1 Cor 6:11).[69] To Paul, the glorified Servant is victorious and believers share

---

66. Note the wording οὐκ ὀρθοποδοῦσιν πρὸς τὴν ἀλήθειαν τοῦ εὐαγγελίου (Gal 2:14). Peter was straight with the nature of the gospel in that his table fellowship actions were inconsistent with that reality. We may also make further observations in Gal 3:10–14. While the passage is notoriously difficult, we may point out that Deut 27:26 and the notion of curse sets the passage not merely in a covenantal membership context, but specifically in a context of obedience and disobedience. The curse in the context of Deut 27 pertains to the issue of disobeying God's law and the nation's judicial standing relative to God and sin. This indicates that the notion of justification in Gal 3:11 may relate more to that vertical issue than just who can belong in God's people. See Craigie, *Book of Deuteronomy*, 327.

67. Dunn, "Justification by Faith," 93: "This reversal is not so clearly mirrored in Philippians 3, where the acceptability of Gentiles to God is not to the fore." The issue of contrast is important in Phil 3. Is the contrast between accepting Gentiles versus an elitist or nationalistic attitude of the Jews or between Paul's boasting in his own accomplishments versus Christ? Since the notion of accepting Gentiles is noticeably absent and Paul's boasting is present, it stands to reason that the latter reading is preferred.

68. Ibid., 92–93; O'Brien, *Philippians*, 394–96; Hawthorne, *Philippians*, 141. Dunn argues that the contrast is not between personal achievement and Christ but rather covenant standing (by covenant practice) and Christ. However, this may be too sharp a distinction between the two. The wordplay on σάρξ in Phil 3:2–4 may indicate the unity that is shared between them. Paul does refer to circumcision in terms of σάρξ. However, in a more universal statement about the nature of believers, he uses the term again (v. 3). In this latter instance, it appears that this use appeals to the Spirit/flesh distinction of relying on one's own effort and self rather than the Spirit's transforming empowerment. The apostle then proceeds to show why this is wrong in his own testimony of having boasted in the flesh (vv. 4–11). If this exegesis is true, then Paul looks at the covenantal membership as a means of personal achievement rather than the actual end.

69. Some have raised the issue of future justification. Regardless of one's interpretation of Rom 2:13 (where the future of δικαιόω occurs), agreement exists that future justification is a pronouncement in congruence with present justification and that the latter exists presently. See Wright, "Justification:

in the salvific benefits that he accomplished. The theological significance of Isaiah's vision has been inaugurated.

Gentiles and the Glory of God

As I have noted, a key element of Paul's ministry is his mission to the Gentiles. We have already observed this in Acts. Luke links Paul's work amongst the nations with the Damascus road and with the Servant's mission (cf. Acts 22:15; 26:17–18; Isa 42:6). Paul extended the Servant's work to the ends of the earth in order that God's glory might fill the earth and thereby fulfill the vision of Isa 6:1–3.

Paul's letters reinforce this paradigm by describing his own mission in terms of the Servant. He discusses his hope that his toil will not be in vain (Phil 2:16), which echoes the Servant's statement in Isa 49:4.[70] That mentality is found in other Pauline texts (Gal 2:2; 4:11; 1 Thess 3:5).[71] God called Paul in the womb, just as the Servant claims himself (Gal 1:15; Isa 49:1). Later in that letter, God shows his glory through Paul, just as God intended to do in the Servant (Gal 1:24; cf. Isa 49:3).[72] The Servant's mission thus becomes Paul's mission.

Other allusions to Isaiah show that Paul thought of his ministry as advancing the impact of the Servant's work towards the fulfillment of Isaiah's vision and theology. Paul quotes Isa 49:8 to encourage his readers not to receive God's grace in vain. Isa 49 deals with how God will grant success to the Servant's endeavors. To Paul, the present has inaugurated that day of salvation, since the Servant's saving work is accomplished (2 Cor 4:1–5; 6:1–2; cf. Rom 4:25; Isa 52:7; 53:11).[73] The Corinthians must live up to the new age (the day of salvation) that they are in (2 Cor 6:2; Isa 49:8).[74] Paul exhorts them not to move backwards in redemptive history, but rather toward the eschatological end of transformation.[75] For Paul, that end goal pertains to every knee bowing before God and every tongue confessing that Jesus is Lord (Rom 14:11; Phil 2:10). Such wording alludes to a variety of passages in Isaiah that discuss God's kingship and the Servant's reward (cf. Isa 45:21–23; 49:18). So it is that the *telos* of Paul's mission is the Servant's glory.

Yesterday," 62–63. For a contrasting viewpoint on Rom 2:13 describing the axiomatic character of God (rather than actually future pronouncement) see Moo, *Epistle to the Romans*, 148.

70. O'Brien, *Philippians*, 300.

71. Ibid.

72. Bruce, *Galatians*, 105.

73. See above discussion concerning Pauline soteriology and the connection to Isa 53.

74. Harris, *Second Epistle to the Corinthians*, 460. Harris offers an excellent discussion on why Paul incorporates Isa 49 into his discussion here. He argues based upon Paul's calling, which is given in terms of the Servant in Isa 49, as well as his mission to Jews and Gentiles, which is also given in terms of the Servant. Although Paul thinks of the Corinthians' experience here of receiving God's grace, he cites Isa 49 because he remembers the reality of the Servant's work.

75. Ibid., 460–61; Garland, *2 Corinthians*, 305; Martin, *2 Corinthians*, 168. Both Garland and Martin share a similar logic with Harris (see above).

The apostle's application of the Servant songs helps us better understand his motivation in ministering to the Gentiles. By taking the mission of the Servant upon himself, Paul labors to reach the nations and to cultivate a community consistent with that which the Servant receives in the end. This is why he is under obligation (Rom 1:14) to preach to the Gentiles even if they consider him and his message foolish (1 Cor 1:22–23) or go so far as to threaten his life (2 Cor 11:26).[76] This is why Paul stresses the unity between Jew and Gentile (Gal 2:11–20; Eph 2:15).

All of this goes back to Paul's calling. In Galatians, Paul states that the revelation of Christ on the Damascus road called him to preach to the Gentiles (1:16). The above discussion aimed to examine what that entailed. Part of Paul's mission stems from his recognition that Jesus is the Servant and so is worthy to receive such worship from all nations. The apostle endeavors to make that a reality. In his mind, it seems that the Damascus road, Isaiah's vision and theology, and the mission to the Gentiles are all tied together.

I can offer one more final and significant example to support this idea. The apostle's thoughts about the offering of the Gentiles to the saints in Jerusalem reaffirm what I have suggested. Schreiner comments that the background of this endeavor originates from the scene in Isaiah in which the Gentiles bring their wealth to Jerusalem (2 Cor 8–9; Isa 2:2–3; 61:6).[77] I have already argued that this eschatological event relates directly to Isaiah's vision.[78] This provides a preliminary association of Isaiah's vision and theology with Paul's own purpose in this specific undertaking.

Rom 15 deepens this idea. That chapter sets the broader context behind the gift to Jerusalem (cf. Rom 15:25–27). The apostle urges his readers towards unity so as to glorify God with one voice (v. 6). This accords with the purpose that the Gentiles will worship God, as seen in Isaiah (vv. 8–12; cf. Isa 2:2–4). Within this, Paul specifically quotes from Isa 11:10 outlining how the Gentiles are to submit and hope in the root of Jesse (Rom 15:12). I noted a variety of substantial parallels between Isa 6 and 11. I even argued that Isa 11 is the fuller depiction of what the prophet witnessed in his vision. In incorporating Isa 11 as part of his mission, the vision and theology of Isaiah has become part of Paul's purpose. Paul's mission to the Gentiles anticipates God's glorious high and lifted up reign through his Servant over all the world.

The rest of Rom 15 reiterates this assertion. Having urged harmony between Jew and Gentile, Paul takes up the issue of the collection for the Jews (vv. 14–27). In his logic, this accords with his broader ministry to the Gentiles, which is grounded in Isa

---

76. Notice in context the allusions to Isaiah. Isa 65:16 is quoted in 1 Cor 2:9, and 1 Cor 2:16 alludes to Isa 40:13. Paul's gospel ties to the same message and content of Isaiah.

77. Schreiner, *Pauline Theology*, 446–47.

78. See previous discussion as well as Hamilton, *God's Glory*, 197, 268; Barker and Bailey, *Micah, Nahum, Habakkuk, Zephaniah*, 341 which imply that Isa 6 is associated with the eschatological realities of the book.

52:15 (quoted in Rom 15:21).[79] This allusion ties together the Servant, Paul's mission, and the vision and theology of Isaiah. In its original context, Isa 52:15 refers to the outcome of the Servant's work in Isa 53. The Gentiles who did not hear or see will now understand the salvation he brought about.[80] As a result, the Gentiles will serve and know God, fulfilling the Lord's reign over all the world; a reality originally described in the prophet's vision (cf. Isa 2:2–4; 11:10; 6:3).[81]

Paul, in referencing Isa 52:15 in this epistle, claims that the Servant's work has been fulfilled. The apostle's role now is to work out the results of his work as it is highlighted in Isa 52:15. Hence, the apostle preaches the gospel (Rom 15:20). This term, drawn from Isaiah, relates to the Servant's victory over sin, death, and exile (40:9; 41:27; 52:7). Paul begins to actualize Isa 52:15 when the apostle preaches this message to unreached regions. People who had not heard or seen will hear what the Servant has done. This work, as Isaiah states, paves the way for God's reign and glory to extend over the entire earth. Paul's mission to the Gentiles has a distinctive contribution to a biblical theology of vision. His ministry to the nations begins to work out the repercussions of the Servant work and thereby aids in fulfilling vision and theology.

Exile and Future Salvation

We have already observed that Paul's ministry moves toward the fulfillment of Isaiah's vision and theology. We can further explore how the apostle still anticipates much of what is seen in Isaiah. The prophet witnesses a time when God will reign uncontested and his glory will fill the earth. This relates to the time when Israel as a nation will be saved and become the center of the world (Isa 2:2–4). Thus, Israel's exile ends (60:1–18) and every enemy (25:1–12) is conquered, including death (25:8).

Paul, using Isaiah's own terminology, makes it clear that such a state has not yet occurred. One example of this is Paul's reference of Isaiah in his discussion of tongues (1 Cor 14:21; cf. Isa 28:11). In Isaiah, Israel, being blind, refuses to understand the prophet's message. Accordingly, the people of Israel are sent into exile, where peoples of foreign tongues will mock them (Isa 28:11). Tongues, then, are a sign of judgment. Paul reiterates that concept to the Corinthians (14:21). Based upon its function, speaking in tongues in church does not lead to conversion, but rather is a sign to

---

79. Schreiner, *Romans*, 765–70. To be specific, Paul is confident in his readers' response to his letter, which is grounded in the authority of his apostolic commission (Rom 15:14–15). This commission resulted in a unique ministry, which itself is purposed to reach the Gentiles per the mission of Isaiah's Servant (vv. 16–24). It also relates to his work with aid from the Gentiles to Jerusalem (vv. 25–27).

80. Moo, *Epistle to the Romans*, 897.

81. Dunn, *Romans 9–16*, 866: "Particularly if Paul did see the Parousia as imminent, as seems most likely, it would simply mean that he saw his own climactic mission toward 'reconciling the world' as a piece with the salvation-history climax spanning the period from Jesus' resurrection to the *Parousia* and final resurrection (11:13–15)." This associates Isaiah's eschatological vision with Paul's *Parousia* and mission, which is precisely what is argued in this chapter.

unbelievers of their alienation from God.[82] This presumes, however, that the exile and the hardened state of Israel and the world continue.[83]

Along that line, Paul recounts the blind and exilic state of Israel. The apostle observes that they do not have eyes to see to this very day (Rom 11:8; cf. Isa 6:9). The present generation needs to heed the same exhortations their ancestors had when first sent into exile: they must trust in the stone that they previously stumbled over (Rom 9:33; 10:11; Isa 28:16). However, at the time, only a remnant was saved, as Isaiah stated (Rom 9:27–28; cf. Isa 10:22). For the rest, a swift judgment awaits (v. 28). That idea alludes to Isa 10:23 and Isa 28:22, which contextually relate to God's punishment in sending Israel into exile. Spiritually and physically, Israel is still in exile, and thus the outcome of the vision has not yet occurred.

All of this awaits a time when the salvation of Israel, promised in Isaiah and glimpsed in his vision, is revealed. Paul's ministry works towards that end. He preaches amongst the Gentiles so as to excite the jealousy of the Jews (Rom 11:13–14). Thus, his labor not only anticipates the repercussions of the Servant's work for Gentiles, but also for Israel.

This culminates in an outcome that fulfills Isaiah's vision and theology. Paul claims that "all Israel" will be saved and cites two texts from Isaiah in support of this idea (Isa 27:9; 59:20–21). Both of these texts are drawn from eschatological contexts associated with Isaiah's vision.[84] They relate to not only Israel's forgiveness of sins, but also to how that facilitates the emergence of God's glory and reign throughout the earth (cf. 27:13; 60:1–19), when all nations will come to Jerusalem in recognition of the centrality of God's majesty and authority (cf. Isa 11:10; 27:13; 60:1–18).[85] Paul, by appealing to these texts, arguably shows that national Israel will be converted to that effect. He thereby shows that "his gospel" resolves all of God's plan.[86]

In addition, Paul states that Israel's salvation results in nothing short of life from death (Rom 11:15). This refers to resurrection and the final victory over death (cf. 1 Cor 15:50–58), which forms part of the portrait of God's eschatological victory in Isaiah (25:1–12). Paul echoes Isaiah in suggesting that resurrection is when God swallows death in victory (1 Cor 15:54; cf. Isa 25:7). All of this also takes place within the wider context of God's ultimate reconciliation of all things to himself (2 Cor 5:19; Col

---

82. Ciampa and Rosner, "1 Corinthians," 741–42.

83. Ibid., 742; Thiselton, *First Epistle to the Corinthians*, 1121.

84. Oswalt, *Isaiah 1–39*, 498–99; Motyer, *Isaiah*, 492–95. The forgiveness of Israel in Isa 27:9 leads to its restoration in verses 10–12. Verse 13 is quite interesting, as it alludes to how Assyria will worship God on his holy mountain. The picture of Assyria coming to worship, as well as the phrase "holy mountain," are tied with the eschatological picture surrounding Isaiah's vision (cf. intertextuality between Isa 6, 11, 19). Similarly, God's deliverance of Israel in Isa 59:20–21 leads to his glory shining upon Israel and the world, which also fulfills Isaiah's vision that God's glory will fill the earth. Paul's allusions to these passages indicate that he shares the same eschatological vision as Isaiah.

85. Oswalt, *Isaiah 1–39*, 498–99; Motyer, *Isaiah*, 492–95.

86. Moo, *Epistle to the Romans*, 350.

1:20). Particularly in Col 1:20, this refers to how God restores the cosmic order back to his own rule and according to his own image (cf. Eph 3:10). Dunn sees that such reconciliation is expressed in Isa 11:6–9.[87] Again, Isaiah's vision of God's glory filling the earth and making all things new and right is Paul's own thought. Paul does not diverge from Isaiah, but rather makes the eschatology of Isaiah's vision his own.

Accordingly, Paul's mission recognizes that the Servant's victory means salvation has emerged into the present. His mission is not only to proclaim that gospel, but also begin to actualize the repercussions of the Servant's work relative to both Gentile and Jew. The whole world must hear the news of Jesus' sacrifice and resurrection so that God's glory will fill the earth. Paul strives towards this end in the present, since Israel (and the world) is still in exile in unbelief. The apostle's work intends to draw Israel to Christ so that the eschatological victory of God described in Isaiah can come to pass. Paul's mission facilitates the time when God's salvation is to extend fully over Israel, the Gentiles, and the entire world.

SPIRIT AND TEMPLE: EZEKIEL IN PAUL

Conversion and the Spirit

In Paul's writings, conversion is one of the major avenues of the Spirit's work (cf. 1 Cor 2:4–5; Gal 3:1–5; Eph 1:13–14; 2 Thess 2:13–14). This is significant, since the apostle ties the believer's conversion with his own experience. Fee argues persuasively for this conclusion based upon the "we" texts in which the apostle includes himself in the Spirit's work at conversion (cf. Rom 5:5; 8:15; Gal 4:6; 1 Cor 2:12; 12:13).[88] To a certain degree, the apostle's experience parallels the believer's experience. This affirms our observations in Acts that Paul is a microcosm of his message. Furthermore, if this is the case, his descriptions of conversion expound upon what he learned and experienced on the Damascus road. Such discussion ties his vision with his understanding of the glorified Christ, the Spirit, and the inauguration of Ezekiel's theology.

The apostle describes conversion in Ezekielian terminology. For example, in Tit 3:5, Paul depicts conversion in terms of washing and regeneration also found in Ezek 36:25–28.[89] In Ezekiel, the people were relationally unclean (4:13) and in fact, dead (3:8; cf. 37:3–5). The Spirit's work, in the context of the new covenant, was to reverse that state by washing Israel to make it acceptable to God and so bring new life, one capable of communing intimately with God. These two ideas seem to relate to the

---

87. Dunn, *Theology of Paul*, 40.

88. Fee, "Paul's Conversion," 177–79.

89. Knight, *Pastoral Epistles*, 343. Notice the parallel wording of cleansing and newness in Ezek 36:25–27 and Tit 3:5.

Pauline ideas of washing (λουτρόν) and renewal (ἀνακαίνωσις).[90] Conversion, then, denotes a powerful internal transformation that makes one relationally alive to God.

Consequently, Paul discusses conversion in terms of resurrection. Eph 2:1–10 states believers were dead and are made alive in Christ. The motif recalls Ezek 37, in which dry bones live.[91] This connection extends beyond a conceptual overlap into shared language, including the terms "peace" (εἰρήνη) and "make alive" (ζωοποιέω). Structural parallels also exist. In Ezek 37, God resurrects Israel (vv. 7–9) so that its people may know he is the Lord (v. 13) and in Eph 2:1–10, God raises believers (v. 5) so that they may know the riches that are in Christ (v. 7). In addition, a rare term, "fitted together" (συναρμολογέω, Eph 2:21), used by Paul, correlates with the LXX of Ezek 37:7, in which the bones "join together" (ἁρμονίαν). Taken together, these elements form distinctive associations between Eph 2 and Ezek 37.[92] Thus, Eph 2 expands upon certain implications of Ezek 37 in the present time.

To be clear, Paul does not claim that the prophecy is fulfilled. He still awaits a future resurrection (cf. Rom 8:23; 1 Cor 15:15–28). Contextually, the apostle appeals to a spiritual transformation in Eph 2 rather than the totality of resurrection envisioned in Ezek 37. He states that believers are dead relative to their trespasses and sins. The contrast, then, is not between the physical and spiritual death Ezekiel portrayed, but rather focuses on the latter. The flow of the chapter affirms this emphasis. The apostle describes believers' transformation relative to their reconciliation with God by the Spirit (Eph 2:18). Accordingly, Eph 2:1–10 reiterates the same reality as Titus 3:5; conversion is the regenerating work of the Spirit's indwelling.[93]

That being said, how does Paul make use of the Ezek 37 motif in Eph 2? Paul seems to evoke this theme to focus on a specific aspect of what occurs in Ezek 37: the Spirit's new covenant work. We recall from Ezekiel that God's indwelling presence was critical to filling the world with his glory (37:28; 43:2). For that reason, the dry bones only become living people when the "spirit" enters them (37:8–9). The Spirit's indwelling facilitates a spiritual aspect of the resurrection that empowers the individual and corporate resurrection described in Ezek 37. In this way, the indwelling and transforming ministry of the Spirit is the linchpin of Ezekiel's theology. Paul's attention to such spiritual rejuvenation in Eph 2:1–10 argues that he believes such work has begun. Eph 2 shows believers the significance of conversion in light of the larger motif that it participates in: resurrection, the presence of God, and the fulfillment of Ezekiel's vision and theology. This makes sense in context. In the flow of argument, Paul parallels Christ's physical resurrection (Eph 1:20) with those who are in Christ

---

90. Ibid.
91. Suh, "Use of Ezekiel 37 in Ephesians 2," 715–33.
92. Ibid.
93. O'Brien, *Letter to the Ephesians*, 153–54; Hoehner, *Ephesians*, 308; Lincoln, *Ephesians*, 86.

(Eph 2:1–10). Being brought to life spiritually is part of the entire scheme of participation in Christ's ultimate physical resurrection.[94]

This resonates with another Pauline text that discusses the Spirit as the "Spirit of life" (τοῦ πνεύματος τῆς ζωῆς, Rom 8:2). Schreiner sees this description as an allusion to Ezek 37.[95] Paul makes such an allusion in the context of the Spirit of life liberating believers from one era, characterized by bondage to sin, to an eschatological era characterized by new life. Such freedom (ἠλευθέρωσέν, Rom 8:2) does not only describe a believer's new position before God (cf. Rom 8:1) but also an entirely new quality of existence[96], which mirrors our consideration of conversion. However, the apostle further argues that the "Spirit of life" ultimately gives believers life from death, which parallels Jesus' resurrection (8:11). Paul's use of the term "Spirit of life" in Rom 8 connects Ezek 37 with conversion and resurrection. Such associations affirm that Paul views conversion as part of a broader complex of events culminating in resurrection, and that all of this stems from the paradigm of Ezek 37.[97]

Notice that the Spirit's work in conversion relates not only to resurrection, but also to the resurrected Lord. This takes us back to the Damascus road, where Paul saw the *resurrected Christ*. Paul's association of conversion with this "bigger picture" seems to have originated from that vision. After all, he claims that the believer's experience of the Spirit's transforming power was his own. On the Damascus road, Paul arguably realized that Christ was the one who fulfilled the agenda of God's presence in Ezekiel and understood that the Spirit's transforming work he presently encountered participated in that scheme. This accounts for the apostle's use of language and motifs from Ezekiel, and further ties his discussion of conversion to resurrection. To Paul, conversion is when the Spirit transforms and indwells believers, which is akin to the Spirit's work as it is depicted in Ezekiel. That part of Ezekiel's theology has been inaugurated.

The Believer as Temple

Such considerations relate directly to the notion of Paul's use of temple language. Paul calls individual believers "the temple" (1 Cor 6:19)[98] in reference to the fact that the Spirit is in them (cf. 1 Thess 4:8; Gal 3:2–3).[99] The apostle extends this language to

---

94. Lincoln, *Ephesians*, 86.

95. Schreiner, *Romans*, 400: "An OT antecedent is found in Ezekiel, where the 'breath of the Lord,' that is, his Spirit, produces life (Ezek. 37:5–6, 9–10, 14), and Paul saw the prophecy of Ezekiel as being fulfilled in his gospel since the resurrection was now assured for believers (cf. Rom. 8:10–11)."

96. Dunn, *Romans 1–8*, 38A:415–16; Schreiner, *Romans*, 400.

97. Moo, *Epistle to the Romans*, 493; Schreiner, *Romans*, 400.

98. Thiselton, *First Epistle to the Corinthians*, 474. In context, the reference to personal behavior (i.e., sexual immorality) argues that Paul has in mind individual believers when calling them the temple of God. This is in contrast with earlier texts in which the apostle seems to label the church/corporate body as the temple. See ibid., 315; Fee, *First Epistle to the Corinthians*, 147.

99. Moo, *Epistle to the Romans*, 493; Thiselton, *First Epistle to the Corinthians*, 474; Garland, *1*

apply to the corporate body. The church as a whole is a temple (1 Cor 3:16–17; 2 Cor 6:16; Eph 2:21).[100] This may derive from the fact that Spirit-filled individuals come together to form Christ's body.[101] This may also function as a proleptic demonstration of the kind of resurrected community envisioned in Ezekiel (cf. 37:16–28; Eph 2:11–20).[102] The flow of Eph 2 supports this idea. Paul writes that God "resurrected" believers per Ezek 37:6–8 and then made them a temple (Eph 2:21), which mirrors the end of Ezek 37, when God will dwell in the midst of his people (vv. 26–28).[103] I suggested that the believer's conversion is *a part of* the Spirit's full resurrecting work described in Ezek 37:1–10 (Eph 2:1–10). Perhaps the same logic extends to Paul's appeal to the temple later in Eph 2. Could it be that the church is the sign that (or, a part of) the entire temple theology prophesied by Ezekiel would come to pass? I will explore this idea further at various junctures throughout the rest of this chapter.

Some scholars see an innovative hermeneutical shift in the way the apostle presents the temple. To these scholars, Paul appears to redefine the eschatological temple presented in Ezekiel from a building to a spiritual people.[104] However, we remember that Ezekiel's theology of presence already included the understanding that God would make individuals a temple (cf. Ezek 2:2; 36:27). That has always been an essential means through which God would fill the world with his glory from the inside out. Rather than viewing Paul as innovating Ezekiel, we can see that the apostle actually seems to work within the prophet's paradigm. He claims that, in light of the Spirit's work of transforming individuals, the indwelling presence of the Spirit has begun.[105] Believers have an intimate relationship with God as envisioned in Ezekiel (cf. 37:23, 27) and should live accordingly. The outcome of God's presence filling the earth has thus begun. As I have suggested, the church may signal that the entire paradigm of Ezekiel will come to pass.

First Fruits for the Future

This moves us to a discussion of the redemptive historical dynamics involved in the Spirit's work. I have stressed the nature of inauguration; however, is there an element

---

Corinthians, 238. Note the wording τοῦ ἐν ὑμῖν ἁγίου πνεύματός ἐστιν οὗ ἔχετε ἀπὸ θεου. Believers have received the Spirit, which implies his indwelling character as the grounds for Paul's use of temple terminology.

100. Thiselton, *First Epistle to the Corinthians*, 315; Fee, *First Epistle to the Corinthians*, 147; Garland, *1 Corinthians*, 120–21.

101. Schreiner, *Pauline Theology*, 344. The language of Eph 2:20–22 indicates that believers are fitted together to become the temple.

102. Beale, *Temple and the Church's Mission*, 245–52. Beale would argue that the church *is* the eschatological temple of the OT. I would qualify this by more a proleptic demonstration. Nonetheless, his observations form the basis of my argument here.

103. Suh, "Use of Ezekiel 37 in Ephesians 2," 730; Hamilton, *God's Indwelling Presence*, 26–27.

104. Suh, "Use of Ezekiel 37 in Ephesians 2," 732–33; Beale, *Temple and the Church's Mission*, 245–68.

105. Hamilton, *God's Indwelling Presence*, 102–20.

of anticipation? Before answering in favor of the latter, I need to make some final comments on the former.

Our discussion so far has argued that an eschatological age has dawned. Paul puts it even more clearly in drawing his distinction between law and spirit (cf. Rom 8:2). Scholars argue that these ideas actually refer to different periods of redemptive history. The former was under the old covenant, and the latter concerns its fulfillment and the consequent operation of the new.[106]

This idea has merit. In Gal 4, Paul observes that people were kept under the law until the fullness of time (τὸ πλήρωμα τοῦ χρόνου, 4:4) when Christ came.[107] The Spirit's work in establishing the intimate relationship envisioned in Ezekiel occurs at this moment (4:6; cf. Ezek 37:23).[108] The Spirit's working signals that the culmination of history has begun.[109] This same paradigm is reiterated in 2 Cor 3. The previous covenant could not transform individuals, but only produced death instead (2 Cor 3:6). Although the law came with glory, the new covenant eclipses that splendor because of the Spirit's transformative work. He enables believers to be brought to conform to the glorious image of the Son (2 Cor 3:18). As I have already suggested, such language relates 2 Cor 3-4 to the Damascus road (2 Cor 3:18; 4:4). By alluding to his experience in this context, the apostle indicates that the mystery unveiled at his calling indicates the beginning of the new era when the people of God are defined by the Spirit (cf. Phil 3:3) and are filled with his presence as a temple, just as Ezekiel predicted (cf. Eph 5:18).[110] They are a form of the eschatological people of God that Ezekiel envisioned. Paul's vision was indeed a vision of inauguration in this regard.

This vision mandates how believers are to live. They cannot live based upon the law, since that era has faded and a new one has begun. If they did, they would in essence build up what was broken down and actually transgress the law (Gal 2:18). Believers cannot begin with the Spirit and end with the flesh (Gal 3:1-4). Rather, the paradigm of this time is that those who trust in Christ receive the Spirit, who causes them to bear much fruit (cf. Gal 3:13-14; 5:17-18). His work in their lives produces what the law could never accomplish: fruit that did not violate any law but instead fulfilled God's requirements (5:23).[111] That is the true transformation envisioned by Ezekiel (cf. 36:26-27;

---

106. Schreiner, *Romans*, 395; Moo, *Epistle to the Romans*, 473-76; Dunn, *Romans 1-8*, 38A:414-16; Schreiner, *Pauline Theology*, 281-82; Fee, "Paul's Conversion," 168.

107. Bruce, *Galatians*, 194; George, *Galatians*, 301; Schreiner, *Pauline Theology*, 96.

108. Fee, "Paul's Conversion," 168.

109. Ibid., 168-69; Longenecker, *Galatians*, 172.

110. O'Brien, *Philippians*, 361; Fee, "Paul's Conversion," 168-70. We can recall that in Ezekiel, the people had confused the present with the eschatological. They thought God's presence and protection guaranteed their safety, despite the fact that they were anything but God's temple personally. Paul, by stressing the worship of God in the Spirit, presents the church as part of the eschatological people of God that will partake in the outcome of Ezekiel's vision and theology.

111. Longenecker, *Galatians*, 263; Schreiner, *Pauline Theology*, 134.

37:23–26) inaugurated at this time.[112] Accordingly, this redemptive historical situation demonstrates that the Spirit is the *modus operandi* of Christian living.

Along that line, the means by which believers are sanctified reflects Ezekiel's concept of God's indwelling presence. In Eph 2:20–22, Paul depicts the church as God's temple, mediating God's presence to the world via the Spirit.[113] This may be the background behind Paul's later command to be filled with the Spirit (Eph 5:18).[114] While this refers to the complete influence of the Spirit over a believer, the metaphor itself may relate to fulfilling the call for believers to be the temple.[115] Just as God was to fill the temple and the world, so the believer is to be a microcosm of such fullness. The broader context of Ephesians supports this. Paul also envisions that Jesus, in the end, will fill the cosmos with glory and that the church is part of that process. God intends the church to be the fullness of Christ, who fills all things in every way (Eph 1:23).[116] By being filled with the Spirit, the church participates in Ezekiel's paradigm of God filling the earth with his glory from the inside out. The way Christians are sanctified points to what Christ has begun.

Because believers are the temple, they must exhibit personal holiness (cf. 1 Cor 6:16–19). Ezekiel condemned Israel for their sexually immoral practices, which desecrated its people's own heart temples (Ezek 14:3) and the physical temple (7:21–22). Paul urges his readers to abstain from such evil, since they have been redeemed (1 Cor 6:20) as God's temple (v. 19). Instead, they are to glorify (δοξάσατε) God in their bodies, which again alludes to how God's glory and presence filled the temple (1 Cor 6:20; cf. Ezek 43:5).[117] Believers, by godly living, exhibit God's presence filling the world from the inside out. Holiness and worship are not merely moral necessities to Paul, but also reflect the believer's function as God's temple at this juncture of redemptive history.

Similarly, on a corporate level, the reality of temple prohibits false teaching. Paul questions what the temple has to do with idols (2 Cor 6:16). Just as Ezekiel warned against placing idols in the heart or in the temple (cf. Ezek 14:3), so too Paul acknowledges that the Corinthians are in danger of doing the same by accepting false teaching (2 Cor 6:16). This carries a warning not to propagate lies. Those who violate

---

112. Schreiner, *Pauline Theology*, 142; Block, *Ezekiel*, 2:356. Interestingly, being filled with the Spirit parallels the indwelling of the word of Christ (Eph 5:18; Col 3:16). The correspondence of Spirit and word also matches what Ezekiel stated (cf. Ezek 1:3; 3:1–3).

113. O'Brien, *Letter to the Ephesians*, 212–13; Beale, *Temple and the Church's Mission*, 261–63.

114. O'Brien, *Letter to the Ephesians*, 391; Lincoln, *Ephesians*, 344.

115. Beale, *Temple and the Church's Mission*, 252, 262. We find a parallel between the church needing to glorify God as the fullness of his temple and being filled with the Spirit who dwells in God's temple.

116. The flow of Ephesians argues for this idea. Being filled with the Spirit relates to walking wisely (cf. Eph 5:15) and thereby accomplishing God's calling (Eph 4:1), which correlates with Christ as the one who fills the church and who fills everything in every way.

117. Beale, *Temple and the Church's Mission*, 252.

the temple sanctity will be destroyed, just like in the days of Ezekiel (1 Cor 3:17; cf. Ezek 9:6).[118] Moreover, this also should compel believers to embrace the truth. Paul reminds believers that they have an exclusive relationship with their God. Because they are the temple, he dwells amongst them and is their God just as they are his people (2 Cor 6:16b). This idea comes as a direct quote from Ezek 37:27 and corresponds with other Pauline statements by which the Spirit facilitates an intimate relationship with the Lord (cf. Rom 8:15; Gal 4:6).[119] Within such communion, it is unthinkable to tolerate a union with any other ideology or idol.[120] Overall, Paul uses Ezekielian theology to show how and why believers live as they do in the current time.

Nevertheless, Paul's discussion of the Spirit and the believer's life does not merely reflect inauguration, but also anticipation. We have already seen hints of future realities yet to come throughout this discussion. The resurrection has not yet happened. The fullness of temple theology has not yet been actualized. Christ is not yet all in all (cf. Eph 1:23). Paul's triumphal proclamation of what the believer now experiences does not contradict those statements. The apostle resolves this tension by reminding us that the Spirit is a kind of down payment (ἀρραβών, 2 Cor 1:22; 5:5; Eph 1:13–14) or the first fruits (ἀπαρχή, Rom 8:23). The Spirit's presence and current work cannot be interpreted as the complete fulfillment of Ezekielian theology. The eschatological has come into the present; conversely, the present ministry points to a greater reality to come. In describing the Spirit with this language, Paul makes reference to the Spirit's ultimate work of resurrection and the fulfillment of all promises.[121] He seals believers for the day of redemption (Eph 4:30).[122] This reiterates what I have said concerning the connections between conversion, resurrection, and Ezek 37. Moreover, it also shows that Paul operates within Ezekiel's paradigm. What occurs now does not override what Ezekiel envisioned but instead pushes forward for its complete fulfillment. The church is the sign that all will come to pass.

Therefore, to Paul, the Spirit's work at this time is not an end to itself. Rather, the Spirit's new covenant ministry directs believers to a future moment. He signifies that God will accomplish his work of resurrection as described in Ezekiel and thereby facilitate the fullness of his glory throughout the entire world (cf. Rom 8:21; Eph 4:30).[123] Accordingly, Paul's present ministry points forward to the eschatological fulfillment of Ezekiel's vision.

---

118. Thiselton, *First Epistle to the Corinthians*, 317; Block, *Ezekiel*, 1:308.
119. Block, *Ezekiel*, 1:419–20; Fee, "Paul's Conversion," 178–81.
120. Harris, *Second Epistle to the Corinthians*, 504.
121. Fee, "Paul's Conversion," 169; Dunn, *Romans 1–8*, 38A:474; Lincoln, *Ephesians*, 39.
122. O'Brien, *Letter to the Ephesians*, 437.
123. Dunn, *Romans 1–8*, 38A:472; Fee, "Paul's Conversion," 169–70. Eph 4:30 is particularly important in presenting this idea in discussing the day of redemption, a time when exile ends and God's glory spreads throughout the earth. See O'Brien, *Letter to the Ephesians*, 430.

THE SON AND SAINTS: DANIEL IN PAUL

Second Adam and the Saints

Acts suggests that the glory of Christ on the road to Damascus created a new paradigm for how Paul views Jesus and the church. One of his primary realizations revolved around the notion of corporate solidarity. Christ and the church are one, just as the Son of Man and the saints are in Daniel. This realization plays out in the apostle's writings. Whether that deals with the "in Christ" metaphor in Ephesians or the notion of substitutionary language in his letters (cf. Gal 3:13; Eph 5:2; 1 Thess 5:10), the link between Jesus and his body is pervasive. In fact, the notions of being Christ's body (Eph 4:12) or his bride (Eph 5:25) are ways to communicate the union or oneness between Jesus and his people.[124]

However, does Paul really associate the notion of corporate solidarity with Dan 7 and the Damascus road? Scholars are more reserved on that matter. Schreiner uses Dan 7 to illustrate that "in Christ" refers to this sort of corporate representation or affiliation.[125] Conversely, he states that we cannot directly employ Dan 7 and a Son of Man Christology, because Paul does not ever use such language in his writings.[126]

The objection is reasonable; nonetheless, we can tie the apostle's conception of Christ and church with Dan 7 and the Damascus road via an Adam Christology.[127] As discussed, Paul's use of "likeness" terminology relates to Dan 7 in contexts describing Christ as the second Adam (cf. 1 Cor 15:22, 45, 49; 2 Cor 3:18; Col 3:10). Thus, although Paul does not use the term "Son of Man" or "one like a son of man," his notion of likeness, image, or Christ as man or as Adam essentially refers to the same reality.[128] In addition, certain texts, like 1 Cor 15 and 2 Cor 3:18, use an Adam Christology to show the solidarity between Christ and his people. Believers are one with Christ as they are made into his image. As already discussed, those texts also refer to Paul's experience on the Damascus road (cf. 1 Cor 15:8). Thus, Paul's Adam Christology bridges Dan 7 with the Damascus road and his conception of corporate solidarity.

Based upon this, we can examine how the Adam Christology specifically impacted Paul's theology concerning the church. Rom 5 and 1 Cor 15, which mention Christ as second Adam, are crucial in this matter. In Rom 5, the parallel between Adam and second Adam exhibits the basis for the church's salvation.[129] In essence,

---

124. Schreiner, *Pauline Theology*, 335; Dunn, *Theology of Paul*, 549–51. We should not confuse the notion of the origin of the body metaphor itself with the concept corporate solidarity that underlies it. I am arguing about the latter, and not the former, when dealing with the influence of the Damascus road.

125. Schreiner, *Pauline Theology*, 158.

126. Ibid., 158–59.

127. Ibid., 157–59; Kim, *Origin of Paul's Gospel*, 260–68. Schreiner actually discusses it as such.

128. Kim, *Origin of Paul's Gospel*, 260–68.

129. Moo, *Epistle to the Romans*, 316; Cranfield, *Epistle to the Romans*, 271–72. δια τουτο may indicate a conclusion to the discussion in verses 1–11. Better yet, it may communicate the basis by which verses 1–11 operate. Paul draws out as his conclusion a required inference upon which verses

death and condemnation are the redemptive historical realities resulting from Adam's transgression (Rom 5:12). Christ's work, while sharing the parallel of union and solidarity, actually exceeds the consequences of Adam's sin by procuring justification and life (Rom 5:15–17). The foundation of a believer's standing before God (cf. Rom 5:10) is secured through union with Christ, which looks forward to the future and final reality of eternal life (5:21).[130] Consequently, as noted, 1 Cor 15 states that believers are ultimately made into the image of that new Adam (cf. 1 Cor 15:45–49). Hence, people are saved in relation to Christ as a new Adam, and their final end is to be remade in the image of that Adam. Adam Christology, which relates back to the Damascus road, shapes Paul's conceptualization of the church from *terminus a quo* to *terminus ad quem*.

In addition, Dan 7 and the second Adam play into Paul's understanding of the church as Jew and Gentile. We can observe this in two ways. First, I noted that Jews and Gentiles are mentioned in Daniel's central vision. Not only will the saints (Israel) worship God and overcome, but also those from every tongue and tribe (cf. Dan 7:14). As will later be argued, the apostle's mission prepares the church to participate in what that scene proclaims. Second, if Paul views the notion of "one like a son of man" in Adamic terms, then the church's conformity with Christ's image means they too are a new humanity. Eph 2:15 makes this connection between Christ, new Adam, and the church as a new humanity. The apostle writes that because believers are in Christ, they are made into a new man such that there is no Jew and Gentile. Gal 3:27–28 and Col 3:10–11 make similar statements. The believer's new identity in the second Adam erases the distinction between Jew and Gentile (Col 3:11). The unity of Jew and Gentile in the church testifies that the categories of old humanity are gone in light of the church's new identity in Christ. Thus, even the composition of the church points to its solidarity with Christ, the new Adam. Thus far, Christ is the pattern for the church from its beginning, in its makeup, and of its end.

For this reason, Paul appeals to Danielic terminology to remind the church to champion the supremacy of Christ. The apostle proclaims Christ's preeminence by reminding his readers how they have been transferred into Christ's kingdom (Col 1:13). He is the one who created and is above all thrones (1:16). He is the image of the invisible God (1:15).[131] All of this language echoes Dan 7:9–14, when God transfers the kingdom to the Son of Man, the image of God.[132] This all takes place as thrones are set up in the heavenly court, but in the end, the Son of Man rules over all creation.[133] Co-

---

1–11 hinge. This specifically regards the certainty of final salvation that Christ has procured.

130. Moo, *Epistle to the Romans*, 316.

131. Kim, *Origin of Paul's Gospel*, 218–23.

132. Dunn, *Theology of Paul*, 107; Dunn, *Colossians and Philemon*, 92.

133. In the context of various angelic authorities and powers (cf. 1 Cor 15:24; Eph 1:21; 3:10), the word appears to refer to the same supernatural beings. Such language originates from passages like 2 *En* 20:1 and *T. Levi* 3:8 which recall the heavenly court in Dan 7:9. This parallels his description of Christ in Eph 1:20–23. See Dunn, *Theology of Paul*, 107.

lossians brings the church back to its foundation in the person and primacy of Christ. Paul's description of Christ's supremacy draws from Danielic imagery as the primary illustration of when such preeminence will be seen. Paul discovered that truth on the Damascus road and uses such language to remind his readers of what they anticipate.

Along this line, the terminology of "saints" is used repeatedly in the greetings of the epistles (cf. Rom 1:7; 1 Cor 1:2; Eph 1:1) and seems to harken to the language of saints in Dan 7:18, 21–22. Perhaps Paul often describes believers with this term, not only to underscore holiness, but also their purpose as it pertains to that future moment.[134] This particularly makes sense in the case of 1 Cor 6:2. Paul reminds his audience of the reality that the saints (ἅγιοι) will judge (κρινοῦσιν) the world. This echoes the language where judgment (τὴν κρίσιν) is given for the saints (τοῖς ἁγίοις) in Dan 7:22. Paul seems to have the notion of the saints in their eschatological role in Dan 7 in view and applies that truth to the church's situation.[135]

Overall, the Damascus road gives the apostle clarity about Jesus and a conviction concerning the nature of the church. In essence, everything about the church is formulated around Christ. The solidarity between Christ and the church exists such that the church is made to look like him, not only in moral practice and holiness, but also in terms of the church's salvation, composition, and resurrection: everything from beginning to end. This stems from the paradigm of corporate solidarity apparent in Dan 7 between the saints and the Son, which Paul understood on the Damascus road and communicates through his Adam Christology. Hence, the apostle urges the church to exalt Christ. He reminds believers of his supremacy in terms of Daniel's vision, and even calls them saints to underscore their purpose in light of that vision. This suggests that the apostle's mission to unify Jew and Gentile relates to the scene of Jews and Gentiles worshipping the Son of Man, the new Adam. All of this demonstrates that the realities of the vision have begun to enter into the present.

Kingdom Delay and the Saints

While components of the vision have begun, the vision of the Son's coronation and consequent dominion has not yet come to pass. Paul's audience still lives under foreign rulers (cf. Rom 13:1–7). This places believers in an exilic situation parallel to Daniel.[136] Paul calls upon the saints to submit under these authorities and live a quiet, godly life (cf. Rom 13:1–8; 1 Tim 2:2). Paul's reasoning is that in resisting these powers, one actually disobeys God, who has ordained every authority (Rom 13:1–4). The

---

134. Ibid., 44–45.

135. Evans, "Daniel in the New Testament," 525. Evans states that this also relates to Matt 19:28 and Luke 22:28–30. Such an observation is valid without being mutually exclusive to the echo of Daniel. They are all linked together.

136. Schreiner, *Pauline Theology*, 449–51; Moo, *Epistle to the Romans*, 791; Dunn, *Theology of Paul*, 676.

language here recalls the concepts and wording in Dan 2:21 and 4:17, 25, 32.[137] God grants authority to whomever he pleases. Accordingly, just as Daniel submitted under foreign rule as a reflection of God's ultimate sovereignty, so believers act similarly for the same purpose in their recognition that Jesus is Lord.[138]

The notion of the delay of the vision and its significance may partially play into Paul's description of present-day suffering. Prior to the resurrection of the saints, believers will groan with all creation at the weight of the suffering they experience (Rom 8:23). Suffering makes one worthy of God's kingdom (2 Thess 1:5, 11). Such hardship only ends with the revelation of Jesus Christ, who comes in the clouds (1 Thess 4:17; 2 Thess 1:7) bringing the hope of eternal life (1 Tim 6:12–15; Tit 3:7).[139] The notions of resurrection, kingdom, eternal life, and even the clouds all resonate with Daniel's vision. In Daniel's paradigm, the persecution of the saints continues until the scene of Dan 7:9–14, when the saints finally have victory. Daniel also states that at that time, the saints will be resurrected to their eternal reward (Dan 12:2). Paul appears to follow the same pattern.

This is affirmed in 2 Thess 2:7. In the passage, Paul mentions that the mystery of lawlessness is already at work. The terms "lawlessness" and "mystery" allude to Daniel.[140] The context also echoes that book. The man of lawlessness seems to be the one that Daniel describes as the horn of the fourth beast. The mystery of lawlessness, then, discusses the satanic activity that culminates in the arrival of this evil man, who exalts himself against God (2 Thess 2:7; cf. Dan 11:36).[141] With this, Paul reminds believers that they are not yet in the time of the Son of Man's final victory and rule. Instead, they are in the time leading up to the final confrontation between false human authority and God's final dominion in his Son, which is precisely why they are suffering at this time (cf. 2 Thess 1:4).[142]

Thus, while Paul could identify elements of the vision that have been actualized, he readily acknowledges that believers do not live in the full eschatological moment. Presently, they await God's kingdom to come and suffer, as Daniel predicted. Nonetheless, believers have hope, and we already see such expectations in terms of Daniel's vision.

---

137. Dunn, *Theology of Paul*, 676. Compare οὐ γὰρ ἔστιν ἐξουσία εἰ μὴ ὑπὸ θεου (Rom 13:1) with τὸν κύριον τοῦ οὐρανοῦ ἐξουσίαν ἔχειν πάντων (Dan 4:17).

138. Moo, *Epistle to the Romans*, 793.

139. Knight, *Pastoral Epistles*, 265–68. In the flow of 1 Tim 6:12–15, Paul commands Timothy to hold onto eternal life, which will be consummated with the appearance of Jesus Christ.

140. Bruce, *1 and 2 Thessalonians*, 170.

141. Fee, *First and Second Epistles to the Thessalonians*, 288; Wanamaker, *Epistles to the Thessalonians*, 257; Bruce, *1 and 2 Thessalonians*, 170; Beale, *Temple and the Church's Mission*, 286–88.

142. Bruce, *1 and 2 Thessalonians*, 146, 163.

I Saw the Lord

Synthesis: Paul's Preparation of the Saints towards the Vision

Just as Paul took on the mission of the Servant to work towards the realities of Isaiah's vision, so part of his labor pertains to preparations towards the fulfillment of Dan 7. This observation helps us synthesize what we have just discussed: on the Damascus road, Paul realized that Jesus was the new Adam and consequently identified that the church were participants in the agenda of Jews and Gentiles worshipping the Son of Man in Dan 7. As a result, he endeavors to minister not only to the Jews, but also to the Gentiles, and calls them saints to associate them with the moment of Daniel's vision (cf. 7:21). He also reminds the people of Christ's preeminence and how the church should worship him. Their job is to magnify Christ as the saints and those from every tongue, nation, and tribe do in Dan 7:14. At the same time, Paul does not tell believers that this time is the fulfillment of vision, but rather states that the kingdom has not yet arrived. They will still suffer as the saints do in Daniel's theology; however, Paul directs believers to place their hope in the final deliverance, which echoes the outcome of Daniel's vision. Paul directs believers' efforts to that end. His mission is one of inauguration and anticipation.

Paul's use of liturgical terminology in Rom 15 and Phil 3 may provide a final example of this (e.g., λατρεύω, λειτουργέω). I will grant that the echoes between Rom 15 and Phil 3 and Dan 7 are fainter than in other instances. Hence, I want to pose these as more suggestive than definitive. The analysis above still stands, regardless of these two texts. Nonetheless, two initial factors signal a connection between Dan 7 and those texts and are therefore worth exploring. First, the terms (particularly λειτουργέω) are relatively rare in the NT (and in Paul), which attracts the readers' attention.[143] Second, Paul's application of these terms to the Gentiles in Rom 15 and Phil 3 is also unique in both OT and NT. In the OT, the only text which uses λατρεύω of the Gentiles in a positive sense is Dan 7:14.[144] Arguably, When Paul uses a rare word in a way found only in one prior text, he may be making a connection with that passage. Hence, as will be discussed, the intertextuality of these words in Paul's writings suggests that his mission prepares for the moment described in Dan 7:9–14.

With this in mind, we return to Rom 15 and the collection of the Gentiles for the Jews. I have already discussed this in relation to Isaiah, but it also contains significant connections with Daniel. This illustrates that even as this analysis attempts to dissect intertextual associations to different prophets, Paul merges them to form a composite picture, which implies the unity of vision and theology that the apostle witnessed on the Damascus road.

In Rom 15, Paul reminds his readers that his writing and ministry is based upon the grace that was given to him from God (διὰ τὴν χάριν τὴν δοθεῖσάν μοι ὑπὸ

---

143. Hays, *Echoes of Scripture*, 29–31. The only other places the verb λειτουργέω is used in Heb 10:11 and Acts 13:2.

144. λειτουργέω occurs in Dan 7:10 of Theodotian and λατρεύω occurs in Dan 7:14 of the LXX.

τοῦ θεοῦ, v. 15). The phraseology recalls Paul's commissioning on the Damascus road.[145] Verse 16 claims that he was called to be a priest (λειτουργός) who ministers to the Gentiles (ἱερουργοῦντα). Perhaps, by using such language, Paul relates himself to the agenda of Dan 7.

This idea is strengthened by our examination of the remainder of Rom 15. In Paul's explanation of his mission stemming from the Damascus road, he states that his goal is for the Gentiles to deliver aid to the Jews (Rom 15:27; cf. 2 Cor 9:12). The way he describes this endeavor in Rom 15:25–27 holds some interesting similarities with Dan 7. Before making these comparisons, we need to recall a fundamental truth about this text; namely, the collection for Jerusalem poses some inherently eschatological overtones. As discussed, this goal anticipates a future time when the Gentiles would bring an offering to Jerusalem, as Isaiah depicted.[146] Hence, the discussion of the collection is not merely for the sake of logistics, but rather makes a statement about the nature of Jew and Gentile, foreshadowing what was prophesied. With this context in mind, the use of λειτουργέω more strongly echoes Dan 7. The word λειτουργέω does not often occur in OT discussions of eschatology. One of the (two) major texts that it does appear in is Dan 7:10,[147] and the setting and the word choice already points to an association with Daniel's vision.

With this in mind, the Jews in Jerusalem are called the saints, echoing Dan 7:18, 27. Paul's mission in bringing the gift from the Gentiles is to demonstrate the unity of saints with those from the nations. This too brings us closer to the scene where the saints (Israel) are associated with people from every tongue, nation, and tribe (cf. Dan 7:14, 18–25). Moreover, the Gentiles are offering up a priestly sacrifice in serving their brethren (λειτουργῆσαι, Rom 15:27). Such language is found in Dan 7:10–14. Thus, Paul appears to cast the harmonious interaction described in Rom 15 in Danielic terms. Rom 15, then, may be a somewhat proleptic scene of Dan 7. Once again, such an agenda in Rom 15 originates from Paul's commission on the Damascus road (cf. Rom 15:6).

Philippians may also support the idea of the church as anticipation of Dan 7. In that book, the apostle stresses how the church should be a unified community for the sake of the gospel. Within this, Paul views his labor as a priestly work to complete the ministry of the Gentiles in that city (Phil 2:17). Their fellowship together for the gospel was itself a priestly service, just like that of their brethren in Rome (Phil 2:30; cf. Rom 15:27). Moreover, Paul characterizes his readers as part of the true people of God because of how they serve (λατρεύοντες) God in the Spirit. The use of the term λατρεύω could allude to Daniel (cf. 7:14). The rest of the chapter seems to point to that conclusion. In Paul's argument, such service relates not only to avoiding legalism

---

145. Dunn, *Romans 9–16*, 38B:859.

146. Schreiner, *Pauline Theology*, 446. The discussion on the intertextuality between Isaiah and Rom 15 already indicates the proleptic nature of this text, which supports the suggestion above as well.

147. The other is Ezek 40–48.

(3:1–16), but also licentiousness (vv. 17–19). Additionally, this service looks forward to the return of Christ (vv. 20–21).[148] The language of Christ's coming reminds us of Pauline language surrounding his vision, and particularly its Danielic elements. Christ will come from heaven, recalling the heavenly nature of his vision (cf. Acts 9:3), which Daniel also describes (7:13). Believers will be conformed to his image (Phil 3:21), language drawn from Jesus as second Adam in the context of Paul's vision on the Damascus road (1 Cor 15:22, 45), which originated from Daniel's vision (7:13). At that time, Christ will subject all things to himself (Phil 3:21) which also reflects Paul's language elsewhere (Eph 1:21; Col 1:16) and relates to Dan 7:9–14.[149]

Accordingly, the flow of Phil 3 argues that the apostle aims for the church to be a worshipping community of Jews and Gentiles to act consistently with the anticipation of the time when that vision is fulfilled. Consequently, the church is a prolepsis awaiting a fullness that stems from the scene of Dan 7:9–14. Believers' conduct anticipates a time when they will worship Christ in full perfection. Again, Paul's mission, then, is to build up the church in preparation for that occasion.

PAULINE ESCHATOLOGY AS THE ANTICIPATION OF THE VISION

Inauguration as Affirmation of Anticipation of Vision and Theology

In the discussions above, inauguration has already left us with a sense of anticipation. Paul's use of Isaiah, Ezekiel, and Daniel establishes that the present has come into the eschatological in order to point to the future consummation of all things. Paul has reiterated Isaiah's paradigm of the end of exile, the salvation of Israel and the Gentiles, and a resurrection and new creation that makes all things right by reconciling the world to God. He has envisioned a time when the first fruit of the Spirit's work is consummated such that God's glory fills the earth, as Ezekiel presented. He has prepared the church to be a part of what takes place in Dan 7, when the Son of Man receives worship from the saints and from people of every tongue, nation, and tribe. As we have observed, Paul links these descriptions with language from the respective visions, as well as with his own experience on the Damascus road. His vision and theology does not diverge from the eschatological paradigms associated with the visions of the prophets. Rather, Paul affirms that their inaugurated theologies all move to those very ends.

I have also briefly noted that Paul associates this culmination with the return of Christ. For the apostle, that is when heaven meets earth, as other visions have implied. Phil 3:20–21 explains how Christ comes down from heaven and transforms believers so

---

148. See O'Brien, *Philippians*, 345. Paul contrasts the Philippians against the false teachers and sets himself as a model against both legalism (vv. 15–16) and licentiousness (v. 17). As such, the apostle exemplifies and explains the nature of being the true people of God in their spiritual service to him.

149. Dunn, *Theology of Paul*, 107.

as to gain sole authority over all the cosmos.[150] An analysis of Christ's return in Paul's writings helps to solidify that the apostle does have the same idea as his predecessors.

The Return of Christ

The Thessalonian epistles contain language similar to Phil 3:20–21. Christ's *Parousia* is associated with heaven and the clouds (1 Thess 4:17), elements found in Daniel's vision (cf. 7:13) as well as Ezekiel's (1:4). Paul's description of the sudden and acute judgment of the wicked echoes Isaiah. While wicked people cry out peace and safety, their destruction will be like the labor pains of a woman (1 Thess 5:3; Isa 13:8). They will receive eternal destruction when Christ comes in his majestic glory (2 Thess 1:9–10).

That last reference is significant in this discussion. The wording of 2 Thess 1:9–10 follows Isa 2:10–17 quite closely.[151] For example, Paul uses the words τῆς δόξης τῆς ἰσχύος αὐτοῦ to describe Christ, a phrase only found (repeatedly) in Isa 2 (vv. 10, 19, 21). Furthermore, the apostle seems to follow the flow of Isa 2. In that passage, Isaiah describes God's judgment as he brings low those who are "high and lifted up" (2:11) such that he alone will be high and lifted up (v. 17) in fulfillment of Isaiah's vision (Isa 6:1).[152] In 2 Thess 1:9–10, Christ punishes the wicked and then is magnified by the saints. With these echoes, Paul affirms that his idea of the end is the eschatological picture of Isaiah's vision. As 2 Thess 1 reveals, Christ's return will cause the wicked to be brought low so that Christ's glory is exclusively magnified, just as Isaiah said.[153]

Isaiah, Daniel, and Ezekiel are interwoven into a unified eschatological portrait in 2 Thess 2. The introduction of the man of lawlessness, or the son of destruction, recalls the horn of the fourth beast in Daniel.[154] For instance, this individual exalts himself above everything (ὑπεραιρόμενος ἐπὶ πάντα λεγόμενον θεὸν), which mirrors Dan 11:36 (ὑψωθήσεται ἐπὶ πάντα θεὸν). This individual also takes his seat in the temple (2 Thess 2:4), which primarily alludes to Daniel's descriptions of how this person will make alterations to law and sacrifice (cf. 7:25). This also implies that Ezekiel's notion of a future physical temple may not be removed from Paul's paradigm.[155]

150. Hawthorne, *Philippians*, 234; O'Brien, *Philippians*, 466.

151. Wanamaker, *Epistles to the Thessalonians*, 229; Bruce, *1 and 2 Thessalonians*, 152.

152. Oswalt, *Isaiah 1–39*, 125.

153. Aus, "Relevance of Isaiah 66," 265–68. We could add Aus' observations to our discussion, for Aus demonstrates that Paul also employs Isa 66 in the background of 2 Thess 1.

154. Green, *Letters to the Thessalonians*, 309; Bruce, *1 and 2 Thessalonians*, 168; Wanamaker, *Epistles to the Thessalonians*, 246; Martin, *1, 2 Thessalonians*, 33:235. Bruce, Green, and Wanamaker link this individual in Dan 11 with Antiochus Epiphanes; however, as I have argued, there is overlap between the horn of the third beast and the horn of the fourth, which accounts for the shift from immediate to eschatological in Dan 11.

155. See my previous discussion of Daniel's use of Ezekiel in the seventy-week prophecy. Daniel envisions a time when the holy place will be consecrated, which probably refers to Ezekiel's idea of a future temple. Daniel incorporates Ezekiel's innertextuality as his own theology. Hence, by supporting Daniel's idea of temple, Paul implicitly supports Ezekiel's.

Some have argued that the temple refers to the church rather than to a physical structure.[156] The major evidence against the notion of a material temple is the use of the term 'temple' (ναός) in Paul and other instances in the NT. To be sure, Paul essentially uses "temple" to refer to the church elsewhere in his writings.[157] However, the term may still refer to a physical building here. Paul's allusion to Daniel implies that he adopts that prophet's paradigm as his own. He does not claim to modify it or offer a new interpretation. Instead, the text from Daniel is stated as a matter of fact, seemingly presuming acceptance of the ideas originally portrayed in Daniel. Arguably, the culture of the time would have read it as a physical temple.[158] Furthermore, Paul's appeal to temple has mainly connected with Ezekiel's theology of indwelling presence. The connection in this text is slightly different in relation to Daniel. The different intertextual background of Paul's use of temple may account for his variant use of the word. Along that line, the apostle may grammatically signal a difference between structural temple and believer as temple. In 2 Thess 2:4, the phrase "temple of God" has the article, while in 1 Cor 3:16 and 2 Cor 6:16, where "temple" is used in reference to believers, it does not.[159] In addition, 2 Thess 2 is one of the earlier uses of temple in the NT, and so reading Paul's later ideas of temple into this text may be anachronistic.

Consequently, the appeal to Daniel in 2 Thess 2 seems to anchor Paul's use of temple in that text to the eschatological and physical entity envisioned by the prophet.[160]

156. Beale, *Temple and the Church's Mission*, 274–84.

157. Ibid. However, 1 Cor 3:17 might be an exception. With the articular construction, it may refer to a principle concerning the structural temple and comparing believers with that building. See note below.

158. Green, *Letters to the Thessalonians*, 312–13; Wanamaker, *Epistles to the Thessalonians*, 247; Bruce, *1 and 2 Thessalonians*, 169. I am not debating here about which temple (Jerusalem versus pagan), but rather a physical structure versus the abstract church. Scholars point out the background of Daniel and Antiochus Epiphanes IV as indication of a physical structure. Furthermore, Gaius Caesar's image being erected in the temple in Jerusalem may have renewed thoughts that the ultimate foe would do so as well. Green points out that establishing a cult relationship within the church as God's presence is theologically problematic.

159. One objection to this view is that 1 Cor 3:17 uses the article and appears to speak about believers. However, 1 Cor 3:17 appears to give the general principle and then associates believers with that reality (notice the last phrase, "which you are"). If Paul makes this comparison, then he consistently uses the article to refer to structural temples and an anarthrous construction when dealing with believers as the temple. See Garland, *1 Corinthians*, 120.

160. See Martin, *1, 2 Thessalonians*, 33:236. Martin argues that while Paul does not designate the temple in Jerusalem, both the historical background of the intertestamental period as well as the textual background of Daniel works to anchor that interpretation. Along the latter line, Beale's appeal that the temple should be non-material stems primarily from the intertextual use of the term in the NT. To be sure, "temple" does refer to Christ as well as to the body of believers; however, as noted in Ezekiel, those tensions and uses of "temple" as God's presence already existed. Ezekiel held those factors in harmony to show how God's glory would fill the entire earth. Hence, those uses of "temple" (some of which do nonetheless refer to the physical building) do not negate what occurs in this text. However, if his suggestion is correct, the way Beale deals with Paul's creative use of Dan 11 is interesting. See Beale, *Temple and the Church's Mission*, 291. However, this contrasts his position on the NT's use of the OT to draw in the OT context as underlying substructure. See Beale, "Did Jesus and His Followers Preach

As many scholars have acknowledged, a physical building appears to be more fitting.[161] Wanamaker sums up the entire argument well:

> The inner sanctuary in question is almost certainly the Holy of Holies in the Jerusalem temple where God was thought by the Jewish people from OT times to dwell. ναόν is made definite by the article and the possessive genitive τοῦ θεοῦ ("of God"), indicating that a specific building was intended. Although it is true that in 1 Cor. 3:16f. Paul employs ναός in a metaphorical sense to refer to the Christian as a temple of God (cf. 1 Cor. 6:19), in the present context where no mention is made of the believer and the indwelling of the Spirit of God as in 1 Corinthians; such an interpretation is highly unlikely. Jewish Christians as well as Gentile Christians undoubtedly would have understood it as a reference to the one true temple of God in Jerusalem, especially since the verse contains an allusion to Dn. 11:31–36 and the desecration of the temple at Jerusalem by Antiochus Epiphanes... The definite nature of this reference makes it impossible to believe that either the creator of the scenario, whether Paul or another, or the original readers of the letter would have understood the reference metaphorically.[162]

If this is the case, then 2 Thess 2 is consistent with the eschatological schemes presented in Daniel and Ezekiel. The desecration of the temple leads to the consecration of the holy place, an idea found in Daniel's thinking (7:25; 9:24–27) that relates to Ezekiel's vision and theology (40–48),[163] and as suggested above, evidences that the church as temple does not override the entire concept in Ezekiel. Rather, the church is the first fruit of the fullest temple reality to come. Even if critics beg to differ, the reference to temple in this eschatological context shows that Paul articulates some anticipation of Ezekiel's and Daniel's visions and theologies.

In 2 Thess 2, we not only find allusions to Daniel and Ezekiel, but also to Isaiah. When the Messiah returns to judge the man of lawlessness, Christ destroys him with the breath of his mouth (v. 8). The wording parallels Isa 11:4 in describing how the son

---

the Right Doctrine from the Wrong Texts?" 390–91.

161. See Green, *Letters to the Thessalonians*, 312–13; Wanamaker, *Epistles to the Thessalonians*, 247; Bruce, *1 and 2 Thessalonians*, 169; Martin, *1, 2 Thessalonians*, 33:236. In addition to Wanamaker's assertion above, Green expresses doubt towards non-physical readings of the temple: "It may be that the *temple* here referred to is the heavenly sanctuary, which is mentioned a number of times, especially in apocalyptic literature (Ps. 11:4 [10:4]; *1 Enoch* 14:8–25; *2 Bar.* 4:3–6; *T. Levi* 5:1–2). But once more the question arises as to whether the Christians in Thessalonica would have understood this rather opaque reference. Moreover, that sanctuary is the domain of the God of Israel, and we have no explanation concerning how the 'man of lawlessness' could establish his cult in relationship to that realm" (312). Finally, Martin contends, "Paul commonly used *naos* metaphorically of the believer as the dwelling place of the Holy Spirit (1 Cor 3:16–17; 6:19; 2 Cor 6:16). But here it must be used literally if the passage is to depict an observable, symbolic event the church could recognize as an indication of the nearness of the day of the Lord" (236).

162. Wanamaker, *Epistles to the Thessalonians*, 246–47. While I disagree with the statement concerning non-Pauline authorship, I hope the point of the argument is clear.

163. Allusions are apparent between the man of lawlessness and the king of Tyre in Ezek 28:1–10. See Bruce, *1 and 2 Thessalonians*, 169; Wanamaker, *Epistles to the Thessalonians*, 247. Paul probably has in mind the evil results of the end time discussed in Daniel and Ezekiel. Just as the king of Tyre fell so that God's glory would fill the earth in the true temple, so Paul appeals to the same notion here.

of Jesse destroys the wicked with the breath of his mouth. I have already discussed Isa 11's connection with Isa 6.[164] Such intertextuality indicates again that Paul sees an end consistent with Isaiah's vision and theology.

Overall, Paul's eschatology draws upon a composite picture of prior visions and theologies. He affirms that those portrayals do not differ from his own. In this way, Kim is correct in saying that Paul sees a *proleptic Parousia* on the Damascus road. Paul witnesses the glorified Christ knowing full well that this glory culminates in one scene: the coronation of the Son of Man. Accordingly, Paul reiterates the same *repercussions* of that visionary event as the Son of Man comes to earth from the heavenly court to judge the wicked, to be exalted, to dwell with his people, and to rule over all, as depicted in Isaiah, Ezekiel, and Daniel.

PAUL'S CONTRIBUTION TO A THEOLOGY OF VISION

Ridderbos' quote may offer an effective summary to much of what I argue in this chapter:

> The whole content of Paul's preaching can be summarized as the proclamation and explication of the eschatological day of salvation inaugurated with Christ's advent, death, and resurrection. It is from this principal point of view and under this denominator that all the separate themes of Paul's preaching can be understood and penetrated in their unity and relation to each other.[165]

Paul, on the Damascus road, beheld the resurrected Lord, whose glory was so distinctive that the apostle knew Jesus was the Servant of Isaiah, the Son of Man in Daniel, and the chariot rider in Ezekiel. That glory also signaled to Paul that Jesus was victorious and worthy of the honor described in the visionary event. As a result, the theological significance of the vision of Paul's predecessors has been inaugurated. Paul personally experienced this inaugurated theology in his own conversion. We initially recognized this reality from the book of Acts and then saw it borne out in the apostle's writings.

Accordingly, Paul begins to expound upon a variety of subjects in his letters. Some scholars rightly acknowledge that perhaps a "center" is impossible to contain the diversity of these topics. Nonetheless, Paul's subjects are not conflicting or random. Instead, much of what Paul states stems from his understanding that the theologies of Isaiah, Ezekiel, and Daniel have begun. This shapes the assortment of theological issues pertaining to Paul's soteriology, pneumatology, ecclesiology, and more. If Jesus is the Servant, then his work to be the sacrifice for Jews and the many shapes Paul's view of salvation. If Jesus has accomplished the work of inaugurating God's presence, then those indwelt by the Spirit are God's temple and are sanctified by the Spirit. If Jesus is the Son of Man, then the church must participate with him in corporate solidarity.

---

164. See Barker and Bailey, *Micah, Nahum, Habakkuk, Zephaniah*, 341; Hamilton, *God's Glory*, 268.
165. Ridderbos, *Paul*, 44.

In this regard, Paul's theology moves from his understanding of Christ. This is where Kim's suggestion that the Damascus road participates in the origins of Paul's gospel has merit.[166] The glorified Lord on the Damascus road becomes the gateway for Paul's exposition of the OT into his own ministry. That influence, as this chapter illustrates, is extensive and may clarify certain issues in Pauline studies.

This influence not only shapes Paul's proclamation, but also his mission. Paul's message celebrates that Christ's work has inaugurated eschatological realities. Nonetheless, he looks forward to the fulfillment of the vision. The apostle understands that current salvation will be fulfilled when the exile ends. Paul sees the Spirit's current work as evidence of a future resurrection through which God's glory will truly fill the earth. Paul recognizes that the church participates in the work of the saints and believers from every people, nation, and tongue, but prepares them for the time when Christ comes down from heaven to be worshipped. Accordingly, Paul's eschatology picks up on different parts of past visions and theologies to show that all that was prophesied will be accomplished in the end, both the heavenly visionary event and its repercussions on earth. Paul's vision, then, is a *proleptic Parousia*. Like his predecessors, he has seen the same end, only with greater clarity of the central person of the vision: Jesus. Thus, he knows and preaches that history is ready for the culmination of theology and history, the fulfillment of prophecies and vision. His vision and mission is one of inauguration and anticipation.

This brings us back to the opening issue of center versus framework, as well as Paul's contribution to a biblical theology of vision. I am not proposing a center here as much as *part* of the framework under which Paul operates. Put differently, the vision of inauguration and anticipation sets the *directionality* of the apostle's mission. To Paul, his ministry to the Gentiles, defense of the gospel, and writing of letters was not an end to itself or merely meant to promote morality amongst his readers. His vision of inauguration and anticipation promotes a mission of preparation. It begins with Christ and ends with Christ. Paul desires believers to live in light of the new covenant realities Christ has inaugurated by his life, death, and resurrection. Living this way brings honor to the Lord, but also points to, anticipates, and prepares for the ultimate time, when God's people will fully participate in a fulfilled reality of salvation, presence, and kingdom. Paul's ministry accelerates redemptive history towards that end. As such, Paul has not only shaped the flow of a biblical theology of vision in showing how the theologies of Isaiah, Ezekiel, and Daniel have begun to emerge in the present day, but also in showing how believers and present history are set in a collision course with the culmination of God's plan for the summation of all things in Christ.

---

166. Kim, *Origin of Paul's Gospel*, 267–68.

8

John's Vision
Vision of the Culmination of History and Theology

THE MOMENTUM OF PAUL'S vision and theology carries us into John's Apocalypse. Paul has proclaimed that redemptive history accelerates toward the eschatological moment when all things are culminated in Christ. John's vision presents us with the full picture of what that entails. The Apocalypse assembles the final portrait under development ever since Isaiah's calling. Each prophet has contributed a unique theological piece of the puzzle that has been intertextually drawn closer and closer together. John's vision becomes that final point of convergence in portraying the consummation of God's salvation, presence, and kingdom.[1] This is solely found in the coronation of the Son, the summing up of all things in Christ. John's vision is therefore the culmination of theology and the dramatic conclusion of a biblical theology of vision.

The apostle also completes a theology of vision by detailing how the heavenly coronation works itself to earth to resolve the prophetic anticipation garnered by John's predecessors. The prophets and Paul have all understood that the visionary event would have massive repercussions across the cosmos. John's work does not disappoint. As a brief survey of Revelation attests, the apostle's viewpoint does not strictly concentrate on the scene itself or an object/person in that scene, but rather upon the entire progression of that moment and how it shapes the end of history and eternity. Accordingly, John's vision is also the culmination of history.

Thus, the book of Revelation is the apex of a biblical theology of vision. The visions of John's predecessors have moved towards an ultimate revelation that unveils the full nature of the vision and its ramifications upon the world. Now, one man on

---

1. Although John does not explicitly quote from the OT, his allusions are frequent. See Hitchcock, "Critique of the Preterist View," 227: "Revelation includes more Old Testament allusions than any other New Testament book. In numbers, Isaiah is first, followed by Daniel, Ezekiel, and Psalms, although the numbers vary from one commentator to another." See also Beale, *Revelation*, 77.

Patmos will see the complete picture of what past visionaries have witnessed and reveal it for us in its entirety.

JOHN'S CALLING AND MISSION

We might be tempted to launch immediately into Rev 4–5; however, the first three chapters do play an important role in understanding John's central vision. Without much surprise, these texts introduce us to John's mentality and purpose in his writing, for John positions his work as a completion of a biblical theology of vision. In essence, the apostle appeals to the visions and theologies of his predecessors in his opening words. These terms will in turn be used in Rev 4–5 itself. Hence, the first three chapters provide a context of convergence, suggesting that John's vision in Rev 4–5 is both central to and the intentional unification of the visions and theologies of those before him.

Revelation as the Presentation of a Vision of Convergence

Rev 1:1–8 begins to show how John pulls past revelation together towards his central vision. Verse 1 announces that John's message, given from God through Christ, pertains to what will occur shortly (ἃ δεῖ γενέσθαι ἐν τάχει, Rev 1:1). This seems to allude to Dan 2:28, 45, when Daniel explains that God has revealed to Nebuchadnezzar the mysteries that were to take place in the latter days (δεῖ γενέσθαι μετὰ ταῦτα).[2] John's change of the wording from "latter days" to "shortly" indicates that the divine message involves the fulfillment of Daniel's theology and vision.[3] History and the plan of God are about to reach their climax. Thus, John has already presented his book as relating to the culmination of a biblical theology of vision.

Throughout the rest of Rev 1:1–8, John draws in a variety of echoes to Isaiah, Ezekiel, Daniel, and Paul. These allusions are juxtaposed together, giving the sense that their messages are converging within John's theology. Thus, even while greeting the church and giving a doxology, the apostle directs his readers to look towards this convergence of vision.

John greets the church with grace and peace, not only from the Father but also from the "seven Spirits before the throne" and the Son who is the "firstborn from the dead." His description of the Spirit is not only consistent with the seven churches, but also with the Spirit's ministry in Isa 11:1; a text linked with Isaiah's vision. His description of the Son as πρωτότοκος ἐκ τῶν νεκρῶν also picks up on the exact same language Paul used in Col 1:18. There, Christ's preeminence not only as victor over death, but also over the cosmos (and even a new creation) is in view.[4] John seems to

---

2. Dan 2:45 of Theodotian's version.
3. Beale, *Revelation*, 180–81.
4. O'Brien, *Colossians, Philemon*, 44:90. See chapter 7 in which I discuss how Col 1:15–18 relates

have the same idea in his writing.⁵ In addressing his audience, John prepares readers to anticipate the outcomes communicated in the vision and the related theologies of Isaiah and Paul (or at least a common tradition).⁶

Likewise, John's doxology worships Christ in terms of a biblical theology of vision and theology. Christ is Isaiah's Servant, who can release Israel from its sins (compare λύσαντι ἡμᾶς ἐκ τῶν ἁμαρτιῶν ἡμῶν in Rev 1:6 with λέλυται αὐτῆς ἡ ἁμαρτία in Isa 40:2).⁷ John also honors Christ because he has made believers a kingdom. This echoes the accomplishment of one like a son of man in Dan 7:14 and 27. In addition, the apostle praises Christ because he has made those in him a priest (Rev 1:6). Conceptually, this may relate to Ezekiel, in which God's people are consecrated to work as priests when his glory fills the earth in his final vision (cf. Ezek 45:17; cf. Exod 19:5–6).⁸ Fittingly, John concludes his doxology by ascribing glory and dominion to Christ in terms similar to Dan 7:14. By establishing the fulfillment of vision as the church's motivation for worship, John directs his audience to consider that motif.

All of this moves to verse 7, where the apostle lays out the summation of his book. He has already stated in verse 1 that his message concerns the fulfillment of Daniel's theology. In verse 7, the apostle proclaims this idea more specifically. The central motif of his work is when Christ "comes with the clouds," which alludes to Dan 7:13, the hallmark moment of Daniel's central vision that becomes the central message of Revelation.⁹ Accordingly, both the beginning of this section and its ending suggest that the Apocalypse presents the fulfillment of Daniel's vision.

How do the allusions to Isaiah, Ezekiel, and Paul in the body of this introduction fit into that paradigm? Arguably, John associates all of them together. They are literarily "sandwiched" in Daniel's vision. Thus, as Daniel's vision will be fulfilled, so they too will come to pass. Not only does the literary structure of Rev 1:1–8 suggest this, it

---

to Danielic imagery and Paul's vision on the Damascus road.

5. Beale, *Revelation*, 191.

6. Schuster Fiorenza, "Revelation and Paul." Although some may argue that John may not be familiar with the writings of Paul, we can at least argue that they referred to the same overarching tradition (especially since Paul may have employed a hymn). They could overlap in that way. Furthermore, the association between these two could be valid, since they ministered in the same area (though at different times). Schuster Fiorenza has demonstrated some interesting affinities between the two that argue for a closer relationship. In any case, while I suggest that John and his readers were likely familiar with Paul, we can at least consider the common thought pattern between John and Paul, which shows their theologies in harmony. We will maintain this idea for the rest of our discussions on the relationship between John and Paul. See also Aune, *Revelation 1–5*, 249. Aune reminds us that Paul influenced both Ephesus as well as Laodicea (via Colossae).

7. Oswalt, *Isaiah 40–66*, 50. Isa 40:2 introduces God's agenda to release Israel from its sins, which only occurs by the Servant's hand.

8. Osborne, *Revelation*, 66. See previous discussion. Commentators have pointed out the fundamental allusion to Exod 19:6 of kingdom and priest, which seems to be in the background of the consecration offerings in Ezek 45:13–17. Osborne also cites Isa 61:6. All Israel was to function as a priest, which shares some parallels with the function of the church per 1 Pet 2:9 and Tit 2:14.

9. Aune, *Revelation 1–5*, 59; Mounce, *Book of Revelation*, 50.

matches Daniel's own intertextuality with all of those books. As I have suggested, since all the visions cohere together, the fulfillment of one is really the fulfillment of them all. By this, Rev 1:7 explicitly states what John has hinted throughout these verses. Revelation is the fulfillment of vision and theology.

I can offer one further observation. Much of the language above is found in Rev 4–5. For example, we are reintroduced to the seven Spirits in Rev 4:5 (cf. Rev 1:4). Rev 5:10 repeats the doxology found in Rev 1:6. The central moment of Rev 4–5 is the coming of the Son of Man on the clouds mentioned in Rev 1:7. Accordingly, John begins to focus his readers' attention on the importance of the visionary event, helping them to see it as the unification of the visions of the past.

John's Calling as the Calling of His Forerunners

John's calling furthers this thesis by casting his calling in the light of the commissioning of his predecessors. The apostle illustrates that their calling becomes his own and by extension, their vision also becomes his own. This too establishes why his vision in Rev 4–5 alludes to Isaiah, Ezekiel, Daniel, and Paul.

John begins to recount his calling in Rev 1:9 and even the first two words echo the experiences of his forerunners. The phrase "I John" (Ἐγὼ Ἰωάννης) matches Daniel's words in Dan 8:1 (ἐγὼ Δανιηλ). John's personal description of partaking in suffering, kingdom, and endurance also echoes Daniel's acknowledgement that the saints in this current time suffer until the kingdom is established (cf. Dan 7:9–27; 11:45—12:2). The fact that John's distress and perseverance are "in Jesus" also suggests a Danielic background. In Daniel, the saints suffer but have victory because of their solidarity with the Son (cf. Dan 7:14, 27).[10] John's wording also indicates that suffering and victorious endurance only ensue in Christ. The apostle's calling puts him squarely within Daniel's vision and theology.

On Patmos, John's commissioning commences with a great sound like a trumpet (Rev 1:10). Such noise recalls Ezek 3:12 and the experience Ezekiel has with God's glory at his own calling.[11] In fact, scholars note a series of parallels between Ezekiel and John in this regard. Bauckham suggests that Ezekiel's calling becomes part of the substructure of Rev 1, 4–10, a claim that revolves around two major similarities. First, John's vision in Rev 4 resembles Ezekiel's call vision. Second, Ezekiel's summoning to eat a scroll corresponds with the Lamb's receiving a scroll in Revelation and later, John's own consumption of that scroll in Rev 10:8–10.[12] While critics might disagree with Bauckham on some points, scholars recognize that his assertion of an Ezekielian backdrop to these chapters in the Apocalypse is undeniable.[13] The correspondence

---

10. Miller, *Daniel*, 216.
11. Beale, *Revelation*, 203.
12. Bauckham, *Theology of Revelation*, 82–84; Bauckham, *The Climax of Prophecy*, 245–48.
13. Baynes, "Revelation 5," 807. See also, Kowalski, "Transformation of Ezekiel," 295. Kowalski

between John and Ezekiel in this first chapter paves the way for John's later use of that prophet in his writing. They thereby share the same calling, message, and ministry.

Just as the great sound reveals God's glory in Ezekiel's vision, so the great sound turns John's attention to "one like a son of man" in the midst of the seven lamp stands (Rev 1:12–13). The phraseology recalls both Ezekiel's vision (cf. 1:4; 1:13) as well as Daniel's (Dan 7:13). The descriptions of Christ further entrench this Christophany within their visions. Christ possesses a golden sash (ζώνην χρυσᾶν) similar to the angelic messenger in Dan 10:5 (περιεζωσμένη ἐν χρυσίῳ Ωφαζ). They also both have eyes of fire and are dressed in linen (Rev 1:14; Dan 10:6). I argued that the angelic messenger appeared in such a way to associate himself with Daniel's previous vision in Dan 7.[14] Now, John meets the one who actually accomplishes all of Daniel's vision and theology.

Jesus also has white hair, just like the Ancient of Days in Dan 7:9. This may imply what we have observed both in Daniel and in Isaiah; namely, that the Father displays his own authority and power in his Son. In Daniel, the one like the son of man possesses the majesty of the Ancient of Days to judge the world (cf. Dan 7:14). In Isaiah, the Servant will be high and lifted up like the Father (cf. Isa 6:1 with 52:13). John beholds the one he knows is equal with the Father as described in the vision and theologies of Daniel and Isaiah.

The apostle's description of Christ echoes Isaiah's theology and vision more explicitly. Out of Christ's mouth proceeds a double-edged sword, which fits the description of the Servant in Isa 49:2 (cf. Isa 11:4). Jesus will have the eschatological victory of the Servant, as portrayed in Isaiah's vision. Also, John further describes Jesus' glory as brilliant like the light of the sun (Rev 1:16b). Such a description recalls Isaiah's description of the Servant's majesty (Isa 42:6), which actually becomes the basis for Paul's own viewpoint of Christ on the Damascus road (cf. Acts 9:3; 2 Cor 4:4–6). The glory John saw was the same glory that Isaiah and Paul beheld.

Christ's glory also echoes what Ezekiel saw in his own vision. Jesus' feet were as burnished bronze, likened to the glow of a furnace (Rev 1:15). The words allude to Ezek 1:27, which discusses the chariot rider as having loins of glowing metal and fire.[15] Both Christ and that individual have a voice similar to "many waters" (Rev 1:15b; Ezek 1:24; 43:2). In Ezekiel, the "voice of many waters" is found not only in the opening vision of the book, but also at the end, when God's presence fills the earth with glory. Jesus is the judging and saving presence of God, who will accomplish this very task. Once again, Ezekiel's calling and his entire theology associated with the vision becomes part of John's own commissioning.

John's reaction to this glory resembles Ezekiel (2:1), Daniel (10:9), and Paul (Acts 9:4). They all fall and then subsequently are summoned to their task. What is that

---

also notes parallels with Rev 18–22 and Ezek 37–48.

14. Goldingay, *Daniel*, 291.

15. Beale, *Revelation*, 208; Osborne, *Revelation*, 88.

mission for John? Christ commands the apostle to write what he has seen, what is, and what is about to come after these things (Rev 1:19). His vision just witnessed (what he has seen) has implications on the present (what is) as it anticipates the climax of history (what is to come).[16]

This command explicitly integrates his encounter with the glorified Christ with John's own mission and theology. Such an experience recapitulates the callings of individuals like Ezekiel, Daniel, and Paul. Such an experience also recapitulates the visions of Isaiah, Ezekiel, Daniel, and Paul. Both of these factors point to one conclusion about John's own mission: his ministry bears the weight of these men, and his theology is the convergence of their visions and theologies. His commissioning is to ultimately explain how their theologies are fulfilled, what is to come. The last phrase of Christ's command ("write... what is to come after these things") supports that conclusion. The phrase "after these things" (μετὰ ταῦτα) recalls the wording in Dan 2:28–29, 45 (μετὰ ταῦτα), which refers to the latter days.[17] John will write about how Daniel's message would come to pass, but Daniel's intertextuality as well as John's own intertextuality indicate that this relates not only to the fruition of Daniel's theology, but also to the entire biblical theology of vision.

The Church's Anticipation of the Completion of Vision and Theology

Thus far, John has indicated both the centrality of the vision and how the visions of his predecessors merge into his own vision. The letters to the churches further this paradigm by asserting that John's vision is not something to be ignored or trivialized. Rather, these letters demand that the churches make the vision of John (and his predecessors) their own. Scholars have rightly detected that the exhortations within these messages are not only about the present, but also interweave themes and motifs found in Revelation within imperatives of how to live in the current age.[18] John directs the church to look to the future, to the fruition of history, for guidance on how to live today. Squarely within this is John's call vision as well as past visions. By making such allusions, John heightens the focus upon the vision in Rev 4–5 and shows its importance to the church's life for all time (an important contribution to a biblical theology of vision in and of itself).

---

16. See Beale, *Revelation*, 216; Thomas, *Revelation 1–7*, 113–17; Aune, *Revelation 1–5*, 105–6; Osborne, *Revelation*, 97. While commentators, for the most part, agree on the general idea of the statement, they disagree about its application to the book. My goal is not to extensively comment upon whether a tri-part or bi-part structure is preferred (although the former, with some qualification, seems to have some advantages) other than to state that the assertion above is somewhat outside this specific debate.

17. Beale, *Revelation*, 155, 216. Compare the text בְּאַחֲרִית יוֹמַיָּא (latter days) with μετὰ ταῦτα (after these things). Other Greek versions translate it as ἐπ' ἐσχάτων τῶν ἡμερῶν.

18. Osborne, *Revelation*, 112; Beale, *Revelation*, 223; Aune, *Revelation 1–5*, 126.

We may begin with certain allusions to Isaiah in Rev 2–3. Christ reminds the church in Pergamum that he bears a double-edged sword (Rev 2:12), an echo both to John's opening vision (Rev 1:16) as well as to Isa 49:2. The Servant will execute judgment against God's enemies so as to bring about the vision of Isaiah.[19] In the same manner, this church must watch its doctrine to avoid that very same condemnation when Christ comes (2:16).[20] They do not want to be on the wrong side when the vision is consummated! In addition, Christ reminds Sardis that he is the ruler who has the seven Spirits (Rev 3:1; cf. Rev 1:4), just as Isaiah envisioned (Isa 11:1). Thus, he alone rules wisely, and has the authority to bestow life, which they desperately need (Rev 3:5).[21] Likewise, Christ is the holy one and the keeper of the keys of David, descriptions (particularly ὁ ἅγιος) found in Isaiah's vision (Rev 3:7; cf. Isa 6:3). Thus, the church in Philadelphia can take heart that they will have final victory over Satan, as the Holy One of Israel will rule high and lifted up in the end. Christ will come to that very end (Rev 3:11).[22] The various letters allude to Isaiah's vision and theology to provide accountability for the church as well as inspiration. The eschatological realities associated with that vision will take place, and so the church must live accordingly.

Certain letters also invoke allusions to Ezekiel. The message to Ephesus echoes Ezekiel's vision. Christ walks "in the midst" of the lampstands, indicating his presence and authority among the church (see also Rev 1:13). The language "in the midst" (ἐν μέσῳ) recalls both the language of presence in Ezekiel's first vision (cf. 1:4, 13) as well as his presence in the city, temple, and amongst the nation (10:7; 43:7). Christ now dwells amongst his church in like manner.[23] Because of this intimate relationship, for the Ephesian church to forsake their first love is inexcusable.[24] Christ threatens to remove his presence from the Ephesian church when he returns (ἔρχομαι, Rev 2:5).[25] However, if they repent and overcome, God guarantees eternal life in paradise. This fundamentally alludes to Gen 2. Nonetheless, we observed that Ezekiel's chariot was itself an allusion to creation and paradise.[26] It denoted that God's presence would, in the end, fill the earth via a resurrection (cf. 37:1–28).[27] Hence, the consummation of

---

19. See my discussion in chapter 4. The Servant songs ultimately relate to Isa 6 (cf. Isa 52:13).

20. Contra Aune, *Revelation 1–5*, 188. While some demur at the possibility of "coming" referring to Christ's final coming in Rev 19, the innertextuality of the term strongly points in that direction. Aune makes Rev 2:16; 3:11 the exception to this use of ἔρχομαι. See Osborne, *Revelation*, 146; Thomas, *Revelation 1–7*, 145. Osborne sees it as both present but still anticipating the judgment at the *Parousia*.

21. Osborne, *Revelation*, 173.

22. Ibid., 194; Aune, *Revelation 1–5*, 240. Once again, "coming" relates to Christ's second coming.

23. This is reminiscent of Paul's theology concerning the inauguration of Ezekiel's message, and thereby serves as support for Paul's own ideology (or at least the tradition) within Rev 2–3.

24. Beale, *Revelation*, 229.

25. Aune, *Revelation 1–5*, 147. Aune argues against this being eschatological because it is negative. However, see Thomas, *Revelation 1–7*, 142–45.

26. Wacholder, "Creation in Ezekiel's Merkabah," 14–32.

27. Block, *Ezekiel*, 2:370–72.

Ezekiel's vision serves as both an incentive for obedience as well as a warning against disobedience. John also articulates such fulfillment to the Philadelphians. Christ promises to establish them in God's temple in the new Jerusalem (cf. Rev 3:12).[28] This reinforces that John additionally views the fulfillment of Ezekiel's theology of presence as part of the motivation for the church to endure suffering (Rev 3:11–12).[29]

The letters are also based upon the paradigm found in Daniel. The promise of resurrection for Smyrna after they suffered ten days (Rev 3:9–11) seems to integrate well with what Daniel describes. That prophet himself suffered for ten days (Dan 1:12–14), and the number in Revelation may allude to this suffering.[30] If this interpretation is legitimate, then John reminds his readers that they too endure with the saints of old and will be delivered when the son of man triumphs and eternal life is granted (cf. Dan 7:14–27; 12:1–2). Along this line, Christ will not remove from the book of life anyone who perseveres (Rev 3:5), recalling Dan 12:1.[31] Jesus also presents himself to Thyatira as the Son of God and as having eyes of fire (Rev 2:18), images found in both John's vision as well as Daniel's (cf. 10:6). He has the authority to allow the saints to rule with him (Rev 2:26–27), just like Daniel describes in his vision (7:27). This takes place from Christ's throne, a place given to him by his Father (Rev 3:21). The throne and the notion that God bestowed honor on Christ is found in essentially every vision of the prophets and apostles (cf. Isa 6:1; Ezek 1:26; Dan 7:9; Eph 1:20), and actually anticipates what we will observe in Rev 4–5. This latter example reinforces that John places the visionary event as a core part of the exhortation to the church.[32]

Allusions to Paul are also present in the letters.[33] Christ as the first of creation (Rev 3:14) echoes John's prior description of firstborn from the dead (Rev 1:5). Interestingly, both the notion of firstborn of creation and from the dead are found in Paul's writing in Col 1:15–18. John is likely following the association that Paul has made.[34] Christ claims that his faithful witness ultimately allowed him to have the throne from his Father (Rev 3:11). Paul discusses this very paradigm (cf. Phil 2:5–11). John uses the hope that Paul shared to spur the Laodeceians to be truly "fruitful" (or produce good water) for the Lord.[35] John's use of crown language (2:10; 3:11) also echoes Paul's

---

28. Thomas, *Revelation 1–7*, 292. Thomas acknowledges that this most likely refers to the new Jerusalem. Since believers are deemed metaphorical pillars, so the temple may be a conceptual (rather than structural) idea as well in this case.

29. Beale, *Revelation*, 294.

30. Ibid., 242.

31. Osborne, *Revelation*, 180; Aune, *Revelation 1–5*, 223.

32. Aune, *Revelation 1–5*, 268; Beale, *Revelation*, 310–11; Bauckham, *The Climax of Prophecy*, 6; Osborne, *Revelation*, 214.

33. See above discussion on overlap of Paul and John. As noted, this at least refers to a common tradition. See Schuster Fiorenza, "Revelation and Paul," 578–81.

34. Osborne, *Revelation*, 204; Beale, *Revelation*, 299–301.

35. Beale, *Revelation*, 303; Osborne, *Revelation*, 205–6. Both Beale and Osborne relate this to being productive for the Lord as opposed to being shallow (and thereby disgusting). See also Thomas,

idea of what surrounds Christ's *Parousia* (1 Cor 9:25). John invokes a paradigm similar to Paul's to encourage the saints to persevere through great trial (Rev 2:9–10; 3:11).[36]

Rev 2–3 do not merely contain practical applications for the church, rather they express how the churches ought to live in light of the upcoming consummation of Christ's eschatological victory. The portrayal of this triumph is not only taken from John's call vision, but also from the visions and related theologies of Isaiah, Ezekiel, Daniel, and Paul. Such imagery serves as a reminder of the church's accountability, its standard of practice, as well as its hope and inspiration to persevere. These descriptions do not only refer to past visions, but also look forward to the vision in Rev 4–5, when John officially explains how God's people overcome (Rev 5:5) as anticipated in these letters (cf. 2:7, 11, 17, 26; 3:5, 12, 21).[37] That is when Christ makes his people a kingdom and priests over the earth (5:10), as I discussed earlier (1:6).[38] Accordingly, Rev 2–3 form an important bridge between John's opening of the letter and past visions to the vision of Rev 4–5.

To be sure, the imagery found in a biblical theology of vision is not the only factor in play in these exhortations. A whole host of intertextual factors are present here and throughout Revelation.[39] Nonetheless, I hope we have seen how the visionary event and its context, as described by John's predecessors, function as a key part of John's exhortations. All the letters allude, to some degree, to the visions and theologies of John's predecessors. As such, to John, a biblical theology of vision is part of the heart of the church's practice and worldview. His vision must become the church's own, which provides further evidence that a biblical theology of vision becomes part of the fabric of Revelation.

Synthesis

As we move towards a discussion of Rev 4–5 itself, the first three chapters establish an important context for our understanding of John's presentation of that vision. First, Rev 1–3 announce that the vision is a *central and controlling reality* within the book. John states that the fulfillment of Dan 7 and what it entails is the summation of his book (Rev 1:7). The apostle also impresses upon his readers that the vision must become their hope and motivation. As we have observed with other biblical writers,

---

Revelation 1–7, 305–6. Thomas argues more traditionally that this refers to spiritual zeal for God. However, all of these views are not far off from what God demands. The Lord desires his people to genuinely seek him and produce good works from the heart. I stress this agreement above.

36. Osborne, *Revelation*, 195.

37. Beale, *Revelation*, 311.

38. Ibid.

39. For example, one could trace the influence of Zechariah and the Psalms throughout these texts (e.g., Rev 1:4, 18; Zech 4:1–14). However, my goal is not to give an exhaustive elaboration on each intertextual instance, but rather to focus on the passages related to this study. See also Beale, *Old Testament in Revelation*.

John's vision is a microcosm of his own theology and message. The entire book flows to and from Rev 4–5.

Second, the context establishes the nature of the vision itself. Namely, intertextual allusions in Rev 4–5 to other books are far from coincidental. Instead, the apostle has already provided us a hermeneutical pattern by which the apostle repeatedly *fuses previous revelation into a final and complete vision.* John alludes both to the imagery of the visions of his predecessors as well as to the theologies associated with those visions. His calling is the continuation and consummation of the calling of those who have witnessed the vision before him. Thus, John will explain how what he has seen shows how all things will be fulfilled, both in vision itself and in its entire theological significance.

All of this prepares the reader to go into Rev 4–5 understanding the importance of those chapters in anticipation of John weaving all these visions (and their respective theologies) together into what they really are: various facets of the same eschatological event and the culmination of history and theology. He thereby provides the conclusion of a biblical theology of vision.

JOHN'S VISION AS THE CLIMAX OF VISION

Rev 4–5 as the Climax of Vision

Before engaging in the details of Rev 4–5, some brief observations on the macro level of these chapters provide important insights into the nature of this text. Specifically, I want to remark upon the intertextuality between Rev 4–5 and past visions. The third chapter of this book discusses the various points of overlap between these visions. My point here is not just to comment that similarities exist; instead, I seek to show that this overlap is a part of John's literary strategy. He intentionally makes his vision the convergence point of the other visions, which is consistent with what we observed in Rev 1–3.

We can initially note this deliberate portrayal by contrasting the intertextuality of John's vision with other visions. Other visions overlap with each other. Daniel contains Ezekiel's throne (cf. 7:9), and Ezekiel mentions the glory of God filling the earth, as Isaiah describes (cf. 43:2–5). However, these connections do not comprise the majority of their descriptions of the visionary event. Instead, only several verses out of their entire accounts allude to another biblical writer's vision. Moreover, we sometimes observe these connections within a vision's innertextuality rather than within the vision itself. For example, Daniel picks up Isaiah's and Ezekiel's notion that God's glory would fill the earth in his vision of the mountain in Dan 2:35. Since Dan 2 is innertextually related to Dan 7, we argued that Daniel incorporates the vision and theology of his predecessors. Hence, while the associations existed, they were not always pervasively, explicitly, or directly *within* the previous visions themselves.

By comparison, the intertextuality of John's vision is its chief feature. Intertextuality completely saturates his account of the visionary event. Numerous commentators note this characteristic. Beale observes fourteen similarities between Daniel and Rev 4–5.[40] He also observes frequent overlapping between John's vision and Ezekiel's.[41] Osborne comments that John draws his imagery from both Ezek 1 and Isa 6.[42] Aune recognizes this similarity as well, and the list goes on.[43] Scholars have substantial grounds to make such claims. At a quick glance, we can see similarities of language from the very beginning of John's account with the phrase "I saw" (εἶδον, Rev 4:1), which is also found in Isa 6:1, Ezek 1:1, and Dan 7:1. Ezekiel's angels (Rev 4:7; cf. Ezek 1:10–14) are present in this throne room scene, singing the song found in Isaiah (Rev 4:8; cf. Isa 6:3). The many thrones set up in Daniel (7:9) and Paul (Col 1:15) are also set up in Rev 4:4. Of course, the one seated on the throne appears in all these visions as well (Rev 4:2; cf. Isa 6:1; Ezek 1:26–28; Dan 7:9). Additional similarities exist beyond these.[44] The extensive intertextuality of Rev 4–5 does not diminish the clarity of the allusions between prior visions. Rather, it demonstrates that the interconnectedness of vision is a key element of John's primary goal. He arguably casts his vision as the convergence of all the past visions.

The apostle not only makes frequent allusions to components of other visions, but also employs the substructure of those visions as well. John brings forth the full storyline of the visionary event variously discussed by his predecessors. Previous writers only saw part of the visionary event and its full ramifications, or implied the nature of this moment through their innertextual expositions. For example, Isaiah suggested that the one who was ultimately high and lifted up was the Servant (52:13; cf. 6:1). Also, Ezekiel associated his vision with the outcome of God's glory filling the cosmos (Ezek 43:1–5). Daniel aided the development of a biblical theology of vision by confirming these implications. The vision did concern the coronation of the Son of Man, as Isaiah indicated. The heavenly vision was to be wrought out on earth, as both Ezekiel and Isaiah suggested (cf. Ezek 43:1–5; Isa 2:2–4; 11:1–16). Conversely, even our analysis of Daniel had to draw upon the innertextuality of his vision and theology to derive some of these connections (see Dan 9:24 for the allusion to Ezek 40–48). Dan 7 did not *by itself* express it all, although it may have interwoven all of these elements together inferentially.

However, John completes what Daniel initiated. The overarching plotline of Rev 4–5 is clear and comprehensive. The account focuses on the coronation of the

---

40. Beale, *Revelation*, 314.

41. Ibid., 315.

42. Osborne, *Revelation*, 220.

43. Aune, *Revelation 1–5*, 279. See also, Thomas, *Revelation 1–7*, 354; Michaels, *Revelation*, 92–96; Walvoord, *Revelation of Jesus Christ*, 110–11; Kowalski, "Transformation of Ezekiel," 297.

44. See previous discussion in chapter 3. See also my later explorations of the theological significance of those allusions.

Son of Man (Rev 5:3–7) that Isaiah and Daniel present. His inauguration will have ramifications upon the cosmos, as Isaiah, Ezekiel, and Daniel portray (Rev 5:8–14). Again, here all of these elements are located in one central passage as opposed to scattered throughout the book. Even if the rest of Revelation further explains these realities, the complete storyline, as implied by Ezekiel and Isaiah, and as further solidified by Daniel, is now fully unveiled by John. The apostle reveals the entire scope of the visionary event.

What do we gain from considering these overarching observations on Rev 4–5? While we have not yet identified the significance of each individual element in this text, we have seen, in part, why they all come together within this one text. John has gone beyond his predecessors in his use of allusions. This heightened intertextuality may be part of John's literary strategy to posit Rev 4–5 as the ultimate presentation of the visionary event. Osborne supports this idea by concluding, "This is the culmination of all throne scenes in the Bible."[45] This culmination does not cancel the interconnectedness between earlier visions we have observed. Instead, it confirms that those prior observations were valid. As such, John's agenda is to bring out these ideas, synthesize them within one text, and thereby disclose the fullest presentation of the visionary event: the climax of a biblical theology of vision. In the immediate context, this serves to show the saints that their hope and expectation will not disappoint.[46] All will be fulfilled.

Vision as Fulfillment of Theology (Rev 4)

As we shift from a survey to a more detailed analysis, we can ask certain questions. What is the significance of Rev 4–5 as the climax of vision? What is John's purpose behind the intertextuality of Rev 4–5? The context already suggests an answer. The apostle was not merely calling on past visions' various imagery, but also on their related theological messages. John most likely continues that task in his vision itself. His vision is the composite of all other visions as well as their theologies. Thus, this moment is concerned with the fruition of God's plan and the fulfillment of theology. The intertextuality of Rev 4 specifically sets this agenda for the visionary event.

The first verse asserts this very idea. The vision takes place "after these things" and will show "what will take place after these things." Such phraseology appears in Rev 1:1 as well as 1:19, which I linked with the concept of Daniel's latter days.[47] Rev

---

45. Osborne, *Revelation*, 226. Osborne compares and contrasts previous visions' scenes, and while he notes their differences, he still sees them all as at least essential background in understanding John's vision. This is not quite the same as saying they are all the same event, but it is close. Furthermore, the differences he has raised are addressed in chapter 3 and will be further addressed later in this chapter.

46. Beale, *Revelation*, 311.

47. Ibid., 416. Beale argues against Rev 4–5 occurring after Rev 1–3 because the phrase "after this" does not necessarily refer to the future per se, but rather to the latter days. That implication may not necessarily be required or true. The wording could still denote sequence while secondarily alluding to

I Saw the Lord

4 establishes that the vision is the official inauguration of the fulfillment of Daniel's vision and theology. Christ summons John into the heavenly courtroom to witness this agenda played out. He will see (εἶδον) just as his predecessors also saw (cf. Isa 6:1; Ezek 1:1; Dan 7:13).[48]

The opening of the vision reveals a familiar scene: God seated upon his throne (Rev 4:2). This scene is at the heart of Isaiah's, Ezekiel's, and Daniel's visions (Isa 6:1; Ezek 1:26; Dan 7:9). In light of the context of fulfillment (v. 1), this means that the theological significance of the throne in these visions will soon be actualized. Thus, God will soon be high and lifted up over all creation, as Isaiah witnessed. God's kingdom will triumph over all human kingdoms, as Daniel portrayed. God's presence will fill the entire cosmos, as the chariot-throne in Ezekiel signified. Along that last point, John describes God's glory in verse 3 in accordance with how Ezekiel describes God's majesty (Ezek 1:26). Both liken his splendor to precious stones. This metaphor continues in Revelation to portray how God's glory will finally dwell in the new Jerusalem (Rev 21:18–21). God's glory in the vision anticipates the time when he will fill the entire cosmos with his majesty. Thus, in sum, the themes of God's kingdom and presence, two major themes in a biblical theology of vision, are about to be consummated.

The scene zooms out to reveal twenty-four thrones and elders surrounding God's throne (Rev 4:4). Part of this image is familiar, deriving from Daniel's (7:9) and Paul's (Col 1:15) descriptions. Some aspects are not familiar; namely, the significance of the twenty-four elders. Most likely, these elders are angels who represent the saints of all time: both Israel (twelve tribes) and the church (twelve apostles).[49] These angels, who wear golden crowns and sit on thrones, signify that the saints will receive the honor and the kingdom in the end, just as Daniel observed (7:27) and Paul anticipated (cf. Col 1:13; Rom 15:14–21; Phil 3:20–21).[50] However, the elders also wear white garments that symbolize ultimate cleansing from sin (cf. Rev 3:4–5). In Revelation, the

---

Daniel. See Joel 2:28 with Deut 4:30; 30:1 for a similar idea. See also VanGemeren, "Spirit of Restoration," 85–87.

48. See Beale, *Revelation*, 416; Mounce, *Book of Revelation*, 118. Note the ειδον language and its similarity with other vision introductions.

49. Osborne, *Revelation*, 229; Thomas, *Revelation 1–7*, 347; Beale, *Revelation*, 322. A variety of views exist on the identity and nature of the elders. Some scholars regard them as people, which seems less likely considering the scene in heaven at this point does not involve anyone else. Moreover, these angels are distinguished from humans (saints), and they function as angels in the heavenly court (cf. Rev 5:5–8). We must also take into consideration the background of thrones in Dan 7:9. However, even as angels, their significance must be accounted for. Why does John mention them? Whenever they do appear in later parts of the Apocalypse, it relates to the victory of the saints (cf. Rev 7:11–13; 11:16; 14:3; 19:4). This would also make sense of the number twenty-four, not only as the priestly order, but also of Israel and the church (cf. Rev 21:12). While Thomas states that this is an inviting possibility, he is cautious. Beale argues strongly for this interpretation.

50. See Beale, *Revelation*, 322–26. Cf. also Col 1:13. Paul and Daniel both mention thrones (Dan 7:9; Col 1:13). They expect that the saints will rule in the end (Dan 7:27; 2 Tim 2:13). Paul's use of Danielic language in Colossians suggests that he based his eschatological expectations upon Daniel, and by extension, his own Damascus road experience.

saints will wear this in order that they may dwell in God's presence (7:9–14; 19:13). Daniel anticipates this transformation (12:2), and Paul looks forward to the time when the saints serve and worship God (Rom 15:14–21; Phil 3:1–21). Hence, these elders seem to illustrate how the saints will share in the blessings of God's fulfilled kingdom and presence. If the above analysis is valid, their appearance in the vision indicates that Paul's theology of Jew and Gentile, as well as Daniel's theology of the victory of the saints, will be soon completed.

The scene zooms out yet again to reveal more of what occurs all around the throne. Initially, this relates to judgment, as lightning and thunder come out from the throne (Rev 4:5a). The imagery resembles the chariot-throne in Ezekiel (1:13). Hence, the judgment conveyed in Ezekiel's vision is now a part of the purpose of John's vision. Similarly, the sevenfold Spirit is also present before the throne. He relates to the outcome of Isaiah's vision, as described in Isa 11:1–10.[51] Accordingly, John's vision incorporates Isaiah's theology, indicating that God will subject the world under the true king of Isa 11.

This judgment is against the cosmos. The lightning and thunder occurs in the context of the glass sea before the throne and the living creatures in the midst of the throne. These descriptions collectively portray a microcosm of the world (Rev 4:6–7). They actually derive from Ezekiel's chariot-throne, which is also a microcosm of the world. Both have four living creatures (compare Rev 4:7 and Ezek 1:10), and the glassy sea in John's vision (Rev 4:6) is like the crystal firmament of Ezekiel's (1:22). Thus, God will judge all creation, fulfilling another important component of Ezekiel's vision and theology.

However, judgment is not the sole purpose of the vision. The chapter ends with the celebration of the triumph of God's salvation in the universe (4:8–11). Ezekiel's cherubim give thanks to God (εὐχαριστίαν, Rev 4:9), implying God's positive redemptive work will also commence.[52] Hence, the presence of the cherubim also positively signals that God's presence will fill the entire earth (Rev 4:8a). John's vision fulfills yet another vital part of Ezekiel's vision and theology. However, these cherubim also have six wings, which recalls Isaiah's seraphim (Rev 4:8b; cf. Isa 6:2). In fact, John records that these angels proclaim God's threefold holiness, just like in Isaiah's vision (Rev 4:8c; Isa 6:3). Hence, Isaiah's vision now merges into John's vision. In Isaiah, those angelic beings were not only the harbingers of destruction, but also transforming holiness (cf. Isa 6:7).[53] In the same way, these angels rejoice not only that God has judged in his holiness, but also that he has saved. John's vision commemorates that same reality (see Rev 5:9, which celebrates the salvation wrought by Jesus and its final culmination) and thereby anticipates the completion of Isaiah's vision and theology. That is precisely why the elders join in and give God glory as Creator (Rev 4:10–11).

---

51. Osborne, *Revelation*, 61, 231.

52. Ibid., 238: "Εὐχαριστία refers to the 'thanksgiving' due him for what he does, for his action on behalf of his people."

53. Motyer, *Isaiah*, 77.

God has created all things (σὺ ἔκτισας τὰ πάντα; Rev 4:11), both the current creation as well as a new creation (cf. Rev 21:1). That new creation is the demonstration of God's transforming holiness by which he brings all things in conformity with himself per Isaiah's vision and theology (cf. Isa 65:17).[54] Such a new creation is also the place where God's presence and kingdom find fulfillment—the very anticipation of Ezekiel (Ezek 37:1-28), Daniel (12:2), and Paul (2 Cor 5:5-17).

In this way, the content of Rev 4 introduces us to the general purpose behind the visionary event. In the span of eleven verses, we have revisited familiar images of past visions. This intertextual activity has not only drawn together familiar elements in the vision, but also the major categories, themes, and concepts found throughout our discussion of a biblical theology of vision. From the throne to the angels, John records how God intends to fulfill the entire biblical theology of vision from heaven to earth, saints to the cosmos, kingdom and presence, and judgment to salvation. As all of these theological ideas and visionary images have merged into a single moment, the apostle has unveiled to us the event that fulfills theology.

Christ as Center of History, Theology, and Vision (Rev 5:1-10)

Thus far, John has exhibited his vision as the climax of all prior visions, their related messages, and the plan of God. In John's vision and theology, all of those realities funnel into one central person: Jesus Christ. As Daniel has already indicated through his vision, the vision of kingdom focuses upon the king. John maintains this paradigm, but shows that this not only concerns kingdom, but rather the entire breadth of theology and history.

If Rev 4 discusses the agenda of this scene as the fulfillment of theology, Rev 5 shows how that will be implemented. Rev 5:1 makes this transition by bringing our attention to a book that comes from the throne. The throne that originally announced God's purpose towards this moment will now accomplish that goal. The context already suggests that this book is endowed with God's authority and supernatural ability to enact the message of the scroll. It is at his right hand.[55] What is the content or functionality of this document? Views range from the Lamb's Book of Life to the Old

---

54. Oswalt, *Isaiah 40-66*, 656. Oswalt's explanation is helpful: "As Delitzsch observes, in speaking of the kingdom of God here Isaiah amalgamates several aspects of it that may be chronologically distinct but are spiritually identical. Thus in its present manifestation in the lives of believers, the kingdom is a 'new creation' (2 Cor. 5:17), 'the world to come' (Heb. 2:5). But there is also the millennial kingdom, in which this world will be redeemed and renewed (Rev. 20:4-6). Finally, there are 'new heavens and a new earth' that will exist after 'the first heaven and the first earth had passed away' (2 Pet. 3:13; Rev. 21:1). All three of these manifestations of the kingdom of God and of his Messiah seem to be telescoped together in the prophet's mind, much as the destruction of Jerusalem and the end of the world seem to have been telescoped for Jesus (Matt. 24; Mark 13; Luke 21)."

55. Thomas, *Revelation 1-7*, 375.

Testament.[56] The best solution is to see this document as God's plan of judgment leading to the fulfillment of salvation, with all its blessings and glories.[57]

This may account for why the book is sealed with seven seals and written on both sides. These characteristics mark a Roman will, or at least some sort of legal contract.[58] The breaking of the seals "activated" the contents of the document and granted the benefits prescribed to its recipient. We can observe this in Revelation. The seals trigger God's judgment, leading to Christ's ultimate inheritance of the earth.[59] Such an explanation also does justice to the Danielic and Ezekielian background of the scroll. In Ezekiel, the scroll contained the message of how God's presence would both judge and create a relationship with his people. Daniel views the book in the context of his vision (7:9), where judgment will be unleashed against the nations. He also mentions the sealing of the book for a future time (Dan 12:4), which appears to be imminent, since the book will be unsealed (Rev 6:1; 22:10). Accordingly, the book itself is part of a motif within a biblical theology of vision. It participates in the completion of God's eschatological agenda set by the vision. In essence, this book enacts the fulfillment of history.

Having seen this incredible book, a mighty angel inquires whether anyone is worthy to open the book and break its seals (Rev 5:2). No created being can do so (v. 3). Already the scene begins to focus the power and significance of the book to one individual. Before he is revealed, John weeps, because without the opening of the book, history will not be consummated.[60] This at best would prolong the agony of the saints, since their victory is postponed, but even worse, could signify the destruction of the hope that John had written about earlier in his book. The anticipation of the church's triumph would vanish, and all would become meaningless. This too demonstrates the unmistakable magnitude of the book and of the one who opens it. Who will be the one who finalizes all of history?

At the moment, when all hope is seemingly lost, the elder points out to John that the Lamb can break the seals (Rev 5:5). This speech-act directs the reader's focus from the breadth of all creation to a single individual. The fulfillment of history has centralized into one man, Jesus Christ.

John introduces Christ in a way that demonstrates his absolute worthiness to receive the scroll; namely, Jesus is in the unique position of *being the fulfillment of theology*. Four observations in Rev 5:5–6 point to this conclusion. First, Christ's titles as the Lion of Judah and Root of David exhibit that he is the outcome of Isaiah's

---

56. See discussions in ibid., 375–78; Beale, *Revelation*, 339–45.

57. Scholars who hold to this view include Thomas, *Revelation 1–7*, 378–79; Beale, *Revelation*, 340; Osborne, *Revelation*, 249.

58. Thomas, *Revelation 1–7*, 378; Beale, *Revelation*, 344–45.

59. Thomas, *Revelation 1–7*, 378; Beale, *Revelation*, 344–45.

60. Thomas, *Revelation 1–7*, 386; Beale, *Revelation*, 348.

vision portrayed in Isa 11:1 (Rev 5:5a).[61] He is the king the prophet foresaw. Second, Christ's victory demonstrates this assertion (ἐνίκησεν, Rev 5:5b). Based upon the Isaianic background, Jesus' overcoming probably refers to his sacrificial death (and resurrection) as the Servant. Rev 5:6 confirms this by describing Christ as the Lamb (cf. Isa 52:13—53:12).[62] Accordingly, Christ is not merely the *telos* of Isaiah's vision and theology, but is also the one who accomplishes it, which gives him the right to receive the scroll.

Third, Christ's physical location in the vision posits him as the fulfillment of theology (Rev 5:6a). Christ is in the midst of the throne, the living creatures, and the elders. These entities all signified certain theological realities and now, even visually, they (and their implied theology) all center upon Christ. He is the one that consummates the theology of the vision. Fourth, he possesses the power to complete the theology of past visions (Rev 5:6b). John describes Jesus with seven horns, which alludes to the horns in Daniel that symbolized the might of various kings. As opposed to those failed kings, the Lamb will have the ultimate strength to rule over all creation and thereby accomplish Daniel's vision. Similarly, Christ also has seven eyes, which represents the sevenfold ministry of the Spirit. The Spirit is the mark of the king who fulfills Isaiah's vision (cf. Isa 11:1) and Christ is precisely that.

Overall, John introduces us to Jesus, who is worthy to open the book because he singlehandedly fulfills the entire biblical theology of vision. His past work has made him worthy to complete the entire work. In this way, the visionary event is the celebration of what he has already accomplished and looks forward to its fulfillment.

Because of this, Christ receives the book from the right hand of God, who sits on the throne (Rev 5:7). This continues the "narrative" that we have observed in visions past. Just as Isaiah implied that the Servant would be high and lifted up, and as Daniel portrayed the Son of Man, and as Paul understood the resurrected Lord, so John presents Jesus as the one who obtains the scroll, giving him the right to fulfill history and theology. As such, the purpose behind the visionary event is complete, and the tensions raised above (concerning who was worthy to open the book) are resolved. Christ, then, is the center and resolution of the vision.

All heaven confirms this interpretation in its response to Jesus' reception of the book (Rev 5:8–10). In fact, heaven's worship substantiates all that I have said about Rev 5 up to this point. The living creatures and elders fall before the Lamb to demonstrate that Christ alone is the worthy and chief character of this event, *the center of vision*. They hold the prayers of the saints because he is about to fulfill the saints' intercession

---

61. Beale, *Revelation*, 349. Recall (from chapter 4) that Isa 11 presents a fuller picture of what Isaiah's vision signified. God, high and lifted up, ultimately relates to his Messiah reigning from Jerusalem. Jesus is that one, according to John, and thereby fulfills Isaiah's theology.

62. Ibid., 351; Osborne, *Revelation*, 255–56.

for God to act and vindicate them (cf. Rev 8:3).[63] Thus, the angels' worship also reflects that Christ is about to resolve the tensions of the world and history.

Their praise also celebrates Christ's fulfillment of theology both past, present, and future. They sing a new song, a term Isaiah used to describe heaven and earth's response to the Servant's work of new creation (cf. Isa 42:10). Heaven sings a new song because the Servant was slain (Rev 5:9), but also in anticipation of the consummation of that new creation (cf. Rev 21:1). Hence, the angels' worship demonstrates the culmination of Isaiah's theology, past, present, and future.

In like manner, the angels celebrate how Christ purchased people from every tribe, tongue, people, and nation (Rev 5:9) and made them into a kingdom (v. 10). That echoes the vision and theology of Daniel (7:27), as well as Paul's proclamation that Christ redeemed the Gentiles (Col 1:20–22). The living creatures and elders reflect how Christ has made his people priests as Ezekiel envisioned (Rev 5:10; cf. Ezek 45:15–17), a reality Paul acknowledged had begun (Tit 2:14). However, all of those ideals have yet to reach their fullness. The angels proclaim that the saints will reign (βασιλεύσουσιν, note future tense) over the earth (Rev 5:10). Such wording reminds readers of Paul's portrayal of the believers' end (cf. 2 Tim 2:12). Christ's coronation signals the beginning of the complete fulfillment of all these theological outcomes. All heaven breaks out into praise because of what this moment signifies: all things are fulfilled in Christ.

Thus, this entire discussion exhibits that within a biblical theology of vision, all theology, history, and the vision itself centers on Christ. He is the one who fulfills God's agenda for the world, because he holds the scroll. He is the one who actualizes the theological realities of God's plan in his past and future work. He is the one who resolves the tensions behind the visionary event as the center of the vision. John's vision has demonstrated how these intertwined themes all find their focus and fulfillment in Christ alone. No one else in all creation occupies this place. This moment celebrates who Christ is, all that he has done, and what he is about to do.

Vision as the Fulfillment of History (Rev 5:11–14)

From here, the inertia of the event can only move in one direction: to earth. The *heavenly* court has decreed that all theology and history is summed up in Christ. The mention of history (via the sealed book) in the above discussion, however, demands that this resolution does not remain in heaven but also is wrought on earth. The ending of Rev 5 announces this intention. The vision, then, is not only the culmination of theology, but also of history.

Thus, John's description of the breadth of the visionary event contributes in another way to a theology of vision. In previous discussions, the distinction between

---

63. Osborne, *Revelation*, 258; Mounce, *Book of Revelation*, 135.

the visionary event and its ramifications on earth may have been blurry. Past writers have used language from the vision of heaven to describe eschatological realities on earth and vice versa.[64] Daniel clarifies that the vision itself concerns the Son of Man's enthronement, which then results in the realities described by other biblical writers. John's theology completes the picture and explains why this "blurring" exists. Rev 5:11–14 exhibits that earth ultimately will be brought into conformity with what is decreed in heaven. This explains why biblical writers applied such terminology to both the heavenly scene and to earth, for they will become mirror images of each other.

Beginning with the structural marker καὶ εἶδον in 5:11, John announces heaven and earth's reaction to the Son's exaltation.[65] Initially, the rest of the heavenly court responds. In addition to the living creatures and the elders, myriads of angels join in a chorus of worship (Rev 5:11). Phraseology like "myriads" and "thousands" is found in Dan 7:10, continuing the plotline of the visions stated in Dan 7 accordingly. They all proclaim that the Lamb was worthy to receive power, riches, wisdom, strength, honor, and glory (Rev 5:12). This initially demonstrates that the Son is equal to the Father.[66] Furthermore, the wording alludes to Dan 7:14. I commented that Dan 7:14 shows that although past kings attempted to gain all honor and sovereignty, these characteristics only truly belong to the Son of Man. In Rev 5:12, the angelic hosts proclaim what Daniel envisioned: Jesus alone rules heaven and earth.[67]

Accordingly, earth's reaction reiterates the declaration of heaven in Rev 5:13–14. However, two observations are quite important at this point. First, verse 13 speaks of the entire cosmos worshipping God. Second, at this point in the Apocalypse, all of heaven and earth does not worship God and the Lamb. God will judge them for this very reason (cf. Rev 6:15–17; 16:10–11). Hence, these verses must be an anticipatory

---

64. For example, Isaiah relates the heavenly courtroom scene in Isa 6 not only to the heavenly enthronement of the Servant, but also to his throne on earth in Isa 2 and 11. God's glory filling the temple and the earth is a bridge between heaven and earth. Ezekiel discusses the chariot-throne in the context of how God's glory fills the earth in Ezek 43:2–4. Daniel also relates the decree of the heavenly court to realities that take place amongst the nations in Dan 7:9–12. Paul ascribes Danielic language to Christ's return from heaven to earth. Accordingly, the biblical writers have applied language of the heavenly courtroom scene to earth and associated earthly eschatological realities with the heavenly scene.

65. Osborne, *Revelation*, 261. Osborne correctly notes that while this looks like it goes with the previous section, it actually is a new one based upon the structural marker.

66. Beale, *Revelation*, 364.

67. While alluding to Dan 7:14, John adds certain words in Rev 5:12 to the description in Dan 7:14 to amplify this reality. The term wisdom (σοφία) may indicate Jesus alone possesses the wisdom that Nebuchadnezzar never had (Dan 2:30), and the same wisdom that belonged only to God, who knew the mysteries of the end (Dan 2:20). Similarly, the words power, strength, and glory (ἰσχύς, τιμή, δόξα) are uniquely found in Daniel and probably denote that Jesus alone retains the power, strength, and glory that God gave Nebuchadnezzar, but then removed (Dan 2:37; 4:30; cf. Rev 5:12). Dan 2:37 reads τὴν βασιλείαν καὶ τὴν ἰσχὺν καὶ τὴν τιμὴν καὶ τὴν δόξαν ἔδωκεν, which is quite similar to τὴν δύναμιν καὶ πλοῦτον καὶ σοφίαν καὶ ἰσχὺν καὶ τιμὴν καὶ δόξαν καὶ εὐλογίαν in Rev 5:12. All of this reinforces the notion that Christ rules the world.

statement about what will ultimately ensue from the visionary event.[68] Heaven's rejoicing will become the reality on earth. This stems from what we have seen in context. Christ's fulfillment of vision and theology becomes the fulfillment of history.

Thus, John describes how everything in the entire cosmos worships the One on the throne and Christ. The term "all" ($πᾶν$) is probably used in an absolute sense. Every creature, whether God's friend or foe, will acknowledge the worthiness of the Son. Such submission is described by Paul in Col 1:20 and Phil 2:10-11, both of which allude to the visionary event, or Damascus road.[69] John reiterates the same picture that Paul portrays. Every knee will bow, because what is declared in heaven will be enforced on earth without exception. Their worship in Rev 5:13b matches much of the terminology found in the angels' song in the previous verse. The entire cosmos will join in the same song. The final verse of the chapter reaffirms this. The heavenly beings say "amen" and worship. This indicates that in the end, heaven and earth are unified in praise. In fact, the juxtaposition of the living creatures and the elders signals this reality from a different perspective. The cosmos (as signified by the living creatures) and the saints (signified by the elders) will worship the Lord.[70] Thus, the ending of Rev 5 announces how the earth will, in the end, mirror heaven in the doxology of the vision,[71] which is how the vision will shape history.

Synthesis

By including a panoply of elements of prior visions, John shows the visionary event in all its complexity. It is the vision into which all other visions converge. Consistently, their theologies come together to be fulfilled by one man, the Lamb of God, Jesus Christ. His work in the past has given him the right to be the center of this moment, and that moment is purposed for him to complete God's entire agenda. Thus, heaven must move to earth, and history must reach its climax, and all that is in Christ.

In this way, John contributes to a biblical theology of vision by displaying the visionary event in all its breadth. It is the intersection at which the past and present meet the future. It is the fulcrum upon which inaugurated theology becomes consummated. It is the celebration of Christ's past works in anticipation of his final work. It is the climax of vision and the culmination of theology and history. Within all of this, Christ is the unmistakable center of this central event. All history and theology will be summed up for his eternal glory, just as the vision proclaims.

---

68. Beale, *Revelation*, 365; Osborne, *Revelation*, 264.
69. Beale, *Revelation*, 365; Mounce, *Book of Revelation*, 137. See previous discussion for the connection on Christ's ascension to glory, Phil 2:10-11, and the allusions of Col 1:20 and Dan 7.
70. Beale, *Revelation*, 366.
71. Mounce, *Book of Revelation*, 138.

I Saw the Lord

JOHN'S THEOLOGY AS THE WORKING OUT OF VISION

The remainder of the book accomplishes the purpose of the vision. Heaven must invade earth to implement the declaration of the visionary event, and that is precisely what occurs. Our discussion (primarily of Rev 6–19) will explore how God's judgments and salvation proceed from the vision and work towards the fulfillment of the vision, as well as its theological significance. Part of John's theology, then, is the actualization of the theologies of his predecessors.

Vision as Source of God's Eschatological Activity

The context has suggested that Rev 4–5 is the controlling text of the book. Furthermore, Rev 4–5 itself claims to be the launching point of the consummation of God's plan for the cosmos. These are not pithy suggestions left behind as the book progresses. Instead, Rev 6–19 intentionally depicts all of God's activity as the fleshing out of the vision. The apostle repeatedly asserts the vision as the source or basis for God's judging and saving work.

Fundamentally, we observe this play out in the way the sealed book (Rev 5:1–2) functions in the rest of the Apocalypse. The unsealing of this book brings on a series of judgments (Rev 6:1–17), the last of which commences a new series of judgments (the trumpet judgments, 8:1–13; 11:15–19). Those in turn cascade into God's final demonstrations of wrath in the bowl judgments (16:1–21). Scholars acknowledge that the sealed book contains this entire schema.[72] In this way, the visionary event of Rev 5 is the origin of all that takes place in the rest of the book.

John also links Rev 6–19 with the vision in other ways. For instance, thunder and lightning accompany the trumpet and bowl judgments (cf. Rev 8:5; 11:19; 16:18–21). Bauckham observes that these relate to the thunder and lightning surrounding God's throne in Rev 4:5.[73] God's wrath in the Apocalypse works out the agenda declared in Rev 4–5, and all the judgments proceed from heaven to earth (Rev 6:1; 8:1; 11:19; 16:1). However, John's descriptions of heaven draw on language that alludes to Rev 4–5. The four living creatures participate in the seal judgments (6:1, 3, 5, 7; cf. 4:6). The angels who stand before God's throne blow the trumpets and pour out the bowls of judgment (8:2, 6; 16:1; cf. 5:11). Judgment comes from the heavenly temple, which is another way to describe the heavenly court in Rev 4–5 (11:19).[74] Thus, these pas-

---

72. Osborne, *Revelation*, 249; Aune, *Revelation 1–5*, 491; Jauhiainen, "Recapitulation and Chronological Progression in John's Apocalypse," 543–59. Beale agrees with this on a literary level, even though he views these series of judgments as recapitulations. Even with that perspective, all those judgments would still issue forth from the visionary event, since the seal judgments themselves do (and the rest of the descriptions repeat those same activities).

73. Bauckham, *Theology of Revelation*, 41.

74. Ibid.; Beale, *Revelation*, 618. John describes this temple as having the glassy sea of Rev 4:6 (15:2). This ties the heavenly temple with the heavenly courtroom scene noted earlier.

sages indicate that God's judgment proceeds not just from heaven, but also from the program set by the heavenly court scene in Rev 4–5. Rev 6:16 can provide yet another example. In language that recalls Rev 4–5, the people cry out to the mountains to hide them from "the presence of him who sits on the throne and the wrath of the Lamb." The judgments of God come from his sovereign might and result from his declaration about the Lamb disclosed in Rev 4–5.[75] Therefore, God's judgments thoroughly emanate from the vision agenda.

Similarly, God's salvation likewise issues from the vision. From the heavenly court, the decree goes forth for the salvation of the 144,000 (Rev 7:2). God's activity in this passage culminates in a scene that mirrors Rev 4–5. The saints are brought together in white robes before God's throne (Rev 7:9; cf. Rev 4:4) and praise him with the elders, living creatures, and angels (Rev 7:11; cf. Rev 4:8–10; 5:14). Rev 7 illustrates that John's vision is the launching point and *telos* of God's saving work.[76]

In the flow of Revelation, God's judging and saving work peaks in the return of Christ. That too directly relates to the vision. John sees heaven opened (Rev 19:11). Previously, a door in heaven was opened for John so that he could see the visionary agenda. Later, the heavenly temple was opened to enact the bowl judgments (11:19; 15:5), which, as discussed, also relate back to Rev 4–5.[77] Heaven opening in Rev 19:11 signals the conclusion of all of the activity that began with Rev 4–5. What John first saw is now going to come to pass when Christ, the Lamb who fulfills all theology and history, descends to conquer the world.[78] The apostle thereby casts Christ's return as part of the visionary agenda.

This last observation is significant for another reason. John does not merely position the vision as central within God's activity in the Apocalypse; rather, in doing so, he places Christ as central. The people fear the wrath of the Lamb (6:16) when reflecting upon God's judgment and the heavenly court. The Lamb opens the seals and unleashes all consequential judgment (6:1; 8:1). The one like a son of man comes on the clouds to inaugurate judgment (Rev 14:14). All of God's work culminates in the return of Christ (Rev 19:11). To John, the centrality of the vision means the centrality of Christ. In this way, the dominance of the vision underscores that Christ is the fulfillment of theology and history, as Rev 4–5 itself claimed.

This discussion highlights that Rev 4–5 is the launching point of the rest of God's activity in Revelation. From judgment to salvation to Christ's return, John continually anchors God's work with the vision of Rev 4–5. This confirms the contextual notion that this passage works as the controlling text of the book. This also casts Rev 6–19 as

---

75. Osborne, *Revelation*, 296.

76. Rev 7:16–17 alludes to Rev 21:4, showing that even if these individuals are coming out of the tribulation, their final state is the upcoming eternal state. Hence, this text is slightly proleptic. It is part of the realization of what is to fully come in the end.

77. Bauckham, *Theology of Revelation*, 41.

78. Osborne, *Revelation*, 679; Beale, *Revelation*, 949; Mounce, *Book of Revelation*, 351.

the actualization of the agenda of the vision. Accordingly, as we examine the way John echoes his predecessors in the Apocalypse, we must keep in mind that these are not just incidental allusions. Instead, they comprise the fulfillment of the agenda of Rev 4–5 and the consummation of the vision and its theology.

God's Eschatological Activity as Actualization of Vision (Isaiah)

Based upon this understanding, God's activity in the rest of the Apocalypse fleshes out the significance of the vision, as the vision itself suggests. However, because John's vision ties the visions and theologies of Isaiah, Ezekiel, Daniel, and Paul together, Rev 6–19 actualizes those realities as well. Before engaging in this discussion, I ought to say that it by no means claims to be an exhaustive treatment of all intertextual allusions between prior revelation and John. The intertextuality is far too dense to cover in a single chapter. Other treatments have broached that field.[79] Instead, these next sections intend to effectively illustrate that a fulfillment of a biblical theology of vision is part of John's message.

Isaiah's vision communicates God's salvation. This salvation involves God's judging and transforming holiness and results in the subjection of all things to himself (6:1–13). He will make a new creation (65:17) where his glory fills the earth such that the nations worship him and he reigns exclusively over the cosmos (65:19–20; 66:22–23; cf. Isa 11:1–16). Not only do these components conceptually emerge in John's Apocalypse, he also echoes Isaiah frequently throughout these texts, signaling that John believes Isaiah's vision and theology are coming to pass.

In Rev 6:10, the saints appeal to God's holiness within the seal judgments. They call him "holy" and so far, the use of ἅγιος in reference to the Lord has had an Isaianic grounding (cf. Rev 3:7; 4:8). This instance is likely no exception.[80] Those who have died urge God to enact holy retribution against their persecutors,[81] foreshadowing God's final response (cf. Rev 16:5–6), which implements God's judging holiness as Isaiah envisioned.

The seal and trumpet judgments also take part in actualizing Isaiah's message. The destruction of plant life (8:7), water (8:8–11), and light (8:12) not only resembles the plagues of the Exodus, but also the reversal of the creation week (cf. Gen 1:1–31). If this is true, then God actually dismantles his creation as part of his judgment, the very imagery we see in Isaiah (cf. Isa 24:1).[82] This, of course, allows for a new creation,

---

79. Beale, *Old Testament in Revelation*; Fekkes, *Isaiah and Prophetic Traditions*; Kowalski, "Transformation of Ezekiel," 281. Kowalski provides a helpful review of the literature dealing with the intertextuality of Revelation with Ezekiel.

80. Beale, *Revelation*, 332, 392.

81. Osborne, *Revelation*, 287.

82. Bauckham, *Theology of Revelation*, 49–53. Bauckham links this with the Flood which itself is a reverse creation. See Hamilton, *Book of Genesis*, 303.

which is also part of Isaiah's theology (42:9; 65:19–20; 66:22). John's specific references to Isaiah support that he operates with this larger paradigm in mind. The great earthquake in Rev 6:12 corresponds to Isa 2:19 and 50:3, and both Revelation and Isaiah describe the disturbance of the heavens (Isa 34:4; 6:13). Both texts also record the same response by the people, who hide from his presence (Isa 2:10; Rev 6:15).[83] The echoes of Isa 2 are particularly important. The latter portion of Isa 2 discussed how God would destroy that which was high and lifted up so that he alone would be high and lifted up (Isa 2:17), which relates to the fulfillment of Isa 6:1. In making these allusions, John shows that God's judgments fulfill specific prophecies tied with Isaiah's vision and therefore also work out the greater agenda stated by that prophet.[84]

Simultaneous with God's judgment is salvation. Rev 7 contextually shows that God's workings during the time of the seal judgments offer not only condemnation, but also deliverance.[85] Some will stand on the day of judgment (cf. Rev 6:10), and these individuals, a great multitude who have come out of the great tribulation, are clothed in white before the Lamb and washed in his blood (Rev 7:9, 14).[86] The notions of cleansing, the Lamb, and blood all echo the sacrificial language found in Isaiah (Isa 1:18; 53:4–8).[87] Moreover, Rev 7:15–16 describes how God will sit on his throne and spread his tabernacle over his people. The language highly resembles Isa 4:5–6, another text related to Isaiah's vision, which discusses how God will transform his people in holiness and how his glory will be cast over them like a tent.[88] Such descriptions in Rev 7 prove that God is fleshing out Isaiah's theology of transformation and salvation, which is precisely what the great multitude proclaims. They acknowledge that salvation (σωτηρία) belongs to the Lord (Rev 7:10) and all heaven joins in (Rev 7:11).[89]

The final display of God's wrath in the bowl judgments shows the fulfillment of Isaiah's vision.[90] Rev 15 makes this clear. The saints say that all the nations will come

---

83. Fekkes, *Isaiah and Prophetic Traditions*, 158–61. Fekkes does an excellent job of showing the linguistic parallels between the passages listed above.

84. Mathewson, "Isaiah in Revelation," 195–97.

85. See Thomas, *Revelation 1–7*, 462–66. Rev 7 serves to show and simultaneously contrast with God's prior judgment. In its use throughout the rest of the book, it does have some proleptic anticipation of God's final victory in Rev 20.

86. This scene marks the working out of the visionary agenda in Rev 4–5. The saints look like the angelic elders who were clothed in white (Rev 4:4). John actually juxtaposes the saints with those beings in a scene that resembles Rev 4–5 to underscore the connection. Thus, God's mission of redeeming and glorifying his people is reaching its culmination.

87. Notice the use of λευκαίνω, a rare term, in Isa 1:18 and Rev 7:14. Isaiah does serve as a significant background to Rev 7.

88. Fekkes, *Isaiah and Prophetic Traditions*, 169.

89. Beale, *Revelation*, 431; Osborne, *Revelation*, 320. In John, salvation refers to God's final conquest over his enemies. However, in context, the saints' reception of that deliverance has a soteriological base. Thus, the concept of salvation in John is grounded upon a soteriological reality, even if it pertains more to conquest and triumph.

90. Note the wording in Rev 15:1. The bowl judgments mark the completion of God's wrath. See Thomas, *Revelation 8–22 Commentary*, 231; Osborne, *Revelation*, 560–61. Contra Beale, *Revelation*, 768.

and worship God (Rev 15:4). The wording is highly reminiscent of Isa 66:23, which depicts the scene found in Isa 2:2–4 and Isa 11:1–16.[91] Thus, the martyrs proclaim that the outcome tied with Isaiah's vision is coming to pass. To underscore this, smoke fills the heavenly temple because of God's glory (ἐκ τῆς δόξης τοῦ θεοῦ, 15:8), just like in Isaiah's vision (6:4). In this way, the rich intertextuality of Rev 15 with Isaiah signifies that God's final workings of judgment are the fulfillment of Isaiah's vision and theology.

What ensues does not disappoint. God's bowl judgments continue the idea of de-creation found in Isaiah (Rev 16:1–21; cf. Isa 24:1). As the waters turn into blood, an angel declares that God is holy because he has punished those who persecuted the saints (Rev 16:5–6). This answers the saints' intercession noted earlier in the seal judgments (cf. Rev 6:10) and shows that God indeed completes his judging holiness in the end.[92] The sixth bowl dries up the great river Euphrates (Rev 16:12), which exactly matches what the Lord does in Isa 11:15–16 as an act of judgment against the nations to free his people.[93] A new Exodus will commence and the exile will end, as Isaiah foresaw. Along this line, "fallen, fallen, is Babylon the Great" (Rev 14:8; 16:19; 18:1–24), as Isaiah prophesied (13:1–22; 21:1–10). Babylon's downfall was part of God's work to make all nations low in order that they might worship him and acknowledge his sovereignty.[94] What Isaiah's vision and theology predicted is being realized.

This climaxes with the return of Christ. He rides in on a white horse, ready to judge in righteousness (Rev 19:11) and the breath of his mouth annihilates his enemies (v. 21).[95] Both of those descriptions actually allude to Isa 11:4. John has already alluded several times to this chapter (Rev 1:4; 3:4; 4:5; 5:6), which is a fuller expression of Isaiah's vision. Jesus here completes God's work of making all things low in holy judgment and de-creation so that the Servant would be high and lifted up. He is the one, as the Servant, who bears the sword from his mouth (Rev 19:15, cf. Isa 49:2) to accomplish this task.

Thus far, we have observed that the flow of Revelation works towards the fulfillment of Isaiah's vision and theology. I have saved two passages for the end of this discussion. They are actually found in the "interlude" sections, which function outside of the narrative structure of the book.[96] Nonetheless, these texts are critically impor-

---

91. Beale, *Revelation*, 799. Compare the wording of Rev 15:4 πάντα τὰ ἔθνη ἥξουσιν καὶ προσκυνήσουσιν ἐνώπιόν σου with πᾶσα σὰρξ ἐνώπιόν μου προσκυνῆσαι ἐν Ιερουσαλημ in Isa 66:23. See Oswalt, *Isaiah 40–66*, 691. The worship of the nations recurs throughout the entire book of Isa, starting in Isa 2.

92. Beale, *Revelation*, 818.

93. Fekkes, *Isaiah and Prophetic Traditions*, 201.

94. Beale, *Revelation*, 894; Osborne, *Revelation*, 635; Mathewson, "Isaiah in Revelation," 198–200. In Isaiah, God empties Babylon's temple so that only his palace would be full of glory. See Isa 13:22.

95. Mathewson, "Isaiah in Revelation," 193.

96. This is also why I did not include them in the above discussion, so as to provide an uninterrupted flow.

tant (Rev 12–14). They provide background, purpose, and further elaboration to the trumpet and bowl judgments.[97] As such, they offer a broader framework for God's workings in Revelation and help us to better see the details under discussion here in light of the whole.

In Rev 12, John situates God's activity in the context of the story of Israel.[98] A woman, symbolizing Israel, gives birth to a child whom a dragon desires to destroy (Rev 12:1–4). The child is rescued and takes the throne, and the woman flees to the wilderness (vv. 5–6). While the woman symbolizes corporate Israel and not Mary per se, Isa 7:14 still seems to be in the background.[99] This account also shares another connection with Isaiah: the wilderness. The prophet mentions that Israel will be in the wilderness prior to its deliverance (cf. Isa 40:1).[100] It appears that John, in Rev 12, follows the storyline of Israel's exile in the wilderness, the virgin birth of their deliverer, and their ultimate rescue from exile within Isaiah's prophecy. By expanding upon the finale of this narrative, the apostle recounts the completion of Isaiah's theology and vision.[101]

In addition to background, the "interlude" sections also provide the purpose driving God's eschatological activities. This too brings out the connection between John's message and the fulfillment of Isaiah. In Rev 14, the Lamb stands on Mount Zion with 144,000. The description echoes Isa 2 and 11, in which the Messiah rules from Jerusalem in demonstration of God's high and lifted up reign.[102] The presence of a remnant also shows that God's saving and transforming holiness has come into effect, as Isa 4 portrays. These people are completely blameless (the effect of transforming holiness, cf. Isa 4:3–4) and follow the Lamb, a title for Christ that alludes to the Servant (Rev 14:4–5; cf. Isa 53:7). Thus, in Rev 14, we observe God's rule, salvation, and the Servant (Lamb) of Isaiah. Altogether, this scene displays the full outcome

---

97. See Osborne, *Revelation*, 29. To be sure, the structure of Revelation is quite complex, and Osborne provides us with a good synthesis of the issues. The notion of "interlude" texts, while still having some faults, can help us grasp how these texts (like Rev 12–14) work as asides from the narrative, yet are important. In their own ways, they set the background and purpose for the main narrative sections.

98. In Rev 11:19, the temple opens up for judgment, which resumes in Rev 15:1–8. Accordingly, the passages between these two texts provide background to the storyline that continues later in the book. See ibid., 452.

99. Ibid., 457; Beale, *Revelation*, 628; Aune, *Revelation 1–5*, 682; Aus, "Relevance of Isaiah 66," 255.

100. Scholars have rightly observed that John depicts God's wrath in light of the Egyptian plagues. This makes sense, considering the wilderness motif. A second Exodus is in view. However, even that notion comes from Isaiah itself (43:2–4).

101. Aus, "Relevance of Isaiah 66," 253–54. Aus states that before all of Rev 13–19 takes place, Rev 12 describes the "conflict to be undergone before the final victory."

102. Aune, *Revelation 1–5*, 804; Walvoord, *Revelation of Jesus Christ*, 214–15; Thomas, *Revelation 8–22 Commentary*, 188–92; Osborne, *Revelation*, 525. The intertextual background points to the fact that this is probably an earthly city. Matching with other proleptic scenes, this may refer to Rev 20. If that is the case, then the fact that the events of Rev 20 take place around the "holy city" supports the notion of an earthly city.

of Isaiah's vision. How does this scene contribute to the flow of the book? In context, the picture found in Rev 14 seems to be proleptic, anticipating what occurs after Christ returns. It contrasts the picture of the beast in Rev 13 and displays the end goal of God's workings (particularly in the bowl judgments).[103] Thus, God's judging and transforming holiness, his de-creation activity, the second Exodus, and his wrath against the nations are designed to accomplish the ideals found in Isa 6 and its related texts. John thus illustrates how God works out the end of history to accomplish Isaiah's vision and theology.

God's Eschatological Activity as Actualization of Vision (Ezekiel)

Ezekiel's vision encapsulates a theology of cosmic, corporate, and indwelling presence. God's glory will fill all creation. This occurs within his people as individual temples (Ezek 3:1; 36:26–27), through his people via a corporate temple (39:27; 40–48), and throughout the world as a cosmic temple (1:1–28). In Ezekiel, God's judgment prepares his people and the world for such fellowship (11:1–25).[104] Also, God's indwelling Spirit creates relationally alive people who can have communion with him via a resurrection (cf. 37:1–28).

Rev 6–19 directly concerns the actualization of Ezekiel's vision and theology by virtue of John's calling. This does not only originate from John's commission in Rev 1, but also from his "recommissioning" in Rev 10. In context, this latter text closely governs the content and purpose of the rest of the Apocalypse.[105] The apostle's recommissioning contains all sorts of associations with Ezekiel's calling. Both are given a book to eat, and both find it sweet to the taste (Rev 10:9–10; cf. Ezek 3:3). One could even argue that both encounter bitterness in some fashion because of God's looming judgment (Rev 10:10; Ezek 3:14).[106] These parallels suggest that John's message pertains to Ezekiel's and actually fulfills it.[107] Thus, God recommissions John to proclaim the latter half of the book of Revelation as the completion of Ezekiel's vision and theology.

As the Lord explicitly tells both Ezekiel and John, they must prophesy against a variety of nations and kings (Rev 10:11; cf. Ezek 3:1–27; 28:1–10), which sets

---

103. Rev 14 seems to contrast the previous presentation of the beast and his activities. See Osborne, *Revelation*, 525. However, this contrast participates on the larger level of placing the final wrath of God (Rev 15:1) in the context of the struggle of God's people with Satan, both in history and its final eschatological form. In the end, God will win, and his judgments will produce that victory. See also, Thomas, *Revelation 8–22 Commentary*, 189; Walvoord, *Revelation of Jesus Christ*, 214–15.

104. Block, *Ezekiel*, 1:356.

105. Bauckham, *Theology of Revelation*, 80–82.

106. Block, *Ezekiel*, 1:138. However, Ezekiel's bitterness relates to his resistance to God's message (as opposed to John, who seems to be compliant to God's will even if he understands the judgment to be hard). The parallel, then, is not exact.

107. Bauckham, *Theology of Revelation*, 83–84.

readers' expectations that the apostle's theology in Rev 10–19 deals with working out Ezekiel's message.[108]

Along that line, John illustrates how God's eschatological activities fulfill prophecies in Ezekiel. This is particularly true of the bowl judgments. For example, the destruction of Babylon echoes Ezekiel's description of the fall of Tyre. The kings of the earth who formerly had conducted business with the city now mourn (Ezek 26:16; 27:35; Rev 18:9). Similarly, the merchants also lament in fear (Ezek 27:12–22; Rev 18:10–19). In Ezekiel's theology, the fall of these types of nations was essential in raising up God's glory amongst the world (cf. 39:21),[109] which is precisely what seems to be happening in John's description. The saints rejoice over Babylon's demise because it will no longer delude the world. Instead, God's people will consummate their relationship with Christ in the marriage supper of the Lamb (Rev 18:21—19:10). Equally, Babylon's fall is characterized by the earth being made bright with the glory of God's messenger (Rev 18:1) This alludes to the wording of Ezek 43:2 which discusses how God's glory will shine in the world as he returns to the temple.[110] Hence, John, in his own way, shows that the judgment of the world leads to the consummation of God's presence.

This culminates with the battle of Gog and Magog (Ezek 38–39), which seems to take place at the return of Christ (19:11–21). There, a massive battle ensues in which the birds eat up all the enemies, just as Ezekiel predicted (Rev 19:17; cf. Ezek 39:4, 17–20). In Ezekiel, God designed the battle such that all would know he is supreme and to establish his presence in the world amongst his people (39:22–23). In the flow of the Apocalypse, John also views the event as having such implications.[111] Thus, the apostle shows that God's judgment against the nations leads to the fulfillment of Ezekiel's vision and theology.

I can add three other important details to this framework. First, when introducing the bowl judgments, John states that they will specifically pave the way for God's glory to fill the earth, the completion of his cosmic presence. In Rev 14:1–2, the picture of the 144,000 worshipping in Jerusalem includes a great sound from heaven that resembles the noise around the chariot-throne (cf. Rev 5:8; Ezek 1:24). As Mounce points out, it specifically alludes to the sound of God's presence returning to earth to display his glory in Ezek 43:2.[112] Revelation 15 portrays this same idea. In Rev 15:3, the chariot-throne appears in the context of the sea of glass. This signifies (as it did in

---

108. Kowalski, "Transformation of Ezekiel," 301; Moyise, "Old Testament," 78.

109. Block, *Ezekiel*, 2:424, 480.

110. Osborne, *Revelation*, 635; Beale, *Revelation*, 892. Beale sees this as an introduction to the theme of God's return to the temple. Perhaps, however, it may relate more strongly to the preparation for the return of God to the temple. See below for further discussion.

111. See Rev 19:1–10, which celebrates what is to be inaugurated with Christ's return. See also Thomas, *Revelation 8–22 Commentary*, 355.

112. Mounce, *Book of Revelation*, 265.

Rev 4:6) that the presence of God will fill the whole earth.[113] Consistently, the martyrs proclaim that all the earth will worship God (Rev 15:4), and then God's glory fills the heavenly temple (Rev 15:8). Together, these ideas signal that God's presence will not only fill the heavenly temple, but also the entire earth (just as Isaiah and Ezekiel envisioned; cf. Isa 6:3; Ezek 43:2).[114] The bowl judgments then commence (Rev 16:1–21) to accomplish all of this. More specifically, in light of what we have just discussed, the bowl judgments deliberately work to fulfill the concept of God's cosmic presence, as Ezekiel described.

Second, in addition to cosmic presence, the Apocalypse also portrays the completion of God's corporate presence. God's return to his temple on earth is part of John's theology. In Rev 11, God tells the apostle to measure the temple, the altar, and the worshippers (11:1). This echoes what Ezekiel did (40:3–4).[115] However, there is a significant difference. Ezekiel measured the outer court (40:9–20), but John does not (Rev 11:2). The reason is that the Gentiles will trample the holy city for forty-two months (Rev 11:2b). We reach two major questions at this point. First, is this an earthly or a spiritual, heavenly temple? Second, what does this imagery precisely signify in the flow of the book (particularly in light of the differences between John and Ezekiel)? Even if critics disagree with my analysis, the allusion to Ezekiel should at least show that whatever is technically taking place in this chapter works out Ezekiel's paradigm.

With this in mind, regarding the first issue, John does use the term ναός for the heavenly courtroom throughout the book (cf. 3:12; 7:15; 11:19; 14:15, 17; 16:1). Thus, some scholars argue that it would be more natural and consistent for such an idea here (or a more spiritual, non-structural idea).[116] However, several factors argue for a more earthly and structural scene:

1. John seems to allude to a variety of texts that anchor the interpretation of the temple as a physical entity. Not only do we have strong allusions to Ezekiel, but also to Daniel (7:25; 9:24–27; cf. 8:12–13; 11:31–35), both of whom arguably envisioned a physical and earthly building.[117] Paul, as noted, also reiterates this same sentiment in 2 Thess 2:4. Of interest, just as in 2 Thess 2:4, the phrase "temple of God" in Rev 11:1 also has the article (τὸν ναὸν τοῦ θεοῦ). This too probably points to a structural entity, as it (likely) did in Paul.[118] By appealing to these

---

113. Recall that the sea of glass resembles the cosmos. This may also relate to the victory of the saints over the beast that comes out of the sea.

114. Mounce, *Book of Revelation*, 289; Thomas, *Revelation 8–22 Commentary*, 244. Thomas argues that God's judgments are complete when he replaces the old order with the new Jerusalem. Thus, God's glory will fill the earth.

115. Mounce, *Book of Revelation*, 211; Strand, "Overlooked Background to Revelation 11," 320–22.

116. Beale, *Revelation*, 558.

117. See previous discussions in chapters 4 and 6.

118. See previous discussion in chapter 7. See Wanamaker, *Epistles to the Thessalonians*, 246–47.

source texts, John anchors our understanding of this temple as a reconstituted physical structure: the representation of God's corporate presence in Ezekiel.

2. In addition to such intertextuality, the innertextuality of the temple in the book seems to parallel Rev 11 with structural entities. The measuring of the temple in Rev 11:1–2 seems to relate to the measuring of the new Jerusalem in Rev 21:15–17. In fact, these are the only two texts in the book in which John uses the term μετρέω. Rev 11 correlates to Rev 21. However, most commentators take the latter chapter as a physical, structural entity.[119] If this is the case, and if Rev 21:15–17 parallels Rev 11:1, then Rev 11:1 more likely describes a physical structure. Other structural items such as the altar and outer courts point in this direction as well.

3. Along this line, the use of the term "temple" (ναός) in the Apocalypse seems to be consistently structural. As noted above, its use in Rev 21 seems to be physical, and its use earlier in Revelation pertains to the heavenly courtroom in its entirety (structure with the worshippers, see Rev 7:15; 14:15; 15:5–8). Accordingly, for Rev 11:1 to refer to a structural entity makes sense as well. Interestingly, the interpretation that the temple refers to the church or to God's people would actually be the exceptional use of the word in this case.[120]

4. At the same time, critics may object by arguing that an *earthly* temple is an exception to the way the word is used of the *heavenly* temple. Contextually, however, claiming that Rev 11:1 is the heavenly temple is difficult. If Rev 11:1 does refer to the heavenly court, it becomes rather hard to see how the Gentiles (presumably on earth) can trample it (Rev 11:2). Moreover, John's theology may actually facilitate the parallel of a heavenly temple with an earthly temple. The apostle describes how heaven invades earth and how the two will mirror each other as they become one. The new Jerusalem is case in point, for it signifies how heaven and earth meet such that the whole cosmos becomes a temple, and thus that there really is no temple in the traditional sense. However, that scheme seems to allow for (if not presume) an earthly temple that merges with the heavenly. In fact, the use of temple and related concepts and motifs actually play well into that paradigm. In the flow of the book, God presents the heavenly temple (Rev 4–5; 14:15; 15:5–8) and then the earthly temple (Rev 11:1), which conceptually merge

---

As Wanamaker points out, Paul's use of the article with temple distinguishes it from later uses of the temple relative to believers, which lacks the article. See 1 Cor 3:16 and 2 Cor 6:16.

119. Beale, *Revelation*, 562. Beale offers an interesting comment on the final temple: "This is not merely a spiritual interpretation of Ezekiel's temple prophecy. It is also a redemptive-historical understanding: what Ezekiel prophesied has begun to find its real, true fulfillment on a spiritual level and will be consummated in fuller form physically and spiritually in a new creation (see on Rev. 21:1—22:5)." If this final temple (or cosmic temple) has a physical nature, then why is it so objectionable that John's use of temple includes that throughout the book?

120. For further examples of those who hold to believers as the temple see ibid., 558; Osborne, *Revelation*, 410.

in the formulation of the new Jerusalem (Rev 21). The wording of Rev 11:1 seems to anticipate this union (see discussion above). Other texts also support this notion. In Rev 14, John describes the throne room with loud rumblings, which correspond with Ezek 43:2 (see Rev 14:2). In that OT text, the earth does not merely display God's glory, his glory also returns to the earthly temple and fills it (Ezek 43:5). Rev 18:1 echoes the same text, confirming this agenda. Rev 15 also reiterates this idea. God's glory fills the heavenly temple, presumably because he will do something similar on earth (Rev 15:8; cf. Isa 6:3).[121] In this discussion, I can offer two important observations. First, John's paradigm of heaven to earth can include (if not assumes) the existence of an earthly structural temple to merge with the heavenly. Second, John holds this earthly temple in tension with the heavenly temple and new Jerusalem. Heavenly and earthly temples must be different entities, otherwise it would be impossible to merge the two into one. Individually, these temples cannot be entirely equated with the new Jerusalem either, since the new Jerusalem only exists when heaven and earth join together. In this way, John, in Rev 11:1, includes this distinctly earthly structural temple in the development of his theology concerning temple and God's presence.

These points suggest that reading Rev 11:1–2 as a physical earthly temple may be what John had in mind. The intertextuality of the description is consistent with John's use of the word "temple," the innertextual connections of the temple passages, and the idea that heaven will meet earth such that the heavenly structural temple will merge with the earthly one in the end. The earthly temple must look forward to that goal.

The above discussion actually begins to answer our second question. Why does John deviate from Ezekiel's original description? Our observations thus far suggest that Rev 11 is slightly proleptic. It anticipates heaven coming to earth per John's paradigm. This helps us resolve the contrasting descriptions in Rev 11:1–2. On one hand, the Gentiles will trample the earthly temple. On the other hand, this earthly temple is measured, signaling its consecration. A consideration of the proleptic tension in Rev 11:1–2 can resolve this supposed conflict. God has John proclaim that a future earthly temple awaits God's people, where he will commune with them intimately and thereby with the entire world, just as Ezekiel prophesied. However, prior to that time (three-and-a-half years), what Daniel predicted will ensue. The outer court of the earthly temple will be trampled. This juxtaposition is nothing new. Daniel himself prophesies that in God's plan to anoint the holy place, an evil prince will desecrate the temple area by stopping the sacrificial system (cf. Dan 9:24–27; see also 11:31–35). Rev 11:1–2 may encompass this very concept.

If this is the case, then we can better see how the earthly structural temple plays in John's theology of temple and God's presence (and in the fulfillment of Ezekiel's vision and theology). Rev 11 serves as the introduction to the nature of the final trumpet

---

121. See Thomas, *Revelation 8–22 Commentary*, 244.

judgment, which in turn launches the bowl judgments.[122] Rev 11 states that the earthly structural temple's defilement is an important element of the background to God's judgment. However, Rev 11:1 also indicates that such sacrilege will not always be. God's judgment via the bowl judgments will facilitate his presence richly dwelling in the world and with his people. Rev 11:1 anticipates that part of this reality concerns God's presence on the corporate level. The desecrated earthly structural temple will become the consecrated earthly structural temple. It will be "measured" in the end, just as Ezekiel foresaw, and the people of God will serve within it as priests (cf. Rev 20:6). Thus, the Lord will dwell with his people in a renewed earthly temple as part of the consummation of his relationship with them. However, ultimately, heavenly and earthly temples will join to comprise the new Jerusalem.[123]

In addition, because the corporate temple signifies God's fellowship with his people, the measuring of the temple, the altar, and those who worship in it does not only signify a future building, as Ezekiel envisioned. Rather, it also anticipates a specific state. Measuring those entities also alludes back to Lev 16, in which temple, altar, and people are consecrated for worship.[124] John understands that after a time of eschatological distress, the holy place will be anointed and the people consecrated (as priests) to enjoy God's presence, just as Ezekiel envisioned (cf. Rev 20:6; cf. Ezek 45:17). Through this allusion, John has cast God's workings as the completion of Ezekiel's vision and theology (and again, since the allusion is not in doubt, we can agree that John does work out Ezekiel's ideas, even if one disagrees with the above analysis).[125]

Third, I can offer a final comment concerning God's indwelling presence with the notion of resurrection in Revelation. Right after God commissions John to extend Ezekiel's message, God not only commands John to measure the temple as Ezekiel did, but also to observe the two witnesses. They die, and then, after three-and-a-half

122. Osborne, *Revelation*, 415. Osborne views this as essentially background to how the church operates during the end time. Thomas, *Revelation 8–22 Commentary*, 85–86. Thomas views this as what the latter half of Daniel's seventieth week entails. That may relate to Rev 11, the seventh trumpet judgment, and the final bowl judgments. Thomas' analysis has the exegetical support of the forty-two months. The frequent mention of a three-and-a-half period argues that Rev 11 refers to the final escalation of end-time activity. Beale acknowledges that the text deals with final realities as well. See Beale, *Revelation*, 556.

123. Recall that Rev 11:1 is held as distinct from the new Jerusalem. It is the earthly temple that ultimately merges with the heavenly and results in the new Jerusalem. Hence, Rev 11:1 as proleptic denotes an earthly temple and not the new Jerusalem, which I will argue further shortly. In sum, Rev 20:6 plays an important role, since it discusses priests during the Millennial Kingdom, which coincides with an earthly temple at the time. Also, the discontinuity between Ezekiel's temple and new Jerusalem supports that Rev 11:1 evidences this.

124. Strand, "Overlooked Background to Revelation 11," 320–25. As I have discussed, while the allusion goes to the Day of Atonement, what is in view is not atonement for sin, but rather consecration of certain objects for worship, as well as the ordination of the priesthood.

125. Beale, *Revelation*, 562. Beale provides such analysis in viewing the temple in Rev 11:1 as a spiritual entity. Ultimately, even if one believes John develops or transforms Ezekiel differently than I have suggested, we can all agree with my thesis that John interacts with Ezekiel to show the fulfillment of his theology and vision.

days, are raised again and taken into God's presence (Rev 11:11–12). How they are raised is quite interesting. The breath of life from God enters into them, phraseology that matches Ezek 37:5.[126] This becomes significant when we consider their role in the flow of the book. These two witnesses serve as a testimony of God's victory in the end times.[127] Their miraculous acts validate their verbal proclamation (11:5–6). In light of this, their experience of death and resurrection most likely becomes a microcosm of their message as well. Just as they overcame the beast in resurrection and are ushered into the presence of God after three-and-a-half days, so the saints will also overcome by resurrection after a three-and-a-half year period (cf. Rev 11:2, 3; 12:6).[128] The two witnesses are a demonstration of and testimony to God's final victory.[129] If these parallels are valid, then such triumph fulfills another part of Ezekiel's vision and theology. God's presence will dwell in his people, resurrect them, and facilitate their communion with his presence on every level. This may be why the 144,000 are labeled as the first fruit in Rev 14:4d. They who are a part of Israel (cf. Rev 7:1–8) signal the resurrection of God's people, just as Ezek 37 envisioned.[130]

All of this shows that the narrative framework above not only fulfills Ezekiel's prophecies, but also fulfills the theological realities the prophet saw in his vision. This makes God's judgments against the nations thoroughly purposed to actualize Ezekiel's theology of vision. God shows his wrath against the nations in fulfillment of specific prophecies and for the sake of establishing his cosmic, corporate, and indwelling presence in this world. In this way, the latter part of the book really does continue Ezekiel's calling, mission, and vision, as John's recommissioning suggests. The apostle thereby incorporates the fulfillment of Ezekiel as his own theology.

God's Eschatological Activity as Actualization of Vision (Daniel)

Daniel's theology of vision related to God's kingdom. Specifically, he describes how all of human history culminates in God's exclusive reign over the cosmos. Within this, the saints will suffer, but in the end they will triumph. That triumph hinges upon the victory of the true king, the one like a son of man.

---

126. Osborne, *Revelation*, 597; Thomas, *Revelation 8–22 Commentary*, 97.

127. Osborne, *Revelation*, 435; Beale, *Revelation*, 572; Thomas, *Revelation 8–22 Commentary*, 87.

128. Aus, "Relevance of Isaiah 66," 254.

129. Osborne, *Revelation*, 430–31; Thomas, *Revelation 8–22 Commentary*, 99. Osborne more explicitly makes this connection. Thomas acknowledges that the imagery echoes the ascension of Christ, as well as those in Christ.

130. Contra Thomas, *Revelation 8–22 Commentary*, 198. However, see Osborne, *Revelation*, 530; Beale, *Revelation*, 744. The term "first fruits" can be used to denote a significant sacrifice without the subsequent larger harvest in mind. However, even in such texts, the notion of an initial or prime harvest is still in view and bases the metaphor off of that idea (cf. Jer 2:3) such that we cannot make too strong of a distinction between the initial gathering and the larger subsequent harvest.

John intertextually intertwines all of these themes into his description of God's eschatological activity. Interestingly, in Rev 6–19, John frequently alludes to the struggle and victory of the saints mentioned in Daniel. This harmonizes well with his overarching emphasis on the Christian's travail and hope.[131] John acknowledges that per Daniel's paradigm, suffering must take place. The two witnesses illustrate that very point. The beast wages war against them just like in Dan 7:21, which describes the beast making war against the saints.[132] In this way, John fleshes out what Daniel envisioned.[133]

To further link his account with Daniel, the apostle even makes reference to the time of three-and-a-half years (Rev 11:2, 3; 12:6), which is precisely how Daniel referred to this era (cf. 9:27; 12:7). Rev 12 also affirms this struggle. The beast, itself a motif derived from Dan 7, will kill many, just as Daniel prophesied in his central vision (Rev 12:13; cf. Dan 7:25; 11:45—12:1). However, the people of God will, in the end, have victory (Rev 12:11; cf. Dan 7:26). In this regard, John describes a beast and a woman (Rev 17:3) who also persecuted the saints (v. 6).[134] These allusions also point out that Daniel's vision and theology become the substance of what John describes concerning the saints' tribulation.

However, in the midst of this hardship, John shows that God still preserves, saves, and works out all things for the saints' victory in the Son, just as Dan 7 depicted. Rev 7 is an important illustration of this. In the midst of his seal judgments (Rev 6:17), God also preserves a remnant. He seals 144,000 people of Israel from his wrath (Rev 7:2–4).[135] This is in conjunction with a great multitude who come from every tongue, tribe, and nation to offer worship to God (Rev 7:9). That is the very description of Jews and Gentiles found in Dan 7:14, 27,[136] and Rev 14:3 depicts a similar scene of worship. The 144,000 sing before the throne, the four living creatures, and the elders in a scene that resembles Rev 4:4–6 and Dan 7:14, 27. In such echoes of Dan 7, John demonstrates that Rev 6–19 moves toward the outcome of what Daniel envisioned: both the saints and the Gentiles will come together to honor the one like a son of man.[137] The visionary event will provide victory for the saints, as Daniel explained.

---

131. Beale, *Revelation*, 171; Osborne, *Revelation*, 42.

132. Beale, *Revelation*, 698.

133. This is particularly true if the two witnesses signal, to some degree, what is happening to the rest of the saints.

134. Osborne, *Revelation*, 615; Beale, *Revelation*, 864. The beast relates to the animal revealed in Rev 13:1–2, which stems back to Dan 7.

135. Thomas, *Revelation 1–7*, 472; Beale, *Revelation*, 404; Osborne, *Revelation*, 304.

136. Other allusions to Dan 7 include the four winds (Rev 7:1; cf. Dan 7:2), the sea (Rev 7:1; Dan 7:2), the throne (Rev 7:11; Dan 7:9), and saints serving God (Rev 7:15; Dan 7:14; note the shared word, λατρεύω).

137. Rev 7:16–17 seems to have a proleptic bent towards Rev 20–22. Hence, Rev 7 is part of the entire goal of the Millennial Kingdom and eternal state.

Why will such victory take place? God's judgments in the Apocalypse are geared towards establishing his kingdom, as Daniel envisioned. The enemies of God will not always be in power. God's wrath will liberate his people. In this way, the narrative flow of God's judgments works towards the end described above. Rev 10–11 state this. An angel arrives on the scene to recommission John (Rev 10:1). Although this moment resembles Ezekiel's vision, the angel himself resembles the angelic figure who gave Daniel an important message about the end (cf. Dan 10:1–6). Hence, John's recomissioning does not merely pertain to the fulfillment of Ezekiel, but also of Daniel.[138] Along that line, when the seventh trumpet is blown, the angels declare that the kingdom of the world has now become the kingdom of the Lord (Rev 11:15). This seems to refer to the implementation of Daniel's kingdom agenda.[139] In addition, the text states that while the nations will war against God, he will overcome and reward the saints (Rev 11:18). Thus, God's kingdom victory provides relief for his people, just as he revealed to Daniel. All of this sets the context for God's dealings in Rev 12–19.[140] In light of our discussion, the fulfillment of Daniel's vision and theology seems squarely within the purpose behind God's activities in those chapters.

Accordingly, as God enforces this agenda, he casts Satan from heaven to earth as part of his conquest for his kingdom (Rev 12:10). Part of this involves Michael, who appeared in Daniel (10:13). The spiritual warfare waged in Daniel now comes to its climax in Revelation (10:13–21; 12:1; Rev 12:7–17).[141] God also announces that "Babylon the Great," the city described in Dan 4:30, will fall (Rev 14:8) and then consequently annihilates it (Rev 18:1–24).[142] In the process, the bowl judgments bring down all other competing authorities. God attacks the throne of the beast (Rev 16:10) because there will only be one throne in the end, the one seen in the visionary event.

This brings us to the center of Daniel's vision: the one like a son of man. The saints' victory over suffering, as well as kingdom, is all on his shoulders. John expands upon that reality. In Daniel, we observed the conflict between kings and the true king, the statue versus the stone (cf. Dan 2:35; 7:1–14). This culminated in an individual who surpassed the evil power of prior rulers (7:25–26; 11:36–38) but is overcome by the Son of Man (7:26). John imports this exact struggle into his writing. The beast of Rev 13 seems to be that ruler (the leader and representative of world powers) who challenges Christ. The metaphor of the beast, as well as its particular descriptions, draws heavily from Dan 7:1–8. Likewise, his corporate solidarity with his nation(s) is

---

138. The description of the angel in Rev 10 affirms this. The angel, both in Daniel and in Rev 10, displays the glory found in the visionary event, signaling that his message pertains to its fulfillment.

139. Beale, *Revelation*, 611. Beale states that if there is any OT background to these statements, it comes from Dan 2 and 7.

140. Bauckham, *Theology of Revelation*, 82–84; Beale, *Revelation*, 520–21.

141. Beale, *Revelation*, 650; Thomas, *Revelation 8–22 Commentary*, 129.

142. Beale, *Revelation*, 754. Note that the phrase "Babylon the Great" is found in Dan 4:30.

also a feature in Dan 7.[143] The entire complex of thought surrounding the beast and its activities is drawn from Daniel.[144] By this, the apostle deliberately addresses the fulfillment of Daniel's theology in his own. In part, Revelation is a showdown between the counterfeit (Rev 6:2) and the king.

Thus, the beast battles the Lamb and the saints, just like Daniel predicted (Rev 13:1–10; cf. Dan 7:25). Even the beast's hubris is put in Danielic terms. The number 666 seems to partially originate from the dimensions of Nebuchadnezzar's statue (Rev 13:18; cf. Dan 3:1).[145] Just as the kings in Daniel were described by the might of the statue, John describes this wicked king in similar terms. Although going through every exhaustive detail of overlap between John and Daniel here would fall outside the scope of this work, Rev 17:14 provides an important summary of the major events in the Apocalypse.[146] It states that the beast, with his coalition, wages war against the Lamb. Nonetheless, the Lamb will triumph along with those who are with him (οἱ μετ' αὐτοῦ). This follows the exact paradigm of Dan 7:21, in which the beast wages war against the saints but is ultimately overcome by their victory in the Son.[147] Hence, the entire complex of events that John describes in Rev 6–19—the suffering of the saints, the appearance of the beast, God's judgments on the kingdoms, and the victory of the Lamb and the saints—are all means by which God works out the repercussions of Dan 7 in history.

Ultimately, Christ will return with flaming eyes (Rev 19:12), a description drawn from one of Daniel's related visions (Dan 10:6; cf. Rev 1:14), to finish the visionary agenda of Daniel and John. He will seize and defeat the beast, just as Daniel described (Dan 7:11; Rev 19:20). Rev 19 thus provides the climactic ending of the conflict prophesied in Daniel and incorporated in John. Jesus definitively shows himself as the only king worthy of honor. He thereby establishes the kingdom of God over the world (cf. Rev 11:15) and completes God's judgments from start (Rev 6:1) to finish (Rev 19:11–21). As a result, the saints, who find victory in him, will complete the purpose of the vision in that every nation will worship him (Rev 14:1–4; cf. Rev 22:2–3). Thus, God's work in the Apocalypse is the actualization of Daniel's vision and theology.

---

143. Thomas, *Revelation 8–22 Commentary*, 154–55.

144. Beale, *Revelation*, 683; Dunn, "Danielic Son of Man in the New Testament," 536–37. See Dunn for a list of parallels between Rev and Dan.

145. Beale, *Revelation*, 727; Thomas, *Revelation 8–22 Commentary*, 185; Walvoord, *Revelation of Jesus Christ*, 211–12. Thomas agrees that the statue motif may be in view, but argues that this does not help identify the individual. This may play a part of the idea (see also 1 Kgs 10:14 of 666 talents of gold) even if the total understanding of the number may not occur until the end.

146. Osborne, *Revelation*, 621. Osborne states, "The events presupposed here relate to an ongoing series of passages in the book." Hence, 17:14 provides an interpretation and summary of the events in the book.

147. Beale, *Revelation*, 880. Beale explicitly states that Dan 7:21 matches Rev 17:14. Compare the wording τὸ κέρας ἐκεῖνο ἐποίει πόλεμον μετὰ τῶν ἁγίων καὶ ἴσχυσεν πρὸς αὐτούς in Dan 7:21 with οὗτοι μετὰ τοῦ ἀρνίου πολεμήσουσιν καὶ τὸ ἀρνίον νικήσει αὐτούς in Rev 17:14.

God's Eschatological Activity as Actualization of Vision (Paul)

Paul's vision was one of inauguration and anticipation. He identified Jesus as the one portrayed in his predecessors' visions and because of Christ's glory, Paul knew that the significance of the vision was inaugurated. At the same time, the apostle awaited the final outcome envisioned by Isaiah, Ezekiel, and Daniel. In a sense, then, what we have observed above also fulfills Paul's theology. For example, Paul's use of Isaiah acknowledges that while salvation has come to pass in Christ, its fulfillment is still yet to come. John in the Apocalypse picks this expectation up. The 144,000 who have washed themselves clean in the Lamb appear blameless (ἄμωμος, Rev 14:5), terminology used by Paul to discuss the end result of salvation (Eph 5:27). Paul's expectation of an ultimate cleansing is now actualized in John.

Similarly, the apostle's appeal to Isaiah also related to the salvation of Israel and a new creation, both of which appear in Revelation (7:1–8; 21:1). The apostle knew that conversion was part of God's greater work of resurrection by the Spirit (Rom 8:11; Eph 2:1–10). This too is demonstrated in John's writing (Rev 11:11). Paul also prepared for a time when Jew and Gentile would worship Christ together (Rom 15:14–21) which figures in John's account (Rev 7:9–10; 14:6). He also knew that just as Daniel and Ezekiel proclaimed, the Antichrist would appear and desecrate the temple (2 Thess 2:3–4), which John also explains (Rev 13:1–18). So it is that John fills out various points of Paul's anticipation.

This climaxes with John's portrayal of Christ. Paul knew that his theology came from his vision of Christ and was for the sake of the glorified Christ (Eph 1:23). John shares this same Christ-centered focus. Paul put his hope in Christ and what he would do at his return (Phil 3:20–21). John portrays Christ coming to slay the Antichrist (2 Thess 2:8; Rev 19:20) and subject all to himself (Phil 2:11; 3:20–21; Rev 19:21). Thus, John displays what Paul's theology waited for.

Synthesis

At this point, it is useful to take a step back and consider a synthesis of our discussion. When looking at Rev 6–19, we may see a general literary flow from God's seal to trumpet to bowl judgments.[148] Within this, God further explains the background and

---

148. Even if they are recapitulations, they literarily still appear to progress this way. See Jauhiainen, "Recapitulation and Chronological Progression in John's Apocalypse." However, there are some problems harmonizing recapitulations, especially in the conflict between Satan's deceiving the nations (Rev 12:9) and his complete inability to do so in Rev 20:3. How can the saints be in heaven (Rev 15:2–3) yet resurrected on earth simultaneously (Rev 20:4)? Or, if Rev 15 and Rev 20 both reference the church age, how can the physical resurrection seemingly portrayed in Rev 20 take place at this time? Similarly, can one really view Satan's casting out from heaven to earth and having freedom on the earth (Rev 12:7–17) as the same thing as Satan being bound on earth in the Abyss and not having freedom to deceive on earth (Rev 20:1–15)? They take place in different places and have different purposes. The harmonization questions we discussed before seem to indicate distinct variations that mean Rev 12

nature of his workings via various "interlude" texts that together paint a composite picture of the Lord's eschatological activity. However, what this discussion has shown is that such judgment and salvation is not random. There is a purpose behind the dense intertextuality in these passages. Much of what happens here, both in the flow of Rev 6–19 as well as its intertextuality, deals with all that is entailed by John's vision in Rev 4–5. As discussed, that vision is the launching point for God's workings in Rev 6–19. The visionary event in heaven must now come to earth. Earth must ultimately mirror the glory and worship seen in the visionary event. Furthermore, Rev 4–5 actually contain the visions and theologies of Isaiah, Ezekiel, Daniel, and Paul. Thus, as Rev 6–19 works out the agenda of Rev 4–5, John alludes to the writings of his predecessors to show how specific prophecies related to their visions are coming to pass to achieve the outcomes that their visions foresaw. Herein lies another contribution John makes to a biblical theology of vision: he shows how God moves in history to actualize that entire theology.

One final thought remains. While I have teased out allusions to prior revelation, John does not categorize the intertextuality of his writing so neatly. Rather, he juxtaposes them all together. Hence, Isaiah's vision of the end merges with Ezekiel and Daniel in Rev 14:1–5. The bowl judgments against the nation simultaneously fulfill Ezekiel's notion of Gog and Magog, as well as Isaiah's new creation and Daniel's establishment of kingdom. They are all intertwined, for indeed, they are all not against each other, but interrelated, theological realities tied together by the same visionary event. This too affirms the unity of visions I have asserted throughout this book.

JOHN'S THEOLOGY AS THE CONSUMMATION OF VISION (REV 20–22)

Millennial Kingdom

The Apocalypse has shown us the birth pains leading up to the fulfillment of the visionary event. The book has already anticipated this moment through a series of proleptic texts. They depict this time as one in which God will reign high and lifted up from Jerusalem (Rev 14:1). His glory will fill the earth (Rev 15:8) and his transforming holiness will make his people blameless (Rev 14:4).[149] As such, God's presence will richly dwell with his people and be displayed to all nations via a temple (Rev 11:1). Moreover, his kingdom will triumph (11:15; 12:10) and the saints will share in the victory of Christ (7:1–17; 14:1–4). All of that has now been produced by God's judgment in salvation seen earlier in the book (Rev 6–19) and these ideas provide important background for our discussion of Rev 20. The fulfillment of vision is in view.

---

and 20 are not angles of the same event.

149. Even though the 144,000 are in view, they are the first fruit of God's people and thus, what happens to them will also occur to the rest of the saints.

It is fitting then that Rev 20:1 begins with an angel descending from heaven (καταβαίνοντα ἐκ τοῦ οὐρανοῦ) to remind the reader that this is a result of heaven invading earth per the agenda of Rev 4–5.[150] Baukham argues that this entire time period falls into the framework of Dan 7:11–12.[151] This is the final resolution of the counterfeit versus the king. God proves that over this creation, his Son and those in him truly reign as opposed to the beast and his kingdom (which itself is the climax of all false authorities in human history).[152] Thus, the Millennial Kingdom is concerned with the demonstration of God's success in implementing the decree of the vision. Does Jesus possess all authority and glory and the kingdom? Does he act as the fulfillment of theology, including being the new Adam that Daniel and Paul portray?

The proleptic texts already suggest a positive answer to these types of questions. The information in Rev 20:1–10 adds to this. Satan is bound, as Isaiah envisioned (Isa 24:21). This shows yet another component of Isaiah's vision completed. God will reign over all his foes, both natural and supernatural.[153] The saints reign on thrones as John anticipated, along with the elders who sat on thrones (Rev 4:4). This not only fulfills John's vision, but also what is intertextually bound in that vision: the victory of the saints in Daniel and in Paul (7:27; Rom 5:17; 8:17). They have overcome the beast, just as the proleptic texts proclaimed (Rev 15:2; 20:4). They will live and reign with Christ (ἔζησαν καὶ ἐβασίλευσαν, Rev 20:4b). This not only alludes to Daniel's and Paul's descriptions of the future rule of the saints (cf. Dan 7:27; 2 Tim 2:12), but also implies the notion of resurrection prophesied by Isaiah, Ezekiel, and Daniel (Isa 26:2; Ezek 37:1–28; Dan 12:2), anticipated by Paul and John (Rom 8:11; Rev 2:10–11), and now manifested in Rev 20:4.[154]

The rule of the saints is accompanied by the fact that they are also priests (Rev 20:6). This too links back with what was proclaimed in John's vision (Rev 5:9). Again, the Millennial Kingdom completes the agenda of the vision. Even more, this relates to Ezekiel's own theology, by which God's people all become priests in the context of the temple (cf. Ezek 45:17). In fact, this was arguably anticipated in Rev 11:1, and so both John's and Ezekiel's vision and theology are fulfilled.[155]

So far, we have observed that God, in Christ, has successfully carried out the purpose of the visionary agenda. History and theology are being fulfilled. In a few short verses, allusions to Isaiah, Ezekiel, Daniel, and Paul point to the conclusion that

---

150. Osborne, *Revelation*, 700.
151. Bauckham, *Theology of Revelation*, 106–7.
152. Ibid.
153. Oswalt, *Isaiah 1–39*, 454.
154. Osborne, *Revelation*, 707. Osborne correctly notes that the term resurrection (ἀνάστασις) more often than not refers to physical resurrection as opposed to merely spiritual. This is indeed what the biblical writers envisioned and supports the notion that this is a period at the end of history as opposed to the church age.
155. What is fascinating is that the people of God are not called priests in the eternal state. This shows that the temple concept in Rev 11:1 most likely anticipates Rev 20:6 and the priesthood of believers.

the Millennial Kingdom functions in part as the actualization of a biblical theology of vision. However, how does the unleashing of Satan and the deception of the nations fit into this? Does that not imply some sort of weakness in Christ's reign, and therefore a flaw in the fulfillment of vision? To the contrary, this moment actually demonstrates the opposite.[156] God allows the devil to attempt to revert history to what God had stamped out by his judgments (cf. Rev 13:3).[157] In fact, Satan's attempt to deceive may even echo what took place in the garden of Eden (Gen 3:13).[158] However, Christ now proves what the vision declares. He is the true Adam, the one who fulfills the salvation, kingdom, and presence of God. He will not falter, but will uphold all that he has accomplished. The agenda and theology of the vision will not be compromised. Hence, Satan will never win and is thereby finally defeated as fire comes down from heaven and he is cast into the lake of fire forever (Rev 20:9–10).

A great white throne then appears, which may echo the familiar throne of the vision.[159] God makes official and final all that he has demonstrated. Heaven and earth flee away as they are dissolved. John states "there is no place for them" (τόπος οὐχ εὑρέθη αὐτοῖ, Rev 20:11). This denotes the complete eradication of this old creation and actually borrows the wording in Dan 2:35.[160] There, God eradicates the statue to set up his kingdom, and in John, we see the full consequences of that reality. There is only one true king who brings salvation, kingdom, and presence, and he alone will reign. Hence, a final sentencing ensues from the throne, completing the notion that as the books are opened (Rev 20:12), some will go to disgrace and everlasting contempt (Rev 20:11–15; Dan 12:2). The vision and its theological significance are unquestionably complete in Christ.

Thus, the Millennial Kingdom and consequent final judgment demonstrate that God, in his judging and saving work in Revelation, successfully accomplishes the

---

156. Bauckham, *Theology of Revelation*, 107: "Finally, to demonstrate that their triumph in Christ's kingdom is not one which evil can reverse, that it is God's last word for good against evil, the devil is given a last chance to deceive the nations again (20:7–8)."

157. Several factors evidence this. Notice the identical wording of συναγαγεῖν αὐτοὺς εἰς τὸν πόλεμον between Rev 20:8 and Rev 16:14. This may also account for the reference to Gog and Magog. This is not a claim to be a fulfillment of the original prophecy, but is more likely referring to the scope of Satan's attempted deception as well as the purpose of his activity. He desires to revert history prior to the victory of the Son. See Thomas, *Revelation 8–22 Commentary*, 423–24: "But the present passage differs from Ezekiel 38–39 in a number of ways that suffice to show this is not the specific occasion foreseen by Ezekiel (Smith). That the prophet equates Gog and Magog with 'the four corners of the earth' is ample reason to refrain from limiting it to one geographical region . . ." Thomas' observation is particularly important. In Ezek 38:1–2, Gog is actually a person and not a place. Magog is a place. John's appeals to the phrase differently than the original context, indicating that this is a slightly different event. It is an echo of the battle that took place before.

158. John's original depiction of Satan supports this conclusion. The devil is the serpent of old, a characterization from the garden, and the deceiver (12:9). These two primary descriptions show that the ideas of Gen 3 are involved in John's theology.

159. Thomas, *Revelation 8–22 Commentary*, 429; Beale, *Revelation*, 1031.

160. Beale, *Revelation*, 1032; Osborne, *Revelation*, 720.

agenda of the vision and fulfills all of its theological outcomes. Most importantly, this displays that his Son is the one whom the vision (in all its diversity) declares him to be. Heaven has successfully invaded earth, history has reached its climax, and theology has been completed in the Son.

Eternal State

In considering Rev 21:1—22:5, several questions come to mind. If the Millennial Kingdom marks the fulfillment of a biblical theology of vision, why does the eternal state seem remarkably similar to the vision? Conversely, why is there such discontinuity as well? How does all of this shape the function of this era, not only in Revelation, but also relative to a biblical theology of vision?

I can begin by pointing out certain dissimilarities between what had previously been associated with the visions and John's description at the end of Revelation. First, it appears that the eschatological outcome brought about by the vision related to the present creation (cf. Isa 11:1–16; Dan 7:1–9; Ezek 40–48; but see Isa 65:17).[161] Conversely, John's presentation concerns a completely new cosmos (Rev 20:11; 21:1). Second, Ezekiel envisions a sea in his presentation (47:8), but John states the complete opposite (Rev 21:1).[162] Third, the measurements (21:16) as well as the material (21:18) of the new Jerusalem do not correspond with the temple in Ezekiel (42:15–20; 45:2). The new Jerusalem is a perfect cube, whereas Ezekiel's temple lacks the height dimension. Osborne suggests that the new Jerusalem is "another degree greater than Ezekiel's temple."[163] Fourth, in fact, John declares that there is no temple, contrary to Ezekiel's presentation. There is also no mention of the priesthood, contrary to what we find in the Millennial Kingdom (cf. Rev 20:6). Accordingly, the eternal state seems to be different and have a different purpose than the Millennial Kingdom.

At risk of oversimplification, the eternal state appears to forever commemorate and celebrate the completed work of the vision. Initial support for this reading includes the various allusions to God's past redemptive work in the structure of the city (e.g., twelve tribes of Israel and twelve apostles, Rev 21:12, 14). The city serves as a museum of sorts to remember the Lord's acts.[164] It also functions, as a temple-like structure, to facilitate the enjoyment of those outcomes as God's people intimately commune with the Lord.[165] Along that line, we may note the contrast between the

---

161. Oswalt, *Isaiah 40–66*, 656. Oswalt highlights that the new creation encompasses inward transformation, Millennial Kingdom, as well as the eternal state.

162. The lack of a sea has theological implications, especially in light of the wickedness associated with water (cf. Rev 13:1). Nonetheless, we acknowledge that this is an eradication of both the physical ocean and what it signified. See Osborne, *Revelation*, 730; Beale, *Revelation*, 1042. See Thomas, *Revelation 8–22 Commentary*, 440. Thomas reminds us that the use of sea conveys comprehensiveness.

163. Osborne, *Revelation*, 752.

164. Thomas, *Revelation 8–22 Commentary*, 463.

165. Beale, *Revelation*, 1062; Osborne, *Revelation*, 745.

saints' activities in the Millennial Kingdom and the eternal state. The saints rule in the former (ἐβασίλευσαν, Rev 20:4), but rule and worship in the latter (λατρεύσουσιν, Rev 22:3, 5). This too points to the notion that the Millennial Kingdom is the demonstration of God's success in implementing the vision, and that the eternal state is the tribute to his completed work. The former proves the agenda of the vision has come to earth, and the latter celebrates that it is finished.

With that, the continuity (intertextuality) between vision and the eternal state serves that purpose. It will remind those present of the spectacular work of God in Christ expressed in the vision and also serve as a stimulus for the saints to engage in the final purpose of the vision: the glorious worship of Christ. Accordingly, a new world commences specifically designed to this end (Rev 21:1). God now dwells with man, as they are his people, and he is present amongst them (Rev 21:3), wording that draws upon Ezek 37:27 and 48:35. To reiterate this reality, God brings John up to a high mountain (Rev 21:10) recalling Ezek 40:2. The new Jerusalem is the bride of the Lamb (Rev 21:9), contrasting Ezekiel's description of Israel's harlotry (Ezek 16:1–23; 23:1–49). Instead, the city is replete with God's glory, as indicated by the various precious stones within it (Rev 21:11). Its gates and foundations remind everyone of God's relationship with his people (Rev 21:12).[166] Its structure echoes the temple of Ezekiel's final vision. There is much overlap between these two entities. This may be indicative of the fact that heavenly and earthly temples have merged per John's paradigm as discussed above. At the same time, as I also noted, differences between John's description of the eternal state and Ezekiel's temple exist, the most predominant of these being that within the eternal state, there is no temple (Rev 21:22). Overall, the continuity serves to recall Ezekiel's vision theology, and the discontinuity shows that this is something beyond what Ezekiel's vision and theology concentrated upon. The eternal state is the enjoyment of Ezekiel's theology totally fulfilled. God's presence and glory have been consummated and can now be fully enjoyed.

Thus, the new world brings an entirely new order. It is heaven and earth completely united (Rev 21:1). There is no sea (Rev 21:1), which not only refers to the body of water, but also to what the sea signified: the presence of evil (cf. Rev 13:1). God's workings in old creation conquered sin, Satan, and death. Along that line, the new world has no tears, death, mourning, or pain (Rev 21:4). What Isaiah envisioned (Isa 25:8), bought by the victory of the Lamb (Isa 52:13—53:12; Rev 5:9), is the permanent experience of believers. Hence, they will drink of the water of life perpetually, as Isaiah offered in the context of the Servant's completed work (Isa 35:5–6; 55:1).[167] The river also recalls the transforming power of God's presence in Ezek 47:3.[168] The city does not require the sun or moon because God's glory fills the earth, as both Isaiah and Ezekiel foresaw (Isa 6:3; 24:23; Ezek 43:1–4). God's glory

---

166. Thomas, *Revelation 8–22 Commentary*, 463.
167. Beale, *Revelation*, 1105.
168. Ibid.

alone pervades the cosmos (Rev 21:23) and his salvation is consummated, as only those who are blameless can enter the city (Rev 21:27). In these ways, the eternal state reminds believers what God accomplished in fulfilling Isaiah's vision and theology, and the saints enjoy those benefits forever.

At the center of all of this is a scene that matches the heavenly courtroom. The throne is there (22:3a) and God's servants worship him (v. 3b). The word for "worship" (λατρεύω) is the same term used in Dan 7:14 when the Son of Man receives authority such that every people, nation, and tongue would serve him. Paul seems to have anticipated that reality in his ministry to Jew and Gentile (Rom 15:14–21; Phil 3:3). The doxological outcome of the vision becomes the perpetual program in the eternal state. This is because the Lamb does rule, as the vision proclaimed (cf. Rev 5:5–10), and the saints rule with him forever (Rev 22:5; cf. 5:10). The eternal state perpetuates the ultimate goals of the visions of Daniel and Paul.

Hence, John concludes a biblical theology of vision explaining that the entire cosmos, heaven and earth, will forever celebrate what the visionary event stood for and will live out its goal: the worship and service of the Lamb who fulfills history and theology. In this way, the vision becomes a perpetual memory for all eternity.

JOHN'S CONTRIBUTION TO A BIBLICAL THEOLOGY OF VISION

As with all our discussions of different visions and theologies, John's theology of vision does not comprise the entire message and purpose of his writing. Much more could be said of the purposes and significance of each part of the book. This analysis does not claim to have exhausted the ideas contained within Revelation or to have explained their complete intent. Rather, I hope to have shown that the vision plays an important role in the book and pieces together a significant amount of the apostle's theological message. More importantly, I have sought to show readers that it makes a substantial contribution to the overarching biblical theology of vision.

With that in mind, John provides the climax of what has developed throughout progressive revelation. He not only discloses the most comprehensive perspective of the visionary event, he also shows how the heavenly courtroom's declaration works out in redemptive history. The apostle seems to intentionally make his writing a hub of intertextual activity to exhibit the convergence of past visions and their theologies. The agenda in John's vision concerns the culmination of that entire theology and all history in the Son.[169] His descriptions of God's consequent judgments and salvation are the actualization of those realities in history. The final outcome of this actualization is the complete realization of the visionary agenda as well as its eternal

---

169. Ruiz, *Ezekiel in the Apocalypse*, 519–20. Ruiz perceptively notes that part of John's theology includes his inner-biblical hermeneutic. John's theology invites the reader to engage "in a dialogue with the text and with the texts within the text," which supports the notion that visions and theology converge in the Apocalypse.

commemoration and celebration. Ultimately, John has intertwined all the visions and theologies into one single storyline, marking the climax of history and theology. The puzzle is now complete.

John does not simply tell believers of this consummation, but instead urges them to make this vision their own (Rev 2–3). Love, endurance, doctrinal fidelity, purity, and fruitfulness all relate to Christians' future hope in the fulfillment of vision and theology. To that effect, the apostle reminds his readers that the fulfillment of Daniel's vision is soon (Rev 22:6).[170] The vision and theology that was previously sealed is now unsealed because of its imminence (Rev 22:10–11).[171] Jesus will return to fulfill Isaiah's theology, carrying reward (22:12; cf. Isa 40:10).[172] Thus, John encourages those who remain faithful. His final words also exhort them to avoid being the immoral persons who, as Paul states, will never inherit the kingdom of God (Rev 22:15; cf. Eph 5:5).[173] Even in the conclusion of his book, the apostle reminds his audience that God is determined to complete the entire vision and theology, just as John (along with all his predecessors) described. Believers look to that moment with an eager, sanctifying expectancy.

---

170. Compare ἃ δεῖ γενέσθαι ἐν τάχει (Rev 22:6) with ἃ δεῖ γενέσθαι ἐπ' ἐσχάτων τῶν ἡμερῶν (Dan 2:28).

171. Osborne, *Revelation*, 784; Beale, *Old Testament in Revelation*, 1129. Compare μὴ σφραγίσῃς τοὺς λόγους τῆς προφητείας τοῦ βιβλίου τούτου in Rev 22:10 with σφράγισαι τὸ βιβλίον ἕως καιροῦ συντελείας in Dan 12:4.

172. Rev 22:12 alludes to God's work to end exile in Isa 40:10. Compare the wording ὁ μισθός μου μετ' ἐμοῦ ἀποδοῦναι ἑκάστῳ in Rev 22:12 with ἰδοὺ ὁ μισθὸς αὐτοῦ μετ' αὐτου in Isa 40:10.

173. Compare οἱ φάρμακοι καὶ οἱ πόρνοι καὶ οἱ φονεῖς καὶ οἱ εἰδωλολάτραι in Rev 22:15 with πᾶς πόρνος ἢ ἀκάθαρτος ἢ πλεονέκτης, ὅ ἐστιν εἰδωλολάτρης, οὐκ ἔχει κληρονομίαν ἐν τῇ βασιλείᾳ τοῦ Χριστοῦ καὶ θεοῦ in Eph 5:5

9

Conclusion

As a discipline biblical-theology often assumes a wide variety of expressions. Yet at the heart of each of these expressions is the overriding presupposition that the rich diversity of Scripture serves its profound unity. Further, this "diversity within unity" is most clearly seen through a consideration of the historical development of theological themes. And, this historical progression of ideas runs from one end of the Bible to the other. In other words, the entire Bible is moving, growing according to a common purpose and towards a common goal (thus we can say that the whole Bible is "eschatological").[1]

A BIBLICAL THEOLOGY OF VISION

Diversity

AS WE SUMMARIZE A biblical theology of vision, I may present it along the lines described by Dumbrell above, starting with its diversity. Isaiah, Ezekiel, Daniel, Paul, and John each had a vision that innertextually relates to a significant portion of their messages and theologies. Our goal here is to summarize such innertextuality. Such a summary can give us a sense of the various theological topics they address and also helps us see how the biblical writers exposit their own visions.

Isaiah's vision encompasses a theology of God's sovereignty, glory, holiness, and salvation. God's holiness will not only judge, but also transform. His glory will tear down competing idols in order to fill the cosmos with his presence alone. This will result in his sole and uncontested dominion over the entire cosmos as he reigns from Zion. Isaiah's vision, however, specifically portrays how the Son is high and lifted up in his saving work. His atoning death brings forth the transforming holiness, glory, and dominion that the vision proclaims. He is the ruler that Isaiah saw.

---

1 Dumbrell, *End of the Beginning*, i.

Ezekiel, in slight contrast, focuses upon the notion of God's presence. His vision of the chariot-throne introduced us to the various dimensions of God's glory. God intends for his glory to fill the entire cosmos. He also desires to display his majesty corporately and within individuals. In sum, the chariot-throne vision exhibits God's agenda to fill the whole earth with glory from the inside out. This is the only solution to Israel's hard heart, which refuses to engage in a relationship with its God. God rides his chariot so that he can save and transform Israel into a relational nation, a transformation that will require a resurrection. In the end, the fullest expression of the vision is the success of God's work in history and in establishing the consummation of his relationship in the future.

Daniel proclaims a message about God's kingdom. The Lord has a plan for history and controls the events of this world from start to finish. That scheme is set to one end: the establishment of God's sole dominion. No kingdom will succeed in thwarting that agenda. The statue will be crushed, as Daniel explains. However, the saints suffer at this time because the fullness of God's kingdom is not yet in the world. Israel is in exile. Such conflict will continue and escalate until one like a son of man comes, as Daniel sees in his central vision. This one will receive all the honor and glory that previous human kings vied for but could never have. This one will establish God's kingdom, just as the stone completely overpowers the statue. This one will grant the saints victory over their persecutors in addition to eternal life and an eternal kingdom. Daniel solidifies the visionary event as the coronation of the Son with massive redemptive historical consequences.

Paul, on the Damascus road, sees the resurrected Christ and understands the realities surrounding the church, salvation, sanctification, and glorification. On the Damascus road, Paul experienced salvation, the reception of the Spirit, as well as the understanding that all history related to Christ. He fleshes these ideas out in his mission and writings. He stresses the atoning work of Christ's death and the soteriological centrality of justification. The apostle explains that sanctification in the church is by the Spirit. His indwelling presence means that the church is the temple and that believers must walk in his transforming power. Jews and Gentiles equally partake of these realities because Christ is worthy of all, he is the second Adam, and all things will be summed up in him. Thus, Paul labors amongst Jews and Gentiles in anticipation of the time when what he saw on the Damascus road becomes the full reality throughout the world. To Paul, that moment will consummate salvation and entail resurrection, new creation, and subjecting all things to Christ. That is what the church hopes for and points to.

John's vision provides a view of what is to come. God's plan of history will unfold as he fulfills all things in Christ. God will judge the world, leading to the climax of history. God will also fulfill prophecies associated with the visionary event that leads to the climax of theology. All of that finds its *telos* in Christ, who is the fulfillment of history, theology, and vision. Overall, the central vision in the Apocalypse becomes the commissioning of God's eschatological activity as well as its final destination. In the end, the world will be brought to conform with the realities in the vision as heaven comes to earth. De-creating judgments will lead to a new Exodus and a new creation. The suffering of the saints will end in victory and eternal life. Eternity will be spent celebrating the success of what God declared through the vision. This is the believer's hope and motivation.

I have deliberately not discussed the interconnections between the visions and theologies to show the assorted theological issues involved in a biblical theology of vision. While some overlap exists even in the above discussion, the matters of sovereignty, holiness, salvation, sanctification, glory, presence, kingdom, suffering, perseverance, the Spirit, Jews and Gentiles, ecclesiology, eschatology, and Christ constitute a wide range of issues. God's workings within a biblical theology of vision are not monolithic, but complex.

Unity

Nonetheless, a biblical theology of vision demonstrates that the diverse topics above do not work against each other or even apart from each other, but rather all together. This is fundamentally because they stem from one visionary event, and thus one agenda, and are ultimately linked to one person: Jesus Christ. The visions all revealed different aspects of the future moment when God crowns his Son and works out all things for his glory. The works of the earliest readers of these texts up to recent scholarship, as well as an exegetical examination of these passages, point us toward that conclusion. The intertextuality between the visions of the prophets and apostles relates to the intertextuality of their theologies.

Moreover, their interconnections tie them into a single storyline, part of God's working in redemptive history. A biblical theology of vision accomplishes this in two ways. First, it demonstrates the role of the visionary event in redemptive history. While the innertextuality of vision and theology shows the nature of the vision itself—its theological meaning, or its eschatological ramification on earth—the intertextuality of vision demonstrates how all of those realities are part of the coronation of the Son and the ramifications of that inauguration. That is the moment that fulfills God's plan in the Son from heaven to earth and from heavenly court declaration to history. History moves to that climax. Second, such intertextuality actually illustrates the way the ministries of the prophets and apostles work together toward this end goal. As I mentioned, the prophets and apostles are a microcosm of their messages. The vision is not merely the starting point for their mission but also the *telos*. They labored and even gave their lives to that very end. As such, their work advances the cause of the vision within redemptive history.

In light of this, we can see how the interconnected theologies and the resulting story unfold. Isaiah begins this by acknowledging that though Israel will soon go into exile as an unholy people, God will one day reverse all of this through his saving work. He points the people of God to the time when the Servant will be high and lifted up. That marks the era when the people will be cleansed and know that God reigns from his throne. They will worship God, whose glory will fill the entire cosmos.

Ezekiel continues Isaiah's work by explaining the significance of the throne in the heavenly court. He thereby expands upon Isaiah's paradigm by explaining how God's glory will fill the earth. God's presence will go even into the heart of man and ultimately, make them a new, resurrected people. He has not left them, but works out all things to dwell within them more richly than ever before. The completion of Ezekiel's theology as God returns to his temple in Jerusalem compliments the completion of Isaiah's theology of God's reign from his house in Zion. So Ezekiel points people to a similar goal as Isaiah had, for their theologies work together.

Daniel integrates the visions and theologies of Isaiah and Ezekiel into his own. His vision includes the Ancient of Days sitting on a throne, as Isaiah saw, and specifically, Daniel portrays that God sits upon the chariot-throne as Ezekiel's envisioned. If the reader did not understand that Isaiah and Ezekiel's visions were directed towards the same eschatological moment, Daniel makes this clear. He explains that the vision pertains to the fulfillment of God's kingdom, which entails the anointing of the holy place, as Ezekiel proclaimed, as well as the fulfillment of atonement and God's reign, as Isaiah foresaw. In essence, Daniel proclaims that the visionary event fulfills vision and prophecy. The prophet not only draws past visions closer together, but also places them along the same storyline. He shows that they all deal with the visionary event that crowns the Son to start the consummation of history, as articulated by his own vision and theology as well as those of his predecessors. Kingdoms and kings will rise and fall, but one day, the Son of Man will be inaugurated and will reign forever, winning victory for the suffering saints. With that, the people of God are given a clear expectation of God's plan and its climax in the visionary event. They await that moment as God moves the present toward the eschatological.

This progresses to Paul, who, seeing Christ after his death and resurrection, understands that he sees the same glorious individual as his predecessors did in their visions and experiences the inauguration of those related theologies. Salvation has come in Christ, as Isaiah envisioned. The Spirit has come in Christ, as Ezekiel proclaimed. Jew and Gentile have come together in Christ, as Daniel saw in his vision. This understanding informs Paul's mission to prepare the church to anticipate the consummation of the vision. Jew and Gentile join together in expectation of unified service to the Son. The radical conversion of believers looks forward to the final resurrection. Salvation will find its full fruition in the end of exile, the deliverance of all God's people, and the establishment of a new creation. Paul's theology, although unique, works with his predecessors' towards their complete fulfillment. The eschatological has come into the present, but at the same time, the present accelerates even more vigorously toward the eschatological.

Such movement paves the way for John, who fills out the substance of that expectation. History will soon reach its climax, as Paul predicted. Daniel's vision and theology will come to pass soon. Past writers have pointed to this moment as the hope of God's people, and John's description lives up to that expectation. The visionary event encompasses the fullness of a biblical theology of vision, and the church will share in that fullness through the victory of their Savior, Jesus Christ. This moment proclaims his right over the entire cosmos in recognition of what he has accomplished. This moment begins his final work to enact all that John's predecessors envisioned. The events that follow testify that this is precisely what occurs. History moves in the direction of fulfilling vision and theology. God's judgments implement Isaiah's concept of new creation, which facilitates the fullness of his glory, as anticipated by Ezekiel. God's workings of salvation also actualize what Isaiah prophesied. As a result, people from every tongue, nation, and tribe come and worship God, as Daniel foresaw. All of that completes what Paul anticipated and moves to the climax of the return of Christ, who establishes his kingdom in fulfillment of prophecy and vision. God's Millennial Kingdom proclaims the success of God and his Son in completing the agenda of the visionary event. The echoes of the vision will be memorialized for eternity as the saints worship God for what he has accomplished in fulfilling vision and theology.

Overall, a biblical theology of vision demonstrates the cohesion of theology and history. The diversity of topics in Scripture is not random, but rather is tied together by a central agenda set by the visionary event. God moves all history to anticipate, inaugurate, and ultimately consummate that agenda in his Son. The entire biblical theology of vision is for his honor and glory.

A START AND NOT A FINISH

Hopefully, this entire discussion has reinforced that the visions play an important role in biblical theology. It helps us better grasp the holistic message of certain prophets and apostles. It also covers a panoply of theological issues that can help to shape or reinforce our convictions. More than that, a biblical theology of vision can also show how these various topics collaborate in their mutual fulfillment and completion. What we have observed affirms the organic unity of diversity, part of the goal of any biblical theology. Finally, the visions can help align these various writers to their contribution and function in the storyline of redemptive history. Such a discussion thereby provides shape to how we view the plotline of Scripture. The visionary event sets a significant agenda within God's plan for the world, and the peak of history should include that eschatological moment in the heavenly courtroom.

Nonetheless, I would be the first to admit that this is a start and not a finish. This is *a* biblical theology of vision and not *the* biblical theology of vision. Further comments can certainly be made about how the vision ties in with the theology of each respective biblical writer. More work can and should be done in examining the intertextuality between the various visions and their respective theologies. More answers will be needed to more questions and objections against the visions' unity. That may lead to more qualifications or better articulations of that idea. Further investigation might take place concerning the background of visionary interpretation in extra-biblical literature. Beyond what is broached here, other visions may relate to this theme. For example, what about the transfiguration of the Lord, which is in the context of seeing the kingdom (Matt 16:28—17:13)? What about Stephen's vision of the Son of Man (Acts 7:56)? How does Zechariah play into this scheme?

My goal is for us to continue study along these innertextual and intertextual lines. Such research may lead us to expand upon or temper my ideas about a biblical theology of vision. *That is welcomed.* My goal is not to defend myself, but to articulate the truth and exalt the Savior. In that vein, this is not the final word, but a word to start a conversation on these issues. Hopefully, this work will compel our eyes to look upon familiar and glorious texts and plumb them for all their beauty and depth. Ultimately, from this, we will see the Lamb who was slain receiving all the glory he is due in recognition of his triumph in theology and history. My hope is that the reader grasps the immense weight of that moment as all the theologies and visions of Isaiah, Ezekiel, Daniel, Paul, and John are summed up in the Son.

BE THOU MY VISION

With that, a biblical theology of vision cannot be lost upon us as readers. Even if readers disagree with various points of this book, the weight of the visions of past prophets is an unmistakable reality. This study has argued that a vision captivated Isaiah, Ezekiel, Daniel, Paul, and John. They anticipated it, wrote about it, and sacrificed their lives because of it. Paul prescribes Christian ministry in light of that vision, and John urges us to accept it as our own to persevere, love, and pursue holiness. We carry on their mission and vision, as the present moves toward the eschatological, to hope as they hoped and to yearn as they yearned for the glory of Christ in all things. May he be our vision above all.

Bibliography

Alexander, Philip S. "Enoch, Third Book Of." In *The Anchor Bible Dictionary*, edited by David Noel Freedman et al., 2:522–26. New York: Doubleday, 1992.
Alexander, Ralph. "Ezekiel." In *The Expositor's Bible Commentary*, edited by Frank E. Gaebelein et al., 6:737–996. Grand Rapids: Zondervan, 1986.
Allen, Leslie C. *Ezekiel 1–19*. Word Biblical Commentary 28. Dallas: Word, 2004.
———. *Ezekiel 20–48*. Word Biblical Commentary 29. Dallas: Word, 2004.
Andersen, Francis I. "Enoch, Second Book Of." In *The Anchor Bible Dictionary*, edited by David Noel Freedman et al., 2:516–22.
Anderson, Robert A. *Signs and Wonders: A Commentary on the Book of Daniel*. International Theological Commentary. Grand Rapids: Eerdmans, 1984.
Archer, Gleason. *A Survey of Old Testament Introduction*. Chicago: Moody, 1994.
Ashley, Timothy R. *The Book of Numbers*. New International Commentary on the Old Testament. Grand Rapids: Eerdmans, 1993.
Aune, David E. *Revelation 1–5*. Word Biblical Commentary 52a. Dallas: Word, 1997.
Aus, Roger D. "Relevance of Isaiah 66:7 to Revelation 12 and 2 Thessalonians 1." *Zeitschrift für die neutestamentliche Wissenschaft und die Kunde der älteren Kirche* 67 (1976) 252–68.
Averbeck, Richard E. "Christian Interpretations of Isaiah 53." In *The Gospel According to Isaiah 53: Encountering the Suffering Servant in Jewish and Christian Theology*, edited by Darrell L. Bock and Mitch Glaser, 33–60. Grand Rapids: Kregel, 2012.
———. "כפר." In *New International Dictionary of Old Testament Theology and Exegesis*, edited by Willem A. VanGemeren, 2:689–711. Grand Rapids: Zondervan, 1997.
Bailey, Daniel P. "The Intertextual Relationship of Daniel 12:2 and Isaiah 26:19: Evidence from Qumran and the Greek Versions." *Tyndale Bulletin* 51 (2000) 305–8.
Baldwin, Joyce G. *Daniel: An Introduction and Commentary*. Tyndale Old Testament Commentaries. Downers Grove, IL: InterVarsity, 1978.
Barker, K. L. "Premillennialism in the Book of Daniel." *Master's Seminary Journal* 4 (1993) 25–43.
Barker, K. L., and W. Bailey. *Micah, Nahum, Habakkuk, Zephaniah*. New American Commentary 20. Nashville: Broadman & Holman, 1998.
Barnett, Paul. *The Second Epistle to the Corinthians*. New International Commentary on the New Testament. Grand Rapids: Eerdmans, 1997.
Barrick, W. Boyd. "The Straight-Legged Cherubim of Ezekiel's Inaugural Vision (Ezekiel 1:7a)." *Catholic Biblical Quarterly* 44 (1982) 543–50.
Barry, John. *The Resurrected Servant in Isaiah*. Milton Keynes, UK: Paternoster, 2010.
Bartelt, Andrew H. "The Centrality of Isaiah 6(-8) within Isaiah 2–12." *Concordia Journal* 30 (2004) 316–35.
Bauckham, Richard. "Apocalypses." In *Justification and Variegated Nomism*, edited by D. A. Carson, Peter T. O'Brien, and Mark A. Seifrid, 1:135–88. Grand Rapids: Baker Academic, 2004.
———. *The Climax of Prophecy: Studies on the Book of Revelation*. Edinburgh: T. & T. Clark, 1993.
———. *The Theology of the Book of Revelation*. Cambridge: Cambridge University Press, 1993.
Baynes, Leslie A. "Revelation 5:1 and 10:2a, 8–10 in the Earliest Greek Tradition: A Response to Richard Bauckham." *Journal of Biblical Literature* 129 (2010) 801–16.

Bibliography

Beale, G. K. *The Book of Revelation: A Commentary on the Greek Text.* New International Greek Testament Commentary. Grand Rapids: Eerdmans, 1999.

———. "Did Jesus and His Followers Preach the Right Doctrine from the Wrong Texts? An Examination of the Presuppositions of Jesus' and the Apostles' Exegetical Method." In *The Right Doctrine from the Wrong Texts?*, edited by G. K. Beale, 387–404. Grand Rapids: Baker, 1994.

———. "The Influence of Daniel Upon the Structure and Theology of John's Apocalypse." *Journal of the Evangelical Theological Society* 27 (1984) 413–23.

———. "Isaiah 6:9-13: A Retributive Taunt Against Idolatry." *Vetus Testamentum* 41 (1991) 257–78.

———. *John's Use of the Old Testament in Revelation.* Journal for the Study of the New Testament: Supplement Series 166. Sheffield: Sheffield Academic, 1999.

———. *The Temple and the Church's Mission: A Biblical Theology of the Dwelling Place of God.* New Studies in Biblical Theology 17. Downers Grove, IL: InterVarsity, 2004.

———. *We Become What We Worship: A Biblical Theology of Idolatry.* Downers Grove, IL: InterVarsity, 2008.

Bergen, Robert D. *1, 2 Samuel.* New American Commentary 7. Nashville: Broadman & Holman, 1996.

Beuken, W. A. M. "The Manifestation of Yahweh and the Commission of Isaiah: Isaiah 6 Read Against the Background of Isaiah 1." *Calvin Theological Journal* 39 (2004) 72–87.

Block, Daniel I. "Beyond the Grave: Ezekiel's Vision of Death and Afterlife." *Bulletin for Biblical Research* 2 (1992) 113–41.

———. *The Book of Ezekiel.* 2 vols. New International Commentary on the Old Testament. Grand Rapids: Eerdmans, 1997-98.

———. "Bringing Back David: Ezekiel's Messianic Hope." In *The Lord's Anointed: Interpretation of Old Testament Messianic Texts*, edited by Philip E. Satterwaite, Richard S. Hess, and Gordon J. Wenham, 167–88. Grand Rapids: Baker, 1995.

———. "Gog and the Pouring Out of the Spirit: Reflections on Ezekiel 39:21–29." *Vetus Testamentum* 37 (1987) 257–70.

———. "Text and Emotion: A Study in the 'Corruptions' in Ezekiel's Inaugural Vision (Ezekiel 1:4–28)." *Catholic Biblical Quarterly* 50 (1988) 418–42.

Blomberg, Craig L. "The Legitimacy and Limits of Harmonization." In *Hermeneutics, Authority, and Canon*, edited by D. A. Carson and John D. Woodbridge, 135–74. Grand Rapids: Zondervan, 1986.

Bock, Darrell. *Acts.* Baker Exegetical Commentary on the New Testament 3. Grand Rapids: Baker Academic, 2007.

———. "A Theology of Luke-Acts." In *A Biblical Theology of the New Testament*, edited by Roy Zuck and Darrell Bock, 87–166. Chicago: Moody, 1994.

Boyarin, Daniel. "Daniel 7, Intertextuality, and the History of Israel's Cult." *Harvard Theological Review* 105 (2012) 139–62.

———. *The Jewish Gospels: The Story of the Jewish Christ.* New York: New Press, 2012.

Brownlee, William Hugh. "The Servant of the Lord in the Qumran Scrolls." *Bulletin of the American Schools of Oriental Research* 132 (1953) 8–15.

———. "The Text of Isaiah 6:13 in the Light of DSIa." *Vetus Testamentum* 1 (1951) 296–98.

Broyles, Craig C. "Traditions, Intertextuality, and Canon." In *Interpreting the Old Testament: A Guide for Exegesis*, edited by Craig C. Broyles, 157–76. Grand Rapids: Baker, 2001.

Bruce, F. F. *The Book of the Acts.* Rev. ed. New International Commentary on the New Testament. Grand Rapids: Eerdmans, 1988.

———. *The Epistle to the Galatians: A Commentary on the Greek Text.* New International Greek Testament Commentary. Grand Rapids: Eerdmans, 1982.

———. *The Epistles to the Colossians, to Philemon, and to the Ephesians.* New International Commentary on the New Testament. Grand Rapids: Eerdmans, 1984.

———. *1 and 2 Thessalonians.* Word Biblical Commentary 45. Waco, TX: Word, 1982.

———. *Paul: Apostle of the Heart Set Free.* Grand Rapids: Eerdmans, 1984.

Bruce, Les P. "Discourse Theme and the Narratives of Daniel." *Bibliotheca Sacra* 160 (2003) 174–86.

Carson, D. A. *The Gospel According to John.* Pillar New Testament Commentary. Grand Rapids: Eerdmans, 1991.

———. "Matthew." In *The Expositor's Bible Commentary,* 8:3–602. Grand Rapids: Zondervan, 1995.

Cate, Robert L. "We Need to Be Saved (Isaiah 1:1-20, 5:1-12, 6:1-13)." *Review & Expositor* 88 (1991) 137-51.

Childs, Brevard. *Introduction to the Old Testament as Scripture.* Philadelphia: Fortress, 1999.

Chisholm, Robert B. "The Christological Fulfillment of Isaiah's Servant Songs." *Bibliotheca Sacra* 163 (2006) 387-404.

———. *Handbook on the Prophets: Isaiah, Jeremiah, Lamentations, Ezekiel, Daniel, Minor Prophets.* Grand Rapids: Baker, 2002.

Ciampa, Roy E., and Brian S. Rosner. "1 Corinthians." In *Commentary on the New Testament Use of the Old Testament*, edited by G. K. Beale and D. A. Carson, 695-752. Grand Rapids: Baker, 2007.

———. *The First Letter to the Corinthians.* Pillar New Testament Commentary. Grand Rapids: Eerdmans, 2010.

Clines, David J. A. *Job 21-37.* World Biblical Commentary 18A. Nashville: Thomas Nelson, 2006.

Collins, Adela Yarbro, and John Joseph Collins. *King and Messiah as Son of God: Divine, Human, and Angelic Messianic Figures in Biblical and Related Literature.* Grand Rapids: Eerdmans, 2008.

Collins, John Joseph. "The Apocalyptic Context of Christian Origins." *Michigan Quarterly Review* 22 (1983) 250-64.

———. *The Apocalyptic Vision of the Book of Daniel.* Harvard Semitic Monographs 16. Missoula, MT: Scholars, 1977.

———. *Daniel.* Hermeneia. Minneapolis: Fortress, 1993.

———. "The Son of Man and the Saints of the Most High in the Book of Daniel." *Journal of Biblical Literature* 93 (1974) 50-66.

Conzelmann, Hans. *Acts of the Apostles: A Commentary on the Acts of the Apostles.* Edited by Eldon Jay Epp with Christopher R. Matthews. Translated by James Limburg et al. Philadelphia: Fortress, 1987.

Cooper, Lamar Eugene. *Ezekiel.* New American Commentary 17. Nashville: Broadman & Holman, 1994.

Craigie, Peter C. *The Book of Deuteronomy.* New International Commentary on the Old Testament. Grand Rapids: Eerdmans, 1976.

Cranfield, Charles E. B. *A Critical and Exegetical Commentary on the Epistle to the Romans.* 2 vols. Edinburgh: T. & T. Clark, 1979.

Culver, Robert Duncan. *Daniel and the Latter Days.* Chicago: Moody, 1954.

Davies, Philip R. "Eschatology in the Book of Daniel." *Journal for the Study of the Old Testament* 17 (1980) 33-53.

Davila, James R. "4QMess Ar (4Q534) and Merkavah Mysticism." *Dead Sea Discoveries* 5 (1998) 367-81.

DeVries, Simon J. *1 Kings.* 2nd ed. Word Biblical Commentary. Dallas: Word, 2004.

Dillard, Raymond B. "Harmonization: A Help and Hindrance." In *Inerrancy and Hermeneutic: A Tradition, a Challenge, a Debate*, edited by Harvey M. Conn, 151-64. Grand Rapids: Baker, 1988.

Dillard, Raymond B., and Tremper Longman. *An Introduction to the Old Testament.* Grand Rapids: Zondervan, 1994.

Dumbrell, William J. *The End of the Beginning: Revelation 21-22 and the Old Testament.* Grand Rapids: Baker, 1985.

Dunn, James D. G. *Christology in the Making: A New Testament Inquiry into the Origins of the Doctrine of the Incarnation.* Philadelphia: Westminster, 1980.

———. "The Danielic Son of Man in the New Testament." In *The Book of Daniel*, edited by John J. Collins and Peter W. Flint, 2:528-49. Leiden: Brill, 2001.

———. "Echoes of Intra-Jewish Polemic in Paul's Letter to the Galatians." *Journal of Biblical Literature* 112 (1993) 459-77.

———. *The Epistles to the Colossians and to Philemon: A Commentary on the Greek Text.* New International Greek Testament Commentary. Grand Rapids: Eerdmans, 1996.

———. "The Justice of God: A Renewed Perspective on Justification by Faith." The Henton Davies Lecture, Regent's Park College, Oxford. *Journal of Theological Studies* 43 (1992) 1-22.

———. "Paul and Justification by Faith." In *The Road from Damascus*, edited by Richard Longenecker, 85-101. Grand Rapids: Eerdmans, 1997.

———. *Romans 1-8.* Word Biblical Commentary. Dallas: Word, 1998.

———. *Romans 9-16.* Word Biblical Commentary. Dallas: Word, 1998.

———. *Theology of Paul the Apostle.* Grand Rapids: Eerdmans, 2006.

Bibliography

Eslinger, Lyle M. "The Infinite in a Finite Organical Perception (Isaiah VI 1–5)." *Vetus Testamentum* 45 (1995) 145–73.

Evans, Craig A. "Daniel in the New Testament: Visions of God's Kingdom." In *The Book of Daniel*, edited by John J. Collins and Peter W. Flint, 2:490–527. Leiden: Brill, 2001.

———. "Isa 6:9–13 in the Context of Isaiah's Theology." *Journal of the Evangelical Theological Society* 29 (1986) 139–46.

Fee, Gordon D. *The First and Second Epistles to the Thessalonians*. Grand Rapids: Eerdmans, 2009.

———. *The First Epistle to the Corinthians*. Grand Rapids: Eerdmans, 1987.

———. "Paul's Conversion as Key to His Understanding of the Spirit." In *The Road from Damascus*, edited by Richard Longenecker, 166–83. Grand Rapids: Eerdmans, 1997.

Feinberg, Charles. "The Virgin Birth in the Old Testament and Isaiah 7:14." *Bibliotheca Sacra* 119 (1968) 251–58.

Fekkes, Jan. *Isaiah and Prophetic Traditions in the Book of Revelation: Visionary Antecedents and Their Development*. Journal for the Study of the New Testament: Supplement Series 93. Sheffield: JSOT, 1994.

Fishbane, Michael. *Biblical Interpretation in Ancient Israel*. Oxford: Clarendon, 1985.

Ford, Desmond. *Daniel*. Nashville: Southern Publishing Association, 1978.

Fung, Ronald Y. K. *The Epistle to the Galatians*. New International Commentary on the New Testament. Grand Rapids: Eerdmans, 1988.

Garland, David E. *1 Corinthians*. Grand Rapids: Baker Academic, 2003.

———. *2 Corinthians*. New American Commentary. Nashville: Broadman & Holman, 1999.

Gathercole, Simon J. "The Justification of Wisdom (Matt 11.19b/Luke 7.35)." *New Testament Studies* 49 (2003) 476–88.

Gentry, Peter J. "Daniel's Seventy Weeks and the New Exodus." *Southern Baptist Journal of Theology* 14 (2010) 26–44.

George, Timothy. *Galatians*. New American Commentary. Nashville: Broadman & Holman, 1994.

Gignilliat, Mark. "Theological Exegesis as Exegetical Showing: A Case of Isaiah's Figural Potentiality." *International Journal of Systematic Theology* 12 (2010) 217–32.

Goldingay, J. E. *Daniel*. Word Biblical Commentary. Dallas: Word, 2002.

———. "Daniel in the Context of Old Testament Theology." In *The Book of Daniel*, edited by John J. Collins and Peter W. Flint, 2:639–60. Leiden: Brill, 2001.

———. "The Stories in Daniel: A Narrative Politics." *Journal for the Study of the Old Testament* 37 (1987) 99–116.

Goswell, Greg. "The Temple Theme in the Book of Daniel." *Journal of the Evangelical Theological Society* 55 (2012) 509–20.

Green, Gene L. *The Letters to the Thessalonians*. Pillar New Testament Commentary. Grand Rapids: Eerdmans, 2002.

Guthrie, Donald. *New Testament Introduction*. Downers Grove, IL: InterVarsity, 1990.

Hafemann, Scott J. "The Glory and Veil of Moses in 2 Corinthians 3:7–14." In *The Right Doctrine from the Wrong Text? Essays on the Use of the Old Testament in the New*, edited by G. K. Beale, 295–312. Grand Rapids: Baker, 1994.

Halperin, David J. *The Faces of the Chariot: Early Jewish Responses to Ezekiel's Vision*. Texte und Studien zum antiken Judentum 16. Tübingen: Mohr, 1988.

Hamilton, James M. *God's Glory in Salvation Through Judgment*. Wheaton, IL: Crossway, 2010.

———. *God's Indwelling Presence: The Holy Spirit in the Old & New Testaments*. Nashville: Broadman & Holman, 2006.

———. "'The Virgin Will Conceive': Typological Fulfillment in Matthew 1:18–23." In *Built Upon the Rock*, edited by Daniel M. Gurtner and John Nolland, 228–47. Grand Rapids: Eerdmans, 2008.

Hamilton, Victor P. *The Book of Genesis: Chapters 1–17*. New International Commentary on the Old Testament. Grand Rapids: Eerdmans, 1990.

Hamm, Dennis. "Paul's Blindness and Its Healing: Clues to Symbolic Intent (Acts 9; 22 and 26)." *Biblica* 71 (1990) 63–72.

Harris, Murray J. *The Second Epistle to the Corinthians*. Grand Rapids: Eerdmans, 2005.

Hartenstein, Friedhelm. "Cherubim and Seraphim in the Bible and in Light of Ancient Near Eastern Sources." In *Angels: The Concept of Celestial Beings: Origins, Development, and Reception*, edited by Friedrich V. Reiterer, Tobias Nicklas, and Karin Schöpflin, 156-88. Berlin: de Gruyter, 2007.

Hartley, John. *Leviticus*. Word Biblical Commentary. Dallas: Word, 1992.

Harvey, Barry. "On Seeing: Isaiah 6:1-12." *Review & Expositor* 97 (2000) 97-104.

Hawthorne, Gerald F. *Philippians*. Word Biblical Commentary. Dallas: Word, 2004.

Hays, Richard B. *Echoes of Scripture in the Letters of Paul*. New Haven: Yale University Press, 1989.

Hitchcock, Mark L. "A Critique of the Preterist View of the Temple in Revelation 11:1-2." *Bibliotheca Sacra* 164 (2007) 219-36.

Hoehner, H. W. *Ephesians: An Exegetical Commentary*. Grand Rapids: Baker, 2002.

Hofius, Otfried. "The Fourth Servant Song in the New Testament Letters." In *The Suffering Servant: Isaiah 53 in Jewish and Christian Sources*, edited by Bernd Janowski and Peter Stuhlmacher, 163-88. Grand Rapids: Eerdmans, 2004.

House, Paul R. "Isaiah's Call and Its Context in Isaiah 1-6." *Criswell Theological Review* 6 (1993) 207-22.

———. *Old Testament Theology*. Downers Grove, IL: InterVarsity, 1998.

Iwry, Samuel. "Masṣēbāh and Bāmāh in 1Q Isaiah 6:13." *Journal of Biblical Literature* 76 (1957) 225-32.

Janowski, Bernd. "He Bore Our Sins: Isaiah 53 and the Drama of Taking Another's Place." In *The Suffering Servant: Isaiah 53 in Jewish and Christian Sources*, edited by Bernd Janowski and P. Stuhlmacher, 48-74. Grand Rapids: Eerdmans, 2004.

Jauhiainen, Marko. "Recapitulation and Chronological Progression in John's Apocalypse: Towards a New Perspective." *New Testament Studies* 49 (2003) 543-59.

Jenni, Ernst. "הֵיכָל." In *Theological Lexicon of the Old Testament*, edited by Ernst Jenni and Claus Westermann, translated by Mark E. Biddle, 1:234-36. Peabody, MA: Hendrickson, 1997.

Johnston, Gordon H. "Messianic Trajectories in Jeremiah, Ezekiel, and Daniel." In *Jesus the Messiah: Tracing the Promises, Expectations, and Coming of Israel's King*, edited by Herbert W. Bateman IV, Gordon H. Johnston, and Darrell L. Bock, 169-90. Grand Rapids: Kregel, 2012.

Joines, Karen Randolph. "Winged Serpents in Isaiah's Inaugural Vision." *Journal of Biblical Literature* 86 (1967) 410-15.

Kaiser, Walter C. *The Messiah in the Old Testament*. Grand Rapids: Zondervan, 1995.

Kanagaraj, Jey J. "Jesus the King, Merkabah Mysticism and the Gospel of John." *Tyndale Bulletin* 47 (1996) 349-66.

Kasemann, Ernst. "God's Righteousness in Paul." *Journal of Theology and Church* 1 (1965) 100-110.

Kee, Min Suc. "The Heavenly Council and Its Type-Scene." *Journal for the Study of the Old Testament* 31 (2007) 259-73.

Keel, Othmar. *Jahwe-Visionen und Siegelkunst: Eine neue Deutung der Majestätsschilderungen in Jes 6, Ez 1 und 10 und Sach 4*. SBS 84/85. Stuttgart: Katholisches Bibelwerk, 1977.

Keil, Carl F., and Franz Delitzsch. *Commentary on the Old Testament*. Peabody, MA: Hendrickson, 2002.

Kidner, Derek. "Isaiah." In *New Bible Commentary*, edited by Gordon J. Wenham, Alec Motyer, and D. A. Carson, 629-70. Downers Grove, IL: InterVarsity, 1994.

Kim, Seyoon. *The Origin of Paul's Gospel*. Tübingen: Mohr, 1981.

———. *Paul and the New Perspective: Second Thoughts on the Origin of Paul's Gospel*. Grand Rapids: Eerdmans, 2002.

Knibb, Michael A. "The Date of the Parables of Enoch: A Critical Review." *New Testament Studies* 25 (1979) 345-59.

———. "Messianism in the Pseudepigrapha in the Light of the Scrolls." *Dead Sea Discoveries* 2 (1995) 165-84.

Knight, George W. *The Pastoral Epistles: A Commentary on the Greek Text*. New International Greek Testament Commentary. Grand Rapids: Eerdmans, 1992.

Köhler, Ludwig, et al. *The Hebrew Aramaic Lexicon of the Old Testament*. 2 vols. Leiden: Brill, 2000.

Korner, Ralph J. "'And I Saw . . .': An Apocalyptic Literary Convention for Structural Identification in the Apocalypse." *Novum Testamentum* 42 (2000) 160-83.

Köstenberger, Andreas J. *John*. Baker Exegetical Commentary on the New Testament. Grand Rapids: Baker, 2004.

Kowalski, Beate. "Transformation of Ezekiel in John's Revelation." In *Transforming Visions*, edited by William A. Tooman and Michael A. Lyons, 279-311. Eugene, OR: Pickwick, 2010.

Bibliography

Kratz, Reinhard Gregor. "The Visions of Daniel." In *The Book of Daniel*, edited by John J. Collins and Peter Flint, 1:91–113. Leiden: Brill, 2001.

Kraus, Hans-Joachim. *A Continental Commentary: Psalms 60–150*. Minneapolis: Fortress, 1993.

Lacheman, E. "The Seraphim of Isaiah 6." *The Jewish Quarterly Review* 59 (1968) 71–72.

Lacocque, André. "Allusions to Creation in Daniel 7." In *The Book of Daniel*, edited by John J. Collins and Peter Flint, 1:114–31. Leiden: Brill, 2001.

———. *The Book of Daniel*. Translated by David Pellauer. Atlanta: John Knox, 1979.

Landy, Francis. "Seraphim and Poetic Process." In *The Labour of Reading: Desire, Alienation, and Biblical Interpretation*, edited by Fiona C. Black et al., 15–34. Atlanta: SBL 1999.

———. "Strategies of Concentration and Diffusion in Isaiah 6." *Biblical Interpretation* 7 (1999) 58–86.

Levenson, Jon D. *Resurrection and the Restoration of Israel: The Ultimate Victory of the God of Life*. New Haven: Yale University Press, 2006.

———. "The Temple and the World." *The Journal of Religion* 64 (1984) 275–98.

Liebreich, Leon J. "The Position of Chapter Six in the Book of Isaiah." *Hebrew Union College Annual* 25 (1954) 37–40.

Lincoln, A. T. *Ephesians*. Word Biblical Commentary. Dallas: Word, 1990.

Lindars, B. *New Testament Apologetic: The Doctrinal Significance of the Old Testament Quotations*. London: SCM, 1961.

Lindsell, Harold. *The Battle for the Bible*. Grand Rapids: Zondervan, 1976.

Longenecker, R. *Biblical Exegesis in the Apostolic Period*. Grand Rapids: Eerdmans, 1975.

———. *Galatians*. Word Biblical Commentary. Dallas: Word, 1990.

Lucas, E. *Daniel*. Apollos Old Testament Commentary. Downers Grove, IL: InterVarsity, 2002.

Martin, D. Michael. *1, 2 Thessalonians*. New American Commentary 33. Nashville: Broadman & Holman, 1995.

Martin, R. *2 Corinthians*. Word Biblical Commentary. Waco, TX: Word, 1986.

———. *Reconciliation: A Study of Paul's Theology*. Atlanta: John Knox, 1981.

Mathewson, David. "Isaiah in Revelation." In *Isaiah in the New Testament*, edited by Steve Moyise and Maarten J. J. Menken, 189–210. London: T. & T. Clark, 2005.

Matthews, K. *Genesis 11:27—50:26*. Nashville: Broadman & Holman, 2005.

Merrill, E. H. *Kingdom of Priests: A History of Old Testament Israel*. Grand Rapids: Baker, 1987.

Michaels, J. *Revelation*. IVP New Testament Commentary Series. Downers Grove, IL: InterVarsity, 1997.

Miller, Stephen R. *Daniel*. New American Commentary 18. Nashville: Broadman & Holman, 1994.

Montgomery, J. *A Critical and Exegetical Commentary on the Book of Daniel*. International Critical Commentary. Edinburgh: T. & T. Clark, 1989.

Moo, Douglas J. *The Epistle to the Romans*. Grand Rapids: Eerdmans, 1996.

———. "Israel and the Law in Romans 5–11: Interaction with the New Perspective." In *Justification and Variegated Nomism: The Teaching of Paul*, edited by D. A. Carson, M. Seifrid, and P. O'Brien, 185–216. Grand Rapids: Eerdmans, 2004.

Morgenstern, Julian. "'Son of Man' of Daniel 7:13f.: A New Interpretation." *Journal of Biblical Literature* 80 (1961) 65–77.

Morris, Leon. *The Gospel According to John*. New International Commentary on the New Testament. Grand Rapids: Eerdmans, 1995.

———. *The Gospel According to Matthew*. Pillar New Testament Commentary. Grand Rapids: Eerdmans, 2000.

Motyer, Alec. *The Prophecy of Isaiah: An Introduction and Commentary*. Downers Grove, IL: InterVarsity, 1993.

Mounce, Robert H. *The Book of Revelation*. Grand Rapids: Eerdmans, 1997.

Mounce, William D. *Pastoral Epistles*. Word Biblical Commentary. Dallas: Word, 2000.

Moyise, Steve. "Seeing the Old Testament Through a Lens." *Irish Biblical Studies* 23 (2001) 36–42.

Muilenburg, James. "The Son of Man in Daniel and the Ethiopic Apocalypse of Enoch." *Journal of Biblical Literature* 79 (1960) 197–209.

Murray, D. F. "Divine Prerogative and Royal Pretension: Pragmatics, Poetics and Polemics in a Narrative Sequence about David (2 Samuel 5.17–17.29)." *Journal for the Study of the Old Testament Supplement Series* 264 (1998).

Nanos, Mark D. "What Was at Stake in Peter's 'Eating with Gentiles' at Antioch?" In *The Galatians Debate: Contemporary Issues in Rhetorical and Historical Interpretation*, edited by Mark D. Nanos, 282–320. Peabody, MA: Hendrickson, 2002.

Nickelsburg, George W. E. "Apocalyptic and Myth in 1 Enoch 6–11." *Journal of Biblical Literature* 96 (1977) 383–405.

———. "Eschatology: Early Jewish Literature." In *The Anchor Bible Dictionary*, edited by David Noel Freedman et al., 2:579–94. New York: Doubleday, 1992.

———. *1 Enoch: A Commentary on the Book of 1 Enoch*. Edited by Klaus Baltzer. Minneapolis: Fortress, 2001.

———. *1 Enoch 2: A Commentary on the Book of 1 Enoch: Chapters 37–82*. Hermeneia. Minneapolis: Fortress, 2012.

Nicol, George G. "Isaiah's Vision and the Visions of Daniel." *Vetus Testamentum* 29 (1979) 501–5.

Niessen, R. "The Virginity of the עַלְמָה in Isaiah 7:14." *Bibliotheca Sacra* 137 (1980) 133–50.

O'Brien, Peter T. *Colossians, Philemon*. Word Biblical Commentary. Dallas: Word, 1998.

———. *The Epistle to the Philippians: A Commentary on the Greek Text*. New International Greek Testament Commentary. Grand Rapids: Eerdmans, 1991.

———. *The Letter to the Ephesians*. Grand Rapids: Eerdmans, 1999.

Odell, Margaret S. "You Are What You Eat: Ezekiel and the Scroll." *Journal of Biblical Literature* 117 (1998) 229–48.

Olley, J. W. "'The Many': How Is Isa 53:12a to Be Understood?" *Biblica* 68 (1987) 330–56.

Osborne, G. R. *Revelation*. Grand Rapids: Baker, 2002.

Oswalt, John N. *The Book of Isaiah: Chapters 1–39*. New International Commentary on the Old Testament. Grand Rapids: Eerdmans, 1986.

———. *The Book of Isaiah: Chapters 40–66*. New International Commentary on the Old Testament. Grand Rapids: Eerdmans, 1998.

———. "משח." In *New International Dictionary of the Old Testament Theology and Exegesis*, edited by Willem A. VanGemeren, 2:1123–26. Grand Rapids: Zondervan, 1997.

Parry, Jason Thomas. "Desolation of the Temple and Messianic Enthronement in Daniel 11:36—12:3." *Journal of the Evangelical Theological Society* 54 (2011) 485–526.

Patterson, Richard D. "The Key Role of Daniel 7." *Grace Theological Journal* 12 (1991) 245–61.

Perrin, Nicholas. *Thomas, the Other Gospel*. Louisville: Westminster John Knox, 2007.

Perrin, Norman. *Rediscovering the Teaching of Jesus*. New York: Harper & Row, 1967.

———. "Son of Man in Ancient Judaism and Primitive Christianity: A Suggestion." *Biblical Research* 11 (1966) 17–28.

Pervo, Richard I. *Acts: A Commentary on the Book of Acts*. Edited by Harold W. Attridge. Hermeneia. Minneapolis: Fortress, 2009.

Peterson, David. *The Acts of the Apostles*. Grand Rapids: Eerdmans, 2009.

Pettegrew, Larry D. *The New Covenant Ministry of the Holy Spirit*. Grand Rapids: Kregel, 2001.

Piper, John. *The Future of Justification: A Response to N. T. Wright*. Wheaton, IL: Crossway, 2007.

Polhill, John B. *Acts*. Nashville: Broadman & Holman, 1992.

Porteous, Norman W. *Daniel: A Commentary*. Old Testament Library. Philadelphia: Westminster, 1965.

Ridderbos, Herman N. *Paul: An Outline of His Theology*. Grand Rapids: Eerdmans, 1975.

Roberts, J. J. M. "Double Entendre in First Isaiah." *Catholic Biblical Quarterly* 54 (1992) 39–48.

———. "Isaiah in Old Testament Theology." *Interpretation* 36 (1982) 130–43.

Robinson, Geoffrey D. "The Motif of Deafness and Blindness in Isaiah 6:9–10: A Contextual, Literary, and Theological Analysis." *Bulletin for Biblical Research* 8 (1998) 167–86.

Robson, James. *Word and Spirit in Ezekiel*. New York: T. & T. Clark, 2006.

Rooker, Mark F. "Evidence from Ezekiel." In *The Coming Millennial Kingdom*, edited by Donald K. Campbell and Jeffrey L. Townsend, 119–34. Grand Rapids: Kregel, 1997.

Rowland, Christopher. *Christian Origins: An Account of the Setting and Character of the Most Important Messianic Sect of Judaism*. 5th ed. London: SPCK, 1993.

———. *The Open Heaven: A Study of Apocalyptic in Judaism and Early Christianity*. New York: Crossroad, 1982.

Ruiz, Jean-Pierre. *Ezekiel in the Apocalypse: The Transformation of Prophetic Language in Revelation 16:17—19:10*. Europäische Hochschulschriften. Frankfurt am Main: Peter Lang, 1989.

Bibliography

Sailhamer, John H. *The Pentateuch as Narrative: A Biblical-Theological Commentary*. Grand Rapids: Zondervan, 1992.

Sanders, E. P. *Paul and Palestinian Judaism: A Comparison of Patterns of Religion*. Philadelphia: Fortress, 1977.

Schafroth, Verena. "An Exegetical Exploration of 'Spirit' References in Ezekiel 36 and 37." *Journal of the European Pentecostal Theological Association* 29 (2009) 61–77.

Schmid, Herbert. "Daniel der Menschensohn." *Judaica* 27 (1971) 192–221.

Schmidt, Johann Michael. "Gedanken zum Verstockungsauftrag Jesajas (Is 6)." *Vetus Testamentum* 21 (1971) 68–90.

Schmidt, Nathaniel. "The 'Son of Man' in the Book of Daniel." *Journal of Biblical Literature* 19 (1900) 22–28.

Schmitt, John W., and J. Carl Laney. *Messiah's Coming Temple: Ezekiel's Prophetic Vision of the Future Temple*. Grand Rapids: Kregel, 1997.

Schreiner, Thomas R. "Is Perfect Obedience to the Law Possible? A Re-examination of Galatians 3:10." *Journal of the Evangelical Theological Society* 27 (1984) 151–60.

———. *The Law and Its Fulfillment: A Pauline Theology of Law*. Grand Rapids: Baker, 1993.

———. *New Testament Theology: Magnifying God's Glory in Christ*. Grand Rapids: Baker, 2008.

———. *Paul Apostle of God's Glory in Christ: A Pauline Theology*. Downers Grove, IL: InterVarsity, 2001.

———. "Penal Substitution View." In *Four Views: The Nature of the Atonement*, edited by James Beilby and Paul R. Eddy, 67–98. Downers Grove, IL: InterVarsity, 2006.

———. *Romans*. Baker Exegetical Commentary on the New Testament. Grand Rapids: Baker, 1998.

Schüssler Fiorenza, Elisabeth. "Apocalyptic and Gnosis in the Book of Revelation and Paul." *Journal of Biblical Literature* 92 (1973) 565–81.

Schweitzer, Albert. *The Mysticism of Paul the Apostle*. New York: Henry Holt, 1931.

Segal, Alan F. *Paul the Convert: The Apostolate and Apostasy of Saul the Pharisee*. New Haven: Yale University Press, 1990.

Smith, Gary. *Isaiah 40–66*. New American Commentary 15B. Nashville: Broadman & Holman, 2009.

Stein, Robert H. "The Benefits of an Author-Oriented Approach to Hermeneutics." *Journal of the Evangelical Theological Society* 44 (2001) 451–66.

Steinmann, Andrew E. "Is the Antichrist in Daniel 11?" *Bibliotheca Sacra* 162 (2005) 195–209.

Stokes, Ryan E. "The Throne Visions of Daniel 7, 1 Enoch 14 and the Qumran Book of Giants (4Q530): An Analysis of Their Literary Relationship." *Dead Sea Discoveries* 15 (2008) 340–58.

Strand, Kenneth Albert. "An Overlooked Old Testament Background to Revelation 11:1." *Andrews University Seminary Studies* 22 (1984) 317–25.

Suh, Robert H. "The Use of Ezekiel 37 in Ephesians 2." *Journal of the Evangelical Theological Society* 50 (2007) 715–33.

Tanner, J Paul. "Is Daniel's Seventy-Weeks Prophecy Messianic? Part 2." *Bibliotheca Sacra* 166 (2009) 319–35.

Thielman, Frank. *Ephesians*. Baker Exegetical Commentary on the New Testament. Grand Rapids: Baker Academic, 2010.

Thiselton, Anthony C. *The First Epistle to the Corinthians: A Commentary on the Greek Text*. Grand Rapids: Eerdmans, 2000.

Thomas, Robert L. *Revelation 1–7: An Exegetical Commentary*. Chicago: Moody, 1992.

———. *Revelation 8–22: An Exegetical Commentary*. Chicago: Moody, 1995.

Thomas, Robert L., and Stanley N. Gundry, editors. *A Harmony of the Gospels*. Chicago: Moody, 1978.

Tull, P. "Intertextuality and the Hebrew Scriptures." *Currents in Biblical Research* 8 (2000) 88–119.

VanGemeren, W. A. "The Spirit of Restoration." *Westminster Theological Journal* 50 (1988) 81–102.

Vanhoozer, Kevin J. *Is There a Meaning in This Text?* Grand Rapids: Zondervan, 1998.

Wacholder, Ben Zion. "Creation in Ezekiel's Merkabah: Ezekiel 1 and Genesis 1." In *Of Scribes and Sages: Ancient Versions and Traditions*, edited by Craig A. Evans, 1:14–32. New York: T. & T. Clark, 2004.

Walker, William O. "The Origin of the Son of Man Concept as Applied to Jesus." *Journal of Biblical Literature* 91 (1972) 482–90.

Waltke, Bruce K. *The Book of Proverbs: Chapters 15–31*. New International Commentary on the Old Testament. Grand Rapids: Eerdmans, 2005.

Bibliography

———. *An Old Testament Theology: An Exegetical, Canonical, and Thematic Approach*. Grand Rapids: Zondervan, 2007.

Waltke, Bruce K., and M. O'Connor. *An Introduction to Biblical Hebrew Syntax*. Winona Lake, IN: Eisenbrauns, 1990.

Walton, John. "Isaiah 7:14: What's in a Name?" *Journal of the Evangelical Theological Society* 30 (1987) 289–306.

Walvoord, John F. *Daniel: The Key to Prophetic Revelation*. Chicago: Moody, 1971.

———. *The Revelation of Jesus Christ*. Chicago: Moody, 1996.

Wanamaker, Charles A. *The Epistles to the Thessalonians: A Commentary on the Greek Text*. Grand Rapids: Eerdmans, 1990.

Watts, John. *Isaiah 1–33*. Word Biblical Commentary 24. Waco, TX: Word, 1985.

Wegner, Paul D. "How Many Virgin Births Are in the Bible? (Isaiah 7:14) A Prophetic Pattern Approach." *Journal of the Evangelical Theological Society* 54 (2011) 467–84.

———. "A Re-examination of Isaiah IX 1–6." *Vetus Testamentum* 42 (1992) 103–12.

Wenham, G. J. *The Book of Leviticus*. New International Commentary on the Old Testament. Grand Rapids: Eerdmans, 1978.

———. *Genesis 16–50*. Word Biblical Commentary 2. Dallas: Word, 1994.

Whitcomb, John C. "Christ's Atonement and Animal Sacrifices in Israel." *Grace Theological Journal* 6 (1985) 201–17.

Witherington, Ben. *The Acts of the Apostles: A Socio-Rhetorical Commentary*. Grand Rapids: Eerdmans, 1998.

———. *Grace in Galatia: A Commentary on Saint Paul's Letter to the Galatians*. Grand Rapids: Eerdmans, 1998.

Wood, Leon. *A Commentary on Daniel*. Grand Rapids: Zondervan, 1973.

Wright, N. T. *Justification: God's Plan and Paul's Vision*. Downers Grove, IL: InterVarsity, 2009.

———. "Justification: Yesterday, Today, and Forever." *Journal of the Evangelical Theological Society* 54 (2011) 49–64.

Young, Edward J. *The Book of Isaiah: The English Text, with Introduction, Exposition, and Notes*. Grand Rapids: Eerdmans, 1965.

———. *Prophecy of Daniel*. Grand Rapids: Eerdmans, 1949.

Zimmerli, Walther. *Ezekiel: A Commentary on the Book of the Prophet Ezekiel*. Translated by Ronald E. Clements. Edited by Frank Moore Cross and Klaus Baltzer with Leonard Jay Greenspoon. 2 vols. Hermeneia. Philadelphia: Fortress, 1979.

Scripture Index

Genesis
1	16, 91
1:1–31	210
1:2	140n92
1:6	89
1:26f	143n102
1:26–28	90
1:28	142, 143n105
2	194
3	227n158
3:13	227
6	10
12:1–3	49
16	129n61
16:11	78n98
22:15–16	136
22:16	128n60
38:26	161n55
45:1	38n77, 39n79
49:10	8

Exodus
3:1–6	37n69
13:21	37n69
19:5–6	190
19:6	111, 190n8
19:18	37n69
23:24	59n46
24:10	52n15, 90
25:19	100
28:33	52n15
40:34–38	105
40:34	57
40:35	32, 57

Leviticus
4	111n87
4:5–7	111n87
9:1–24	110
9:7	111
16	219
16:16	110
16:18–19	110
25	8
25:10–55	14

Numbers
5:14	99
11:1–2	37n69
14:21	34, 34n58, 54, 57, 57n36, 62
22:18	57n35

Deuteronomy
4:24	66
4:30	200n47
27	164n66
27:26	164n66
28:15–68	96
28:63–65	96
30:1	200n47
33:26–28	143

Joshua
24:26	59n46

Judges
3:19	38n77, 39n79
9:6	59n46
13:5	78n98

1 Samuel
17:4	23
25:37	104

2 Samuel

7:8–14	49
7:14	8
8:18	112n92
13:9	38n77, 39n79
18:8	59n46
21:19	23, 24n9

1 Kings

6:23	100
6:32	89
7:44	89
8:10–12	105
8:10	32
8:11	57
8:32	81n108, 161n55
8:44	95
8:48	95
10:14	223n145
11:13	95
14:23	59n46
22:14–19	45n105
22:19–23	44
22:19–22	17, 45n104
22:19	44, 44n103, 54
22:20	45
22:36–40	45

2 Kings

15:13–19	49
24:13	54n21

1 Chronicles

18:17	112n92
20:5	23, 24n9

2 Chronicles

5:14	57
7:1–2	57

Job

33:12	161n55

Psalms

2:6	8
2:7	8
8:4	142
11:4	185n161
18:2	118n14
18:10–11	143
27:4	54n21
42:9	118n14
68:15–16	95
68:29	95
71:3	118n14
72:19	34, 34n58, 54, 54n20, 57, 57n36, 62
82	8
82:1	14
82:3	161n55
82:4	161n55
87:1–7	95
97:2	143
99:5	31n45
104:3	143
110	8
132:13	95

Proverbs

17:15	81n108, 161n55
30:19–20	78n98

Isaiah

1–12	53
1–5	48
1	53
1:1–18	51, 159
1:1	49
1:2	50
1:3	50
1:4	50, 50n8, 56, 63
1:7	49, 55, 56, 66
1:8	49
1:10	50
1:12–14	66, 69
1:16–19	67
1:17	49
1:18	63, 211, 211n87
1:19—2:5	55
1:19–31	51
1:21	74
1:24	49
1:25	50n9
1:26–27	74, 74n90
1:26	49, 124n43
1:28–31	55
1:29	69
1:30	63, 69
1:31	66
2–12	55n27
2	34n57, 53, 54, 54n22, 55, 56, 62, 77, 119, 183, 206n64, 211, 212n91, 213
2:1–4	34, 34n57, 40, 51, 53, 55, 118, 124n43
2:1	53, 58

Scripture Index

2:2–4	7, 56, 74n90, 121n30, 145, 166, 167, 198, 212
2:2–3	166
2:2	11n29, 14, 34, 34n57, 35, 49, 51, 54, 61, 76, 80n105, 83n2, 95, 109, 118, 119, 121, 121n30
2:3–4a	49
2:3	49, 54, 109
2:4	76
2:4a	49
2:4b	49
2:5—4:1	51
2:6—4:5	55
2:6	65, 67
2:7–8	61
2:8	67
2:9	76
2:10–17	183
2:10	183, 211
2:11	73, 74, 75, 76, 84, 183
2:12	50, 76
2:13–14	65
2:13	63
2:17	67, 76, 183, 211
2:18	67
2:19	183, 211
2:20–21	67
2:20	74
2:21	183
3:1–7	49
3:8	49, 50
3:9	63
4	57, 57n39, 58, 70, 77, 213
4:2–5	51, 69, 76
4:2–4	52
4:2	58, 149
4:3–4	213
4:3	50, 50n8, 57, 84, 162
4:4–6	84n2
4:5–6	211
4:5	50, 57
5	55
5:1–30	51
5:1–4	51
5:2	65
5:3	70
5:5–30	51
5:5	49
5:7	74
5:8–30	75
5:13	50, 67
5:14	49
5:16–19	50
5:16	50n8, 66, 160
5:18	63
5:19	50, 50n8, 56
5:24	50, 50n8
5:26–30	49
5:30	51
6	1, 6, 16, 17, 18, 30, 34n57, 45, 52n15, 53, 54, 54n22, 55, 55n26, 55n27, 56, 57, 57n39, 58, 61, 62, 63, 64, 68, 70, 73, 74n90, 77, 78, 79, 108, 119, 124, 166, 166n78, 168n84, 186, 194n19, 198, 206n64, 214
6:1ff	16
6:1–13	26, 210
6:1–8	6
6:1–6	30
6:1–3	26, 27, 29, 40, 52, 60n48, 62, 76, 84, 165
6:1	10, 28, 30, 31, 31n45, 35, 39, 44n103, 48, 51, 52, 53, 54, 55, 55n26, 56, 57, 62, 68, 73, 74, 75, 79, 80, 83n2, 84, 84n2, 84n3, 108, 109, 118, 156, 183, 192, 195, 198, 200, 211
6:1b	31
6:2–3	51, 56
6:2	10, 11, 21, 21n1, 36, 38, 39, 40, 56, 66, 201
6:3–4	36
6:3	13, 30, 34, 36, 42, 50, 52, 54, 56, 57, 57n37, 58, 59, 61, 62, 63, 65, 68, 69, 70, 71, 73, 75, 80, 84, 84n2, 84n3, 88, 89, 108, 109, 119, 145, 148, 149, 156, 156n33, 167, 194, 198, 201, 216, 218, 229
6:3b	31, 62
6:4–13	26, 58
6:4	27n26, 28, 54n21, 58n41, 60n48, 66, 69, 212
6:5–13	52
6:5–7	30, 52
6:5	13, 29n39, 52, 58, 63, 68, 69, 73, 77
6:6–7	39
6:6	29, 39, 64n63, 67, 68
6:7	29n36, 63, 71, 80, 123, 201
6:8	63
6:9–13	50, 60
6:9–10	159
6:9	50, 63, 149, 156, 156n33, 159, 168
6:10–13	63
6:10	30, 63, 64, 68, 69, 71, 80, 84
6:11–13	12, 53, 55, 66
6:11	37, 55, 56
6:13	52, 57n39, 59, 59n46, 63, 64, 69, 123, 149, 211
6:13b	60
7–12	78, 81

I Saw the Lord

Isaiah *(cont.)*

7	78
7:1–3	74
7:1	74, 77
7:3	74, 76, 78n98, 79n99
7:11	74
7:13–18	74
7:13	74, 78
7:14	78, 78n98, 79, 79n99, 213
7:15–16	78
7:20	74
7:22	78
8:1–4	79n99
8:8	79n99
8:13	65
8:14	69
8:18	79n99
9:6	78, 79, 79n103, 80n105
9:7	74, 75
9:13	65
10:3	65
10:12	75
10:21	76
10:22	168
10:23	168
11	8, 61, 62, 68, 72, 74n90, 79, 124, 124n39, 124n41, 166, 168n84, 186, 201, 204n61, 206n64, 213
11:1–16	75, 114, 118, 145, 198, 210, 212, 228
11:1–15	84
11:1–10	7, 76, 124n43, 201
11:1–5	61, 62, 73, 79, 80n105, 84
11:1–3	78, 79, 80n105
11:1	75, 79n105, 80n105, 124, 189, 194, 204
11:4–5	124
11:4	8, 14, 15, 185, 192, 212
11:5–8	61
11:6–9	77, 169
11:6	79n99
11:8–9	77
11:8	62, 79n99
11:9	11n29, 61, 62, 73, 77, 118
11:9b	61, 62
11:10	166, 167, 168
11:13	81
11:15–16	212
11:16	72
12:1–6	58n40, 70
12:6	69, 70
13–27	71, 82
13:1–22	212
13:8	183
13:11	71, 75, 76
13:22	75, 212n94
14:1	74
14:7	71
14:14	74
14:15	74
14:25–26	71
16:1	76
16:4	76
16:5	74, 75, 79
16:12	66
17:3	74
17:7	68
18:7	73, 76
19	72, 168n84
19:11–12	71
19:18–21	71
19:18	73, 76
19:19	59n46
19:20–21	73
19:22	71
19:23	72, 76
19:25	71
21:1–10	212
22:1	65
22:8–13	74
22:14	63, 123
22:18	67, 74
22:20–21	75
22:23–25	67
22:23	75
22:25	75
23:7	71
23:17–18	76
24:1—27:13	76
24:1–5	159
24:1	210, 212
24:4–10	75
24:15–16	72
24:16a	76
24:20	66, 71
24:21	75, 77, 226
24:23	70, 229
25:1–12	167, 168
25:3	72
25:6–10a	77
25:6	72
25:7	168
25:8–10	77
25:8	167, 229
26:2	226
26:15	70
26:19	77, 130, 131
26:21	71
27:1	77
27:6	65, 70

Scripture Index

27:9	63, 71, 123, 168, 168n84	37:36–38	74
27:10–12	168n84	38:1—39:8	82
27:13	76, 168, 168n84	40–48	82
28–35	68, 82	40:1—48:22	64
28:1—35:10	64	40:1–2	124n37
28:11	66, 167	40:1	213
28:16	118, 134, 168	40:2	63, 190, 190n7
28:17	74	40:3–5	70
28:22	168	40:3	66, 70
29–32	64	40:5	70
29:1–8	64	40:9	167
29:8	64	40:10	231, 231n172
29:9–15	64	40:13	79n102, 166n76
29:9	64, 159	40:23	75
29:10–12	64	41:6	70
29:11–12	64	41:8	59n46, 69
29:13	64n63	41:12–16	118
29:18	68	41:18	76
29:19	68	41:20	64
29:23	66, 68, 160	41:27	167
30:1–2	63, 64	42:1–9	82
30:11–12	64, 66, 69	42:1–4	80n105, 84
30:12	64	42:1–3	80n105
30:15	66, 68	42:1	15, 30, 30n41, 79n105
30:20	68	42:3–4	80n105
30:26	69, 70	42:4	8, 30, 80
30:27	66	42:6–7	149
30:30	66	42:6	148, 163, 165, 192
30:33	66	42:7	79, 149
31:1	64	42:8	65, 67, 80
32	68, 74n90	42:9	211
32:1–8	75, 82	42:10	205
32:1–6	73	42:11	66
32:1–5	61, 76	42:14	80n105
32:1–3	79	42:18—43:21	124n37
32:1	68, 75, 124n43	42:18–19	65
32:3	68	42:19	64
32:16	74, 74n90, 75	42:20–21	64
33:5	76	43:2–5	197
33:10	75	43:2–4	213n100
33:14	66	43:3	67
33:17	76	43:4a	70
33:22	76	43:4b	70
33:24	67	43:5	69
34:1—35:8	82	43:8	70, 149
34:4	211	43:14	67
35:2	72	43:4–20	76
35:5–6	229	43:6	76
35:8	69	43:11	80
35:10	69	43:18–20	76
36:1—37:38	64	43:22—44:23	124n37
37:16	56, 82	43:23	65
37:21–28	82	43:27	66
37:23	74, 75	43:28	66
37:31–32	76	44:14	64, 69

Isaiah *(cont.)*

44:16–17	64
44:17	64
44:18–19	64
44:18	64, 159
44:22	67
45:6	72
45:17	124
45:21–23	165
45:22–23	154
45:22	72
45:23	72, 135, 156n34
45:25	69
47:4	68
48:2	69
48:8	64, 80
48:11	70
48:17	68
48:20	68
49–56	82
49	165, 165n74
49:1–13	82
49:1–3	61
49:1	165
49:2–3	30, 30n41
49:2	30, 192, 194, 212
49:3	80, 80n107, 81, 84, 156, 156n33, 165
49:4	30n41, 165
49:6	42, 80, 156, 156n33
49:7	80
49:8	80, 165
49:14–26	80
49:18	165
49:22	76
50:3	211
50:4–5	80n105
50:4b–5	80
50:4	80
50:6	159
50:7–9	30n41
51:9	80n106
51:16	69
51:17	80
52	45
52:1	69, 80
52:5	159
52:7	8, 14, 165, 167
52:10	68, 72
52:11	68
52:12	159n43
52:13—53:12	30, 40, 67, 80, 124, 138, 204, 229
52:13	30, 34, 35, 80, 81, 82, 114, 130, 138, 192, 194n19, 198
52:15	80, 81, 159n43, 167
53	125, 160, 162, 165n73, 167
53:1–11	72
53:1–10	34
53:1	80n105
53:2–8	159
53:3	159
53:4–8	211
53:5–6	160
53:5	30, 159, 160, 161
53:6–8	160
53:7	80, 213
53:8	124
53:9	80
53:10–11	124
53:10	59n46, 69, 160, 161
53:11–12	30
53:11	8, 11, 67, 80, 81, 81n108, 124, 125, 130, 148, 159, 160, 161, 161n55, 162, 164, 165
53:12	30, 80, 81, 118, 159
54:1–17	34, 35
54:1–10	75
54:1–5	34n57
54:1	34, 80, 80n106
54:4	78n98
54:5–12	78n98
55:1	229
55:4	137
55:5	72
56:1	74
56:7	72, 76
56:10	65
56:11	65
57:13a	65
57:15	69, 73, 76
57:19	69
58–66	82
58:8	70
59:1–2	65, 82
59:1	65
59:2	63, 65, 159
59:6	63
59:7	159
59:9–11	65
59:16	80
59:20–21	168, 168n84
59:21	69
60:1–19	168
60:1–18	61, 167, 168
60:4	76
60:5	76
60:9	70
60:10	76
60:13	31n45, 70, 70n81, 80n107

Scripture Index

60:14	76
60:21	124
61:1–11	82
61:2–3	8
61:3	59n46, 69, 70, 70n81
61:4	76
61:6	111, 166, 190n8
62:1–2	124n43
62:2–11	70, 72
62:12	69
63:18	162
64:6	63
64:8–9	66
64:10	66
65:9	59n46, 69, 76
65:13–25	61
65:16	166n76
65:17	7, 202, 210, 228
65:18–25	76, 77
65:19–20	210, 211
65:20	77
65:23	69
66	183n153
66:5	70
66:6	75
66:19–20	72
66:20	76
66:22–23	210
66:22	69, 211
66:23–24	7
66:23	212, 212n91
66:24	66

Jeremiah

1	48
2:3	220n130
7:4	95
23:5	8, 124
25:11–12	123
25:11	7

Ezekiel

1–3	85, 85n7, 87
1:1—3:13	87
1–2	18n66
1	1, 13, 16, 17, 18, 40, 41, 43n98, 45, 48, 129n61, 143n103, 198
1:1–28	27, 214
1:1–3	86
1:1–2	31, 35
1:1	28, 29, 31, 83, 83n1, 96, 112, 113, 198, 200
1:3	85n7, 93, 96, 101, 174n112
1:4	10, 21, 28, 87, 90, 150, 183, 192, 194
1:5–24	36
1:5–14	87
1:5–12	142
1:5–8	88
1:5	36, 38, 88, 104
1:6–8	97
1:6	36, 38, 104
1:7	37, 88
1:8	38, 39, 104
1:9	88
1:10–14	198
1:10	88, 104, 201
1:11	38, 39, 88
1:12	39n79, 87n13, 88, 92
1:13	39, 90, 192, 194, 201
1:14	88
1:15–26	39
1:15–21	17, 28, 42n91, 87, 89
1:15	11, 89, 104
1:17	38, 89
1:18	94
1:20	17, 89, 92
1:21	92
1:22–27	87, 89
1:22	10, 36, 89, 201
1:23–24	39
1:23	39, 89
1:24–25	89n24
1:24	17, 192, 215
1:26–28	35, 128n60, 142, 150, 198
1:26–27	90
1:26	8, 10, 28, 39n79, 42, 83n2, 90, 150, 195, 200
1:26b	90
1:27	10, 35, 88, 90, 192
1:28	44, 83, 87, 90, 150
2:1—3:5	101
2:1–3	103, 150
2:1–2	98, 107
2:1	26n25, 91, 144n109, 150, 192
2:2–3	92
2:2	94, 102, 172
2:2b	94
2:3–7	91
2:3	93
2:4	91, 101
2:5	94n39
2:6–7	93
2:6	93
2:7	93, 103
2:8—3:3	93, 94
2:10	94
3–7	97

I Saw the Lord

Ezekiel (cont.)

3:1–27	214	8:1–8	98n51
3:1–3	93, 174n112	8:1	101
3:1	214	8:2	101
3:3	214	8:3–16	102
3:3b	94	8:3–5	29
3:4–10	93	8:3	99
3:5	91	8:4—11:25	86
3:6–7	92	8:4–18	95
3:7–11	12	8:4	31, 83, 86, 89, 99
3:8	93, 97, 169	8:5–18	84
3:9	91, 91n32, 96, 101	8:5–6	99
3:10–11	93	8:10–12	99
3:10	94, 101	8:16	54n21
3:11	93	8:17	101
3:12–13	16	9:1—48:35	87
3:12	87, 94, 99, 110, 191	9:1—11:25	86, 89, 100
3:13	94, 96	9:1–2	100
3:14—8:18	87	9:3	100
3:14–27	95	9:4	100
3:14	87, 214	9:6–7	100
3:16–21	86n12, 96	9:6	175
3:17–20	85n7	9:7	100
3:17	96	10:1–22	29n35
3:22–27	96	10:1–3	10, 11
3:22–23	86, 99	10:1	36, 37, 100
3:22	96	10:2	28, 29, 39, 42n91
3:23	87, 96	10:7	194
3:24	96, 97	10:12	36n66, 39
3:25	97	10:15–18	29
3:26–27	86n12	10:15	31
3:26	96, 97	10:16	39
3:27	96	10:19	16
4–24	85n7	10:22	100
4–7	85n7	11:1–25	214
4:1	97	11:1–20	112n91
4:3	97	11:1–12	86n12
4:7	97	11:1	87
4:13–14	98	11:9	84n2
4:13	169	11:10	94n39
4:14	98	11:13	100
5:7	98	11:14–21	100
5:10	102n64	11:14–16	100
5:11	98n51, 99	11:14	85n7
6:4	98	11:15–16	106n71
6:9	98, 102n64, 103	11:16–17	108
6:10	98	11:16	105
6:13	103	11:17–20	106
7:1	85n7	11:17–18	100
7:9	98	11:19–20	108
7:21–22	174	11:19	101, 103, 104
7:22–24	98, 100	11:20	101, 104
7:27	94n39	11:20a	101
8–11	28, 85, 85n7, 86, 87, 105, 107	11:22–25	101
8	86, 99, 101	12–24	101
		12–19	85n7

12:2	84	26:2	105
12:15	103	26:16	215
12:22–28	101	27:12–22	215
13:1–16	101	27:13	84n2
13:7–23	101	27:35	215
13:21	103	28:1–19	86n12
13:23	94n39	28:1–10	105, 185n163, 214
14	101	28:22–25	84
14:1–2	101	28:22	84, 105
14:1	101	28:25	84
14:2	101	29:1–8	86n12
14:3	84, 101, 102, 103, 174	33–48	85n7
14:3b	101	33–39	86n7
14:14	43n99	33:1–33	103
15:7	103	33:1–9	85n7, 86n12
16	86n12	33:1	86n7
16:1–63	84	33:10–20	86n12
16:1–23	229	33:21–22	96
16:15–20	102	33:21	96
16:21	102	33:22	86n12
16:24–25	102	34–37	31
16:30	102, 103	34:1–22	112n91
16:33	102	34:1–11	35
16:38	103	34:10	112n91
16:42	99, 103	34:11–22	31
16:49–63	103	34:23	112n91
18:1–32	86n12	34:24	84, 112, 112n91
18:31	102, 103	34:25	31, 32
19:1–14	112n91	34:30	31
20–23	85n7	36:20–23	84
20:1–49	102	36:23	105
20:12	103	36:25–28	169
20:22–24	109	36:25–27	103, 169n89
20:40	84n2	36:25	103
20:44	94n39	36:25b	103
21:1	85n7, 102	36:26–27	92, 104, 173, 214
21:5	103	36:26	101, 104, 108, 110
22:1–31	84, 102	36:27	104, 107, 109, 172
22:4–8	109	37–48	192n13
22:16	103	37	101n60, 104, 104n68, 105, 130n64, 170, 171, 172, 175, 220
22:26	84		
23	86n12	37:1–28	34, 35, 194, 202, 214, 226
23:1–49	102, 112n91, 229	37:1–14	92, 104
23:28–29	84	37:1–10	172
23:30	109	37:1–3	104
23:38–40	102	37:3–5	169
24	85n7	37:5–6	171n95
24:1–14	86n12	37:5	220
24:15–19	102	37:6–9	103, 105
24:21	102	37:6–8	172
24:24–27	102	37:6	104
24:27	103	37:7–9	170
25–32	85n7, 105	37:7–8	104
25:3	105	37:7	104, 170
25:6–7	105	37:8–9	170

Ezekiel *(cont.)*

37:9–10	171n95
37:11	104
37:13	104, 170
37:14	104, 171n95
37:15–28	104
37:16–28	172
37:21	105
37:22	105
37:23–28	105
37:23–26	174
37:23	172, 173
37:24	105
37:26–28	172
37:26–27	105
37:26	105
37:27	108, 172, 175, 229
37:28	84, 108, 108n79, 109n80, 170
38–39	35n59, 105, 215, 227n157
38:1–2	227n157
38:1	85n7
38:16	35, 40, 105
39:4	215
39:7	105
39:13	105
39:17–20	215
39:21–28	35n59
39:21–22	105
39:21	84, 145, 215
39:22–23	215
39:22	106
39:25	105
39:27	214
39:29	35n59, 103
40–48	35n59, 86, 86n7, 106, 106n71, 107, 108, 109n80, 110, 125, 181n147, 185, 198, 214, 228
40–43	84, 85
40:1—42:20	108
40:2	11n29, 14, 83n2, 109, 111, 119, 121, 229
40:3–4	216
40:9–20	216
40:12b	111
40:13	111
40:22	108
41:18–25	111
41:18–22	108
42:15–20	228
43	16n53, 28, 31, 45, 87
43:1–7	29, 34, 40
43:1–5	105, 112, 198
43:1–4	229
43:2–7	83n2, 84, 86
43:2–4	206n64
43:2	31, 34, 83, 84n2, 119, 170, 192, 215, 216, 218
43:3–7	29n35
43:3	31, 86, 87, 106, 106n71
43:4–7	108
43:4–5	108
43:5	87, 94, 174, 218
43:5b	31
43:7	31, 84, 87, 95, 108, 109, 194
43:20	110
43:26	110
44:1–5	114
44:2	111
44:3	31, 35, 112, 114
44:15–31	111
44:24	110
45:1–9	108
45:2	228
45:7	112
45:13–17	111, 190n8
45:15–17	205
45:15	110
45:17	110, 190, 219, 226
45:20	110
46:9	110
46:11	110
47:1–12	111
47:3	229
47:8	228
48:8–10	108
48:35	84n2, 111, 229

Daniel

1:12–14	195
1:19–20	135
2–7	116
2	32–33, 33n49, 115, 116, 118, 119, 120, 120n21, 121, 122, 132, 133, 134, 137, 140, 197, 222n139
2:6	135
2:18	157
2:19	157
2:20–22	117
2:20	206n67
2:21	179
2:22	157
2:25	123
2:26–27	134
2:27	157
2:28–29	33, 193
2:28	33, 35, 40, 120, 189, 231n170
2:29	33
2:30	206n67
2:31	117, 118, 132, 133

Scripture Index

2:32–33	132
2:32	115, 120
2:33	33n50, 115
2:34–35	33, 34, 118, 121n30
2:34	12, 33n50
2:35	7, 11n29, 14, 31, 109n82, 117, 118, 121, 127, 129, 133, 134, 145, 197, 222, 227
2:37–39	120
2:37–38	143n105
2:37	132, 135, 143, 206n67
2:38–39	140
2:38	122, 132, 133
2:39–40	132
2:44–45	118, 121n30
2:44	33n49, 33n50, 114, 122, 144
2:45	135, 189, 189n2, 193
2:46	135
2:48–49	135
3–6	117
3	116, 135n75, 136, 137
3:1–15	117
3:1	119, 132, 133, 223
3:2	152
3:4–5	132
3:4	117, 133
3:23–26	134
3:25	136
3:28	136
3:29	134
3:33	143
4	115, 116
4:1	117, 133, 134
4:3	114
4:5	117
4:8	145n110
4:10–11	132
4:11–12	119
4:11	132, 133
4:12–14	132
4:14	133n70
4:17	15, 152, 179, 179n137
4:22	143
4:25	135, 143, 179
4:27	135, 141
4:29	117
4:30	133n70, 206n67, 222, 222n142
4:31	133n70
4:32	179
4:33	134, 135
4:35	134
4:37	133n70, 134
5	116
5:1	141
5:3–4	117, 133
5:11	145n110
5:18	135
5:19–23	133
5:19	117
5:20	135
5:21	135
5:30	134
6	116
6:1	135
6:14	133
6:22	133, 134
6:24	133n72
6:25	117, 134
6:26	134
6:27	143
7	1, 6, 8, 9, 10, 11, 12, 13, 14, 18, 20, 27, 29, 31, 33n49, 40, 41, 42, 43, 43n98, 44, 115, 116, 117, 118, 119, 120, 122, 126, 126n51, 127, 128, 128n60, 129, 129n61, 130, 131, 132, 135n75, 136, 137, 139, 140, 143n102, 143n106, 144, 146, 151, 152, 176, 177, 178, 180, 181, 182, 192, 196, 197, 198, 206, 207n69, 221, 221n134, 221n136, 222n139, 223
7:1–28	32
7:1–14	222
7:1–9	228
7:1–8	27, 27n28, 140, 142, 222
7:1–4	117
7:1	116, 140, 198
7:2–8	119, 140
7:2	221n136
7:3–8	127
7:4–8	27n28
7:4	140
7:5	115, 120
7:6	115, 140n95
7:7–14	33
7:7–8	33n50, 35, 141
7:7	115, 141
7:8	33n50, 121, 127, 129, 141
7:9–27	191
7:9–14	27, 27n28, 33n50, 129, 131, 135, 137n87, 138, 141, 177, 179, 180, 182
7:9–13	29, 128
7:9–12	27n28, 206n64
7:9–10	35
7:9	10, 17, 28, 29, 31, 35, 43, 113, 126, 141, 177n133, 192, 195, 197, 198, 200, 200n49, 200n50, 203, 221n136
7:10–14	181
7:10	10, 11, 36, 180n144, 181, 206
7:11–14	34n56
7:11–12	226
7:11	27n28, 33n49, 130, 142, 223

I Saw the Lord

Daniel (cont.)

7:12	27n28
7:13–27	43n95, 130
7:13–22	32
7:13–14	27n28, 43n95, 131, 138, 145, 146, 151, 154n24
7:13	7, 8, 10, 11, 40, 42, 129n61, 135, 136, 142, 143, 182, 183, 190, 192, 200
7:14–27	152, 195
7:14	27n28, 31, 40, 114, 117, 126n51, 132, 135, 137, 138, 139, 142, 143, 144, 145, 152, 154n24, 177, 180, 180n144, 181, 190, 191, 192, 206, 206n67, 221, 221n136, 230
7:15–28	27, 27n28, 144
7:15	27n28
7:17	132, 140, 141
7:18–25	181
7:18	144, 178, 181
7:21–22	131, 178
7:21	127, 180, 221, 223, 223n147
7:22	178
7:24–26	131n67
7:25–27	145
7:25–26	222
7:25	126n51, 129, 138, 183, 185, 216, 221, 223
7:26–27	131, 145
7:26	114, 142, 221, 222
7:27	145, 152, 181, 190, 191, 195, 200, 200n50, 205, 221, 226
8–12	116, 126, 129, 131
8	115, 116, 117, 120, 125n45, 127, 128, 129, 131
8:1	116, 191
8:2–5	117
8:2	142
8:3–19	121
8:3–9	121
8:3	115, 120
8:4	127
8:5	117
8:6–7	127
8:7–8	127
8:8	115, 117, 140
8:9	117, 121, 133
8:10	127, 131, 133
8:11	127, 133
8:12–13	216
8:12	127
8:13–14	125n45, 128
8:13	129
8:14	130, 131
8:17	120, 121, 135, 144n109
8:19	120, 127
8:20–21	120
8:21	127
8:24	127, 145n110
8:25	128, 130, 134
8:27	127
9–12	115
9	115, 121, 123, 125n45, 125n48, 126, 126n51, 128n58, 128n59
9:2	123, 124
9:16–17	125
9:16	121, 123, 134, 145n110
9:18–19	129
9:20–23	129n61
9:20	134
9:23–27	7
9:24–27	124, 185, 216, 218
9:24–26	121, 128, 137, 138, 141, 144, 145n110
9:24	117, 123, 124n37, 124n43, 125, 125n45, 126, 127, 128, 130, 131, 137n87, 139, 141, 143, 145n110, 198
9:24b	130
9:25–26	126n51, 137, 138
9:25	8, 126n51, 138
9:26–27	128, 138, 138n89
9:26	124, 128, 138
9:26a	139
9:27	128, 138, 221
10–12	115, 128, 129n61
10	43n98, 44n100
10:1–8	43
10:1–6	222
10:1	116
10:5–6	128
10:5	142, 192
10:6	192, 195, 223
10:7	43, 151
10:8–9	44
10:9	192
10:11	128n60, 129n61
10:12	129n61
10:13–21	222
10:13	128n60, 222
10:14	129n61
11–12	117, 129
11	129, 138n89, 183, 184n160
11:3–4	117
11:3	138n89
11:10	138n89
11:13	133
11:31–36	185
11:31–35	216, 218
11:31	138n89
11:34–35	129
11:35–45	129
11:35	129

11:36—12:3	121, 129
11:36-45	133, 146
11:36-38	222
11:36	129, 133, 138n89, 179, 183
11:37-38	133
11:37	133
11:38	129
11:39-44	129
11:40	121, 129
11:45—12:2	191
11:45—12:1	221
11:45	129, 130, 134, 141
12	130, 131
12:1-3	117
12:1-2	195
12:1	129, 195, 222
12:2-3	131, 145n110
12:2	130, 141, 179, 201, 202, 226, 227
12:2a	7
12:2b	7
12:3	7, 127, 130, 131, 138
12:3b	130
12:4	203, 231n171
12:7-9	33
12:7	128n60, 221
12:11	138n89
12:13	130, 146, 152

Hosea

1-2	78n98
6:2	130n64

Joel

2:28	200n47

Amos

9:11	34n57

Habakkuk

2:14	34, 34n58, 54, 54n20, 57, 62

Zechariah

3:8	8
4:1-14	196n39
8:9	54n21

Matthew

4:18-22	25
8:28-34	38, 38n73
14:15-21	23
16:28—17:13	237
17:1-13	23
19:28	178n135
21:12-13	24
21:18-22	24
22:1	17
24	202n54
24:37-38	11
25:31	17
26:69-75	25
26:71-72	25n21
26:73	25n21
28:2	38n73
28:5-8	23

Mark

1:16-20	25
5:1-17	38, 38n73
6:35-44	23
9:2-8	23
11:12—14:25	24
11:15-18	24
13	202n54
14:66-72	25
14:69	25n21
14:70-71	25n21
16:2-8	23
16:5	24

Luke

5:1-11	25
8:26-37	38, 38n73
9:12-17	23
9:28-36	23
19:45-48	24
21	202n54
21:27	17
22:28-30	178n135
22:54-62	25
22:58	25n21
22:59	25n21
22:69	43, 151n16
24:1-8	23
24:4	24, 38n73

John

1:35-51	25
2:13-22	24
6:4-13	23
12	46
12:38-41	30
18:15-18	25
18:18	25n21
18:25-27	25
19:25	25n21
20:1	23

Acts

1:9	17
1:11	17
2:1–4	17, 151
2:4	151n13
4:8	151n13
4:31	151n13
7:54–56	151n16
7:55–56	43
7:56	237
7:57–60	43
8:1–4	43
9	44n100
9:2–8	43
9:3	26, 150, 155, 182, 192
9:4	26, 150, 192
9:5	150
9:7	43, 43n100, 151
9:8	149, 155
9:17	149, 150, 151n13
9:20–22	152
9:24–28	152
10:44	151
13:2	180n143
13:9	151n13
13:38	160
13:47–48	149
13:47	42
13:52	151n13
19:1–6	151
22:3–21	148n5
22:4–10	148
22:6–11	151
22:6	148, 150
22:7	154
22:9	43, 43n100, 151
22:11	148
22:14	148, 149
22:15	147, 163, 165
22:16	149, 163
26:9–18	148n5
26:12–19	43
26:12–18	148
26:13	150
26:16	147, 150
26:17–18	163, 165
26:17	149
26:18	149, 152, 163
26:18b	149
28:26	149

Romans

1:7	178
1:14	166
1:18—3:20	159
2:13	161, 164n69, 165n69
2:24	159
3:15	159
3:20–30	158
3:20	159
3:23	159
3:25	158, 160
3:26	160, 161, 162
4:25	159, 161, 165
5	176
5:1–11	176n129, 177n129
5:1	158, 159, 164
5:5	169
5:8	160
5:9	158
5:10	177
5:12	177
5:15–17	177
5:17	226
5:19	160, 162
5:21	177
6	162
6:7	160, 162
8	171
8:1	171
8:2	171, 173
8:10–11	171n95
8:11	171, 224, 226
8:15	169, 175
8:17	226
8:21	175
8:23	170, 175, 179
8:29–30	159n45
8:29	40
9:27–28	168
9:28	168
9:33	168
10:11	168
11:8	159, 168
11:13–15	167
11:13–14	168
11:15	168
13:1–8	178
13:1–7	178
13:1–4	178
13:1	179n137
13:11	164
14:11	165
15	166, 180, 181, 181n146
15:6	166, 181
15:8–12	166
15:12	166
15:14–27	166
15:14–21	200, 201, 224, 230

15:14–15	167n79
15:15–28	170
15:15	181
15:16–24	167n79
15:16	181
15:20	167
15:21	159n43, 167
15:25–27	166, 167n79, 181
15:27	181

1 Corinthians

1:2	178
1:22–23	166
1:30	160
2:4–5	169
2:9	166n76
2:12	169
2:16	166n76
3:16f.	185
3:16–17	107, 172, 185n161
3:16	184, 217n118
3:17	175, 184n157, 184n159
6:2	178
6:11	160, 164
6:16–19	174
6:19	107, 171, 174, 185, 185n161
6:20	174
9:1	18, 154, 156
9:25	196
12:13	169
14:21	167
15	155, 156, 176, 177
15:3	159
15:8	18, 154, 156, 176
15:22	156, 176, 182
15:24	177n133
15:45–49	177
15:45	156, 176, 182
15:49	40, 155, 176
15:50–58	168
15:54	168

2 Corinthians

1:22	175
3–4	154, 155, 155n26, 156, 173
3	173
3:3	158
3:6	173
3:8	40
3:18	18, 155, 155n26, 158, 173, 176
4:1–5	165
4:4–6	18, 42, 155, 192
4:4	40, 154, 155, 156, 158, 159, 173
4:6	154, 155, 155n26
5:5	175
5:15–17	202
5:17	156, 158, 160, 202n54
5:18–19	159
5:19	168
5:21	161
6:1–2	165
6:2	165
6:16	172, 174, 184, 185n161, 217n118
6:16b	175
8–9	166
9:12	181
11:26	166
12	154n21

Galatians

1:4	163
1:8	163
1:11–12	154
1:12–16	154
1:15	165
1:16	147n3, 154, 155n26, 156, 157, 157n36, 158, 163, 166
1:24	165
2:2	165
2:11–20	166
2:11–13	163
2:14–16	164
2:14	164n66
2:16	159, 162, 163
2:18	173
3:1–5	169
3:1–4	164, 173
3:2–3	171
3:10–14	164n66
3:11	159, 161, 162, 164n66
3:13–14	173
3:13	160, 176
3:27–28	177
4	173
4:4	173
4:6	169, 173, 175
4:11	165
5:17–18	173
5:23	173

Ephesians

1:1	178
1:7	158
1:10	157, 158
1:13–14	169, 175
1:20–23	154, 177n133
1:20	170, 195
1:21	154n24, 177n133, 182

Ephesians (cont.)

1:23	174, 175, 224
2	170, 172
2:1–10	170, 171, 172, 224
2:5	170
2:7	170
2:11–20	172
2:15	166, 177
2:16	159
2:18	170
2:20–22	174
2:20–21	107
2:21	170, 172
3:1–10	154
3:3–5	157, 158
3:3	157
3:5	157
3:10	169, 177n133
4:1	174n116
4:12	176
4:30	175, 175n123
5:2	160, 176
5:5	231, 231n173
5:15	174n116
5:18	173, 174, 174n112
5:25	176
5:27	224

Philippians

2:5–11	156n34, 195
2:5–8	159
2:6	40
2:7–8	160, 161
2:7	159
2:10–11	135, 154, 207, 207n69
2:10	165
2:11	224
2:16	165
2:17	181
2:30	181
3	164n67, 180, 182
3:1–21	201
3:1–16	182
3:2–4	164n68
3:3	164n68, 173, 230
3:4–11	164n68
3:7–9	162, 163, 164
3:9	164
3:15–16	182n148
3:17–19	182
3:17	182n148
3:20–21	182, 183, 200, 224
3:21	159n45, 182

Colossians

1:13	177, 200, 200n50
1:14	158
1:15–18	189n4, 195
1:15	177, 198, 200
1:16	177, 182
1:18	189
1:20–22	205
1:20	159, 169, 207, 207n69
1:25	40
3:10–11	177
3:10	176
3:11	177
3:16	174n112

1 Thessalonians

1:10	41
3:5	165
4:8	171
4:17	158, 179, 183
5:3	183
5:10	176

2 Thessalonians

1	183, 183n153
1:4	179
1:5	179
1:7	179
1:9–10	183
1:11	179
2	183, 184, 185
2:3–4	224
2:4	183, 184, 216
2:7	179
2:8	185, 224
2:13–14	169

1 Timothy

2:2	178
3:16	154
6:12–15	179, 179n139

2 Timothy

2:12	205, 226
2:13	200n50

Titus

2:14	160, 190n8, 205
3:5	169, 169n89, 170
3:7	159, 179

Scripture Index

Hebrews

2:5	202n54
10:10	107
10:11	180n143

1 Peter

2:9	190n8
3:20	11

2 Peter

3:13	202n54

Revelation

1–3	196, 197, 199n47
1	40, 191, 214
1:1–8	189, 190
1:1	189, 190, 199
1:4	191, 194, 196n39, 212
1:5	195
1:6	190, 191, 196
1:7	190, 191, 196
1:9	191
1:10	191
1:12–13	192
1:13	194
1:14	192, 223
1:15	192
1:15b	192
1:16	194
1:16b	192
1:17	44
1:18	196n39
1:19	33, 35, 40, 193, 199
2–3	194, 194n23, 196, 231
2:5	194
2:7	196
2:9–10	196
2:10–11	226
2:10	195
2:11	196
2:12	194
2:16	194, 194n20
2:17	196
2:18	195
2:26–27	195
2:26	196
3:1	194
3:4–5	200
3:4	212
3:5	194, 195, 196
3:7	194, 210
3:9–11	195
3:11–12	195
3:11	194, 194n20, 195, 196
3:12	195, 196, 216
3:14	195
3:21	195, 196
4–10	191
4–5	1, 6, 18n66, 27, 29, 35, 189, 191, 193, 195, 196, 197, 198, 199, 199n47, 208, 209, 210, 211n86, 217, 225, 226
4:1—5:14	32
4	191, 199, 200, 202
4:1–2	30
4:1	198, 200
4:2–3	35
4:2	29, 31, 198, 200
4:3	28
4:4–6	39, 221
4:4	28, 36, 198, 200, 209, 211n86, 226
4:5	191, 208, 212
4:5a	201
4:6–8	36, 36n66
4:6–7	39, 201
4:6	38, 201, 208, 208n74, 216
4:7	198, 201
4:8–11	201
4:8–10	209
4:8	21, 30, 35, 36, 39, 198, 210
4:8a	201
4:8b	201
4:8c	201
4:9	30, 35, 201
4:10–11	201
4:11	202
5	202, 204, 205, 207, 208
5:1–10	35, 40, 202
5:1–2	208
5:1	18, 202
5:2ff.	18n66
5:2–5	27n29
5:2	203
5:3–7	199
5:3	203
5:4–5	27
5:5–10	230
5:5–8	200n49
5:5–6	203
5:5	196, 203
5:5a	204
5:5b	204
5:6	27n29, 204, 212
5:6a	204
5:6b	204
5:7	29, 31, 204
5:8–14	199
5:8–10	204

Revelation *(cont.)*

5:8	215
5:9	201, 205, 226, 229
5:10	191, 196, 205, 230
5:11–14	205, 206
5:11–13	31
5:11	36, 206, 208
5:12	206, 206n67
5:13–14	206
5:13	30, 40, 206
5:13b	207
5:14	209
6–20	33n52
6–19	208, 209, 210, 214, 221, 223, 224, 225
6:1–17	208
6:1	203, 208, 209, 223
6:2	223
6:3	208
6:5	208
6:7	208
6:9	29
6:10	210, 211, 212
6:12	211
6:15–17	206
6:15	211
6:16	209
6:17	221
7	209, 211, 211n85, 211n87, 221, 221n137
7:1–17	225
7:1–8	220, 224
7:1	221n136
7:2–4	221
7:2	209
7:9–14	201
7:9–10	224
7:9	209, 211, 221
7:10	211
7:11–13	200n49
7:11	209, 211, 221n136
7:14	211, 211n87
7:15–16	211
7:15	216, 217, 221n136
7:16–17	209n76, 221n137
8:1–13	208
8:1	208, 209
8:2	208
8:3	29, 205
8:5	208
8:6	208
8:7	210
8:8–11	210
8:12	210
10–19	215
10–11	222
10	214, 222n138
10:1	222
10:7	35
10:8–10	191
10:9–10	214
10:10	214
10:11	214
11	216, 217, 218, 219, 219n122
11:1–2	217, 218
11:1	216, 217, 218, 219, 219n123, 219n125, 225, 226, 226n155
11:2	216, 217, 220, 221
11:2b	216
11:3	220, 221
11:5–6	220
11:7	35
11:11–12	220
11:11	224
11:15–19	208
11:15	222, 223, 225
11:16	200n49
11:18	222
11:19	208, 209, 213n98, 216
12–19	222
12–14	213, 213n97
12	213, 213n101, 221, 224n148
12:1–4	213
12:4	35
12:5–6	213
12:6	220, 221
12:7–17	222, 224n148
12:9	224n148, 227n158
12:10	222, 225
12:11	221
12:13	221
13–19	213n101
13	214, 222
13:1–18	224
13:1–10	223
13:1–2	221n134
13:1	228n162, 229
13:3	227
13:18	223
14	213, 214, 214n103, 218
14:1–5	225
14:1–4	223, 225
14:1–2	215
14:1	225
14:2	218
14:3	200n49, 221
14:4–5	213
14:4	225
14:4d	220
14:5	224

Scripture Index

14:6	224
14:8	212, 222
14:14	209
14:15	216, 217
14:17	216
15	211, 212, 215, 218, 224n148
15:1–8	29, 213n98
15:1	211n90, 214n103
15:2–3	224n148
15:2	208n74, 226
15:3	215
15:4	212, 212n91, 216
15:5–8	217
15:5	209
15:8	216, 218, 225
16:1–21	208, 212, 216
16:1	208, 216
16:5–6	210, 212
16:10–11	206
16:10	222
16:12	212
16:14	227n157
16:18–21	208
16:19	212
17:3	221
17:6	221
17:10	35
17:14	223, 223n146, 223n147
18–22	192n13
18:1–24	212, 222
18:1	215, 218
18:9	215
18:10–19	215
18:21—19:10	215
19	194n20, 223
19:1–10	215n111
19:4	200n49
19:11–21	215, 223
19:11	209, 212
19:12	223
19:13	201
19:15	212
19:17	215
19:20	223, 224
19:21	212, 224
20–22	221n137, 225
20	211n85, 213n102, 224n148, 225, 225n148
20:1–15	224n148
20:1–10	226
20:1	226
20:3	224n148
20:4–6	202n54
20:4	224n148, 226, 229
20:4b	226
20:6	219, 219n123, 226, 226n155, 228
20:7–8	227n156
20:8	227n157
20:9–10	227
20:11–15	227
20:11	227, 228
20:12	227
21:1—22:5	217n119, 228
21	217, 218
21:1	202, 202n54, 205, 224, 228, 229
21:3	229
21:4	209n76, 229
21:9	229
21:10	229
21:11	229
21:12	200n49, 228, 229
21:14	228
21:15–17	217
21:16	228
21:18–21	200
21:18	228
21:22	229
21:23	230
21:27	230
22:2–3	223
22:3	229
22:3a	230
22:3b	230
22:5	229, 230
22:6	231, 231n170
22:10–11	231
22:10	33, 203, 231n171
22:12	231, 231n172
22:15	231, 231n173

1 Enoch

6–16	10
10:12	7
14	9, 10, 11, 12
14:3	17
14:8–25	185n161
14:18–21	11n29
14:18	10, 17
14:19	10
14:20	10
14:21	10
15:1—16:3	17
24–25	9, 11, 11n29
25:3–4	11n29
25:3	11n29
38:2	8, 11
39:6	15
40:4	8
45:3	8

I Saw the Lord

1 Enoch (cont.)

46–48	9
46	11, 12, 40
46:1	11
46:5	12
46:6	12
46:6b	12
46:7–8	12
46:7	8
47:1–4	12
47:3	11
48:2	7
61:2–16	12
61:5	8
61:8	8
61:10–12	11
62	11
62:2	12
62:7	11
71	9, 11
71:2	11
71:7	11
71:15–17	12
90:30	7
91–93	7
91:14–16	7

2 Enoch

20:1—25:5	13
20:1	177n133
21:1	13
21:2	13
21:3	13
22:1	13
22:2–7	13

3 Enoch

1:1	13
1:8	13
3:4	13
4:1	13
10:1–6	13

Jubilees

23:12–31	7
23:27–29	7

Assumption of Moses

5–10	7
10:9	7

4 Ezra

7:28	8
12:12	14
13	40
13:1–4	14
13:4	14
13:6–7	8
13:9	8
13:12	14

T. Levi (Testament of Levi)

3:8	177n133
5:1–2	185n161

2 Baruch

4:3–6	185n161
4QpGena	
4Q252 5:1–7	8
4QpIsaa	
4Q161 3:11–25	8
11QMelchizedek	8, 14
10	14
16	14
23	14
4QMess Ar (4Q534)	15
1.9	15
2.16–18	15n52

www.ingramcontent.com/pod-product-compliance
Lightning Source LLC
Chambersburg PA
CBHW080546230426
43663CB00015B/2726